THE BLUE GUIDES

12C sculpture from Cambodia from the Musée Guimet (see p 217)

BLUE GUIDE

Paris and Versailles

Ian Robertson

Maps and plans by John Flower

A & C Black
London

WW Norton
New York

Eighth edition

Published by A & C Black (Publishers) Limited
35 Bedford Row, London WC1R 4JH

© A & C Black (Publishers) Limited 1992

ISBN   0–7136–3581–9

A CIP catalogue record for this book
is available from the British Library

Published in the United States of America by
WW Norton & Company, Incorporated
500 Fifth Avenue, New York NY 10110

Published simultaneously in Canada by
Penguin Books Canada Limited
2801 John Street, Markham, Ontario L3R 1B4

ISBN 0–393–30889–8   USA

Printed and bound in Great Britain by
Butler & Tanner Ltd, Frome and London

The publishers and the author have done their best to ensure the accuracy of all the information in Blue Guide Paris and Versailles; however, they can accept no responsibility for any loss, injury or inconvenience sustained by any traveller as a result of information or advice contained in the guide.

Please write in with your comments, suggestions and corrections. Writers of the best letters will be awarded a free Blue Guide of their choice.

Ian Robertson was born in Tokyo, in 1928, and educated in England. After spending some years in publishing and specialist bookselling in London, he was commissioned to rewrite Blue Guide Spain. He has since rewritten and revised several editions of Blue Guides to Ireland, France, Paris and Versailles, Portugal and Switzerland and has compiled Blue Guide Austria and Cyprus.

PREFACE

'To visit Paris at random is a most foolish and dangerous thing' wrote Thomas Cook in 'The Excursionist', and the same advice still applies.

This eighth edition of the Blue Guide incorporates numerous revisions and additions, to reflect the changes which have taken place in the French capital and its immediate surroundings since the publication of the previous edition. The section on Practical Information and amenities has been up-dated. The Historical Introduction summarises the relationship of Paris to French history in general, and provides a chronological framework for a better understanding of her past.

This new edition also contains full descriptions of St.-Denis, Vincennes, Ecouen, Sceaux, Malmaison and St.-Germain-en-Laye, the Musée Condé at Chantilly, Senlis, and the Château at Fontainebleau, as they are often visited in day trips from central Paris.

The 32 routes in Paris itself are described for sightseeing on foot, almost always the most convenient and enjoyable way of getting about, while some of the nearest métro stations are also indicated along each route. Visitors to Paris are warned that, because of the sheer scale of many of the monuments, and the extensive sweep of many of the vistas, it is only too easy to underestimate distances, and it is advised not attempt too much sightseeing in a day. Indeed, the Musée du Louvre alone deserves and physically demands several visits.

A number of the major museums of Paris continue to undergo radical reorganisation, as with the Musée du Louvre itself, where whole departments are being moved around and certain sections are likely to be closed entirely for long periods of time. Others may well be shut temporarily for partial re-arrangement. The museums will attempt to keep a proportion of their collections on view during this period of upheaval, but in certain cases the author has little alternative but to list a selection of important works which may be seen somewhere in the building rather than specify their precise whereabouts, an unsatisfactory situation which it is hoped will be improved by the time the next edition of this Guide is published.

Visitors returning to Paris after a period of years will find many changes, not all for the good. Certainly the cleaning of façades (even if only the façades in some cases) has improved its general appearance, and indeed, in spite of traffic flowing along the quais of the Seine (unobtrusively underground in some stretches), much of the centre still retains its immense charm.

The transformation of the area formerly occupied by the old Halles has been completed, and many have suffered from agoraphobia after visiting the commercial Forum but at least you now have a better view of both St.-Eustache and the nearby Bourse du Commerce, which is some compensation. Many familiar views and horizons have been broken by the erection of vast blocks of buildings, which, dominating the surrounding area, have also irreparably affected the cityscape. Certain squalid outlying districts continue to be transformed out of all recognition; others of considerable architectural interest—such as the Marais—continue to be tastefully restored, although the new opera-house in the Pl. de la Bastille has been much criticised on several counts. Unfortunately the view of many monuments is spoiled by shoals of blatantly parked coaches, but there is still a great deal to see not far off the beaten track.

The practice of 'starring' the highlights has been continued, even if the system is subjective and inconsistent, for such asterisks do help the hurried visitor to pick out those things which the general consensus of opinion (modified occasionally by the author's personal prejudice, admittedly) considers should not be missed. In certain cases a museum has been starred, rather than individual objects among those described, when the standard of its contents is remarkably high.

Selection remains the touchstone by which guide books are judged. It is hoped that this edition will provide a balanced account of most aspects of a great city and its immediate surroundings without neglecting any that might appeal to the resident or visitor, and without being so exhaustive as to leave him no opportunity of discovering additional pleasures for himself.

In addition to those providing facilities and material assistance, or offering information and advice, who were listed at this point in the previous edition, the following must be mentioned: Nicolle Roques (Office de Tourisme de Paris); Hélène Lefevre (Etablissement public du Grand Louvre); Henri de Cazals (Direction des Musées de France) and Hélène Lassalle; Sylvie Poujade; Clemence Berg and Marc Plocki; Françoise Mardras and Bertille Lanne (Musée du Louvre); François Reynaud and Anhe Isabel Vignaud (Musée de Carnavalet); Mme Lebreton (Musée Cognacq-Jay); Isabelle d'Andlau (Académie des Beaux-Arts); Nathalie Manuel (Musée Camondo); Beatrice Saule and Ariane de Lestrange (Château de Versailles); Béatrice Uey; Jérome Rouselle (EPAD, at La Défense); Pierre Billotey and Nathalie Marthe (IGN); Derek Brown (Michelin); Richard Wilkinson; Marie-France de Peyronnet; Dilys MacCrindle; John Tomes; and Fabienne de Sèze.

The street-atlas, maps and plans have been corrected; the cartography has again been undertaken by John Flower.

The author must yet again thank Arthur and Marion Boyars and Charles and Lizette Amar for their generous hospitality.

Susan Benn has taken a number of fine photographs with which to illustrate this edition. The author and publishers would also like to thank the Musée Marmottan for permission to reproduce the photograph of Berthe Morisot's Au Bal.

My wife has continued to criticise and encourage while joining me on several sorties both in Paris and its vicinity.

A NOTE ON BLUE GUIDES

The Blue Guides series began in 1915 when Muirhead Guide-Books Limited published 'Blue Guide London and its Environs'. Finlay and James Muirhead already had extensive experience of guide-book publishing: before the First World War they had been the editors of the English editions of the German Baedekers, and by 1915 they had acquired the copyright of most of the famous 'Red' handbooks from John Murray.

An agreement made with the French publishing house Hachette et Cie in 1917 led to the translation of Muirhead's London Guide, which became the first 'Guide Bleu'—Hachette had previously published the blue-covered 'Guides Joanne'. Subsequently, Hachette's 'Guide Bleu Paris et ses Environs' was adapted and published in London by Muirhead. The collaboration between the two publishing houses continued until 1933.

In 1931 Ernest Benn took over the Blue Guides, appointing Russell Muirhead, Finlay Muirhead's son, editor in 1934. The Muirheads' connection with Blue Guides ended in 1963 when Stuart Rossiter, who had been working on the Guides since 1954, became house editor, revising and compiling several of the books himself.

The Blue Guides are now published by A & C Black, who acquired Ernest Benn in 1984, so continuing the tradition of guide-book publishing which began in 1826 with 'Black's Economical Tourist of Scotland'. The Blue Guide series continues to grow: there are now more than 40 titles in print, with revised editions appearing regularly and many new Blue Guides in preparation.

'Blue Guides' is a registered trade mark.

EXPLANATIONS

Type. The main routes are described in large type. Smaller type is used for deviations, for historical and preliminary paragraphs, and for descriptions of greater detail or less importance.

Asterisks indicate points of special interest or excellence: two 'stars' are used sparingly.

Street Numbering. In Paris, in streets parallel to the river, the houses are numbered from E to W; in those at right-angles to the Seine, from the end nearest the river.

The **Population** figures given (in round figures) are based on those of the last census, of 1982, or revisions of them.

Anglicisation. For the sake of consistency, place-names and the names of kings, etc. have retained their French form.

CNMH after certain monuments and buildings indicates that the *Caisse Nationale des Monuments Historiques* is responsible for them; see p 172.

CONTENTS

EXCURSIONS FROM PARIS

MAPS AND PLANS

HISTORICAL INTRODUCTION

The foundations of modern France may be said to date from the crossing of the Alps by the Romans in 121 BC and the establishment of the province (Latin provincia; modern Provence) of Gallia Narbonensis. Important remains such as the Pont du Gard and the theatres and amphitheatres at Nîmes, Arles and Orange are still extant. But the whole of France as we now know it did not become subject to Rome until after Julius Caesar's decisive defeat of Vercingetorix at Alésia in 52 BC. In the previous year Caesar had first mentioned—under the name of Lutetia—the fortified capital of the Parisii, an insignificant Gallic tribe, confined on islands in the Seine, which he nominated as the rendezvous of deputies from conquered Gaul.

In spite of occasional local revolts, Rome gradually imposed her government, roads, speech and culture on Gaul. By c AD 250 the country had become partially Christianised, St. Dionysius (Denis) being its first bishop, but within a few years the first of a series of Barbarian invasions began. In 292 Paris became a base of the Emperor Constantius Chlorus, although it was not until 360 that the name was applied to the river-port. Barbarian mercenaries (among them Visigoths and Burgundians) were employed to defend the frontiers of the Empire in its decline, but they wearied of their alliance with the degenerate Gallo-Romans, and after the repulse of Attila and his Huns at the Catalaunian Fields (451) became virtually masters of the land, the most powerful tribe being the Salian Franks under their leader Merovius.

Merovius's grandson Clovis I (481–511) defeated Syagrius (the Roman governor of Soissons) in 486, and the Alemanni at Tolbiac in 496, after which he adopted the Christian religion. In the following year Paris opened her gates to him (traditionally on the advice of Ste. Geneviève), although he did not make it his official capital until 508. According to Frankish custom, the kingdom was divided on his death between his three sons into Austrasia (between the Meuse and the Rhine), Neustria (the territory to the NW, from the Meuse to the Loire) and Burgundy (to the S), and although the Merovingians remained in control, the dynasty was weakened by internecine warfare during the next two centuries.

Eminent among the Merovingians was Chilperic I (king of Neustria from 561–84) and Dagobert (king of Austrasia from 622 and of all France from 628 until his death in 638). Paris remained the political centre of conflicting Frankish interests, its growing population overflowing to form suburbs around monasteries situated on both banks of the river; but after the death of Dagobert, who refounded the abbey of St.-Denis, most of the power passed into the hands of the 'maires du Palais', one of whom, Charles Martel (714–41), an Austrasian, was to defeat the invading Moors at Poitiers in 732. In 751 Pepin, Martel's son, deposed Childéric III, the last of the Merovingians, and founded a new dynasty.

Carolingians

Pepin, le Bref   (751–68)
Charlemagne   (768–814)
Louis I, le Débonnaire   (814–40)
Charles, le Chauve (the Bald)   (840–77)
Louis II, le Bègue (the Stammerer)   (877–79)

Louis III (879–82)
Carloman (882–87)
Charles, le Gros (the Fat) (884–87)
Count Eudes (887–98)
Charles, le Simple (898–923)
Louis IV, d'Outremer (Beyond the Son) (936–54)
Lothaire (954–86)
Louis V, le Fainéant (the Lazy) (986–87)

Although Pepin resided occasionally at Paris, his son Charlemagne, in alliance with the Pope, extended his dominion over Germany and Italy, and was crowned 'Emperor of the West', or 'Holy Roman Emperor'. He moved the seat of government from France to Aix-la-Chapelle (present-day Aachen). Not only a great ruler, Charlemagne also presided over a remarkable revival of learning and education. However, the system of dividing territories on the death of kings was to cause the eventual disintegration of the empire, and in 843, by the Treaty of Verdun, those areas which were to form modern France were transferred to his grandson Charles 'le Chauve'. Further division ensued, and France became little more than a collection of independent feudal states controlled by dukes and counts.

The situation was further disturbed by the invasion of Scandinavian or Norse pirates. By 912 the Vikings had settled in Rouen and had carved out the duchy of Normandy for themselves, in 885 having besieged and pillaged Paris itself from their encampment (possibly on the present site of the Louvre). The Cité had been successfully defended by Eudes, Duc de France and comte de Paris, who in 888 deposed Charles 'le Gros', but the Carolingian dynasty continued to stagger on for another hundred years. It was to be a century of disunity for France, distinguished politically by the growth of Norman power, and religiously by the foundation in 910 of a Benedictine abbey at Cluny, later to gain fame and influence.

Capetians

Hugues Capet (987–96)
Robert, le Pieux (996–1031)
Henri I (1031–60)
Philippe I (1060–1108)
Louis VI, le Gros (1108–37)
Louis VII, le Jeune (1137–80)
Philippe Auguste (1180–1223)
Louis VIII, le Lion (1223–26)
Louis IX (St. Louis) (1226–70)
Philippe III, le Hardi (the Bold) (1270–85)
Philippe IV, le Bel (the Handsome/Fair) (1285–1314)
Louis X, le Hutin (the Quarrelsome) (1314–16)
Jean I (1316; died 4 days old)
Philippe V, le Long (the Tall) (1316–22)
Charles IV, le Bel (1322–28)

Hugues Capet was elected by the nobles at Senlis in preference to any more incapable Carolingians, and he and his successors proceeded to make Paris the base of a centralising policy by which they might control the disunited country. But this policy frequently brought them into conflict with independent spirits, one of whom, William, duke of Normandy, in 1066 invaded and conquered England. Paris grew steadily in size and importance, particularly on the North Bank, and during the reign of Louis VI, if not earlier, a second town wall was thrown up. The 'Hanse Parisienne', a league of merchants, was established, marking the foundation of the municipality.

The marriage in 1152 of the future Henry II of England to Eleanor of Aquitaine (the divorced wife of Louis VII), whose dowry brought Henry about one-third of France, was to cause a power struggle between the two countries which lasted three centuries. Meanwhile, in 1095 Urban II preached the First Crusade at Clermont; in 1198 the Abbey of Cîteaux was founded; in c 1115 Clairvaux was founded by St. Bernard, who in 1146 was to preach the Second Crusade at Vézelay. In 1163 the foundation-stone of Notre-Dame was laid and some years later Philippe Auguste built the fortress of the Louvre. This religious enthusiasm was in part the reason for the expulsion of the Jews. The cathedral schools of Paris (at which Guillaume de Champeaux and Abélard had taught) were united to form one University, which was granted its first statutes by Pope Innocent III in 1208. This was established on the Left Bank of the Seine, where the growing student population settled; the Right Bank became the centre of commerce, industry and administration. Some streets were paved; the two ancient wooden bridges were replaced by ones of stone; and the city was enclosed by an extensive line of fortifications.

In the political field Philippe Auguste won back a large part of the lost provinces (Normandy and Anjou), inflicting a heavy defeat on the allies of John of England at Bouvines in 1214. The bloody Albigensian Crusade of 1209–13 eventually restored Languedoc to French rule.

During the long reign of Louis IX, the Hospice des Quinze-Vingts and the theological college of the Sorbonne were founded, the latter to become a dominant influence in the University. The Palais de la Cité was rebuilt (parts of which, notably the Ste.-Chapelle, still exist), and the office of Provost was reformed; statutes were drawn up for the many guilds, which were to remain in force until the Revolution. Louis, canonised in 1297, was a great crusader, and eventually lost his life at Tunis. With the death of Charles IV in 1328 the direct branch of the Capetian dynasty became extinct.

House of Valois

Philippe VI (1328–50)
Jean II, le Bon (the Good (1350–64)
Charles V, le Sage (the Wise) (1364–80)
Charles VI, le Bien-Aimé (the Well-beloved) (1380–1422)
Charles VII, le Victorieux (1422–61)
Louis XI (1461–83)
Charles VIII, l'Affable (1483–98)
Louis XII, le Père du Peuple (1498–1515)
François I (1515–47)
Henri II (1547–59)
François II (1559–60)
Charles IX (1560–74)
Henri III (1574–89)

The claim of Philippe de Valois to the throne was disputed by Edward III of England, who invaded France, precipitating the Hundred Years' War (1337–1453). He routed the French army at Crécy (1346) and inflicted a further defeat on Jean II at Poitiers in 1356. The ravages and depredations of both French and English soldiery roused the peasants (the Jacquerie) and the burgesses to revolt. In Paris, Etienne Marcel (Maire du Palais and provost of the merchants) took advantage of the situation to increase the influence of the municipality, but he offended public opinion by attempting to hand over the city to Charles of Navarre, and was assassinated in 1358. Two years later, by the Treaty of Brétigny, England renounced her claims, but before long desultory warfare between the two countries broke out again and continued until the French had won back a large part of their lost territory, largely due to the tactics of Du Guesclin.

Charles V was able to bring back some order to the kingdom. He built the fortress of the Bastille, but anarchy returned during the following reign, when his weak-minded son Charles VI provoked the citizens of Paris—at that time numbering some 280,000—by excessive taxation. Although the resulting revolt of the 'Maillotins' was bloodily suppressed, the king became the pawn of rival regents and for the next 40 years France suffered from dissensions between the aristocratic party, the Armagnacs, and the Burgundians, the popular party (Jean II had made his fourth son, Jean sans Peur, Duke of Burgundy).

Seizing the opportunity, Henry V of England invaded France, and supported by the Burgundians, defeated a French force at Agincourt (1415). By the Treaty of Troyes (1420) he received the hand of Catherine, Charles VI's daughter, together with the right of succession to the throne. But in 1422 Henry died at Vincennes, only seven weeks before the death of Charles VI. Charles VII, by himself no match for the English and Burgundians, found a champion in Jeanne d'Arc (Joan of Arc; 1412–31). But the English continued to control Paris until 1436. In 1429 John, Duke of Bedford repelled an assault led by Joan, who, after a brilliant campaign, defeated the English at Orléans in May of that year. Captured at Compiègne by the Burgundians in 1430, she was handed over to the English, condemned as a heretic by a court of ecclesiastics, and burned at the stake in Rouen. But the successful revolt she had inspired continued, and by 1453 only Calais remained of the once extensive English possessions in France. A vivid account of conditions prevailing in Paris during the years 1405–49 is given in the anonymously compiled 'Journal d'un Bourgeois de Paris'. The poet Villon was born here in 1431.

With the reign of Louis XI the change from a medieval social system to the modern state was accelerated. A brilliant and unscrupulous politician (and relieved of the menace of England, then occupied with the domestic 'War of the Roses'), he proceeded to crush the great feudal lordships which encroached on his territory, the most threatening being that of Charles the Bold ('le Téméraire') of Burgundy. The Peace of Péronne (1468) gave the Burgundians a momentary advantage, but Louis managed to alienate Charles' English allies by the Treaty of Picquigny (1475). After Charles' death before the walls of Nancy in 1477, Louis soon overwhelmed his lesser adversaries, and brought Arras, the Franche-Comté, Anjou, and Maine into direct allegiance to the crown. In 1469/70 the first printing-press in France was set up in the Sorbonne; and in 1484 the first meeting of the Estates-General was convened at Tours, near which, in the Loire valley, several châteaux were being rebuilt as royal residences.

The following half century was principally occupied with indecisive campaigns in Italy, the only tangible result of which—particularly during the reign of François I—was the establishment in France of the cultural concepts of the Italian Renaissance. Among the more important literary figures of the period were Marot, Rabelais, Du Bellay, and Ronsard, the last two being members of the circle known as La Pléïade.

Charles VIII and Louis XII were successive husbands of Anne de Bretagne, whose dowry, the important duchy of Brittany, was formally united to France in 1532 on the death of her daughter, wife of François I. The reign of Henri II saw the acquisition by France of the Three Bishoprics (Metz, Toul, and Verdun), while Calais fell to the Duc de Guise in 1558. In 1559 Henri II concluded the treaty of Cateau-Cambrésis with Felipe II of Spain, thus ending the Italian wars. In 1564 an edict fixed the beginning of the year as 1 January, inaugurating the 'new style' of dating.

The short reign of François II, who while still dauphin (aged ten) had married Mary Stuart, Queen of Scots, was followed by that of his brother Charles IX. At the instigation of Catherine de Médicis (1519–89), his bigoted and domineering mother, Charles signed the order for the massacre of protestant Huguenots on the Eve of St. Bartholomew (23 August 1572). (Catherine was mother also of Henri III, and of Marguerite de Valois, the first wife of Henri of Navarre.) From 1560 until the promulgation of the Edict of Nantes in 1598, the country was ravaged, sporadically, by the Religious Wars of the League (La Ligue). In 1589 the ultra-Catholic Henri, Duc de Guise, was murdered at Blois by Henri III, against whom he had been an overt rebel. The king himself was assassinated at St.-Cloud the following year.

House of Bourbon

Henri IV, le Grand   (1589–1610)
Louis XIII, le Juste   (1610–43)
Louis XIV, 'le Roi Soleil'   (1643–1715)
Louis XV, le Bien-Aimé   (1715–74)
Louis XVI   (1774–92)
Louis XVII   (never reigned)
Louis XVIII   (1814–24)
Charles X   (1824–30)

The parents of Henri IV (of Navarre) were Jeanne d'Albret (daughter of Marguerite of Navarre) and Antoine de Bourbon, of the Bourbon branch of the Capetian dynasty, descending from Robert of Clermont, sixth son of Louis IX. A Protestant, Henri eventually defeated the Catholics at Ivry (1590), but was unable to enter the besieged capital until 1594, after he had ostensibly abjured his faith with (it is said) the cynical remark that 'Paris vaut bien une messe'. Despite his conversion, he granted Protestants freedom of worship by the Edict of Nantes. Among the many who joined in the general recognition of Henri as the legitimate heir to the throne was Montaigne, whose 'Essays' were published in part in 1580.

Peace established, Henri set about enlarging the palaces of the Louvre and the Tuileries, planned several squares including the Place Royale, and completed the Pont Neuf. However, with his assassination by Ravaillac in 1610, religious restlessness returned, and the admirable reforms and economies instituted by Sully, his able minister, were brought to nothing by the extravagant favourites of young Louis XIII (whose mother, Marie de Médicis, Henri had married in 1600 after his divorce from Marguerite de Valois). On Henri's death, Marie became Regent, but in 1624 Cardinal Richelieu (1585–1642) took over the reins of government. His main aim was the establishment of absolute royal power in France, and of French supremacy in Europe. He suppressed all Protestant influence in politics, capturing their stronghold, La Rochelle, in 1628. Anyone defying Richelieu suffered severe penalties, and numerous fortresses throughout the country were dismantled in the process of repression. The cardinal then turned his attention to the House of Habsburg, which under the Emperor Charles V had been encroaching on the frontiers of France, and, in alliance with Gustavus Adolphus of Sweden, Richelieu involved France in the Thirty Years' War. The campaigns of the Grand Condé (1621–86; a member of a collateral branch of the Bourbons) resulted in the temporary acquisition of Picardy, Alsace and Roussillon.

In 1635 and 1640 respectively, the Académie Française and the Imprimerie Royal were founded; a fifth wall was erected around Paris, where several new quarters arose, such as the Pré-aux-Clercs (Faubourg St.-Germain), the Ile-St.-Louis and the Marais, which became a favourite residence of the nobility. Marie de Médicis built the Palais du Luxembourg; Anne of Austria, consort of the king since 1614, founded the church of Vâl-de-Grace in thanksgiving for the birth of a son (later Louis XIV) in 1638; and Richelieu built for himself the Palais-Cardinal, later the Palais-Royal.

Richelieu had been succeeded meanwhile by Cardinal Mazarin (1602–61), who carried on his predecessor's policies. Although France was assured of the possession of Alsace and the Three Bishoprics by the Treaty of Westphalia in 1648, the expenses of campaigning were crippling. Civil war broke out, known as 'La Fronde', from which no one—the insurgents, Mazarin, Condé or Marshal Turenne (1611–75)—emerged with much credit. During the Fronde, Condé (who had defeated the Spaniards at Recroi in 1643), allied himself with Spain (who had not subscribed to the Treaty of Westphalia), but Turenne's victory at the Battle of the Dunes (1658) forced Spain to accept the Treaty of the Pyrenees the following year.

On Mazarin's death in 1661 Louis XIV, who had succeeded as a minor in 1643, decided to govern alone, duped by the conviction that 'L'État c'est moi'. The nobility were reduced to being ineffectual courtiers, and the king selected his ministers from the *haute bourgeoisie*, some, such as Colbert (1619–83), being very able. He then launched a series of costly wars of self-aggrandisement, which although they eventually increased the territory of France—its frontiers fortified by Vauban (1633–1707)—were to bring his long reign to a disastrous close. At the same time his indulgence in such extravagant projects as the building of a palace fit for the 'Roi Soleil' at Versailles (extended by Hardouin-Mansart, with gardens laid out by Le Nôtre and its lavish decoration supervised by Le Brun), where Louis had chosen to transfer his court in 1672, further beggared the country. At Versailles most of the great artists of this and succeeding epochs were gathered, while among composers Lully (from 1652 until his death in 1687), Couperin and (in the following reign) Rameau provided music to entertain the court.

In Paris, which had now grown to a metropolis containing some 500,000 inhabitants and 25,000 houses, boulevards were laid out on the lines of Etienne Marcel's wall. The Hôtel des Invalides was founded in 1671. The University quarters were incorporated within the city, which had become one of the cultural centres of Europe—Corneille, Molière, La Fontaine, Boileau and Pascal (the latter associated with the activities of the reforming Jansenists of Port-Royal) making their home there—while the salons of Mme de Rambouillet and Mme de Sablé, among others, had become the influential intellectual rendezvous of such figures as La Rochefoucauld, the Scudérys, and Bossuet. Meanwhile, in 1685, Louis had revoked the Edict of Nantes, which again imposed Catholicism on the country.

The king's preoccupation with 'La Gloire' involved him first in the rapid campaign of 1667–68, which secured the possession of several towns in Flanders; while the Dutch War of 1672–78 ended in the Peace of Nijmegen and the absorption of the Franche-Comté. Less successful were the campaigns against the League of Augsburg (or the Grand Alliance; 1686–97), and of the war of the Spanish Succession (1701–13), in which French forces suffered repeatedly at the hands of Marlborough and Prince Eugène (at Blenheim in 1704; Ramillies in 1706; Oudenaarde in 1708; and Malplaquet in 1709), although Marshal Villars won a victory at Denain (1712) after the withdrawal of the English from the war.

'If greatness of soul consists in a love of pageantry, an ostentation of fastidious pomp, a prodigality of expense, an affectation of munificence, an insolence of ambition, and a haughty reserve of deportment; Lewis certainly deserved the appellation of Great. Qualities which are really heroic, we shall not find in the composition of his character.' Such was Smollett's condemnation. Life at court during the latter part of the reign and subsequent regency (under Philippe, duc d'Orléans; 1715–23) is brilliantly recorded in the 'Mémoires' of the Duc de Saint-Simon. Several bad harvests (particularly in 1726, 1739 and 1740) decimated the peasantry—who formed four-fifths of the population of 20,000,000 in 1700—but colonial trade improved, and merchants thrived in such provincial centres as Bordeaux, Nantes, and Marseille.

The marriage in 1725 of Louis XV to Marie, daughter of Stanislas Leczinski (the deposed king of Poland) drew France into the War of the Polish Succession (1733) and further ruinous wars followed, including that of the Austrian Succession (in which Louis was allied with Frederick the Great of Prussia in opposition to England and Holland, who supported the cause of Maria Theresa, Empress of Austria). In spite of Saxe's brilliant victory at Fontenoy (1745) the French gained little, while the English improved their position as a maritime power, and Prussia likewise gained in strength. The Seven Years' War (1756–63), in which France was allied to Austria, was disastrous for France, and saw the loss of flourishing colonies in India, North America and the West Indies. By 1788 the cost of these wars had created a situation whereby three-quarters of the State expenditure was being spent on reducing the national debt and on defence.

Nevertheless, grandiose buildings continued to be erected in Paris, such as the Panthéon and the Palais-Bourbon; but a sixth wall, raised as a customs-barrier by the powerful and rapacious farmers-general of taxes, only fostered further discontent ('Le mur murant Paris rend Paris murmurant'). In spite of the general degradation of his court and the corruption and negligence rife among his administrators, the reign of Louis XV was made illustrious by some of the great names in French literature: Voltaire, Rousseau, Montesquieu, Marivaux, the Encyclopédistes (Diderot, Condillac, Helvetius, d'Alembert, *et al*), who frequented the fashionable salons of the Marquise de Lambert, Mme de Tencin, Mme du Deffand, Mlle Lespinasse, Mme Geoffrin, or Baron d'Holbach, and others of lesser influence. But many of the philosophers vehemently attacked both the establishment and the clergy, and their ideas undoubtedly helped to sow the seeds of revolution. At the same time the expulsion of the Jesuits in 1764, after years of struggle with the Jansenists, removed one of the pillars of the Ancien Régime.

On his succession Louis XVI found the populace critical of his predecessor's extravagance and lack of military success, but was too weak to cope with the interminable financial crises (in spite of the reforms initiated by

Turgot from 1774 and of Necker from 1777). 'This man is rather weak but not imbecile, but there is something apathetic about both his body and his mindêhe has no taste for instruction and no curiosity', wrote teh Austrian Emporer Joseph I, after visiting his brother-in-law, while he urged Marie-Antointette to abandon 'the vortex of dissipation around her' and seek 'rational company', prophetically remarking that otherwise 'the revolution will be cruel'. Economic problems were precipitated by bad harvests, particularly in 1787–88, when there were grain riots in many French towns, including Paris and Grenoble. These crises inspired reforms, which, if accepted, would have adversely affected the privileged estates ('Les Privilégiés')—the upper ranks of the clergy (the First Estate), and the majority of the nobility (the Second Estate)—who therefore rejected them. Louis' foreign policy, which supported the American colonies in their struggle for independence from England, was not only financially disastrous, but indirectly did much to disseminate democratic ideals.

In an attempt to reform methods of taxation—for Les Privilégiés held innumerable hereditary rights by which they avoided paying taxes, yet levied them to their own advantage—the king convoked an assembly of the Etats généraux. The 1165 deputies elected met at Versailles on 5 May 1789, for the first time since 1614. The first political act of the Third Estate, the Non-Privilégiés (which numbered almost 600) was the creation of a National Assembly (17 June), which, meeting separately in the Jeu de Paume on the 20th, swore not to disband until a constitution had been given to the country which would limit royal autocracy and guarantee liberty, equality and fraternity. Three days later Mirabeau defied the king: 'Nous sommes ici par la volonté du peuple etêon ne nous arrachera que par la force des baïonnettes'; and on 9 July, reinforced by many of the clergy and a minority of the nobility, the renamed Assemblée constituante set to work to frame such a constitution. But two days later Necker, who had promised further financial reforms, was dismissed by the king, and it was feared that this gratuitous act would be followed by the dissolution of the Assembly.

The **Revolution**. The citizens of Paris—and also in the provinces at Dijon, Rennes, Lyon, Nantes, and Le Havre—were provoked into a more open rebellion, culminating in the storming of the Bastille on 14 July; but while the next few months saw numerous reforms, there was little political or economic stability, and tensions heightened. In an attempt to avoid bankruptcy, church lands were nationalised, which produced some opposition. Many of the nobility—a class shortly, but temporarily, to be abolished—sought asylum abroad. The king and his unpopular consort, Marie-Antoinette, were virtually prisoners in the Tuileries; they attempted to flee the country but were arrested (at Varennes in June 1791) and brought back to Paris. On 1 October 1791 a new Legislative Assembly was formed, which in the following April declared war on Austria to forestall foreign intervention. The Assembly was at first swayed by the moderate Girondins, but the following year the extreme Jacobins under Danton, Robespierre and Marat, seized power and, as the National Convention, meeting on 20 September (the day on which the victory of Valmy turned the tide of war in France's favour), established the Republic.

On 21 January 1793 Louis XVI was executed in the Place de la Révolution, an act followed by the setting-up in March of the dictatorial Committee of Public Safety, which, suspicious of the moderate party, ruthlessly suppressed all those suspected of royalist sympathies. The guillotine was in constant action. In July Marat was assassinated, and even the Dantonists found themselves to be a moderating force, opposed to the even more bloodthirsty Hébertists. But Robespierre, chief architect of the Reign of Terror, brooked no rivals, and early in 1794 both Hébert and Danton were guillotined. However, after further weeks of ferocious intimidation, the reaction came and on 27 July (9 Thermidor; see below), Robespierre's own head fell.

A **Republican Calendar**, the object of which was to make a break with Christian tradition, was instituted during the autumn of 1793, the mathematician Romme being responsible for its chronology. It was to remain in force until January 1806, when France officially reverted to the Gregorian Calendar (introduced in 1582). It was antedated, as it was considered that the first year (An I) had begun at the autumnal equinox (22 September) of 1792, to coincide with the proclamation of the Republic. The year was divided into 12 months of 30 days each; each month being sub-divided into three periods of ten days or décades; and five days ('sansculottides') were added at the end of each year (six in leap years) to be observed as national festivals.

The days were named in numerical order: *primidi, duodi, tridi, quartidi, quintidi, sextidi, septidi, octidi, nonidi, and décadi* (the day of rest). More poetic names, devised by Fabre d'Eglantine, were given to the months: *Vendémaire, Brumaire*, and *Frimaire* being the autumn months of vintage, fog, and frost; *Nivôse, Pluviôse*, and *Ventôse* the winter months of snow, rain, and wind; *Germinal, Floréal*, and *Prairial*, the spring months of seed-time, flowers, and meadows; while *Messidor, Thermidor*, and *Fructidor* were the summer months of harvest, heat, and fruit.

By 1795 the Girondins were again in control, although the Royalists continued to make determined efforts to change the course of events, particularly in the Vendée, where they were eventually suppressed by Hoche. On 28 October 1795 a Directory of five members assumed power. One of the five was Barras, to whom the young Corsican general, Napoléon Bonaparte (1769–1821), owed his promotion as general of the Interior. During the next four years French republican armies under Bonaparte won notable successes abroad, especially in campaigns against the Austrians (whom he was to crush at Marengo on 14 June, 1800). Returning to Paris after his failure to destroy the British fleet at the Battle of the Nile, Bonaparte found the tyrannical Directory generally detested, and with the help of the army and of Siéyès, established the Consulate by a coup d'état on 9–10 November 1799. Bonaparte became First Consul, assisted by Siéyès and Roger Ducos. A new constitution awarded him the consulate for life but such was his personal ambition that he declared himself 'Emperor of the French', and was crowned Napoléon I (1804–15) in Notre-Dame by Pope Pius VII (18 May 1804). A Civil Code, largely retaining the liberal laws of the Revolution, was laid down. Paris was embellished with monuments and bridges, as befitted the capital of an expanding empire, and was further enriched by the spoils of conquest.

First Empire. Faced by a new coalition of England, Austria, and Russia, Napoléon shattered the last two at Austerlitz in 1805, and imposed on them the humiliating Peace of Pressburg, but his fleet had been virtually destroyed at Trafalgar only six weeks earlier. In the following year Prussian armies were cowed at Jena and Auerstadt, and a further campaign against Russia was ended by the Treaty of Tilsit, which brought temporary peace to the Czar. Austria attempted to renew the struggle, but suffered disastrous defeats at Essling and Wagram. The subsequent Peace of Vienna (1809) marked perhaps the apogee of the emperor's power.

Meanwhile, his brother Joseph had been imposed on the Spaniards, whose guerrilla methods of carrying on the war in the Peninsula were to cause a continual drain on Napoléon's reserves of power. England sent out two expeditionary forces to assist the incapable Spaniards, and under

Wellington they inflicted a series of defeats on the French, among them Salamanca, and culminating in the battles of Vitoria (1813) and—on French territory—Toulouse.

Napoléon himself had just returned from the suicidal invasion of Russia, where the 'Grande Armée' although successful at Borodino, was virtually annihilated at the crossing of the Beresina by 'Generals January and February'. The Prussians, recovered from their previous defeats, were able to retaliate at Leipzig (October 1813), and also entered France. Paris itself surrendered to the Allies (31 March 1814) after skirmishing on the heights of Montmartre. The emperor abdicated at Fontainebleau, and retired to the island of Elba.

The **Bourbons** were restored, but the Treaty of Paris (30 May 1814) cut the empire down in size. During 'the Hundred Days' (26 March–24 June 1815), Napoléon made a desperate attempt to regain absolute power, having claimed at Grenoble (en route to Paris from Elba) that he had come to deliver France from 'the insolence of the nobility, the pretensions of the priests and the yoke of foreign powers'. His defeat at Waterloo (18 June) and subsequent banishment to St. Helena, where he died in 1821, enabled the king—Louis XVIII—to resume his precarious throne, which he was only able to retain by repressive measures: the University was supervised by the clergy. The reign of his successor, Charles (1824–30)X, under whom were passed the reactionary Ordinances of St.-Cloud, suppressing the liberty of the press and reducing the electorate to the landed classes, only proved that the bigoted Bourbons could 'learn nothing and forget nothing'. The 'July Revolution' of 1830 lost him his throne.

House of Orléans. Louis-Philippe (1830–48; son of Philippe-Égalité d'Orléans of the Revolution) was chosen as head of the 'July Monarchy', and the upper-middle class, who had striven for power since 1789, now achieved it. Most of the urban populace, however, still lived in pestilential conditions: some 19,000 Parisians of a total of about 900,000 died in an outbreak of cholera in 1832. The total population of France was then about 32,500,000. The only other towns of any size were Lyon and Marseille, with about 115,000 each, and Bordeaux and Rouen with about 90,000 each. France was still essentially a country dominated by agriculture and by a rural population.

The king devoted himself, with perhaps more energy than taste, to the further embellishment of the capital, and many pretentious buildings date from this period. Gas lighting had first been installed there in 1829. In 1840 the body of Napoléon was transferred with much pomp to its last resting-place under the Dôme des Invalides. The city was surrounded by a ring of fortifications in 1841–45, but these could not defend the 'citizen-king' against the mass of his people. Socialist ideas were spreading, but the conservative policy of Guizot opposed any reforms, and in the 'February Revolution' of 1848 Louis-Philippe was overthrown. In June 1848, during the brief military dictatorship of Général Cavaignac, some 4000 workmen were killed, another 1500 shot, and 11,000 imprisoned or deported to Algeria. In the elections which followed, which introduced universal male suffrage, the electorate leapt from 250,000 to 9,000,000. Among famous literary figures during the first half of the century were Balzac, Chateaubriand, Hugo, George Sand, Stendhal, Flaubert, Gautier, and Sainte-Beuve.

A **Second Republic** was set up by the provisional government, and Louis Napoléon (Bonaparte's undistinguished and indolent, but shrewd and cynical nephew, who as pretender had already made two abortive attempts to regain the throne), was elected Prince-President by almost 75 per cent of those who voted; but such was the sentimental prevalence of the idea of Empire, that in December 1851 a coup d'étât (involving the temporary imprisonment of some 30,000 in opposition) led to his election as the Emperor Napoléon III (1852–70) some months later, thus inaugurating the Second Empire.

Having adopted the clever but misleading motto of 'L'Empire c'est la paix', he proceeded to embroil the country in a succession of wars, firstly in the Crimea (1854–56), and then in Italy, which he undertook to deliver from Austrian oppression, afterwards unchivalrously demanding Savoy and Nice in recompense. Meanwhile he continued the expedient policy of his predecessor, by clearing the mass of congested, evil-smelling, and tortuous lanes of old Paris, which had so favoured the erection of barricades in 1830 and 1848. In their place Baron Haussmann laid out a number of broad boulevards which are still characteristic of much of the centre, while from 1861 Garnier's Opera-house, representative of the expansive taste of the time, was being built, and the Bois de Boulogne and the Bois de Vincennes were transformed into public parks.

But these peaceful projects were halted abruptly in 1870 when Napoléon III declared war on Prussia. The inglorious campaign ended with the capitulation of Sedan, where the emperor was taken prisoner and deposed. He died in exile at Chislehurst (England) in 1873.

Third Republic

Presidents
1871–73   Adolphe Thiers
1873–79   Maréchal MacMahon
1879–87   Jules Grévy
1887–94   Sadi Carnot
1894–95   Jean Casimir-Périer
1895–99   Félix Faure
1899–1906 Émile Loubet
1906–13   Armand Fallières
1913–20   Raymond Poincaré
1920   Paul Deschanel
1920–24   Alexandre Millerand
1924–31   Gaston Doumergue
1931–32   Paul Doumer
1932–40   Albert Lebrun

Gambetta and Thiers were largely instrumental in forming the Third Republic, which had been proclaimed (4 September 1870) while German troops advanced on Paris, which was invested on 19 September, its defenders commanded by Trochu. After a four-month siege and much suffering and famine, Paris capitulated on 28 January 1871. At this time the fortified enceinte of Paris almost 34km long, and had 67 entrances or gates. A circle of 17 detached fortresses were built at strategic points beyond this boundary wall. The Louvre had been turned into an armament workshop, the Gare d'Orléans (now Austerlitz) into a balloon factory, and the Gare de Lyon into a cannon-foundry; but the army was ill-prepared. Order was not re-established until the Communard Insurrection (18 March–29 May) had been crushed at the cost of pitched battles in the streets, in which 3000–4000 Communards were killed, and the destruction of parts of the Tuileries and other public buildings such as the Hôtel de Ville. Retaliatory measures included the summary execution of 20,000–25,000 Parisians, including women, mostly of the working classes; and the deportation of a further 4000–5000. Thiers, who was ultimately responsible for these mass killings, was then declared Président. An amnesty bill, introduced by Gambetta, was not adopted until 1880.

By September 1873 the last occupying troops had gone, but France was left to pay a heavy war indemnity and lost the provinces of Alsace and Lorraine. Various political crises, embittered by the reprehensible 'Dreyfus affair' (1894–1906), coloured much of the period up to the outbreak of the First World War. An 'Entente Cordiale' between Britain and France was established in 1904, putting an end to colonial rivalry and paving the way to future co-operation. In 1903 the 'Loi sur les Associations' was passed, and in 1905 the Church was separated from the State, both essential measures to counteract the pernicious influence the ecclesiastics and religious orders still had on education. During these decades building continued apace, even if much of it was of a meretricious nature. The 'Grand Palais' and 'Petit Palais', a new Hôtel de Ville, the Gare d'Orsay, the Eiffel Tower and the basilica of Sacré-Coeur exemplify the taste of an age, differing facets of which were well described by Zola and later by Proust. In 1910 extensive areas of Paris were inundated by the flooding of the Seine.

War with Germany broke out on 3 August 1914. French troops were dramatically reinforced at the Marne by some 11,000 men rushed to the front in Parisian taxis: citizens had the satisfaction of hearing the din of battle gradually recede and little damage was done to the capital by air raids or long-range bombardment. But although Paris was saved from another occupation, ten departments were overrun, and the attrition of three long years of trench warfare followed. In 1916, with the Battle of the Somme and the French stand at Verdun, the tide began to turn against Germany. On 11 November 1918 an armistice was signed. The provinces lost to France through the Treaty of Versailles in 1871 were restored, although Clemenceau, the 'Tiger', France's Prime Minister, wanted more. Nothing, however, could compensate for the staggering loss of life during the war years. For every ten Frenchmen aged between 20 and 45, two had been killed—a total of over 1,300,000. Slowly the country recovered her strength, even if politically she showed little initiative. In Paris, Thiers' fortifications were demolished in 1919–24, affording an opportunity to lay out a new ring of boulevards. A number of new buildings were erected for the Exhibition of 1937, including the Musées d'Art Moderne and the Palais de Chaillot. Meanwhile France's defensive policies were concretely expressed in the construction of a costly and supposedly impregnable barrier along the German frontier—the Maginot Line (named after a minister of war)—which was immediately side-stepped by invading armoured divisions at the outbreak of the Second World War (September 1939), underlining the sagacity of the French high command.

Demoralised French forces, in no state to resist and not capable of mounting a successful counter-attack, ostensibly capitulated to the triumphant Reich, while a high proportion of the British army was able to re-cross the Channel from Dunkerque (27 May–4 June 1940) in a fleet of open boats sent to their rescue. The Germans proceeded to occupy the northern half of the country and the Atlantic coast, overrunning the rest of France after 11 November 1942. For the rest of the war, the underground Resistance Movement did what it could to thwart the collaborating policies of the 'Vichy Government' (1940–44) presided over by the octogenarian Marshal

Pétain, hero of Verdun, and Pierre Laval, among others.

Meanwhile, a provisional government had been set up in London by Géneral Charles de Gaulle (1890–1970), and Free French forces co-operated in the liberation of France. Allied troops disembarking in Normandy and in the South of France (6 June and 15 August 1944 respectively) converged on Paris, which was free by late August. But an armistice with Germany was not signed until 8 May 1945. The occupying troops were, after a fierce campaign, driven from French soil, and France was able to participate in the victory celebrations.

In October 1946 the **Fourth Republic** was proclaimed, of which Vincent Auriol (1947–54) and René Coty (1954–58) were presidents. Women now had the vote and proportional representation was adopted. Slowly, despite many changes in government and despite defeat in Indo-China and revolt in Algeria, the country was restored to economic prosperity after the physical and moral devastation of war. In 1957 a Common Market (EEC) was established, in which France, West Germany, Italy and the Benelux countries were founder members.

Fifth Republic

1958–69	Charles de Gaulle
1969–74	Georges Pompidou
1974–81	Valéry Giscard d'Estaing
1981–	François Mitterrand

In 1958 de Gaulle prepared a new constitution, which was approved by a referendum, and the general was elected the first president of the new republic by universal direct suffrage, for a period of seven years. The powers of the head of state were considerably—some would say inordinately—increased: he nominates the prime minister, who in turn recommends the members of the government; he can make laws and refer decisions of major importance to popular vote by referendum; in extreme cases he has the power to dismiss the National Assembly.

In 1962 Algerian independence was proclaimed and a remarkable number of Algerians can still be seen in the industrial towns of France. In 1965 de Gaulle was returned to power with enthusiasm but with a reduced majority. In May 1968 a serious 'Student Revolution' took place in Paris, which precipitated overdue educational reforms. The following year de Gaulle was succeeded by Pompidou, who died in office in 1974. His successor was Giscard d'Estaing whose somewhat cavalier attitude to the mass of his countrymen produced a reaction, and a swing to the Left, with Mitterrand moving into the Elysée. But, like the Bourbons, the Socialist regime appears also to have 'learnt nothing and forgotten nothing'. Mitterrand immediately alienated many of his supporters by the inclusion of Communist ministers in the government, a devious manoeuvre which in turn provoked reaction. In spite of instituting changes in the electoral system in an attempt to retain Socialist control, they lost the election of March 1986, when Jacques Chirac, who had been the right-wing *maire* of Paris since 1977 (when the title was changed from that of Préfet de la Seine) became Prime Minister, inaugurating what was called a period of 'cohabitation' with the Socialist President, who in 1988 was re-elected, and the Socialist party returned to power.

In 1989, the bicentenary of the Revolution was celebrated by the inauguration of a prestigious opera house at the Place de la Bastille.

Glossary of Architectural and Allied Terms

ACAJOU, mahogany

ARC-BOUTANT, flying buttress

ARCHIVOLT, the series of mouldings which form the ensemble of an arch

ARDOISES, slates

AUTEL, altar

BOISERIES, decorative woodwork

CAISSONS, EN, coffered

CARREFOUR, crossroads

CARRELAGES, floor tiles

CASERNE, barracks

CHEVET, exterior of an apse; also ABSIDE

COLONNETTE, little column for a vaulting shaft

CONTREFORTS, buttresses

CORBELS, wooden or stone projections supporting a beam or parapet, and often elaborately carved.

DESSUS DE PORTE, a painting above a door

DONJON, keep

DOUVES, moat; wet or dry

EBENISTE, cabinet-maker

EGLISE, church

EMAIL, enamel

ESCALIER, staircase, *à vis*, spiral

FLECHE, spire

HOTEL, mansion

HOTEL DE VILLE, town hall, also MAIRIE

HOTEL-DIEU, principal hospital in many towns

JEU DE PAUME, a real tennis-court

JUBE, rood-screen

MANSARDE, roof of which each face has two slopes, the lower steeper than the upper, named after the architect François Mansart (1598–1666)

NACRE, mother of pearl

NARTHEX, an ante-nave, porch or vestibule to a church or basilica

NEF, nave

OEIL-DE-BOEUF, small circular, sometimes oval, window (bull's eye)

PIECE D'EAU, an expanse of water, usually ornamental

PORTE-COCHERE, carriage gateway

POUTRES, beams or joists

REZ DE CHAUSSEE, ground floor

TIERCERON, curved rib in Gothic vaults springing from the same point as the intersecting diagonal rib, and rising to the end of the ridge-rib

TYMPANUM, space, often decorated, between door lintel and arch

VERMEIL, silver-gilt

VITRAIL, stained-glass window

VOUSSOIRES, wedge-shaped stones used in constructing arches or vaults

Select Bibliography

General and Topographical: Pierre Couperie, Paris through the Ages (an illustrated historical atlas of urbanism and architecture); Jacques Hillairet, Connaissance du Vieux Paris; John Russell, Paris; Theodore Zeldin, The French.

Historical: Alain Decaux and André Castelot, Dictionnaire d'Histoire de France PERRIN; Saint-Simon, Historical Memoirs (3 vols., trans. and ed. Lucy Norton); John Lough, France Observed in the 17C by British travellers, and France on the Eve of Revolution: British travellers' Observations 1763–1788; Arthur Young, Travels in France; Harold Nicolson, The Age of Reason (1700–1789); William Doyle, The Oxford History of the French Revolution; Theodore Zeldin, France, 1848–1945; J. Ardagh, France Today; R.D. Anderson, France 1870–1914; Alistair Horne, The Fall of Paris; J. Huizinga, The Waning of the Middle Ages; and several studies by Richard Cobb.

Literary: Paul Harvey and J.E. Heseltine, The Oxford Companion to French Literature (new edition in preparation); D.G. Charlton (ed.), France: a Companion to French Studies; J.M.H. Reid, The Concise Dictionary of French Literature; P.E. Charvet (ed.), A Literary History of France (6 vols.).

Art and Architecture: Anthony Blunt, Art and Architecture in France, 1500–1700; W.G. Kalnein and M. Levey, Art and Architecture of the 18C in France; Vivian Rowe, Royal Châteaux of Paris; Ian Dunlop, Versailles, Royal Palaces of France, and The Cathedral's Crusade; Allan Braham, The Architecture of the French Enlightenment; Joan Evans, Art in Medieval France; Pierre Lavedan, French Architecture; Otto von Simson, The Gothic Cathedral; Michel Gallet, Paris Domestic Architecture of the 18C; David Thomson, Renaissance Paris.

Maps

For Paris and its immediate surroundings the following are recommended to supplement the Atlas section at the end of this Guide.

Michelin, *Plan de Paris* (No. 10, at 1:10,000), also available with street references as No. 12. Perhaps more convenient when walking, and containing métro and bus maps is their *Paris Atlas* (No. 11), which also includes a list of names, addresses and telephone numbers of organisations likely to be useful to visitors. Nos 10, 11 and 12 show the position of underground car-parks and 24-hour petrol stations. Other maps published annually by Michelin are *Outskirts of Paris* (No. 101, at 1:50,000), *Environs of Paris* (No. 196, at 1:100,000), *Paris Region* (No. 237, at 1:200,000). Map No. 170 covers the same area as No. 196, but concentrates on sport and open-air recreation. The **suburbs of Paris** (with street indexes) are covered in nos. 18, 20, 22 and 24. Map no. 9 concentrates entirely on forms of transport in Paris.

The **Institut Géographique National** (IGN) map of the *Environs de Paris* (No. 90, at 1:100,000) may be preferred by some to the Michelin map of the same area as it gives a better indication of contour and the general lie of the land. Paris is covered in more detail in two of their *Serie Bleue* (No. 2314 est, and ouest, at 1:25,000); and the environs by four sheets of their *Série Verte* at 1:100,000, Maps Nos 8, 9, 20 and 21. Also of use are the IGN map of *Région d'Ile de France: patrimoine artistique* at 1:150,000, which will help with the pin-pointing of monuments and, covering a more extensive area, No. 103 in their *Série Rouge* (Carte de l'Environnement Culturel et Touristique) at 1:250,000. IGN also produce an excellent series of *Forest Maps* at 1:25,000: Nos 401 (Fontainebleau), 404 (Chantilly) and 419 (St.-Germain-en-Laye) cover the wooded areas described in this Guide.

For planning your route to Paris, or on from Paris, Michelin's No. 236 for the area between the Channel ports and Paris is recommended, and also *France-Grandes Routes* (No. 989), or the IGN *France-Routes: autoroutes* (No. 901), both at 1:1,000,000. Also available are the Michelin *Motoring Atlas France* at 1:200,000, and their hardback *Road Altas France*. Collins publish a *Road Atlas France* at 1:250,000, based on IGN maps.

It is always advisable to have the latest editions of maps, which can be found at Edward Stanford Ltd, 12–14 Long Acre, London WC2E 9LP, or McCarta Ltd, 122 King's Cross Road, London WC1X 9DS, and at most good booksellers in the UK or France. The London offices of the Michelin Tyre plc are at Davy House, Lyon Road, Harrow, Middlesex, HA1 2DQ. In Paris the offices of Pneu Michelin are at 46 Av. de Breteuil, south of Les Invalides. IGN's Paris address is 107 Rue La Boétie (the Champs-Elysées end of the street: Métro. Franklin Roosevelt).

PRACTICAL INFORMATION

Formalities and Currency

Passports are necessary for all British and American travellers entering France. British passports, valid for ten years, are issued at the Passport Office, Clive House, Petty France, London SW1, and from certain provincial offices, or may be obtained for an additional fee through any travel agent. British Visitors' Passports (valid one year), available from Post Offices in the UK, are also accepted. **Visas** are not required for British or American visitors to France.

If you intend staying in France for more than three months, you should apply in advance for a *carte de séjour* to the nearest French Consulate, or if already in France, to the Préfecture de Police (Service des Etrangers) in Paris (7 Blvd du Palais, 4e). Procedures are at present in the process of revision.

British subjects wanting to work in France should write to the Consular Section of the Embassy (see below), but it should be emphasised that it is not an employment agency, nor can they help to find accommodation. They will advise on the procedure to be followed, according to the status of the person concerned under EC regulations.

Customs. Travellers by air pass through customs at the airport of arrival; those travelling on international expresses, have their luggage examined on the train, for those travelling by road, luggage is still liable to be scrutinised at the frontier or at ports of departure and disembarkation. Check with your local travel agent about current duty-free allowances.

Embassies and Consulates, etc. French Embassy, 58 Knightsbridge, London SW1X 7JT, tel. 071 235 8080. French Consulate (Visa Dept), 6A Cromwell Place, London SW7, tel 071 823 9555.

British Embassy, 35 Rue du Faubourg St.-Honoré, 75383; the Consulate is at 8 Av. Hoche, 75008; but the office issuing visas is at 16 Rue d'Anjou (near the Embassy). The Franco-British Chamber of Commerce, 8 Rue Cimarosa, 75116; British Council, 9 Rue De Constantine, 75007.

American Embassy, 2 Av. Gabriel, 75008 (just north of the Pl. de la Concorde); Canadian Embassy, 35 Av. Montaigne, 75008; Australian Embassy, 4 Rue Jean Rey, 75015; New Zealand Embassy, 7ter Rue Léonard-de-Vinci, 75016; Irish Embassy, 4 Rue Rude, 75016.

Money. The monetary unit is the *franc*, subdivided into 100 *centimes*. Bank notes of 20, 50, 100, 200 and 500 francs are in circulation, and there are also coins of 5, 10, 20 and 50 centimes, 1 franc, 2 francs, 5 francs, 10 francs and 100 francs.

Branches of most French **banks** are open from 09.00 to 16.00 from Monday to Friday; most branches close on Saturday morning, but central branches of the principal banks may have a bureau de change open from 09.00 to 12.00. Banks are likely to shut at noon on days preceding public holidays. At the Gare du Nord and Gare de Lyon the *bureaux de change* are open daily from 06.30 to 22.00 or 23.00; that at the Gare Montparnasse, from

09.00 to 19.00. Those at the international airports operate a daily service from 06.00 to 23.00.

Larger hotels will also accept and exchange travellers' cheques, but they will give a lower rate of exchange than banks. It is advisable to obtain enough French currency for incidental expenses before leaving home, particularly if arriving in France during a weekend. It is also usually worthwhile to 'shop around', for different banks give different rates of exchange. Most credit cards are generally accepted.

Currency Regulations. There is no restriction on the amount of sterling you can take out of Great Britain. However, it is advisable to check in advance at a bank on the latest regulations for the export or re-export of money from France; proof in the form of a 'declaration of entry' may be required if the sum involved is in excess of 50,000 francs.

Insurance. As members of the EC, British subjects are entitled to French health services (you will probably be refunded about 70 per cent of medical expenses) but you must take a form E111 (available from DHSS offices and post offices) as this is necessary for any refund you will apply for in France. You are also strongly advised to take out private insurance (available from travel agents and banks) which will not only cover the cost of any medical expenses but also loss of luggage, cash and other valuables. Europ Assistance, 252 High St., Croydon, tel. 081 680 1234 offers insurance cover.

Security. No objects of any value should be left inside parked cars. Beware of bag-snatchers and pickpockets. Note that any parcels or luggage left about and apparently abandoned may be destroyed by the authorities. In general, you should deposit any valuables with the manager of your hotel.

Getting to Paris

There are various ways of getting to Paris from Great Britain, and a car is not essential if only Paris and its immediate surroundings are to be visited. There are rapid rail services from London to Paris, while the quickest but least interesting way is by air: see below. Car hire facilities are available at the airports and rail termini or in central Paris.

Tourist Offices. General information, including how to get to Paris, suggestions for accommodation and how to travel around, may be obtained from the **French Government Tourist Office**, 178 Piccadilly, London W1V 0AL, tel. 071 491 7622 (lines are often engaged) and in the United States at 610 Fifth Av., New York, NY 10020 (tel. 212 757 1125), with branches at Suite 630, 645 N Michigan Av., Chicago, IL 60611 (tel. 312 337 6301); 9401 Wilshire Blvd, Beverly Hills, CA90212 (tel. 213 272 2661); and World Trade Center No. 102, 2050 Stemmons Freeway (Box 58610), Dallas, TX 75258 (tel. 214 742 7011); their Canadian office is at 1840 Ouest rue Sherbrooke, Montreal, Quebec H3H 1E4 with a branch at 1 Dundas Street W, Suite 2405 (Box 8), Toronto, Ontario M5G 1Z3 (tel. 461 593 4717).

Travel Agents. Any accredited member of the Association of British Travel Agents will sell tickets and book accommodation. Among tour operators specialising in holidays to Paris are: Eurocities, 22 Queens Rd., Southend,

SS1 1LX, tel 0702 35116; French Selection, Chester Close, Chester St. London SW1X 7BQ, tel. 071 235 0634; Paris Travel Service, Bridge House, Ware, SG12 9DF, tel. 0920 467467; Travelscene, Travelscene House, 11/15 St. Anne's Rd., Harrow HA1 1AS, tel. 081 427 4445. If you are booking a flight only, some agents will impose an additional charge for open-dated return air tickets not originally issued by themselves, and it is preferable to visit the individual airline's offices in such cases.

By Rail. Numerous and frequent passenger, car and coach ferry services are operated by British and French Railways, etc. and for the latest information on services, inquiries should be made to British Rail International, Victoria Station, London SW1, tel. 071 834 2345. The quickest sea journey is by Hovercraft (approx. 6 hours from London to Paris) though bad weather conditions can cause considerable delays or cancellations. The journey-time from London to Paris by ferry is between 8 and 11 hours.

British Rail International (tel. 071 834 2345) provide tickets, sleeping-berth tickets, seat reservations, etc. on Continental services. All trains leave from Victoria and arrive at Gard du Nord.

The French Railways Ltd (SNCF, or Société Nationale des Chemins de Fer Française), 179 Piccadilly, London W1V 0BA, tel. 071 491 1573 (next to the French Government Tourist Office) provide full details of the variety of services available, together with their cost, and sell tickets to personal callers.

To avoid considerable inconvenience and irritation on train journeys, you should check your tickets carefully at the point of issue, particularly their validity (including the return trip). You should make sure that the 'global' charge has been made, including all possible supplements, etc.

The Paris office of British Rail International is at 57 Rue St.-Roch, 75001 (tel. 42 61 85 40).

For railway stations in Paris, see p 32.

The **Channel Tunnel**. In February 1986 the Channel Tunnel Treaty was signed by representatives of the British and French governments, committing them to go ahead with the long gestating project of constructing a tunnel below the Strait of Dover/Pas de Calais. Of the several projects submitted, that of a twin-bored rail and shuttle tunnel was chosen. The immense project is being carried out under the direction of the Channel Tunnel Group Ltd in conjunction with France Manche SA, and it is expected that the tunnel will be completed and the rail link in operation by 1993.

The terminal in England is at Cheriton, just west of Folkestone, directly approached by the M20; the French terminal is near Coquelles, some 5km south west of Calais, with a link road to the A26.

By Bus/Coach. There are several regular bus or coach services from the UK to Paris, and details may be obtained from Victoria Coach Station, 164 Buckingham Palace Rd, London SW1, tel. 071 730 0202; Euroways Euro-lines, 52 Grosvenor Gardens, London SW1W 0AU, tel. 071 730 8235; Supabus, bookable through any National Express office or agent, tel. 071 709 6481, and travel agents.

By Car. Motorists driving to Paris should apply to any of the automobile assocations: Automobile Association, Fanum House, Basingstoke, Hants RG21 2EA, tel. 0256 24872; the Royal Automobile Club, Marco Polo House, 3–5 Landsdowne Rd., Croydon, tel. 081 686 2314; or the Royal Scottish Automobile Club, 17 Rutland Sq., Edinburgh. The American Automobile Association is at 8111 Gatehouse Road, Falls Church, Virginia 22042.

These organisations will provide any necessary documents, as well as suggesting routes, information on rules of the road, restrictions on caravans and trailers, availability of spare parts, insurance etc.

Comprehensive motor insurance is advisable. Driving on a provisional licence is not allowed. At junctions, where there are no signs, trafiic from the right has priority. The use of safety belts is compulsory, while crash helmets must be worn by motorcyclists. Children under ten may not travel in the front seat (unless the car has no back seat).

Both the AA and RAC have offices in Paris, the former c/o the Touring Club de France, 6–8 Rue Firmin Gillot, 15e; the latter at 8 Pl. Vendôme. The insurance facilities offered by *Europ Assistance*, 252 High St., Croydon (tel. 081 680 1234) should be taken advantage of.

The area between the French Channel ports and Paris is described in detail in Blue Guide France.

The most rapid approach to Paris from Calais or Boulogne is via the A26 autoroute. This now starts at the port of Calais or, if approaching from Boulogne, is joined at St.-Omer. The A1 from Lille crosses the A26 south east of Arras and this leads into Paris. There are tolls–*péages*–to pay on these roads. Those disembarking at **Dunkerque** should take the toll-free A25 to Lille and there join the A1 or join the A26 at St.-Omer by taking the D928 just south of Dunkerque.

There are of course a variety of alternative roads, the most frequented being the N1 from **Calais** to **Boulogne**, bypassing Montreuil, and passing through Abbeville, then following the D901 to Beauvais, also bypassed, and there regaining the N1 for Paris. Alternative routes from Abbeville are the continuation of the N1 via Amiens and Breteuil to Beauvais; or from Amiens on the D934 to meet the A1 motorway 108km north of Paris; or bearing south east from Breteuil via Clermont to either Chantilly or Senlis (see Rte 39) for Paris.

Travellers arriving at **Dieppe** may follow either the D915 via Gournay-en-Bray and the N31 to Beauvais, also bypassed, or continue on the D915 via Gisors and Pontoise, both of which may be bypassed. Another route from Dieppe is the N27 driving south to Rouen, following the N14 south east past Magny-en-Vexin to Paris (or the slower N15 south of the Seine via Vernon and Mantes); or alternatively joining the A13 autoroute south of Rouen for Paris. The A13 may also be reached from **Le Havre** via the Pont de Tancarville, or via Rouen.

It is as well to have a good idea of exactly where in Paris you are making for, and to familiarise yourself as to which exit (*sortie*) to aim for prior to entering the *Ceinture* or *Blvd Périphérique*. Exits are usually well indicated some distance in advance, but care must be taken to be in position to make your exit well before bearing off the motorway.

By Air. Regular scheduled air services between England and France are operated by Air France working in conjunction with British Airways. Full information about flights from London and other cities in the UK can be obtained from British Airways, 156 Regent St, London W1 (tel. 071 434 4700), and from Air France, Colet Court, 100 Hammersmith Rd., London W6 7JP (tel. 081 742 6600). There are also daily flights from Gatwick.

Cheaper charter flights to Paris are also available. These are advertised in the small ads of national newpapers and magazines. Among companies offer ing competitively-priced charter flights are: Dan Air, Newman House, 71 Victoria Rd., Horley, Surrey, tel. 0293 820222, Holidaymaker, 49–51

Carnaby St., London W1, tel. 071 734 3737 and Nouvelles Frontières, 11 Blenheim St., London W1, tel. 071 629 7772. The Air Travel Advisory Bureau, tel. 071 629 5000, gives up-to-date information on the best-priced flights available.

There are regular international flights from most European capitals and larger cities to Paris, and direct services from New York, Montreal, etc., and from many other non-European countries.

British Airways has a Paris office at 12 Rue Castiglione, 75001, tel. 47 78 14 14; Air France has an office at 119 Av. des Champs-Elysées, tel. 42 99 23 64.

Internal or domestic services are operated by Air Inter, 49 Av. des Champs-Elysées (tel. 45 49 25 25) and branches.

Paris is served by two international airports: **Charles de Gaulle** (near the village of Roissy-en-France, 23km north east of the capital), comprising two separate terminals; and **Orly** (South and West), 14km south of the city.

Charles de Gaulle is linked by a RER train service with the Gare du Nord and Denfert-Rochereau; Orly with the Gare d'Austerlitz and Les Invalides. They are also connected by an Air France bus service leaving each terminal every 20 minutes between 06.00 and 23.00.

A frequent and regular bus service is also provided between Charles de Gaulle, via Porte Maillot, to Etoile; and between Orly and the town terminal of Les Invalides. They run during the same period, and also operate later at night to meet scheduled flights, even if delayed.

Taxis can be found at the airports and car-hire firms have offices there.

Railway termini in Paris. The main stations, all on métro lines, have left-luggage offices (*consigne*) or lockers, trolleys, information bureaux, etc. Some, such as Gare d'Austerlitz and Gare du Nord, are also connected by regular bus services.

The main stations of the SNCF, which provide a remarkably efficient service, are:

Gare d'Austerlitz (Pl. 15; 6–8), serving the Région Sud-Ouest (Tours, Bordeaux, Toulouse, Bayonne, the Pyrenees, Madrid, etc.).

Gare de l'Est (Pl. 9; 3) for the Région Est (Reims, Metz, Strasbourg, Frankfurt, Bâle, Zürich, etc.).

Gare de Lyon (Pl. 15; 6) for the Région Sud-Est (Lyon, Dijon, Provence, Côte d'Azur, Italy, etc.), including the *Trains à Grande Vitesse* or TGV.

Gare Montparnasse (Pl. 12; 8), terminus for the Région Ouest (Brittany, La Rochelle, etc.), including the TGV, and to the west south west of France.

Gare du Nord (Pl. 9; 3) for the Région Nord (Lille, Brussels, Amsterdam, Cologne, Hamburg, etc., and also for boat-trains to Boulogne, Calais and Dunkerque).

Gare St.-Lazare (Pl. 7; 4), another terminus of the Région Ouest (Normandy lines, Rouen, and boat-trains from Dieppe, Le Havre, Cherbourg, etc.).

Note. French Railways do not have ticket control at platform barriers. Passengers purchasing a ticket in France **must** punch-and-date-stamp (or *composter*) their ticket in an orange-red-coloured machine at the platform entrance before boarding the train. Those failing to do so are liable to pay a supplementary fee/fine to the inspector. This procedure does not apply to tickets purchased outside France.

A telephone information service in English is available at (Paris) 45 82 08 41.

Transport in Paris

Public Transport in Paris. Buses (*autobus*) and the underground railway (*métro*) in Paris are controlled by the RATP (Régie Autonome des Transports Parisiens), with offices at 53 bis Quai des Grands-Augustins (just south of the Pont Neuf, with a branch in the Pl. de la Madeleine (on the eastern side of the church). For enquiries, call 43 46 14 14 (English spoken). They issue useful maps of the métro and bus systems (including lines of the RER: see p 34), and also a leaflet giving details of various summer excursions. (The Michelin Map No. 9 (Paris Transports) is handy.)

RATP also sell a 1, 3 or 5-day *Paris-Visite ticket* (available at the main railway stations, at some 70 of the more important métro stations, from the Tourist Office at 127 Av. des Champs-Elysées and from several suburban stations; also from French Railways in London), allowing unlimited travel on the RATP system; this can be useful and comparatively cheap if used constantly. The yellow weekly ticket is known as a *coupon hebdomadaire jaune*. Visitors staying more than a few days should buy a *Carte Orange* (available at any métro station), for which a passport-size photograph is required. Another convenient method is to buy a *carnet* of ten tickets at any booking office of the métro. Tickets, which operate a turnstile, should be retained until the end of the journey. They may be necessary to operate an an exit or interchange turnstile.

The **Métro** (*Métropolitan*) provides a rapid means of transport throughout Paris, and its modernisation continues. The most convenient métro stations are listed at the beginning of each route described in this Guide. Trains glide silently on rubber wheels through impressively clean stations, which lie approx. 500m apart. Platforms at the Louvre station are decorated with casts from the collections of the museum; at Varenne are casts from the adjacent Musée Rodin. The service, from 05.30 in the morning until approx. 01.30 at night, is normally frequent and regular.

As in most large cities, women should avoid travelling alone late at night, and all travellers should beware of bag-snatchers and pickpockets. The fare is the same for any distance on the main inner network, including all necessary changes, making long journeys reasonably inexpensive in comparison to the shorter distances covered—and certainly cheaper than the London underground.

The first line of the métro was opened in 1900, and certain stations, notably the Bois de Boulogne entrance of Porte Dauphine, retain their Art Nouveau decoration. The various lines are called by the names of the terminal stations: e.g. Ligne 1, Château de Vincennes–Pont de Neuilly. The direction in which the train is running is indicated by a sign naming the terminal station. At interchange stations, the passages leading to the line concerned are clearly indicated by an orange-lighted sign marked *Correspondance*, followed by the name of the terminal stations of the connecting line. Certain changes necessitate an inordinately long walk.

The fast overground lines of the RER (*Réseau Express Régional*) have been extended. Line **A** runs west to east across Paris from St.-Germain-en-Laye to Boissy St.-Léger or Torcy (connected to the métro at Etoile, Auber, Châtelet-Les Halles, Gare de Lyon and Nation). The transverse line **B** leads south from Châtelet-Les Halles to Sceaux and Robinson, and to St.-Rémy-lès-Chevreuse (the latter connected to the métro at Châtelet and Denfert-

One of the few remaining Art Nouveau signs at the entrance of the Paris métro

Rochereau). It leads north from Châtelet-Les Halles via the Gare du Nord, to the airport of Roissy-Charles de Gaulle, or Mitry-Claye.

A third line (**C**), running south of the Seine, connects St.-Quentin-en-Yvelines and Versailles-Rive-Gauche with Orly, on the line to Massy-Palaiseau, and to other suburban lines, and is connected to the métro at Javel, Champ-de-Mars, Invalides, Musée d'Orsay (Solférino), St.-Michel and Gare d'Austerlitz. Those making the excursion to Versailles will find this a convenient means of transport, but should make sure that they are on the correct branch line. Line B is useful if visiting Sceaux.

The otherwise inclusive métro ticket is valid on these three lines within Central Paris but if travelling further afield a separate one must be bought at the interchange stations, which have elaborate automatic ticket machines.

Buses. Bus-stops, which are all request stops (*arrêt facultatif*), are indicated by small placards showing the numbers of the routes and their destinations. Depending on the length of the journey, one, two or more tickets of the *carnet* will be required, the tickets for buses and the métro being interchangeable. Buses therefore are generally more expensive than the métro; ask the driver-conductor if in doubt as to the fare.

Owing to the large number of one-way streets, buses do not necessarily return along the same route, which can be confusing.

Smoking is forbidden on both buses and the métro. Where possible, avoid the use of public transport during 08.00–09.00, and during 17.30–19.30, when the rush-hour is at its height. In some areas traffic is also heavy between 12.00 and 14.00.

Parking is severely restricted in central Paris (being prohibited in many streets), and use should be made of its underground car-parks (but see Security, above). While traffic wardens are not always in evidence, a meter system does operate. In some streets tickets are obtained from machines and must then be placed behind the windscreen. Certain areas in which you may see a number of cars parked may not necessarily be legal parking places and the police, if feeling officious, may either fine you or have your car towed away. Badly-parked foreign cars are removed as ruthlessly as native ones, and may take hours to recover from the '*fourrière*' or pound, and at a considerable charge; there will also be a heavy fine to pay. Alternatively, a clamp or *sabot* may be attached to a wheel. In either case, the owner should apply to the nearest *gendarme* or *Commissariat de Police*.

River Trips. *Les Bateaux-Mouches* (Pont de l'Alma) and *Les Bateaux-Parisiens* (Pont d'Iéna or Pont Neuf) run trips along the Seine both during the day and after dark, which can offer some unusual and attractive low-level vistas as the launch emerges from beneath the numerous bridges. (The importance of the river in the growth and planning of Paris is, perhaps, made more apparent by taking a leisurely walk, between the Pont d'Iéna and the Pont de Sully, along the Quais. Unfortunately, these are less attractive than they once were since traffic has been diverted along the water's edge.)

Taxis will be seen cruising or waiting at a rank, marked 'Tête de Station', and with a telephone. Visitors making regular use of taxis should make a note of the telephone number of the nearest rank.

Some taxi-drivers expect a tip of 10 per cent in addition to the charge on the meter. Rates are displayed inside the vehicle. Note that the night tariff (between 22.00 and 06.00) is considerably higher than the day. There is an additional charge for luggage placed in the boot, and—unaccountably—taxis waiting (or merely arriving at a queue) at a railway terminus, are also allowed to charge extra.

Parisian taxi-drivers have gained a reputation for truculence and rapacity, but usually their bark is worse than their bite. Female taxi-drivers are escorted by their Alsatians. Any complaints should be addressed to the *Service des Taxis de la Préfecture de Police*, 36 Rue des Morillons, 70015.

Topography of Paris

Paris, the capital of France, lies on both banks of the Seine, near the centre of the so-called Paris Basin. Its height above sea-level varies from 25 to 130m, and its distance from the sea is 150km (or over 320km by the windings of the river). The Seine, the third in length of the four great rivers of France, enters the capital some 500km from its source, and describes a curved course through the city, at the same time forming two islands, the Ile St.-Louis and the larger Ile de la Cité.

Much of the attraction of central Paris stems from the way the river, with its numerous bridges, has been used to unite rather than divide the northern or Right Bank (*Rive Droite*) and the southern or Left Bank (*Rive Gauche*); indeed, the two are much more nearly of equal importance than the north and south banks of the Thames. Unlike London, Paris was bounded by a definite line of ramparts, which, although they have long been demolished and their sites built over, served to contain the population, denser than in any other European city (recently over 21,800 inhab. per square kilometre), and enclosed an area of 7800 hectares. The line of the 19C defensive walls can be imagined by following the exterior Blvd Périphérique, and remains of certain forts still survive some distance beyond, although largely engulfed by *banlieues* (suburbs).

The total municipal population of Paris, according to the census of 1990, was—in round figures—2,176,000, with 10,600, 000 in greater Paris, while the total population of France was approx. 54,257,000. (A century or so earlier the figures were 2,269,000 for Paris and 39,238,000 for France.) Some 20 per cent of the population of Paris is made up of foreigners, many from the poorer nations of Europe, but also including large numbers of Algerians, Tunisians, Moroccans, and others from Black Africa, as confirmed by recent demographic surveys. Those interested in such figures and many other statistics should contact the *Institut National de la Statistique et des Etudes Economiques* (INSEE), its head offices at 18 Blvd Adolphe Pinard, 70014e, and with its centre for the Ile-de-France in Tour Gamma A, 195 Rue de Bercy, Paris 70012 (easily approached from the level of the Gare de Lyon).

With the growth of Paris, the old department of the Seine, by a decree which took effect in 1968, was subdivided into four new departments: Ville-de-Paris (75; again with a *Maire*); Hauts-de-Seine (92; préfecture Nanterre); Seine-St.-Denis (93; préfecture Bobigny); and Val-de-Marne (94; préfecture Créteil). The old dpartment of Seine-et-Oise was similarly divided into three: Val-d'Oise (95; préfecture Cergy-Pontoise); Yvelines (78; préfecture Versailles); and Essonne (91; préfecture Évry). At the same time the department of Seine-et-Marne (77; préfecture Melun) was incorporated to make up the District de la Région Parisienne, now known as La Région d'Ile-de-France.

The topography of Paris can perhaps be best understood by taking Pl. de la Concorde (Pl. 7; 7) as a focal point, although historically the Pl. du Parvis-Notre-Dame (from which kilometric distances in France are measured) might be more appropriate. Here (and elsewhere) you can appreciate the artistic town-planning of the past, which deliberately allowed vistas from one bank of the river to extend to the far bank. These great perspectives are one of the most memorable features of Paris.

Turning to the north west, you can see the Arc de Triomphe (and La Défense beyond), at the far end of the Av. des Champs-Elysées: in the opposite direction, the immense bulk of the Louvre beyond the gardens of the Tuileries. This is flanked, to the north, by the Rue de Rivoli, which with its continuation, the Rue St.-Antoine, leads to the Pl. de la Bastille; and further E, by the Rue du Faubourg St.-Antoine, to the Pl. de la Nation, and Vincennes beyond. It is perhaps this transverse road axis which, more than the river, cuts Paris into two almost equal parts.

The **Arrondissements**. These municipal districts, of which there are 20 in central Paris, each with its *Maire* and *Mairie*, or town hall, are important administrative and topographical entities, and their names and numbers convey far more than that of a municipal borough or postal district in London. You can make yourself familiar with the position of some of them: see plan on pp 2–3 of the Atlas.

As in London, certain areas are known more familiarly by their unofficial titles. Their numbering follows a spiral working out clockwise from the centre. When addressing correspondence to Paris the arrondissements should be written as 75001, 75002, etc. rather than 1er, 2e., etc., the prefix 75 indicating the *department*.

75001; Louvre: the western half of the Cité, the Louvre, Pl. Vendôme, Palais-Royal and St.-Eustache.

75002; Bourse: also the Bibliothèque Nationale.

75003; Temple: comprising the north half of the Marais, the Temple and Archives.

75004; Hôtel de Ville: includes the eastern half of the Cité, with Notre-Dame, the Ile St.-Louis and the Centre Pompidou, and the southern part of the Marais, with the Pl. des Vosges, and is bounded by the Pl. de la Bastille to the east.

75005; Panthéon: the 'Quartier Latin', with the Sorbonne, Panthéon, Val-de-Grâce and Jardin des Plantes.

75006; Luxembourg: with St.-Germain-des-Prés, St.-Sulpice and the Palais du Luxembourg.

75007; Palais-Bourbon: comprising the Faubourg St.-Germain, the Musée d'Orsay, Les Invalides, the Ecole Militaire and bounded to the west by the Eiffel Tower.

75008; Elysée: with the Pl. de la Concorde, the Madeleine, the Champs-Elysées and Faubourg St.-Honoré, and including the Parc Monceau to the north, and containing the Av. George-V to the west.

75009; Opéra: reaching up to the Blvd de Clichy and Pl. Pigalle.

75010; Enclos St.-Laurent: with the Gares du Nord and de l'Est, and Hôpital St.-Louis.

75011; Popincourt: the area north east of the Pl. de la Bastille and reaching to Pl. de la Nation.

75012; Reuilly: the area south east of the Pl. de la Bastille, including the Gare de Lyon and Bercy.

75013; Gobelins: the area south of the Gare d'Austerlitz, including the Gobelins and Pl. d'Italie.

75014; Observatoire: including the Cimetière de Montparnasse, Parc de Montsouris and Cité Universitaire.

75015; Vaugirard: the area south west of the Tour Montparnasse and Av. de Suffren.

75016; Passy: between the Seine and Bois de Boulogne, its northern half crossed by the Avenues Foch, Victor-Hugo and Kléber, radiating from the Etoile, and containing the districts of Chaillot, Passy and Auteuil.

75017; Batignolles Monceau: the area north west of the Etoile.

75018; Butte Montmartre: the area north east of the Pl. de Clichy and reaching as far east as the Rue d'Aubervilliers.

75019; Buttes-Chaumont: and including La Villette.

75020; Ménilmontant: including Père Lachaise.

Few of the *banlieues* of Paris merit the attention of the visitor, unless you are interested in *urbanisme*. Whatever one may feel about the vast schemes of *aménagement* and *rénovation* taking place in all areas, the efforts of the road engineers have clearly been successful.

Employment of Time

A good deal of Paris may be seen in a week by the energetic visitor, but this will allow only a superficial glance at some of its museums. With the information on opening times given on pp 50–55 you will be able to plan your campaign and, using the index and atlas section, devise an itinerary of your own. The routes in this Guide have been designed to assist you to explore the city systematically.

A list of convenient métro stations is given at the beginning of most routes: see also Atlas, pp 4–5.

For those with the time and curiosity, an interesting general view of much of Paris may be had, for the price of a single ticket, by taking the métro at the Etoile (for example, or indeed anywhere on Ligne 6), direction Nation; then changing onto Ligne 2, direction Porte Dauphine (two stops beyond Etoile). Much of the journey is made overground rather than under, so you can get a glimpse of areas which you would not otherwise have any particular reason for visiting. The journey can of course be made in the reverse direction.

For those spending only a short time in central Paris, and with no particular priorities, it is perhaps advisable to visit first the Cité, Rtes 1–2, before crossing to the Left Bank, where you might concentrate on the 'Quartier Latin' (including the Musée de Cluny) and the Faubourg St.-Germain (including the Musée d'Orsay, if only for the Impressionists; Rte 9); nor should Les Invalides be overlooked (Rte 11).

Crossing to the Right Bank, you can follow Rte 13 (taking in the Musée des Arts Décoratifs, Rte 16) to the Louvre, the contents of which are described in Rte 15. You can combine Rte 17 with a view of the Madeleine and the Opéra, but of more interest is the Marais (Rte 21; including the Pl. des Vosges and the Musée Carnavalet), the Musée d'Art Moderne at the Centre Pompidou should be seen (Rte 20). The excursion to the Château of Versailles, at least, should be made (see Rte 34), and—depending on your preferences—either the Musée Condé at Chantilly or the Château de Fontainebleau; see Rtes 39 and 40.

Hotels and Restaurants

Hotels of every class, size and price abound in Paris, but it is prudent to book rooms in advance either directly or through a travel agency, for they are often full in the tourist season, particularly at Easter and during the course of exhibitions, trade fairs, etc. Branches of the *Office de Tourisme de Paris* (see p 48) will try to make on-the-spot bookings, which are automatically cancelled if not taken up within 11/2 hours. They can also provide an up-to-date *Guide des Hôtels* for Paris and region. Among other useful lists is that published by *Michelin*, entitled *Paris and environs: Hotels and Restaurants*, which includes well-equipped hotels by arrondissements, together with other useful information.

The latest edition of the annual publications of *Michelin, Kléber, Gault-Millau,* the *Logis de France* or the *Guide des Relais Routiers* are useful in the selection of accommodation and restaurants to suit your taste and pocket. Local Syndicats d'Initiatives can also provide a brochure listing hotels in their area. It is wise, during certain seasons, to book in advance if a weekend excursion is planned.

All hotels are officially classified and are graded by stars, depending on their amenities and the type of hotel, from 4-stars 'L' (Luxury) to 1-star (plain but comfortable). Hot and cold running water will be found in all bedrooms, but only a proportion of hotels in the 1-, 2- and even 3-star categories have rooms with a private bath and WC en suite, although many more will provide a shower and bidet. Similarly, many hotels have no restaurant, although almost all will provide a continental breakfast: but see below.

Charges vary, of course, according to the grade of hotel and the time of year, being at their highest from mid June to mid September. In most hotels (especially when quoting 'en pension' terms) 15 per cent is now added to the bill for 'service'—whether provided or not—and certainly when the bill is marked 'service et taxes compris' (s.t.c.) no additional gratuity is expected.

Most of the more expensive hotels in Paris are situated in the 1st, 6–10th and 16–17th arrondissements. Large hotels outside the centre are used by groups and those attending trade fairs but are inconvenient for the tourist. It is important to check the hotel's location and room price when booking, particularly since many appear to be geared to the 'expense-account' visitor.

Only a few hotels are listed below; omission does not imply any adverse judgement.

Hotels in Paris

LUXURY CLASS: Meurice, 228 Rue de Rivoli, 75001 (42 60 38 60); George V, 31 Av. George V, 75008 (47 23 54 00); Plaza Athénée, 25 Av. Montaigne, 75008 (47 23 78 33); Résidence Maxim's de Paris, 42 Av. Gabriel, 75008 (45 61 96 33); Royal Monceau, 37 Av. Hoche, 75008 (45 61 98 00).

4-STAR HOTELS: Jeu de Paume, 54 rue St.-Louis-en-l'Ile, 75004 (43 26 14 18); Le Bristol, 112 Rue du Faubourg St.-Honoré, 75008 (45 61 97 22); Terrass, 12 Rue Joseph de Maistre, 75018 (46 06 72 85); Ritz, 15 Pl. Vendôme, 75001 (42 60 38 30); Le Raphaël, 17 Av. Kléber, 75016 (45 02 16 00); Pullman St.-Jacques, 17 Blvd St.-Jacques, 75014 (45 89 89 80); La Trémoille, 14 Rue la Trémoille, 75008 (47 23 34 20).

3-STAR HOTELS: Lutèce, 65 Rue St.-Louis-en-l'Ile, 75004 (43 26 23 52); Colbert, 7 Rue de l'Hôtel-Colbert, 75005 (43 25 85 65); Abbaye St.-Germain, 10 Rue Cassette, 75006 (45 44 38 11); Regents Garden, 6 Rue Pierre-Demoins, 75017 (45 74 07 30); Bretonnerie, 22 Rue St.-Croix-Bretonnerie, 75004 (48 87 77 63); Les Jardins d'Eiffel, 8 Rue Amélie, 75007 (47 05 46 21); Ministère, 31 Rue Surène, 75008 (42 66 21 43)Lenox St.-Germain, 9 Rue Université, 75007 (42 96 10 95).

2-STAR HOTELS: Esmeralda, 4 Rue St.-Julien-le-Pauvre, 75005 (43 54 19 20); Chopin, 45 Passage Jouffroy, 75009 (47 70 58 10); Timhotel Montmartre, 11 Rue Ravignan, 75018 (42 55 74 79); Hotel des Celestins, 1 Rue Charles V, 75004 (48 87 87 04); Belle Vue et Charoit d'Or, 39 Rue de Turbigo, 75003 (48 87 45 60); Solferino, 91 Rue de Lille, 75007 (47 05 85 54); Du Vieux Paris, 9 Rue Gît-le-Coeur, 75006 (43 54 41 66); Prima Lepic, 29 Rue Lepic, 75018 (46 06 44 64).

1-STAR HOTELS: Floridor, 28 Pl. Denfert Rochereau, 75014 (43 21 35 53); Hotel de Nice, 42 bis Rue de Rivoli, 75004 (42 78 55 29).

Hotels in Versailles

LUXURY CLASS: Trianon Palace, 1 Blvd de la Reine, 78000 (30 84 38 00);

Pullman Versailles, 2 bis Av. de Paris 78000 (39 53 30 31).

3-STAR HOTELS: Hotel Bellevue, 12 Av. de Sceaux, 78000 (39 50 13 41); Hotel de Versailles, 7 Rue Ste.-Anne, 78000 (39 50 64 54); Residence du Berry, 14 Rue d'Anjou, 78000 (39 49 07 07).

2-STAR HOTELS: Paris Hotel, 14 Av. de Paris, 78000 (39 50 56 00); Clagny, 6 impasse de Clagny, 78000 (39 50 18 09).

Restaurants of every kind and category are plentiful in Paris, and have likewise been officially graded to indicate that they adhere to certain criteria. Although the prices tend to be comparatively high, very often (but by no means always) you will get better value for money than in some other countries where the ritual and etiquette of eating is not taken quite so seriously.

At most restaurants the day's set menu, '*à prix fixe*', is available, with a choice of dishes, and at a much lower price than '*à la carte*', even if somewhat unimaginative in the more modest establishments. Both menus, with prices, are displayed at the entrance. Frequently there is more than one selected menu to choose from, apart from the recommended 'plat du jour'.

The **wine**, either *rouge, blanc* or *rosé*, in bottles or carafes, is usually very fair at most restaurants, while many can provide a liberal choice of superior wines at relatively high prices. When dining *à la carte*, be careful not to add more dishes to the meal than you really want; the slightest addition (of vegetables, for example) can easily swell the bill by a disproportionate amount. Check the bill (*l'addition*), which should be in writing, carefully. The gratuity is now usually included in the price of a set menu but this is not so for à la carte. Any misunderstanding can be avoided by asking if service is included, *Le service est-il compris?*. If no tip has been included, the waiter may be given an additional 10 per cent or so of the bill, according to the quality of service: less where a considerable proportion of the total is for a single bottle.

There are, of course, a number of French gastronomic guides (see above) listing a great range of eating-places in Paris and elsewhere, among them the better-known 'de luxe' restaurants where French cookery should reach its perfection—at a price which few can afford—but you will often get better value for money at the less pretentious establishments.

Unfortunately there is a tendency, particularly in areas frequented by tourists rather than by a regular clientele, to serve stereotyped meals of a mediocre quality for the prices charged. Many restaurants are closed on Sundays, and during August. It is advisable to book a table in advance at the better-known or more fashionable restaurants.

Only a few restaurants are listed below; omission does not imply any adverse judgement.

Restaurants in Paris

Luxury class: Lucas-Carton, 9 Pl. de la Madeleine, 75008 (42 65 22 90); La Tour d'Argent, 15–17 Quai de la Tournelle, 75005 (43 54 23 31); Prunier Madeleine, 9 Rue Duphot, 75001 (42 60 36 04); Le Grand Véfour, 17 Rue de Beaujolais, 75001 (42 96 56 27); Jamin, 32 Rue Longchamp, 75116 (47 27 12 27), Drouant, Pl. Gaillon, 75002 (42 65 15 16).

Medium priced: La Bûcherie, 41 Rue de la Bûcherie, 75005 (43 54 78 27);

L'Embellie, 19 Rue des Ursins, 75004 (46 33 26 29); Dodin-Bouffant, 25 Rue Frédéric Sauton, 75005 (43 25 25 14); Le Mercure Valent, 15 Rue de Petits-Champs, 75001 (42 97 53 85); Flo, 7 Cour des Petites-Ecuries, 75010 (47 70 13 59); La Coupole, 102 Blvd du Montparnasse, 75014 (43 20 14 20); Brasserie Balzar, 49 Rue des Ecoles, 75005 (43 54 13 67); La Macadam, 23 Rue de Turbigo, 75002 (42 36 52 32). Port Alma, 10 Av. New York, 75116 (47 23 75 11); Beauvilliers, 52 Rue Lamark, 75018 (42 54 54 42).

Modestly priced: La Vieux Chêne, 69 Rue Mouffetard, 75005 (43 54 79 22); Le Petit St.-Benoît, 75006 (no telephone bookings); Au Charpentiers, 10 Rue Mabillon, 75006 (43 26 30 05); Le bateau Lavoir, 8 Rue Garreau, 75018 (46 06 02 00); Chartier, 7 Rue de Faubourg Montmartre, 75009 (47 70 86 28); La Timonerie, 35 Quai Tournelle, 75005 (43 25 44 42).

Restaurants in Versailles

Luxury class: Les Trois Marches, Hotel Trianon Palace, 1 Blvd de la Reine, 78000 (30 84 38 00).

Medium priced: Le Chesnoy, 24 Rue Pottier, 78000 (39 54 01 01); Le Champfagou, 3 Rue des eux-Portes, 78000 (39 50 64 04).

Modestly priced: Brasserie du Théítre, 15 Rue des Réservoirs, 78000 (39 50 03 21); L'Instant Jardin, 27 Rue de Satory, 78000 (39 53 85 54).

The many **Cafés** of Paris—there were said to be as many as 300 as early as 1715—are more numerous in the larger streets and squares of Paris, and in many cases tables and chairs are set out on the adjacent pavement (known as the *terrasse*—or behind a glazed conservatory/observatory—where you can spend an entertaining hour watching the passers-by.

The *café* or *café crème* is usually very good, but tea-making is still a perfunctory performance. A 'Coninental' breakfast (*petit déjeuner*) may be obtained in the mornings at many cafés, with fresh rolls, *croissants*, or *brioches*, and butter, with coffee or—less frequently—chocolate.

The usual order for a small beer is a *demi*; draught beer is *à la pression*. It is cheaper to stand at the bar; prices are automatically raised if you take a seat. The waiter should not be paid after each drink but just before you leave. Prices charged at some pretentious cafés or *patisseries* are quite exorbitant and it is always wise to check prices before ordering, to avoid an unpleasant shock.

Menu

Many French culinary terms and processes are universally known, but to assist those not so well acquainted with some of the more common foods, etc., a representative list is appended with their English equivalents.

Les Potages, Soups

Bouillon, broth
Consommé, clear soup
Crème, thick soup

Hors-d'Œuvre and Salads

Crudités, raw vegetables, usually sliced, chopped, or grated
Tapénade, a purée of black olives, capers, anchovies, tunny-fish, etc., from the provençal *tapéno*, for capers
Salade Niçoise, with tomato, anchovy, onions and olives
Salade Cauchoise, of potatoes, celery and ham
Salade panachée, mixed salad
Salade verte, green salad; also
Salade simple, or *de saison*
Salade de riz aux tomates, rice and tomato salad
A *Salade Lyonnaise* in fact consists of a variety of meats, seasoned and with an oil, vinegar, shallot and parsley dressing, and served on separate dishes.

Les Oeufs, Eggs (including some hot hors d'oeuvre)

à la coque, soft-boiled; *mollets*, medium-boiled; *durs*, hard-boiled; *sur le plat*, or *au plat*, fried; *pochés*, poached; *en cocotte*, baked in a ramekin; *brouillés*, scrambled
Omelette aux fines herbes, savoury omelette; *au jambon*, ham omelette, etc., and an infinite variety of others
oeufs durs soubise, hard-boiled eggs with an onion and cream sauce
Quiche Lorraine, cream and bacon tart
Pissaladière, provençal onion and anchovy pie
Gratin Dauphinois, sliced potatoes cooked in cream
Gratin savoyard, similar, but with the addition of eggs and cheese

Les Poissons, les Coquillages et Crustacés (or **Fruits de Mer**), etc., Fish and Shellfish

not forgetting such delicacies as *Cuisses de grenouilles*, frogs' legs; and *Escargots*, snails
Alose, shad
Anchois, anchovies
Anguille, eel
Bar, bass
Barbou, brill
Baudroi, angler fish
Bellon, a type of oyster
Blanchaille, whitebait, a dish of which is *friture*, deep fried
Brochet, pike, often the base of *quenelles Calmars*, inkfish
Carpe, carp
Chipirones, squid
Colin, hake
Coquilles St.-Jacques, scallops
Crevettes, prawns or shrimps
Daurade, sea bream
Ecrevisse, fresh-water crayfish
Encornet, squid
Eperlans, smelts
Espadon, swordfish
Harengs, herrings
Homard, lobster
Huîtres, oysters

Lamproie, lamprey *Langouste*, crawfish or lobster; *langoustine*, Dublin Bay prawn
Lotte, burbot, monkfish
Loup, a kind of sea bass
Maquereau, mackerel
Merlan, whiting
Mérou, brill
Morue, salt cod (see *brandade*, below); fresh cod is *Cabillaud*
Moules, mussels *Mulet*, grey mullet
Omble-Chevalier, char
Palourdes, clams; also *Praires*
Poulpe, octopus
Raie, skate (often served '*au beurre noir*', with black butter)
Rouget, red mullet
St.-Pierre, John Dory
Saumon, salmon; *fumé*, smoked
Thon, tunnyfish or tuna
Truite, trout
Aïoli, a mayonnaise of vinegar, oil and pulverised garlic, often eaten with fish
Quenelles, fish (often pike) or meat dumpling roll, served in a sauce

Les Viandes, Meat

Agneau, lamb; *gigot*, leg of lamb; *carré d'agneau*, cutlets
Boeuf, beef; *queue de boeuf*, ox-tail; *Rosbif*, roast beef; (*Bifteck* is a *franglais* word which has been in use since 1786)
Cochon de lait, sucking-pig
Mouton, mutton
Porc, pork; see below
Veau, veal; *ris de veau*, sweetbreads
Viandes froides, cold meats

Meat may be ordered *bleu*, very rare; *saignant*, underdone; *à point*, medium; or *bien cuit*, well done
Daube, a stew; other forms are *pot-au-feu* and *marmite*
Cassoulet, a stew of mutton, pickled pork, sausages and possibly goose, and haricot beans, originating in Castelnaudary

Among general terms are:
Basquaise, with tomato and pimento
Bercy, with wine and shallots
Bourguignonne, cooked in red wine, with bacon, mushrooms and small onions
Cauchoise, with cream, calvados and apples
Chasseur or *forestière*, with mushrooms
Lyonnaise, with onions
à la meunière, cooked slowly in butter
à la nivernaise, with a glazed carrot and onion garnish
Normande, with a cream sauce
Parmentier, with potatoes
Périgourdine, with truffles and/or *foie gras*
Povençale, with oil, tomatoes and garlic

La Charcuterie, Pork products and cooked meats, etc.

Andouille, smoked chitterling sausage; *andouillettes*, a smaller version
Boudin, black pudding (or white if pork-based); *boudin blanc*, chicken mousse
Cervelles, brains
Foie, liver
Jambon, ham; *jambon cuit*, York Ham; *fumé* or *cru*, smoked; *de Bayonne*, salt-cured
Pieds de porc, pigs' trotters
Rillettes, potted shredded pork; in *Rillons* the pieces of pork are larger
Rognons, kidneys
Saucisses, sausages; *saucisson*, salami sausage
Terrines, potted meats

Les Volailles et le Gibier, Poultry and Game

Alouettes, larks
Bécasse, woodcock
Caille, quail
Canard, duck; *canard sauvage*, wild duck; *caneton*, duckling (those of Duclair and Nantes are reputed)
Cerf or *Chevreuil*, venison
Dinde or *dindon*, female and male turkey
Faisan, pheasant
Grives, thrushes
Lapin, rabbit
Lièvre, hare
Oie, goose; *paté de foie gras* is made from goose liver; a *confit d'oie* is a conserve of goose preserved in its own fat
Palombes, wood-pigeons
Perdreau or *perdrix*, partridge
Pintade, guinea-fowl
Pluviers, plovers
Poulet, chicken; *poularde*, capon
Sanglier, wild boar; *marcassin*, a young wild boar
Sarcelle, teal

Les Légumes et Aromates, Vegetables and Herbs

Ail, garlic; *aïoli*, a mayonnaise of pulverised garlic, vinegar, oil, etc.
Artichauts, globe or leaf artichokes; *fonds*, hearts; *Topinambours*, Jerusalem artichokes
Asperges, asparagus
Aubergine, egg plant
Betterave, beetroot
Blettes, chard
Céleris, celery
Carottes, carrots
Céleri-rave, celeriac; *céleri-rave rémoulade*, in mustard sauce
Cerfeuil, chervil
Champignons, cultivated mushrooms. Other common edible fungi are *Cèpes* (boletus edulis), *Chantarelles* or *Girolles*, and *Morilles Chicorée*, Belgian endive (or witloof); *chicorée frisée* or *scarole*, curly chicory

Chou, cabbage; *chou rouge*, red cabbage; *choux de Bruxelles*, Brussels sprouts
Choucroute, sauerkràut
Choufleur, cauliflower
Ciboulettes, chives
Concombre, cucumber
Cornichon, gherkin
Courge, marrow; *Courgettes*, baby marrows
Cresson, watercress
Echalotes, shallots
Endives belges; see above
Epinards, spinach
Estragon, tarragon
Fenouil, fennel
Fèves, broad beans
Genièvre, baies de, juniper berries
Haricots blancs, white haricot beans; *haricots verts*, French beans; *Flageolets*, green beans
Huile d'Olive, olive oil; *huile de noix*, walnut oil
Laitue, lettuce; *salade*, green salad
Lentilles, lentils
Míche, lamb's-lettuce or corn-salad
Navets, turnips
Oignons, onions
Oseille, sorrel
Persil, parsley
Petits pois, green peas
Pissenlits, dandelions
Poireaux, leeks
Pois chiches, chick peas
Poivre, pepper
Poivrons, sweet peppers (pimentos)
Pommes de terre, potatoes
Raifort, horseradish
Riz, rice
Romarin, rosemary
Truffes, truffles

Les Fromages, Cheeses

There are numerous regional varieties, and the initials c, e, and g indicate whether they are produced from cow (*vache*), ewe (*brebis*), or goat-milk (*chèvre*). Only some of the more usual types are listed.

Normandy: *Bondon, Camembert, Livarot, Pont-l'Evêque, Boursin* (all c)
  Northern France and Ile-de-France: *Mimolette, St.-Paulin, Brie, Coulommiers* (all c)
  Brittany: *Port-du-Salut* (c)
  Touraine and Poitou: *St.-Paulin* (c), *Chabichou* and *Ste.-Maure* (both g)
  Berry and Burgundy: *Valençay* (g), *St.-Florentin* and *Epoisse* (both c)
  The Pyrenean region produces several, mostly cow, but also ewe-cheeses
  The Causses, to the north east, produce the renowned *Roquefort* (e) and *Pelardon des Cévennes* (g)

The Auvergne is noted for the *Bleu-d'Auvergne, Cantal, St.-Nectaire* and *Fourme-d'Ambert* (all c)

Alsace and Lorraine: *Carré-de-l'Est, Munster* and *Rocollet (all c)*

The Franche-Comté produces the *Comté*, and further south, the *Bleu-de-Bresse* (both c)

Savoy is noted for *Beaufort, Emmental, Reblochon* and *Tomme* (all c); in the Lyonnais and Dauphiny, the *Rigotte-de-Condrieu* (c), the *Picodon* and *St.-Marcellin* (both g) are reputed; and in Provence, the *Banon* (g)

There are of course any variety of cream cheeses, such as the *Petit-Suisse*, and numerous processed forms, some encrusted with grape-pips, or walnuts, or dusted with pepper, etc.

The *Fondue Savoyarde* consists of melted cheese (often the *Vacherin*), wine and kirsch, kept at a sizzling temperature, into which cubes of bread are dipped.

Note that cheese is always eaten before the dessert in France.

Les Desserts, Dessert (and also fruit and nuts, etc.)

Abricots, apricots
Ananas, pineapples
Bananes, bananas
Cannelle, cinnamon
Cassis, black current
Cerises, cherries
Citron, lemon
Coings, quinces
Figues, figs
Fraises, strawberries; *fraises des bois*, wild strawberries
Framboises, raspberries
Fruits confits, crystallised fruit; *fruits en compote*, stewed
Groseilles, red or white currants; *Groseilles à Maquereau*, gooseberries
Marrons, chestnuts; *marrons glacés*, candied chestnuts
Mendiant, a plate of mixed almonds, raisins, etc.
Miel, honey
Mûres, mulberries; *mûres de ronce*, blackberries
Myrtilles, bilberries
Noisettes, hazel-nuts
Noix, walnuts
Pamplemousse, grapefruit
Pêches, peaches
Poires, pears
Pommes, apples
Pruneaux, prunes
Prunes, plums; *Mirabelles*, small yellow plums; *Reine-claudes*, greengages
Raisins, grapes; *raisin sec*, raisin
Sucre, sugar
Crème brulée, caramelised cream; *crémets*, a confection of thick cream and egg yolks
Flan, cream caramel
Glaces, ice-creams
Pâte d'amande, almond paste or marzipan; *pâte des prunes*, plum paste; *pâte de coings*, quince paste, etc.
Soufflés hardly require introduction

Patisseries et Confiseries, Pastries, Cakes and Confectionery

Berlingots, pyramid-shaped sweets
Confiture, jam; *confiture d'orange*, marmalade
Crêpes dentelles, pancakes
Croissant, a crescent-shaped rich bread roll
Dragées, sugared almonds
en brioche, baked in dough
en croute, baked in a pastry case
Galettes, a biscuit
Gâteaux, cakes, *gâteaux secs*, biscuits
Gaufres, waffles
Macarons, almond paste macaroons
Nougatines, caramelised ground almonds
Pain d'Epices, spiced honey-cake or gingerbread
Petits fours, fancy biscuits
Pain, bread, is usually bought at *Boulangeries*; there are numerous forms and varieties, the most common perhaps being the *baguette*, a long roll of medium thickness, also thinner, known as a *ficelle*; the *épi* is of more irregular shape; there is also the larger *pain campagne*, etc.

Postal and Other Services

Post Offices, indicated by the sign **PTT** (prounounced Pay Tay Tay), are open from 08.00 to 19.00 on weekdays, and until 12.00 on Saturdays. The main Post Office in Paris is at the Hôtel des Postes, 52 Rue du Louvre, 1er, which provides a 24-hour service in some departments, while that at 71 Av. des Champs-Elysées, 8e, is open from 08.00 until 22.00. The main post office is the destination of all letters, etc. marked merely 'Poste Restante, Paris', without any arrondissement number being given. When the arrondissement number is given, the head post office in the appropriate district should be visited. Correspondence marked 'poste restante' may be addressed to any post office, and is handed to the addressee on proof of identity (passport preferable). Letters may be sent registered (*recommandé*) for a small fee, and are only delivered with proof of identity.

Telegrams in English may be telephoned to 42 33 21 11. There are *Telex* offices at 7 Rue Feydeau and 9 Pl. de la Bourse, both 2e. Telex message can be telephoned to 42 47 12 12; many post offices now have FAX machines.

Letter-boxes are painted yellow. Postage-stamps (*timbres*) are on sale at all post offices and most tobacconists.

Telephones. Public call-boxes can be found at most post offices, métro stations, cafés, restaurants and at some bus stops (taxiphones). With patience, sufficient small change or a *Télécarte*, you should have little difficulty in making the right connection. You can buy télécartes at post offices, France Telecom agencies, tobacconists and railway stations. Reversed-charge calls ('PVC') are accepted. Some call-boxes only take *jetons*, which have to be bought. Note that the charge for calls made from hotels may be as much as 40 per cent higher than for those made from public telephone boxes. When calling abroad, you must wait after dialling the prefix 19 (international) for a change in the dialling tone before continuing.

At present the full tariff applies from 08.00–12.30, 13.30–18.00 on week days, and until 12.30 on Saturday. It is 30 per cent less between 12.30–13.30 and 18.00–21.30 Monday–Friday and between 12.30–13.30 on Saturday; 50 per cent less between 06.00–08.00 and 21.30–22.30 Monday–Friday, 06.00–08.00 and 13.30–22.30 on Saturday and 06.00–23.00 on Sunday. The charge is 65 per cent less between 22.30–06.00 daily (or rather, nightly); these reductions only apply within France.

When telephoning the UK from France, first dial 19, then 44 after the tone change, followed by the area code (but omit the zero) and then the number required. It is a sensible precaution to carry a list of essential telephone numbers with you when you travel. When calling the provinces from Paris, the prefix 16 is first dialled followed, after a change of tone, by a 2-figure department code and then the 6-figure number. (Both the department and 6-figure number are required when dialling from one department to another or within a department.) Telephone-boxes displaying a 'bell' sign may be dialled to. For directory enquiries, dial 12; for operator, 13; Telecom services (complaints etc.), 14; SAMU (ambulance) 15; police, 17; fire, 18.

Information Bureaux. The *Office de Tourisme de Paris*, with its headquarters at 127 Av. des Champs-Elysées, open daily from 09.00–20.00), has English-speaking staff who will answer queries concerning Paris and the environs. Otherwise known as *Le Bureau Central d'Accueil* ('Welcome' reception office), it has subsidiary branches at the Gare d'Austerlitz, Gare de l'Est, Gare du Nord, Gare de Lyon and Gare Montparnasse, and in summer at the Tour Eiffel.

A more central office near the Louvre may be opened in the not too distant future, which will supersede the municipal office in the northern vestibule of the *Hôtel de Ville*, 29 Rue de Rivoli, 4e.

For a comparatively small charge, depending on the category of hotel, they will book accommodation in Paris and, from the head office, in the provinces. They also supply visitors with information leaflets on temporary exhibitions, entertainment, inexpensive restaurants, swimming pools, etc.

Most towns in the environs of Paris have a *Syndicat d'Initiative*.

Medical Services. Hospitals with English-speaking staff: the *British Hospital (Hertford)*, 3 Rue Barbès, Levallois-Perret, north west of the Porte de Champerret, with an entirely new wing; and the *American Hospital*, 63 Blvd Victor-Hugo, Neuilly. In an emergency, dial 17 for the Police, and 15 for SAMU (Service Aide Médicale d'Urgence).

The Disabled. The French are to be commended for their consideration for the disabled, who will find 'Access in Paris' useful. This booklet is available from 'The Paris Survey Project', 68b Castlebar Road, Ealing, London W5. Helpful advice is also be given by RADAR, 25 Mortimer St., W1, tel. 071 637 5400.

Lost Property Office. Articles lost on the métro or in buses (in which case they are held for claiming for the first 48 hrs at the terminus of the route concerned), in the street, theatres or cinemas, etc., should be enquired for at the *Bureau des Objets Perdus*, 36 Rue des Morillons, 15e (open Mondays–Fridays, 08.30–17.00 and on Thursdays until 20.00 except July–August); the nearest métro is *Convention*. The telephone number is 48 28 32 36. Property lost on trains, at stations, on planes and at airports should be reclaimed at the Lost Property office of the terminus or airport in question.

Museums, Collections and Monuments

A table giving hours of admission etc. is printed below, but it should be noted that the times shown are liable to be changed without warning. As a general rule, the **National Museums** are closed on Tuesdays, and the **Municipal Museums** are closed on Mondays; but see below. Many museums still open late and close early, and may be shut between the sacred hours of 12.00–14.00 (sometimes 15.00). This also applies in the case of some churches and other monuments. In many cases the admission fee is reduced on Sundays, when in a few cases entry may be free (but they may also be uncomfortably crowded, as are the Centre Pompidou and Musée d'Orsay most of the time). All national museums are free on Wednesdays.

Museum Pass (La Carte Musées et Monuments). This card gives direct entry to some 60 museums and monuments in Paris and environs can be bought at many museums and métro stations. It is available for 1, 3 or 5 consecutive days.

Lecture tours are organised by several bodies; those promoted by the *Caisse Nationale des Monuments Historiques* (who also publish a number of informative guides, and edit a magazine entitled *Monuments historiques*) are listed in a bi-monthly brochure entitled *Musées, Monuments historiques, Expositions, Visites Conféferences in Paris and the l'Ile de France*, obtainable from the Hôtel de Sully, 62 Rue St.-Antoine, 75003; the Bureau d'Action Culturelle de la Direction des Musées de France, Palais du Louvre, 34 Quai du Louvre, 75001; and Tourist Offices, etc.

A list of such guided visits can also be found in some newspapers. No advance booking is usually necessary: just turn up at the right place at the time stated, and pay the fee. The group is conducted by a competent official French-speaking guide-lecturer; guided tours by English-speaking lecturers can be arranged.

Museums charge an entry fee. Few of the important museums—perhaps because so many of them are undergoing drastic reorganisation—publish good general catalogues or inventories of their permanent collections. There are signs of improvement, with the publication by the *Editions de la Réunion des musées nationaux* of illustrated summary catalogues of the paintings in the Musée du Louvre, issued in five volumes—but also expensive. A list of catalogues in print by this organisation is available from the bookstalls of any of the national museums.

Hours of Admission to the principal Museums, Collections and Monuments

The more important are printed in **bold** type. Some museums will not allow entry some 45 minutes before closing time—even mid morning, before closing for lunch. Sections of some museums may be closed at times other than those indicated. Many are closed on Bank Holidays (*jours fériés*). All times of admission are liable to change without notice and it is wise to check in advance.

Tourist Offices can provide a museums and monuments guide for Paris and the Ile de France (in English) giving up-to-date admission times. You can also get a Bulletin des Musées et Monuments Historiques at most museums. See also Museum Card, p 49.

GT indicates guided tour only.

Arabe, Institut du Monde Quai St.-Bernard, 5e.	13.00–20.00. Closed Mon.
Arc de Triomphe Pl. Charles de Gaulle, 8e	10.00–17.00/17.30
Archives Nationales 60 Rue des Francs-Bourgeois, 3e	13.45–17.45. Closed Tues.
Arènes de Lutèce 47 Rue Monge, 5e	10.00–17.30/20.30
Armée, Musée de l': see Invalides	
Art Moderne de la Ville de Paris 11 Av. du Prés.-Wilson, 16e	10.00–17.40; Wed. till 20.30. Closed Mon.
Arte Moderne: see Pompidou	
Arts Africains et Océaniens 293 Av. Daumesnil, 12e	09.45–12.00; 13.30–17.30; Sat./Sun. 12.30–18.00. Closed Tues.
Arts Décoratifs 107 Rue de Rivoli. 1er	12.30–18.00; Sun. 11.00–18.00. Closed Mon./Tues.
Arts de la Mode Rue de Rivoli, 1er	12.30–18.00 109 Sun. 11.00–18.00. Closed Mon./Tues.
Arts et Traditions Populaires 6 Av. du Mahatma-Gandhi 16e (Bois de Boulogne)	09.45–17.15. Closed Tues.

Assemblée National 107 Rue de Rivoli, 1er	09.00–11.00; 14.00–17.00; when in session, Sat. 09.00–11.00, 14.00–16.00. Closed Sun.
Bagatelle, Château de Bois de Boulogne	08.00/09.00–16.00/20.00
Balzac, Maison Honoré de 47 Rue Raynouard, 16e	10.00–17.30. Closed Mon.
Beaubourg: see Pompidou	
Cabinet des Médailles, Bibliothéque Nationale 58 Rue de Richelieu, 4e	13.00–17.00. Closed Sun.
Camondo, Nissim de 63 Rue de Monceau, 8e	10.00–12.00; 14.00–17.00. Closed Mon./Tues.
Carnavalet 23 Rue de Sévigné, 3e	10.00–17.40. Closed Mon.
Catacombes 1 Pl. Denfert-Rochereau, 14e	Tues.–Fri. 14.00–16.00 Sat., Sun. 09.00–11.00; 14.00–16.00. Closed Mon.
Cernuschi 7 Av. Velasquez, 8e	10.00–17.40. Closed Mon.
Chapelle Expiatoire Sq. Louis XVI, 8e	10.00–16.00/18.00
Chasse (hunting) 60 Rue des Archives, 3e	10.00–12.30; 13.30–17.30; Closed Tues.
Cinema/Henri Langlois Palais de Chaillot, 16e	**GT** at 10.00, 11.00, 14.00, 15.00, 16.00. Closed Tues.
Cluny 6 Pl. Paul-Painlevé, 5e	09.45–12.30; 14.00–17.15. Closed Tues.
Cognacq-Jay 8 Rue Elzévir, 3e	10.00–17.40. Closed Mon.
Conciergerie 1 Quai de l'Horloge, 4e	09.30/10.00–16.30/18.30
Delacroix, Musée 6 Rue de Furstenberg, 6e	09.45–12.30; 14.00–17.15. Closed Tues.
Eiffel Tower Champs de Mars, 7e	09.30/10.00–23.00/24.00

Egouts (sewers)
South end of Pont de l'Alma, 7e

11.00–17.00.
Closed Thurs./Fri.

d'Ennery (oriental art)
59 Av. Foch, 16e

Thurs./Sun. 14.00–17.00.
Closed Aug.

Freemasonry
16 Rue Cadet, 9e

14.00–18.00. Closed Sun.

Gobelins (tapestries)
42 Av. de Gobelins, 13e

GT at 14.15, 14.45.
Closed Fri.–Mon.

Guimet
6 Pl. d'Iéna, 16e and with
extention at 19 Av. d'Iéna

09.45–17.15. Closed Tues.

Histoire Naturelle: see Jardin
des Plantes

Homme, Musée de l'
Palais de Chaillot, 16e

09.45–17.15. Closed Tues.

Hugo, Maison de Victor
6 Pl. Des Voges, 4e

10.00–17.40. Closed Mon.

Instrumental (musical instruments)
Cité de la Musique,
(La Villette)

(temporarily closed)

Invalides, Les (army museum)
Esplanade des Invalides, 7e
also Plans-Reliefs

10.00–17.00/18.00

10.00–16.45/17.45

Jacquemart-André
158 Blvd Haussmann, 8e

(temporarily closed)

Jardin des Plante
(Histoire Naturelle)
57 Rue Cuvier, 5e

10.00–17.00;
Sat./Sun. 11.00–18.00.
Zoo open daily
09.00–19.00

Legion d'Honneur
2 Rue de Bellechasse, 7e

14.00–17.00. Closed Mon.

Louvre, Musée du
Pyramid (Cour Napoléon)
Palais du Louvre, 1er

09.00–18.00; Mon.,
Wed. 09.00–21.45
Closed Tues.

Marine
Palais de Chaillot, 16e

10.00–18.00. Closed Tues.

Marmottan
2 Rue Louis-Boilly, 16e

10.00–17.30. Closed Mon.

Monnaie (Mint)	13.00–18.00;
11 Quai de Conti, 6e	Wed. 13.00–21.00.
	Closed Mon.
Montmartre	14.00/14.30–18.00.
12 Rue Cortot, 18e	Closed Mon.
Monuments Français	09.00–18.00. Closed Tues.
Palais de Chaillot, 16e	
Notre-Dame, Cathedral	08.00–19.00
Crypte Archéologique	10.00–17.00/18.00
Pl. du Parvis Notre-Dame, 4e	
Observatoire	**GT** by appointment.
61 Av de l'Observatoire, 14e	Closed Aug.
Opéra	11.00–17.00. Closed Aug.
Pl. de l'Opéra, 9e	
Orangerie des Tuileries	09.45–17.15. Closed Tues.
Pl. de la Concorde, 1er	
Orsay, Musée d'	09.00/10.00–18.00;
1 Rue de Bellechasse, 7e	Thurs 09.00/10.00–21.45.
	Closed Mon.
Palais de Justice	09.00–17.00. Closed Sat./
2 Blvd du Palais, 1er	Sun.
Petit Palais	10.00–17.40. Closed Mon.
Av. Winston Churchill, 8e	
Picasso	09.15–17.15;
5 Rue de Torigny, 3e	Wed. 09.15–22.00.
	Closed Tues.
Plans-Reliefs: see Invalides	
Pompidou, Centre (CNAC)	12.00–22.00; Sat./Sun.
4e	10.00–22.00. Closed Tues.
Postal Museum	10.00–17.00. Closed Sun.
34 Blvd Vaugirard, 15e	
Rodin, Musée	10.00–17.00/17.45.
77 Rue de Varenne, 7e	Closed Mon.
Romantique, de la Vie	10.00–17.40. Closed Mon.
16 Rue Chaptal, 9e	
Sainte-Chapelle	09.30/10.00–17.00/18.30
Blvd du Palais, 4e	

Sciences et de l'Industrie 30 Av. Corentin-Cariou, 19e (La Villette)	10.00–18.00. Closed Mon.
Serrure, La (locksmiths) 1 Rue de la Perle, 3e	10.00–12.00; 14.00–17.00. Closed Sun./Mon., Aug.
Sully, Hôtel de 62 Rue St.-Antoine, 4e	Gardens 09.00–19.00
Techniques (science museum) 292 Rue St.-Martin, 3e	10.00–17.30. Closed Mon.
Termes: see Cluny	
Villette, La: see Science et de l'Industries and Instrumental	
Vincennes, Château de	10.00–17.00/18.00

ENVIRONS OF PARIS

Champs, Château de	10.00–12.00; 13.30–16.30/ 17.30. Closed Tues.
Chantilly (Musée Condé)	10.00–18.00. Closed Tues.
Défense, La; Grande Arche de Parvis de la Défense	09.00–18.00 Sat./Sun. 10.00–20.00
Ecouen, Château de (Musée de la Renaissance)	09.45–12.30; 14.00–17.15. Closed Tues.
Fontainebleau, Château de	09.30–12.30; 14.00–17.00. Closed Tues.
Petits Appartements	4 **GT**s daily. Closed Mon./Wed.–Fri.
Maisons-Laffitte, Château de	10.00–17.00/18.00
Malmaison and Bois-Préau	10.00–12.30; 13.30–17.00/17.30. Closed Tues.
St. Denis, Basilique de Musée d'Art	10.00–17.00/19.00. 10.00–17.30; Sun. 14.00–18.30. Closed Tues.
St.-Germain-en-Laye Antiquitiés Nationales Pl. du Château	09.00–17.00. Closed Tues.
Preiuré (Nabis) 2bis Rue Maurice-Denis	10.00–17.30/18.30. Closed Mon./Tues.

Sceaux, Château de (Musée de l'Ile de France)	Mon., Fri. 14.00–17.00; Wed., Thurs., Sat., Sun. 10.00–12.00; 14.00–17.00. Closed Tues.
Sèvres, Céramique de	10.00–17.15. Closed Tues.
Versailles, Château de	Oct.–Apr. 09.00–17.30; May–Sept. 09.00–19.00 but several apartments may only be visited on a **GT.** Closed Mon.
Grand Trianon	Oct.–Apr. 09.45–12.30; 14.00–17.30; May–Sept. 11.00–16.30. Closed Mon.
Petit Trianon	Oct.–Apr. 14.00–17.30; May–Sept. 11.00–18.30 Closed Mon.
Gardens/Park	07.00–dusk

Although this table includes many of the principal attractions of Paris and environs, it by no means exhausts the list of things to see or the heights to which one can ascend (such as the terrace of the Arc de Triomphe, the Tour Montparnasse or Tour Eiffel). The visitor is reminded of the following additional points of interest, to mention only a few which deserve a visit, details of which will be found in the text: Palais-Royal; the Hôpital St.-Louis and Hôpital de la Salpêtrière; Ecole Militaire; and the churches of Val-de-Grâce, St.-Eustache, St.-Etienne-du-Mont, St.-Germain-l'Auxerrois, St.-Germain-des-Près, St.-Roch, St.-Médard, St.-Séverin, St.-Sulpice, Ste.-Ursule de la Sorbonne; the cemeteries of Père Lachaise, Montmartre, Montparnasse and Picpus; Pl. Vendôme and Pl. des Vosges, without listing individually the numerous hôtels of the Marais and the Faubourg St.-Germain.

The cemeteries are normally open from 07.30–18.00 in summer, and from 08.00–17.00 in winter; that of Picpus is open during the afternoon only.

A torch and a pair of binoculars, will be found useful when exploring the recesses of churches and cathedrals, and studying the details of capitals and stained-glass windows, etc.

Entertainment

Topical information about theatres, cinemas, cabarets, night clubs, 'manifestations', sporting events, fairs, exhibitions, etc., are advertised in the press, or may be found in any of the magazines and guides devoted to what is on, available from most tourist offices, agents and kiosks.

Theatres. The National, or State-subsidised, theatres are the Comédie-Française, Pl. André-Malraux, 1er; the Théâtre de France (de l'Odéon), Pl. Paul-Claudel, 6e; Théâtre National Populaire (TNP), Palais de Chaillot, 16e; Théâtre de l'Est Parisien (TEP), 17 Rue Malte-Brun, 20e; Théâtre de la Ville and Théâtre du Châtelet, the latter devoted to ballet, and concerts (see below), both in the Pl. du Châtelet, 4e; and the 'Théâtre Lyrique', better known as the Opéra, Pl. de l'Opéra, 9e; and (since July 1989) the new Opéra Bastille. The once-famous Opéra-Comique is now used as an experimental theatre.

Some smaller establishments, music halls, *Chansonniers*, etc., also survive, often devoted to revues of no very refined nature. Many specialise in political satire, for there are targets in plenty (cf. 'Le Canard Enchaîné', a periodical wittier than most), but these can only be appreciated by those with a fairly thorough knowledge of the language and the latest *argot*.

Few cabarets leave much to the imagination, although some purport to offer 'artistic performances', and attempt to provide something to suit all tastes in their entertainment, from the exotic (or simply *érotique*) to the grossly vulgar; but the curious visitor is warned that the announcement of *entrée libre* (free admission) to any of these *boîtes*, night-clubs, and other tourist traps simply means that the price of admission is added to the already exorbitant charge for *consommations* which he is expected to order. The obscure world of 'dancings', cafés-théâtres, discothéques and what not, lies outside the scope of this Guide.

Cinemas of all types, many of the larger converted to show various films in the same building, abound—Paris claims to contain 500—and most of them run continuously from 12.00. Programmes normally change on Wednesdays. Prices charged in the better-known cinemas are high, and yet ushers still expect a tip, although the practice is progressively ignored. The same applies in theatres.

Many theatres close for some weeks in the summer, and on one evening a week, usually Monday or Tuesday. Smoking is forbidden. Note that tickets bought through an agency will cost as much as 25 per cent more than at the box-office of the theatre concerned, usually open between 11.00 and 18.30 or 19.00.

Concerts take place at the Théâtre des Champs-Elysées, 15 Av. Montaigne; the restored Théâtre du Châtelet, Pl. du Châtelet; Salle Gaveau, 45 Rue La Boétie; Salle Pleyel, 252 Rue du Faubourg-St.-Honoré; Salle Cortot, 78 Rue Cardinet; the Palais de Chaillot, Pl. du Trocadero; the Maison de l'ORTF (or 'de la Radio'), 116 Av. du Président-Kennedy; at the Palais des Congrès, Porte Maillot and elsewhere.

Church Music and **Organ Recitals** may be heard at Notre-Dame, St.-Eustache, St.-Germain-des-Prés, St.-Louis des Invalides, St.-Séverin, St.-Sulpice, St.-Roch, St.-Clotilde, St.-Etienne-du-Mont and the Madeleine, among other churches, and any special concerts are usually well advertised.

Art Exhibitions. Although smaller shows devoted to individual artists can be seen at any number of galleries and art-dealers' shops, many of them in the 6e *arrondissement*, the more important temporary exhibitions are held in the Grand Palais, Petit-Palais, Musée d'Orsay, Palais de Tokyo, Musée des Arts Décoratifs, etc., while the Centre National d'Art et de Culture Georges Pompidou (CNAC, or Centre Beaubourg) is an important focus of exhibitions of modern art, 'pop' and otherwise, etc.

General Information

Directories. Almost any address can be found in 'Le Bottin' (the *Annuaire-Almanach du Commerce et de l'Industrie Didot-Bottin*), which may be consulted at post offices, hotels, restaurants, shops, etc., where a notice may be displayed: 'Ici on consulte le Bottin'. Residential and official addresses may be found also in the 'Bottin Mondain'. *Le Bottin* was initiated in 1819 by Sébastien Bottin (1764–1853), who took over an earlier *Almanach du Commerce* founded in 1798. At Bottin's death it merged with the *Annuaire général du commerce* published by Didot. Although a somewhat ponderous example of Gallic methodology, it can be useful on occasions.

Climate. The main characteristic of the weather in Paris is changeability, particularly in the winter and spring, although long periods of fine weather occur each year. Perhaps because of its long wide boulevards, which sometimes act as wind tunnels, the wind is more noticeable than in London, and bitterly cold blasts can be experienced in some quarters in certain seasons, and it can remain cold until well after Easter. Its mean temperature is 11.6°C; only for a few days a year does it become oppressively hot (30°C). The average number of days a year on which the temperature falls below freezing-point is about 35; the number of days of snowfall has averaged 15 in recent decades. In spring and autumn, although the days are shorter, the weather is better for the active sightseer, for in summer (June–August) Paris is packed with tourists. In August the city is deserted by a high proportion of its regular residents, and many theatres, libraries, and even restaurants, are closed.

Language. The visitor who only speaks English can usually get along without too much trouble in Paris, although you will probably pay in cash for your ignorance. Any attempt to speak some French is always appreciated.

Manners. Forms of politeness in France are still less casual than in some other countries, and there is more handshaking at meeting and parting. It is also polite to use 'Monsieur', 'Madame' or 'Mademoiselle' as a form of address (without the surname) even after some acquaintance, but such standing on ceremony is becoming progressively relaxed in most circles.

Public Holidays. 1 January (*Jour de l'An*); Easter Monday; Whit Monday (*Pentecôte*); Ascension Day; 1 May (with Lily-of-the-Valley sold in the streets); 8 May (commemorating the end of World War II in Europe); 14 July (Fête Nationale; Bastille Day); 15 August (*Assomption*); 1 November (*Toussaint*; All Saints' Day); 11 November (Armistice Day); and 25 December (*Noël*; Christmas).

Shopping and **Markets**. Many of the smartest and most expensive shops are to be found in the 1er, 6e, 8e and 16e *arrondissements*, particularly in the area of the Rue du Faubourg-St.-Honoré, but in fact good shops and department stores (among which are *Les Galeries Lafayette* and *Au Printemps*, at 40 and 69 Blvd Haussmann respectively) can be found in most districts of central Paris, and their prices are usually less extravagant. Many of the antique shops and *brocanteurs* (second-hand dealers) are to be found in the 6e, while the so-called *Village Suisse* (shut Tuesday–Wednesday; west of the Ecole Militaire), and the extensive *Marché aux Puces* (open Saturday–Monday; a few minutes' walk north of the Porte de Clignancourt Métro), sometimes produce bargains among the bric-à-brac. A recent—but more expensive—attraction is the *Louvre des Antiquaires*, between the Palais du Louvre and Palais-Royal.

Auctions are held regularly at the rebuilt *Salle Drouot*, 6 Rue Rossini, 9e. Nearby, in the Rue Drouot and further south in the arcades of the Palais-Royal, are the haunts of philatelists; while an open-air stamp market is held at weekends and Thursday mornings at the junction of the Av. de Marigny and Av. Gabriel. Other colourful markets are devoted to flowers: in the Pl. Louis-Lépine (not far east of the Conciergerie), on the east side of the Madeleine, at the Pl. des Ternes, and Pl. de la République. On Sundays the flowers of the Pl. Louis-Lépine give way to a bird market, while opposite, on the Quai de la Mégisserie, is a pet market (not Sunday).

On the north side of the Pl. de la Madeleine some superbly displayed food shops may be seen, although less sumptuous establishments will tempt the eye and palate throughout Paris; indeed, one of the great pleasures of wandering about the city is the quality and display of the merchandise seen in many of the smaller shops: the *fromageries, pâtisseries,* and *charcuteries.*

Food markets not too far from the centre may be visited in the Rue de Montorgueil (leading north from Les Halles métro); the Rue Mouffetard, 5e; Rue des Martyrs, 9e; Rue de Lévis (north east of the Parc de Monceau); Rue Cler, 7e; and Rue Buci (just north of the Odéon métro); and there are of course many others. Food shopping on a Sunday morning at one of the street markets of Paris is almost always an agreeable occupation.

Bookshops and Libraries. Bookshops continue to proliferate throughout central Paris, but differ widely in the range of books stocked, and in the quality of their service. English newspapers and magazines can be found at a price at many kiosks near the centre. A selection of books in English is provided by *Brentano* (37 Av. de l'Opéra), *Galignani* (224 Rue de Rivoli: near the Tuileries métro) and *W.H. Smith* (248 Rue de Rivoli), among others.

Working Hours, etc. In France work starts earlier than in the UK, and generally meals are also taken at an earlier hour. Although there is a movement towards the English weekend, most food shops are open on Sunday mornings, and remain open later on weekday evenings; but they are likely to be shut on Mondays.

Sports. General information about a variety of sporting events, sporting facilities, addresses of tennis-clubs, squash-courts, golf-courses, swimming-pools, etc. in Paris and environs, may be obtained from the *Office de Tourisme de Paris*, 127 Av. des Champs-Elysées, and its branches, and from the *Direction de la Jeunesse et des Sports*, 17 Blvd Morland, 4e. They can also advise on the capacities of the French sporting federations to assist the visitor, who is recommended to apply well in advance to the offices of his own home club or sporting organisation, which may well be able to give more practical information.

Street markets are a feature of Paris

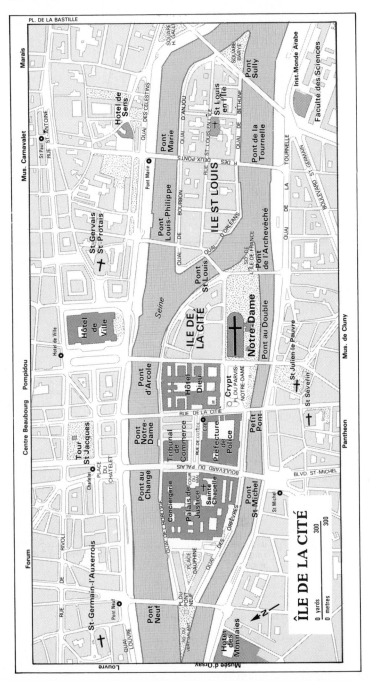

ÎLE DE LA CITÉ

ILE DE LA CITE AND ILE-ST-LOUIS

1 Ile de la Cité
The Conciergerie; Ste. Chapelle

METROS: Cité, St.-Michel, Pont-Neuf, Châtelet.

The **Ile de la Cité** (Pl. 14; 2–4 and opposite), the earliest inhabited part of Paris, lies in the river like a ship, the 'Pointe' as its prow and Notre-Dame as its poop, moored to both banks by numerous bridges: the freighted vessel on a sea argent, which has always figured in the arms of Paris, with the device 'fluctuat nec mergitur' (tossed but not engulfed), is indeed appropriate. The Cité was the site of the original Gallic settlement of *Lutèce* or *Lutetia Parisiorum,* and after the destruction of the later Roman city on the Left Bank, became the site of Frankish Paris. It remained the royal, legal and ecclesiastical centre long after the town had extended onto both river-banks, and—for the visitor with little time—even a brief wander around the Cité will give a good idea of its importance in the historical development of Paris.

The Cité derives its importance from its situation at the crossroads of two natural routes across northern France. The Capetian kings were the great builders of the Cité, and it remained little changed from 1300 to the Second Empire, when Haussmann, after massive demolition, left it more or less with its present appearance.

From the Quai du Louvre the picturesque **Pont-Neuf** crosses the western extremity of the island. It is, in spite of its name, the oldest existing bridge in Paris, begun by Baptiste du Cerceau, completed in 1607, and several times repaired since. It was also the first to be built without houses lining each side, and with pavements. This 'Pointe de la Cité' is occupied by the Sq. du Vert-Galant, so-called in allusion to the amorous adventures of Henri IV, a statue of whom, by Lemot (1818), stands adjacent, replacing another, by Giambologna and Tacca, which stood here from 1635 to 1792.

East of the Pont-Neuf, entered by the Rue Henri-Robert, is the ***Pl. Dauphine**, retaining two rows of houses, some dating from the reign of Louis XIII, but many have been altered since. Unfortunately the east wing of the triangle was demolished in 1874 to provide an unmerited view of Louis Duc's west façade of the Palais de Justice (see below).

During the 17C and 18C the Pl. du Pont-Neuf and the bridge swarmed with pedlars and mountebanks. Tabarin set up his 'théâtre' in the Pl. Dauphine. Here, too, was the original site of the Samaritaine, one of the earliest hydraulic pumps, constructed by a Fleming for Henri IV to supply water for the royal palaces of the Louvre and Tuileries. It derived its name from a figure of the Good Samaritan on the fountain.

Other bridges connecting the Cité to the Right Bank of the Seine are the Pont au Change (1858–59), replacing a stone bridge dating from 1639 lined with money-lenders' shops; the Pont Notre-Dame, rebuilt in 1913 on the site of the main Roman bridge; and beyond is the Pont d'Arcole (1855), named after a youth killed in 1830 leading insurgents against the Hôtel de Ville.

To the south, the Cité is connected to the Left Bank by the Pont St.-Michel, rebuilt several times since the late 14C (last in 1857), affording a fine view of the façade of Notre-Dame. Beyond is the Petit Pont (1853), on the site of another Roman bridge.

Until 1782 it was defended at the southern end by the Petit Châtelet, the successor of the Tour de Bois, which in 886 held Viking or Norman marauders at bay. From the west front of Notre-Dame, the Pont-au-Double (1882) replaced a mid 17C bridge, for crossing which the toll of a diminutive coin known as a 'double' was charged; while from the eastern extremity of the Cité, near the site of the archbishop's palace (pulled down in 1831), is the Pont de l'Archevêché (1828), providing a good view of the apse, with its profusion of flying buttresses.

Following the Quai de l'Horloge (north of the Palais de Justice), and entered just beyond twin towers (see below), is one of the world's most infamous prisons, the ***CONCIERGERIE** (CNMH), occupying part of the lower floor of the Palais, and originally the residence of the 'Concierge', chief executive of the Parlement.

Its historical associations are numerous. In 1418 the Comte d'Armagnac was massacred here with many of his partisans by the hired assassins of the Duc de Bourgogne. The Marquise de Brinvilliers, the poisoner, was held here. During the Revolution, Marie-Antoinette, Bailly, Malesherbes, Mme Elisabeth, Mme Roland, Mme du Barry, Camille Desmoulins, Charlotte Corday, Danton, André Chénier and Robespierre passed their last days in the Conciergerie. 288 prisoners perished here in the massacres of September 1792. Later prisoners were Georges Cadoudal (died 1804) the Chouan leader, Marshal Ney, Mérimée (for a fortnight in 1852) and the Duc d'Orléans (1890).

The Salle des Gardes, a handsome vaulted room of the 14C (restored 1877), where you wait for the guide, contains two stairs (no admission) ascending (right) to the Tour de César, where François Ravaillac, the murderer of Henri IV, was imprisoned (1610); the other leads to the Tour d'Argent, which served as a prison for Robert François Damiens, who attempted to assassinate Louis XV (1757). The spiral staircase in the right-hand corner as you leave the room was climbed by Marie-Antoinette and some 2275 other prisoners on their way from their cells to the Tribunal (see below).

The impressive four-aisled Gothic ***Salle des Gens-d'Armes** (restored in 1868–80), was the original 'Salle des Pas-Perdus', said to be so called because the victims of the Revolution walked through it on their way to the Cour du Mai and execution; the name has since been transferred to the hall above (and to the waiting-rooms of other public buildings accommodating various functionaries).

Near the far end, to the left, a curious open spiral stair leads to the so-called ***Cuisines de St.-Louis** (14C), also vaulted, and with four huge fireplaces.

Returning to the first bay, you turn left past a grille flanking the Rue de Paris, reserved for the *pailleux* (prisoners who slept on straw, being unable to bribe their gaolers). You next enter the diminutive Galerie des Prisonniers, the windows of which look out onto the Cour des Femmes where the female prisoners took exercise, and also the scene of the massacres of September 1792. A railing, which still exists, divided off a section for men. To the left in the Galerie des Prisonniers was the cell where the condemned had their hair shorn while awaiting the departure of the tumbril for the guillotine. At the end is the iron wicket which was the only entrance to the prison in Revolutionary times.

At the opposite end of this gallery is the original door (but in a different position) of Marie-Antoinette's cell, where the queen remained from 2 August to 16 October 1793. Adjacent, and now communicating with it, is Robespierre's cell.

The Chapel (with a gallery for the prisoners) where the Girondins were incarcerated, now displays a collection of souvenirs. These include a blade of the guillotine, a crucifix said to have been found in Marie-Antoinette's cell and orders for arrest.

On leaving the Conciergerie, turn right into the Blvd du Palais passing the Cour du Mai, on the east side of the Palais de Justice, named after the maypole set up here annually by the 'Basoche' or society of law clerks.

The **Palais de Justice**, a huge block of buildings occupying the whole width of the island, also includes within its precincts the Ste.-Chapelle (see below) which, with the four towers on the northern side, are the oldest surviving parts.

The site was occupied as early as the Roman period by a palace in which Julian the Apostate was proclaimed emperor in 360. The Merovingian kings divided their time between the Thermes (see Rte 5) and this Palais de la Cité, which was within the walls, when not in the country. Louis VI died in the palace in 1137; Louis VII in 1180; and in 1193 Philippe Auguste was married here to Ingeborg of Denmark. Louis IX altered the palace and built the Ste.-Chapelle. From 1431 it was occupied entirely by the Parlement, which had previously only shared it with the king, but it was not until the Revolution that it acquired its present function.

Here, in the 16th Chambre Correctionelle, the trials of Flaubert's 'Madame Bovary' and Baudelaire's 'Les Fleurs du Mal' (29 January and 20 August 1857 respectively) took place.

The 18C buildings were greatly enlarged in 1857–68 and again in 1911–14. In the mid 19C, the 14C Tour de l'Horloge, at the north eastern corner (with a clock copied from the original dial designed c 1585 by Germain Pilon), was virtually rebuilt; and likewise, the upper part of the north façade, in an attempt to reproduce the original 14C work by Enguerrand de Marigny. The domed Galerie Marchande, dominating the Cour du Mai, is embellished with sculptures by Pajou.

The more interesting part of these law courts may be entered directly from the boulevard just north of the Cour du Mai, by stairs up to the *Salle de Pas-Perdus**. This magnificent hall, which replaced the great hall of the medieval palace (where in 1431 the coronation banquet of Henry VI of England was celebrated), was rebuilt in 1622 by Salomon de Brosse, and restored in 1878 after being burned by the Communards. At the far end of the room, divided in two by a row of arches, and to the right, is the entrance to the Première Chambre Civile, formerly the Grand' Chambre or Chambre Dorée (restored in the style of Louis XII), perhaps originally the bedroom of Louis IX. Later it was used by the Parlement, in contempt of which Louis XIV here coined his famous epigram 'L'état, c'est moi'. The Revolutionary Tribunal, with Fouquier-Tinville as public prosecutor, sat here in 1793 (see Conciergerie, above).

A vaulted gateway leads from the Cour du Mai to the Cour de la Ste.-Chapelle.

The *SAINTE CHAPELLE** (CNMH) was built in 1243–48 by Louis IX as a shrine for miscellaneous relics, among them those purporting to be the Crown of Thorns and fragments of the True Cross. It is ascribed to Pierre de Montreuil (cf. St.-Denis and St.-Germain-en-Laye), and is remarkable for the impression of lightness it conveys. It was often the scene of royal marriages, and Richard II of England was betrothed here in 1396 to Isabelle of France. It was 'restored' in 1837–57 by Duban, Lassus (who reconstructed a leaden flèche in the 15C style; the fifth on this site) and Viollet-le-Duc.

36m long, 17m wide and 42.50m high, the building gives an impression of great height in proportion to its length and breadth. It consists in fact of two superimposed chapels; the lower for servants and retainers and the upper reserved for the royal family and court. The lofty windows of the upper chapel, an innovation, are surmounted by delicately sculptured gables and a graceful balustrade. The portal consists of two porches, one above the other; the statues are 19C restorations. Marc-Antoine Charpentier (c 1645–1704) was mâitre de musique here from 1698 and composed several important works for the chapel.

The interior of the Chapelle Basse, with carved oak bosses
and 40 columns supporting the upper chapel, is darkened by the decoration of Emile Boeswillwald (1815–96), who attempted to reproduce its medieval paintwork. There are a number of 14–15C tombstones in the pavement.

A spiral staircase leads to the Chapelle Haute (20.50m high), certainly one of the outstanding architectural achievements of the Middle Ages. Its *stained-glass was restored in 1845.

The 86 panels from the Apocalypse in the large rose-window were a gift of Charles VIII. The first window on the right depicts the Legend of the Cross and the removal of the relics. The other windows in the nave and apse illustrate scenes from the Old and New Testaments. Beneath the windows on either side runs a blind arcade; of the apostles against the pillars, the 4th, 5th and 6th on the left, and the 3rd, 4th and 5th on the right, are original.

The two deep recesses under the windows of the 3rd bay were the seats reserved for the royal family. In the centre of the restored arcade across the apse is a wooden canopy beneath which the relics used to be exhibited on Good Friday; those few surviving the Revolution are in the treasury of Notre-Dame.

You leave by the second spiral stair.

To the south, at 36 Quai des Orfèvres, is a Museum of Police History, with a room devoted to the part they played in the Resistance and in the Liberation of Paris.

Opposite the Cour du Mai, the Rue de Lutèce leads between (right) the Préfecture de Police and (left) the domed Tribunal de Commerce (by Bailly; 1860–65), behind which the Marché aux Fleurs offers a colourful contrast. A bird market is held here on Sundays.

2   Notre-Dame

METRO: Cité.

On the eastern side of the Rue de la Cité, you turn right and then left into the Pl. du Parvis Notre-Dame, a space which Haussmann increased sixfold by his demolitions. To the left is the Hôtel-Dieu, rebuilt here in 1868–78 to the north of its original site. The first hospital was founded here by St. Landry, Bp of Paris, in c 660.

John Northleigh, writing in 1702, refers to it as then accommodating 4000 men: 'tended and looked after by the Religious of the Order of St.-Augustine, young perfect Nuns, and for the generality very comely Women, whom they venture among Men when infirm, though perhaps sometimes too far; for one of our infirm Irish-men was grown on a sudden so lusty, that he made a shift to run away with one of the pretty Tenders'.

The ecclesiastical authorities brought heretics to trial on the Parvis here, where the condemned knelt before execution to acknowledge their sin and beg absolution. In 1314 Jacques de Molay, grand master of the Templars, summoned to repeat his confession publicly and accept sentence of imprisonment, unexpectedly protested the innocence of his Order and was hustled off to the stake.

Near the west end of the Parvis is the entrance to the ***Crypte Arché-ologique** (CNMH), displaying architectural remains of all ages of the Cité's past uncovered in 1965 when the area was being excavated for the construction of the adjacent underground car-park. The site is exceptionally well exhibited, and dioramas and models explain the growth of the district prior to the ravaging fire of 1772. Sections are illuminated by press-button lighting, and explanatory notes are printed both in French and English.

The path followed leads above the foundations of the Gallo-Roman rampart (late 3C), a section of which is later seen. Further to the east, beyond the excavated area, lie the foundations of the west end of the Merovingian cathedral of St.-Etienne (6C). After passing display cases of artefacts uncovered here, you follow the foundations of the demolished Hospice des Enfants-Trouvés and other medieval buildings once flanking the Rue Neuve Notre-Dame, some (to the right as you approach the exit) as early as the 2C, and (left) relics of hypocausts, etc.

To the east rises ***NOTRE-DAME** (Pl.14; 4). It was started when Gothic art was beginning to throw off the traditions of the Romanesque style, and was completed in the 13C. It is possible, therefore, to follow in this building the gradual progress of the new style until its decadence in the 14C.

Road distances in France are calculated from its west door.

The idea of replacing the cathedral of St.-Etienne (founded by Childebert in 528: see above) and that of Notre-Dame, further east, by a single building, on a much larger scale, was due to Bp Maurice de Sully, who died in 1196. The former edifice replaced a Roman temple of Jupiter more or less on the site of the present cathedral, the foundation stone of which was laid by Pope Alexander III in 1163. The choir was finished by 1182, except for the roof; followed by the nave in 1208; and the west front with its towers c 1225–50. Meanwhile, in 1235–50 a series of chapels was added to the nave; and later, in 1296–1330, to the apse (by Pierre de Chelles and Jean Ravy). The side porches were begun in 1258; the crossings of the transept were built by Jean de Chelles and Pierre de Montreuil (1250–67).

The School of Music at Notre-Dame was influential during the late 12C and 13C. In 1176 Geoffrey Plantagenet (4th son of Henry II) was buried here, in front of the altar, having died suddenly while in Paris.

In 1431 Henry VI of England (aged 10) was crowned king of France here (by Henry Beaufort, Bp of Winchester, and son of John of Gaunt). Here too the marriages of James V of Scotland and Madeleine of France (daughter of François I, on 1 January 1537), François II to Mary Stuart (1558), Henri of Navarre (later Henri IV) to Marguerite de Valois (1572) and Charles I of England (by proxy) to Henrietta Maria (1625) were celebrated.

Until the end of the 17C Notre-Dame had preserved intact its 14C appearance but the reigns of Louis XIV and Louis XV brought deplorable alterations, particularly in the destruction of tombs and stained-glass Much of what survived in the way of sculptures and treasures were lost during the Revolution. In 1804, Napoléon I was crowned Emperor here by Pius VII; Napoléon III and Eugénie de Montijo were married here in 1853. In 1845 a thorough 'restoration' was begun under the direction of Lassus (died 1857) and Viollet-le-Duc. It narrowly escaped serious damage in 1871, for piled chairs were ready to be set ablaze by the Communards, when they received orders to evacuate the church.

On 26 August 1944 the thanksgiving service following Général de Gaulle's entry into liberated Paris was interrupted by sniping from internal and external galleries. Notre-Dame continues to be the scene of occasional ceremonial functions, state funerals, etc.

EXTERIOR. The *west front consists of three distinct storeys. The central

Porte du Jugement, ruined by Soufflot in 1771, has a 19C Christ on the pier, and in the tympanum, the Last Judgment, restored by Viollet-le-Duc. Only the upper tier of sculptures is ancient.

The Porte de la Vierge (left) contains a restored Virgin on the pier; three kings, three prophets and the Resurrection of the Virgin in the lower part of the tympanum; above is the Coronation of the Virgin.

The sculptures of the Porte de Ste.-Anne (right) are mostly of 1165–75, designed for a narrower portal, with additions of c 1240. On the pier is St. Marcellus (19C); above, scenes from the life of St. Anne and the Virgin, and the Virgin in Majesty, with Louis VII (right) and Maurice de Sully (left). The two side doors retain their medieval wrought-iron hinges.

Above the portals is the Gallery of the Tree of Jesse (reconstructed by Viollet-le-Duc), its statues destroyed in 1793 because the Parisians assumed that they were of kings of France (cf. Musée de Cluny). The magnificent rose-window, 9.6m in diameter, is flanked by double windows within arches. Higher still is an open arcade.

The towers, originally intended to be surmounted by spires, can be ascended for the view; entrance in the north tower. In the south tower hangs the great bell, recast in 1686 and weighing 13 tonnes; Victor Hugo's bell-ringer, Quasimodo, may be remembered. The *chimières* (gargoyles), grotesque figures of devils, birds and beasts, were redesigned by Viollet-le-Duc.

The side façades and apse likewise consist of three distinct and receding storeys; the bold flying buttresses of the latter, by Jean Ravy, are also admired for their elegance. The south porch, according to a Latin inscription at the base, was begun in 1257 (1258 new style) under the direction of Jean de Chelles. The story of St. Stephen depicted in the tympanum, and the medallions of student life, are original. The north porch, of the same period, has an original statue of the Virgin and, in the tympanum, the story of Theophilius. Just to the east of this porch is the graceful Porte Rouge, probably by Pierre de Montreuil. To the left, below the windows of the choir chapels, are seven 14C bas-reliefs. The *flèche* (90m above the ground), a lead-covered oak structure, was rebuilt by Viollet-le-Duc in 1860, the original having been destroyed in the 18C.

The best view of the INTERIOR is obtained from beneath the organ (1733, by Cliquot; rebuilt in 1868 by Cavaillé-Coll, electrified in the 1960s and now under restoration), at the west end. The cathedral (130m long, 48m wide, and 35m high) consists of a nave of ten bays, flanked by double aisles continued round the choir (of five bays). 37 chapels surround the whole. A vaulted gallery overlooks the nave; the windows above were altered in the 13C. The vaulting is supported by 75 piers, surmounted by bold yet graceful capitals. New glass, with an abstract design, was placed in the nave in 1964. Of the three *rose-windows with their original 13C glass, the north is the best preserved and finest.

At the crossing, 'Notre-Dame de Paris', a 14C image, stands against the south east pillar; against the north east pillar is St. Denis by Nicolas Coustou. Seven paintings (by Charles le Brun, Sebastian Bourdon and others), presented by the Goldsmiths' Guild of Paris in 1634–51, hang in the side-chapels of the nave.

The choir, modified in 1708–25 by Louis XIV in fulfilment of his father's vow of 1638, attracted Viollet-le-Duc's 'restoring' hand. Of the original 114 *stalls 78 remain, adorned with bas-reliefs from the designs of Jules Degoullons (1711–15). Canopied archiepiscopal stalls stand at either end.

The bronze angels (1713) against the apse-pillars escaped the Revolutionary melting-pot.

Behind Viollet-le-Duc's altar is a Pietà by Nicolas Coustou, with a base sculptured by Girardon, part of the 'Voeu de Louis XIII'. The statue of Louis XIII (south) is also by Coustou; that of Louis XIV (north) by Coysevox.

In the first four bays of the choir are the remains of the mid 14C screen which, until the 18C, extended round the whole apse; the expressive bas-reliefs on the exterior were unfortunately restored and repainted by Viollet-le-Duc. In the blind arches below are listed some of the eminent people buried in the church.

The ambulatory contains the tombs of 18–19C prelates. Behind the high altar is the tomb-statue of Bp Matiffas de Bucy (died 1304). In the 2nd chapel south of the central chapel is the theatrical tomb, by Pigalle, of the Comte d'Harcourt (died 1769); here also are the restored tomb-statues of Jean Jouvenel des Ursins and his wife (died 1431, 1451).

On the south side of the ambulatory is the entrance to the sacristy, now containing the treasury, a somewhat indifferent collection of ecclesiastical plate, reliquaries and cult objects.

In the Rue du Cloître Notre-Dame, adjacent to the north tower of the cathedral, the chapel of St.-Jean-le-Rond stood until 1748. The natural son of Mme de Tencin (1682–1749) was found abandoned on the steps of the church. Baptised Jean-le-Rond, he grew up to become famous as the Encyclopaedist, D'Alembert (1717–83). At No. 10 is the Musée Notre-Dame de Paris (which may close), with collections relating to the history of the cathedral.

The Rue Massillon turns north into the Rue Chanoinesse: the poet Joachim du Bellay died in 1560 in a house which stood at the junction of these two roads in 1560; the anatomist M.-F.-X. Bichat (1711–1802) died opposite. Parallel to the north (at 19 Rue des Ursins) stands part of the nave of St. Aignan (1118) where mass was celebrated in secret in 1789–91. Nicolas Boileau (1636–1711) died nearby in a house destroyed when the Sq. de l'Archeveche was laid out.

In the Sq. de l'Ile-de-France, at the extreme east end of the Cité, is a Memorial to some 200,000 Frenchmen deported to German concentration camps during the 1939–45 war.

3   Ile St.-Louis

METRO: Cité, Pont-Marie, Sully-Morland.

The **Ile St.-Louis** is reached from the Ile de la Cité by crossing the Pont St.-Louis (dating from 1614, but replaced in 1969). Still a comparatively quiet backwater, although in danger of exploitation, it was formerly two islets and was not built over until the 17C, when as an annexe of the Marais to the north, it became the site of a number of imposing mansions. It is connected to the north bank by the Pont Louis-Philippe (rebuilt 1862); beyond stands the Pont Marie (1635; named after its builder), crossing to the Quai des Celestins. Further east, the island and river are crossed obliquely by the Pont de Sully (1876), at the northern end of which, beyond the Sq. H.-Galli, stands the striking Hôtel de Fieubet (see Rte 19).

On the south side of the island, the Pont de la Tournelle (built of wood in 1369; rebuilt in 1654 and again in 1928) crosses from the Rue des Deux-

Ponts (in which the writer Restif de la Bretonne once lodged) to the Quai de la Tournelle.

To the south east is the Institut du Monde Arabe (see Rte 6), and the adjacent Science Faculty Building, with its tower, built on the site of the old Halles aux Vins.

In the transverse Rue St.-Louis-en-l'Ile is the Hôtel Chenizot (No. 51, with a balcony), of 1730, residence of Teresa Cabarrus (later Mme Tallien) in 1788–93. **St.-Louis-en-l'Ile** was begun by Le Vau in 1664 and finished in 1726 by Jacques Doucet. The tower and curious openwork spire were added in 1765. The ornamental stone-carving in the interior was executed under the direction of J.-B. de Champaigne (died 1681, and buried here). It contains six Nottingham alabasters from the same series as those in St.-Leu-St.-Gilles (see Rte 19).

At No. 12 in this street lived Philippe Lebon (1769–1804), who first introduced into France the principle of lighting by gas (1799). Between Nos 9 and 7 is an arch of the Hôtel de Bretonvilliers, finished by Jean I du Cerceau in 1640. Fénelon (1651–1715) lived at No. 3. No. 2 is the **Hôtel Lambert** (c 1650, by Le Vau), once a residence of Voltaire and Mme du Châtelet, and from 1842 the home of the Czartoryski family and a rendezvous of Polish émigrés.

On the north eastern side of the island, No. 3 in the Quai d'Anjou, belonged to Le Vau; No. 9 was the home of Honoré Daumier (1808–79) from 1846. No. 17 the **Hôtel de Lauzun** or de Pimodan (1657, by Le Vau), was the residence in 1682–84 of the Duc de Lauzun, commander of the French contingent at the Battle of the Boyne, who lived here with 'la Grande Mademoiselle'.

Baudelaire lived on the third floor in 1845, and Gautier had apartments here in 1848, where meetings of the 'Club des Haschichins' took place. The artists responsible for its splendid decoration were Le Brun, Le Sueur, Patel and Sébastien Bourdon. For admission apply to the Municipal Tourist Office, Hôtel de Ville (tel. 42765404).

Ford Madox Ford's 'Transatlantic Review' was published from No. 29 on the quai.

Further west, 13 and 15 Quai de Bourbon were the Hôtel Le Charron (17C); No. 11 was owned by Philippe de Champaigne. No. 1 was the Franc-Pinot, an inn kept during the Revolution by the father of Cécile Renault, who had attempted to murder Robespierre.

Turning south, you pass at No. 6 Quai d'Orleans, the Musée Adam Mickiewicz, with a Polish library and souvenirs of the poet (1798–1855), and also of Chopin. Further east, Nos 16–18 in the Quai de Bethune, was the home of Armand, Duc de Richelieu, great-nephew of the cardinal.

At the eastern extremity of the island is the triangular Sq. Barye.

THE SOUTH OR LEFT BANK:
LA RIVE GAUCHE

4 'Quartier Latin'
St. Séverin; St.-Nicholas-du-Chardonnet; St.-Etienne-du-Mont; Panthéon; the Sorbonne

METROS: St.-Michel, Maubert-Mutualité, Card. Lemoine, Luxembourg.

This area, the site of Roman *Lutetia*, on the south bank of the Seine opposite the Ile de la Cité (see Rte 1), derives its present name (conferred by Rabelais) from the language spoken by the students who congregated here. It grew up with Abélard's removal in c 1200 from the school attached to Notre-Dame to the Montagne Ste.-Geneviève. Originally known as the Université, the Quartier Latin still contains the majority of the educational and scientific institutions of Paris.

In the mid 19C the Blvd St.-Germain was driven east through the old streets and many ancient buildings were swept away. In 1968 its paving-blocks were found to be useful missiles during the 'student revolution'. Cafés and bookshops abound, and the students appear to spend more time in the former than in the various faculty buildings.

The Pl. St.-Michel (Pl. 14; 4) is linked to the Cité by the Pont St.-Michel, with the Fontaine St.-Michel at its south end, erected by Davioud in 1860, and incorporating a memorial of the Resistance of 1944. From the Place the busy Blvd St.-Michel (popularly known as the 'Boul Mich') leads south to the Carrefour de l'Observatoire, in part following the Roman Via Inferior (see pp 74 and 84). The boulevard was laid out by Haussman as a direct continuation of the Blvd de Strasbourg and the Blvd de Sébastopol, and shortly crosses the Blvd St.-Germain, running roughly parallel to the Seine. The architectural and historical character of the Quartier is found in the side-streets.

Immediately to the east of the Pl. St.-Michel, in a still decrepit corner of Old Paris, is the Rue de la Huchette, off which run the Rue Xavier-Privas and Rue du Chat-qui-Pêche, an alley named after an old shop-sign. Théophile de Viau composed his 'Parnasse Satirique' at No. 1 Rue de la Huchette and at No. 8 (or 10) Napoléon lodged in 1795; here also is the diminutive Théâtre de la Huchette.

Turn right along the Rue de la Harpe, and take the first turning left, which brings you to *ST.-SEVERIN*. Rebuilt in the 13–16C on the site of an oratory of the time of Childebert I, Foulque of Neuilly-sur-Marne preached the Fourth Crusade here (c 1199).

The lower part of the west front and the west bays of the nave date from the early 13C; the outer south aisle was added c 1350, the outer north aisle and the eastern part of the church were in construction in 1450–96, the chapels in 1500–20. The main west portal, of the early 13C, was brought piecemeal from St.-Pierre-aux-Boeufs in the Cité in 1837. The upper two storeys date from the 15C. On the left is a tower of the 13C, completed in 1487, with a door which was once the main entrance; the tympanum dates from 1853, but in the frame is a 15C inscription: 'Bonnes gens qui par cy passés, Priez Dieu pour les trespassés'. To the left of the tower, a niche holds a statue of St. Séverin.

The interior impresses by the breadth of its double ambulatory. The most striking details are the ribs of the vaulting and the choir triforium, which approach English Perpendicular in style. The apse was partially classicised in the 17C at the expense of Mlle de Montpensier. In the nave, the first three bays contain late-14C glass from St.-Germain-des-Prés, but much restored; from the fourth bay on the glass is mid 15C. One of the subjects on the south side of the nave is the murder of Thomas à Becket. The west rose-window contains a Tree of Jesse (c 1500) masked by an organ of 1745.

On the far side of the Rue St.-Jacques is the Rue Galande, one of the oldest existing streets in Paris (14C). On No. 42 is a carved representation of the life of St. Julian.

The church of **St.-Julien-le-Pauvre** (right) rebuilt c 1170–1230 and used in the 13–16C as a university church and in 1655–1877 by the former Hôtel-Dieu for various secular purposes, has been occupied by Melchites (Greek Catholics subject to papal authority) since 1889. The present west front was built in 1651. Note the foliated capitals within; an iconostasis obscures the east end.

There is an impressive *view of Notre-Dame the adjacent Sq. Rene-Viviani.

From the north east side of this square runs the Rue de la Bûcherie, where No. 13 was occupied by the Ecole de Médecine from 1483 to 1775, with a rotunda built in 1745 by the Danish doctor Jacques-Bénigne Winslow. The writer Restif de la Bretonne (1734–1806) died at No. 16 (previously No. 27).

South of the Sq. René-Viviani is the Rue du Fouarre (named after the 'straw' on which the students sat), the centre of four 14C schools of the University, and referred to by Dante, who is supposed to have attended lectures here. The Rue Lagrange leads south east to meet the Blvd St.-Germain at the Pl. Maubert ('la Maub'), where Etienne Dolet (1509–46) was burnt as a heretic. Crébillon *fils*, the novelist, (1707–77) was born here.

From just east of the Place, the ancient Rue de Bièvre, in which Dante is said to have written part of the Divina Commedia, runs north east. To the west is the Rue des Anglais, infested by English students in medieval times.

A short distance along the Rue Monge, leading south east, is (left) **St.-Nicolas-du-Chardonnet** ('of the thistle-field'), a Renaissance church built mostly in 1656–1709; the clumsy tower (1625) is a relic of an earlier building. Some of the statues and stucco work are by Nicolas Legendre.

The dark interior contains, in the 1st chapel on the right, Corot's study for the Baptism of Christ; the 2nd chapel on the right of the choir, beyond the transept, contains a monument by Girardon of Bignon, the jurist (died 1656). In the 8th chapel (round the apse) is the tomb of Le Brun's mother, by Tuby and Collignon, designed by Le Brun in the theatrical style of Bernini; against the window is a monument of Le Brun (died 1690) and his widow, by Coysevox. Note the 18C organ-case. A Crucifixion by Brueghel the Younger is in the Sacristy.

Turn left along the Rue St.-Victor to reach (left) the Rue de Poissy. At No. 24 are the remains of the 14C refectory of the ancient Collège des Bernardines; it was occupied by firemen from 1844 to 1970.

At the far end of this street, where it meets the Quai de la Tournelle, stands the 17C Hôtel de Nesmond (Nos 55–57), restored, and containing the offices of La Demeure Historique. This association of proprietors of privately-owned historic residences throughout France, founded in 1924, is devoted to promoting public interest in this aspect of their architectural and cultural patrimony. It publishes a map of c 330 châteaux, with opening hours, etc.

At No. 47 in the quai is the former convent of the 'Miramiones' or Filles Ste.-Geneviève, founded by Mme de Miramion (died 1696), now with a small museum devoted to the hospitals of Paris. No. 15 is La Tour d'Argent, which gained its gastronomic reputation in the Second Empire, and which was built on the site of a tavern dating from 1582.

At 32 Rue du Card.-Lemoine, the next main street running south from the *quai*, stood the Collège des Bons-Enfants, where Vincent de Paul founded his congregation of mission-priests. Further south, No. 49 is the Hôtel le Brun, built by Boffrand for the artist in 1700, and later occupied by Watteau and by Buffon.

Climbing south west at the junction of the Rue du Card.-Lemoine with the Rue Monge, you reach the Rue Clovis, where a section of Philippe Auguste's perimeter wall may be seen.

65 Rue du Card.-Lemoine, the Institution Ste.-Geneviève, was the **Scots College** (Collège des Ecossais; apply to the concierge), re-founded in 1662 by Robert Barclay. George Buchanan graduated in 1528 at the earlier Scots College, founded in 1326. He remained teaching in Paris until 1534, again in 1544–47 and in 1553.

The Chapel, on the first floor, contains the tomb of Frances Jennings, Duchess of Tyrconnel (died 1730), the spirited elder sister of Sarah, Duchess of Marlborough; a memorial erected to James II (who bequeathed his brain to the college) by James Drummond, Duke of Perth, with a long Latin epigraph; and the tomb of Sir Patrick Menteith, who died in 1675 in the service of Louis XIV.

At 5 Rue Descartes (crossing the Rue Clovis) is the entrance to the influential **Ecole Polytechnique**, founded by Monge in 1794 for the training of artillery and engineer officers, transferred in 1805 to the old buildings of the Collège de Navarre, which stood here and were extended in 1929–35.

Founded in 1304 by Jeanne de Navarre, queen of Philippe le Bel, the Collège numbered among its pupils Gerson, Ramus, Henri III, Henri IV, Henri de Guise, Richelieu, Bossuet, Condorcet and André Chénier. The Collège de Boncourt (No. 21), taken over by the Collège de Navarre in the 17C, had earlier contained perhaps the first theatre in Paris. In 1792 Giovanni Battista Piranesi's sons established their engraving works in the building.

At 34 Rue Montagne-Ste.-Geneviève, further down the hill, are remains of the Collège des Trente-Trois, founded in 1633 by Claude Bernard, friend and follower of Vincent de Paul, and named after its 33 scholarships (one for each year of Christ's life).

At 23 Rue Clovis is the entrance to the Lycée Henri-IV. The restored tower, with a Romanesque base and two Gothic upper storeys (14–15C), is a relic of the church (demolished 1802) of the Abbaye Ste.-Geneviève.

Nearly all the conventual buildings were rebuilt in the 18C but the former refectory (now the chapel) is an over-restored 13C building. The kitchens are also medieval. The fact that the abbey came under papal jurisdiction, not that of the Bishop of Paris, influenced Abélard's choice of this area.
Bernardin de Saint-Pierre lived from 1781 to 1786 at 4 Rue Rollin, where he wrote 'Paul et Virginie'. The street is named after Charles Rollin (1661–1741; the historian), who died at No. 8; Descartes lived at No. 14 in 1644–48. Mérimée (1803–70) was born at 7 Carré de Ste.-Geneviève, which was adjacent.

On the right is ***ST.-ETIENNE-DU-MONT** (Pl. 14; 6), showing the incongruous transition from the Gothic to the Renaissance style. It was almost continuously in construction from 1492 to 1586. Marguerite de Valois laid the foundation stone of the portal in 1610 and even this retains certain Gothic motifs. The tower, begun in 1492, was completed in 1628. The north side, with its picturesque porch, dates from 1632.

It replaced an earlier parish church dependent upon and entered through the abbey church of Ste.-Geneviève (see below). During the Revolution, it was known as the 'Temple of Filial Piety'.

The INTERIOR has lofty columns, a wide ambulatory and ribbed vaulting with pendent keystones. Its originality lies in the balustrade which runs along the supporting pillars of the nave and choir, and the beautiful fretted *rood screen, built in 1525–35, is a masterpiece of design and carving (the date 1605 on the side refers only to the door to the spiral staircases by which it is ascended). The organ-case by Jean Buron dates from 1631–32; the pulpit of 1651 is the work of Germain Pilon, with sculptures designed by Laurent de la Hire. The *stained glass ranges in date from c 1550 to c 1600; the oldest windows are those in the apse.

Between the 6th and 7th chapels in the south aisle a tablet commemorates the Jacobins, an order of preaching friars established in the Rue St.-Jacques in 1218. Above the 1st chapel in the choir is an ex-voto to St. Geneviève, with the provost and merchants of Paris, by François de Troy (1726), while higher, to the right, is a similar painting by Largillierre of 1696. On either side of the chapel are the epitaphs of Pascal and Racine (by Boileau), whose graves are at the entrance to the Lady Chapel. Also buried in the church are Charles Rollin (1661–1741), the historian, and the artist Eustache le Sueur (1616–55). In the next chapel south of the choir is the copper-gilt shrine of St. Geneviève (1853), containing a fragment of her tomb; her remains were burned by the mob in the Pl. de Grève in 1801.

From the next bay runs a corridor, at the end of which (right) is the Presbytery, built in 1742 for Louis d'Orléans (son of the Regent), who died here in 1752. On the left is the Charnier, or gallery of the graveyard, with 12 superb *windows of 1605–09; note one depicting the Mystic Wine-press. Most of them are after the designs of Léonard Gautier.

To the west of the Pl.-Ste.-Genevieve (Pl. 14; 6) rises the grandiose bulk of the **PANTHEON** (CNMH), situated on the 'Mont de Paris', the highest point on the Left Bank (60m) and the legendary burial-place of Geneviève (5C), a *pucelle* of Nanterre, later regarded as the patron saint of Paris.

In 1744, lying ill at Metz, Louis XV vowed that if he recovered he would replace the former church, and the present building was begun 20 years later, although not completed until 1789. Its architect, Jacques-Germaine Soufflot (1714–80), died of anxiety, it is said, owing to criticism that subsidence of the walls (noticeable near the choir) would occur because their foundations had been laid on clay pits dug by Roman potters.

In 1791, after the death of Mirabeau, the Constituent Assembly decided that the building should be used as a Panthéon or burial-place for distinguished citizens, and the pediment was inscribed with the words 'Aux Grands Hommes la Patrie reconnaissante'. From the Restoration to 1831 and from 1851 to 1885 it was again used as a church, but on the occasion of Victor Hugo's interment it reverted to the name and purpose decreed in 1791.

The Panthéon, built in the shape of a Greek cross, is 110m long, 82m wide and 83m high to the top of its majestic dome. The pediment above the portico of Corinthian columns is a masterpiece of David d'Angers, representing France between Liberty and History, distributing laurels to famous men. Forty-two windows were walled up during the Revolution.

The interior is coldly Classical, adorned with paintings, among which are some pallid works by Puvis de Chavannes, while in the transepts are monuments by Landowski. The colossal group of the Convention, at the east end, is by Sicard.

The *dome, supported by four piers united by arches, contains three distinct cupolas, of which the first is open in the centre to reveal the second, with a fresco by Gros. By the first pillar (right) is a monument to Rousseau by Bartholomé: on the left, another to Diderot and the Encyclopaedistes by Terroir. Other tablets commemorate Antoine de Saint-Exupéry (1900–44) and Henri-Louis Bergson (1859–1941). Within the dome, in 1852, the physicist Léon Foucault gave the first public demonstration of his pendulum experiment proving the rotation of the Earth.

Most parts of the Panthéon are now closed to the public because of danger from falling masonry. Restoration is expected to take at least 10 years but among the tombs contained within its imposing walls are: Rousseau (died 1778; transferred here in 1794); Voltaire (died 1778; transferred 1791), with a statue attributed to Houdon; and Soufflot, the architect. The heart of Gambetta (1838–82) is contained within a shrine. Of men whose remains have been reinterred in the vaults, the most eminent are Victor Hugo (1802–85) and Emile Zola (1840–1902); Marcelin Berthelot (1827–1907), the chemist; Jean Jaurès (1859–assassinated 1914), the socialist politician; Louis Braille (1809–52), benefactor of the blind; the explorer Bougainville (1729–1811); and Jean Moulin (1899–1944), the Resistance hero. Mirabeau and Marat were interred here with great state, but their remains were soon cast out with ignominy: the former now rests in the cemetery of Ste.-Catherine, the latter in the graveyard of St.-Etienne-du-Mont. Jean Monnet (1888–1979), the 'Father of Europe', was buried in the Panthéon on the centenary of his birth. In the north west corner of the Pl. du Panthéon was the Ecole de Droit, begun by Soufflot in 1771, and subsequently enlarged.

The **Bibliothèque Ste.-Geneviève**, on the northern side of the Place, orig-inated in the library of the Abbaye Ste.-Geneviève. The present building, (1844–50, by Labrouste) is on the site of the Collège de Montaigu, founded in 1314, where Loyola, Erasmus and Calvin were students. It was also known as the 'Hôtel des Haricots', as it was presumed that beans were the staple fare of its inmates. It was in later years a prison.

The library contains c 700,000 vols (nearly 4000 MSS) and over 30,000 prints and engravings (including 10,000 portraits). Rooms are devoted to Scandinavian literature (c 90,000 vols) and the Bibliothèque Jacques Doucet, comprising c 8000 vols of late 19C and 20C French authors, including MSS of Rimbaud, Verlaine, Baudelaire, Gide and Valéry. Illuminated MSS are occasionally exhibited. The building also contains a number of busts by Coysevox, J.-J. Caffieri, Lemoyne and Houdon.

On the right, in the Rue Valette, are the remains of the Collège Fortet (No. 21), dating from 1397. Calvin was a student here in 1531.

Further downhill to the right, in the Rue des Carmes, is St.-Ephrem, a Syrian Catholic church. It was formerly the chapel (1760) of a community of Irish priests who established themselves in the 17C buildings of the Collège des Lombards.

To the left of the library, on the right in the Rue Cujas, is the Collège Ste.-Barbe, founded in 1460, the oldest existing public educational estab-lishment in France, at which Francisco Xavier was a scholar.

Descending west from the Panthéon towards the Luxembourg Gardens is the wide Rue Soufflot, where (right) at No. 14 a tablet commemorates the site of the Dominican or Jacobin convent (1217–1790) where Albertus Magnus and Thomas Aquinas taught.

The Rue St.-Jacques, which is crossed first, was an important thoroughfare in medieval times. It follows the course of the Roman road—the Via Superior—from Lutetia to Orléans, and formed part of the pilgrim route to Santiago de Compostela, and so attracted many convents. Its southern section is described on p 69.

Turning right along the Rue St.-Jacques, you pass (right) the Lycée Louis-le-Grand, formerly the Jesuit Collège de Clermont, founded in 1560. Molière, Voltaire, Robespierre, Desmoulins, Delacroix and Hugo studied here. It was rebuilt in 1887–96.

You next pass the **Collège de France**, with its entrance in the Pl. Marcelin-Berthelot (Pl. 14; 4–6). In the courtyard, with its graceful portico, is a statue of Guillaume Budé (Budaeus; 1468–1540), under whose influence it was founded by François I in 1530 with the intention of spreading humanism and counteracting the narrow scholasticism of the Sorbonne. It was independent of the University, and its teaching was free and public. The present building was begun in 1610, completed by Chalgrin c 1778 and since enlarged. During excavations in 1894 traces of Gallo-Roman baths were found.

In a garden to the north eastern side is a monument to the 'Pléïade', the 16C poetical coterie (notably Du Bellay and Ronsard) which originated in the vanished Collège Coqueret, founded on this site in 1418 but which survived only until 1643. Other members of the group, formed in 1549, were Antoine de Baïf, Rémy Belleau, Jodelle, Pontus de Tyard and Jean Dorat (who took the place of Jacques Peletier).

To the west of the Collège de France is the **SORBONNE**, founded as a theological college in 1253 by Robert de Sorbon (1201–74), chaplain to Louis IX. It was rebuilt at Richelieu's expense by Jacques Lemercier in 1629 but, with the exception of the church, the present buildings date from 1885–1901.

The **University of Paris**, which disputes with Bologna the title of the oldest university in Europe, arose in the first decade of the 12C out of the schools of dialectic attached to Notre-Dame. (Josse de Londres is said to have endowed the College des Dix-Huit in 1180.) Transferred by Abélard to the Montagne Ste.-Geneviève, the university obtained its first statutes in 1208, and these served as the model for Oxford and Cambridge and other universities of northern Europe. By the 16C it comprised no fewer than 40 separate colleges. In 1550 John Dee, the mathematician and astrologer, lectured on Euclid at the Collège de Reims, the first ever to do so in Paris. In 1577 James Crichton (1560–83) 'The Admirable Crichton', is said to have disputed on scientific questions in 12 languages at the university.

Before the end of the 13C the Sorbonne had become synonymous with the faculty of theology, overshadowing the rest of the university and possessing the power of conferring degrees. It was distinguished for its religious rancour, supporting the condemnation of Joan of Arc, justifying the massacre of St. Bartholomew and refusing its recognition of Henri IV. Nevertheless in 1469 it was responsible for the introduction of printing into France, by allowing Ulrich Gering and his companions to set up their presses within its precincts.

Marlowe refers to its 'blockish Sorbonests'; in 1713 it was visited by George Berkeley, who was present at a disputation there, 'which indeed had much of the French fire in it'. Later in the 18C it attacked the 'philosophes' and in 1792 was itself suppressed. It was refounded by Napoléon, and in 1821 became the official headquarters of the University of Paris. The student 'revolution' of May 1968 eventually had the effect of instigating overdue reforms in the university system, and in 1970 the University of Paris was replaced by the formation of 13 autonomous universities in the region.

The ponderous buildings, which still house the university library of 700,000 volumes, the Académie de Paris and minor learned institutions, include the Grand Amphithéâtre (the main lecture hall, containing Puvis de Chavannes' mural, 'Le Bois sacré'), which may be visited on application at the main entrance in the Rue des Ecoles.

Apply here also to visit *Ste.-Ursule de la Sorbonne, facing the Pl. de la Sorbonne founded in the 13C and rebuilt by Lemercier in 1635–59 at the expense of Richelieu. The dramatic *tomb of the great cardinal (1585–1642) was designed by Le Brun and sculptured by Girardon (1694). The *dome was the first example of a true dome in Paris.

5 Musée de Cluny

METROS: Maubert-Mutualité, Odéon, St.-Michel.

Opposite the entrance to the Sorbonne is the Square Paul-Painlevé (Pl. 14; 3–4; with a statue of Montaigne by Landowski). It is flanked to the north by the *Hôtel de Cluny, built at the end of the 15C on the site of Roman ruins, known as the Palais des Thermes, and one of the finest extant examples of medieval French domestic architecture. It houses the **MUSEE DE CLUNY, devoted to the arts and crafts of the Middle Ages, and one of the most rewarding museums in Paris. The entrance is in the right-hand corner of the courtyard, beyond an archway surmounted by the Amboise arms.

The museum is open Wed.–Mon. 09.30–12.30; 14.00–17.15.

The property was bought in 1340 by Pierre de Chalus, Abbot of Cluny in Burgundy, and the mansion was built c 1490 by Abbot Jacques d'Amboise as the town house of the abbots, although rarely occupied by them. On the death of Louis XII in 1515, it became the residence of his widow, Mary Tudor (1496–1533; the daughter of Henry VII), who was known as 'La Reine Blanche' from the white mourning she wore as queen-dowager of France. James V of Scotland was lodged here in 1537 immediately before his marriage to Madeleine, daughter of François I. Later occupants were the Cardinal de Lorraine, Claude de Guise, Mazarin, and the papal nuncios (1600–81).

In the 18C the tower was used as an observatory by the astronomer Messier. At the Revolution the mansion became national property but in 1833 it was bought by Alexandre du Sommerard (1771–1842) and filled with the treasures which he spent his lifetime collecting. These were bought by the State and supplemented by many new acquisitions, during the long curatorship of his son, Edmond du Sommerard (died 1889), and since.

GROUND FLOOR. R1 is devoted to the accessories of medieval costume, such as buckles, clasps and ornamental trinkets; shoes—one à la poulaine, with a pointed toe (late 14C); and metal and leather caskets, etc. Outstanding in this and the next four rooms is the collection of tapestries, mostly 15C, although that of The Resurrection is early 14C. Among them are The Legend of Augustus and the Sibyl (early 16C); The Concert; The Miracle of St. Quentin; Vintage Scenes and the set of six scenes illustrating the activities of a noble household of c 1500, entitled 'La Vie seigneuriale' in R4. Also remarkable are the carved head of the funeral effigy of Jeanne of Toulouse (c 1280) in R2; the textiles and embroidery in R3, some Coptic or Byzantine, others of French, Italian, English and Spanish origin, including examples of Hispano-Moresque fabrics. R5 is largely devoted to carpentry and woodwork, including misericords (from St.-Lucien, Beauvais) and a chest front on which a jousting scene is depicted. Also displayed here are several Nottingham alabasters, and a charming statue of St. Ursula sheltering some of her 11,000 companions under her capacious cloak. **R6** contains examples of stained-glass, including panels from St.-Denis (1144), Troyes (c 1200), and medallions from the Ste.-Chapelle.

The following rooms **(RR7–11)** display sculptural fragments from the central portal of Notre-Dame; mutilated heads from the Tree of Jesse gallery of the cathedral, and statues of the Apostles from the Ste.-Chapelle (1248); carved capitals, some of Catalan workmanship, others from St.-Denis (7C) and St.-Germain-des-Prés (mid 11C); tombstones; a 7C sarcophagus; and a number of fine examples of medival statuary in wood and stone, notable among which is an Adam of c 1260.

Below **R12** is the *Frigidarium* of the **Gallo-Roman baths**, remarkable in that it still retains its vault, unique in France. The room (20m by 11.5m and 14m in height) with the *Piscina* probably on the northern side, is all that remains in its entirety of the baths, assumed to have been built during the reign of Caracalla (212–17): only slight ruins remain of its *Tepidarium* and *Caldarium*. The museum's collection of Gallo-Roman sculpture is displayed here.

On the FIRST FLOOR, and in circular **R3**, are displayed the series of six exquisite *millefleurs* tapestries known as **La Dame à la Licorne** (or Unicorn), probably woven in the southern Netherlands for Jean le Viste between 1484 and 1500: the arms of the family—gules, a band azur with three crescents argent—being frequently seen. They had long hung in the Château of Boussac, and were first brought to public notice by both Mérimée (when Inspector of Historical Monuments) and George Sand, and were eventually acquired by the museum in 1883.

They illustrate the Senses and their disposition is the same as when originally hung: to the right, Sight, in which the unicorn gazes into the mirror held before him by the Lady; and Hearing, in which the Lady plays a portative organ: to the left, Touch, in which the Lady gently grasps the horn of the unicorn; and Smell, in which a monkey sniffs a flower, while the Lady weaves a garland: beyond is Taste, with the Lady feeding the monkey and a parakeet from a bowl of sweetmeats; while further to the right the Lady stands before a tent-like pavilion, while returning jewels to a casket held by her maid, a gesture said to indicate 'Free Choice' and the non-submission to the senses; the top of the pavilion is embroidered with the motto '*A mon seul désir*'.

Outstanding among the statues in **R14** are a Magdalen from Brussels; an early 16C Virgin reading to the Child, from the Lower Rhine; the group of the Virgin swooning; a marble Virgin; a painted Pietà from Tarascon (mid 15C); the Averbode altarpiece (1513; by Jan de Molder), among others, including a painted and gilded panel from The Prodigal Son series.

In a corridor (**R15**) are a variety of medieval artefacts, among them domestic utensils; mirrors; riding accessories; games-boards; stamps, dies, and seals; and writing equipment. **R16** displays part of the Treasure of Gurrazar, including three Visigothic votive crowns with their pendent crosses, dating from the late 7C, discovered near Toledo in 1858; the Golden Rose (1330), given by the Avignon Pope John XXII to a count of Neuchâtel; Gallo-Roman and Merovingian jewellery, including gold torques, bracelets, buckles, ornamented belts and fibulas; Late Roman and Byzantine cloisonné enamelwork; two rock crystal lionheads (5C), which probably once decorated a consular chair, found on the banks of the Rhine; enamels from the Rhineland and Meuse; and notable examples of late 12C–14C Limoges enamelwork, among them reliquaries, chalices, pyxes, shrines, plaques, croziers and crucifixes; the Reliquary of the Ste.-Chapelle, commissioned by Louis IX (showing, on the reverse, three decapitated saints); the so-called Colmar Treasure of early 14C coins and jewellery found in a wall of the Rue des Juifs, Colmar in 1853; processional crosses, including one from Barcelona (mid 14C) and another from Siena (mid 15C); a collection of cameos, intaglios and glyptics; and the Reliquary of St. Anne (1472; by Hans Greiff of Inglostadt). **R17** is devoted to ceramics, including a fine collection of Hispano-Moresque ware, and other examples of lustreware from Manises (Valencia).

R18 contains the reassembled choir-stalls from the abbey of St.-Lucien at Beauvais (1492–1500), some misericords from which are shown in R5. **R19** displays the gold altar-frontal from Basle cathedral (c 1030), made for the Emperor Heinrich II; a collection of Byzantine and consular ivories, including a large figure of Ariadne (c 500); a richly mounted reliquary casket; a 15C Italian bust reliquary, etc.

Adjacent is the **Chapel (R20)**, a masterpiece of Flamboyant vaulting from a central pillar, with a filigree of delicate moulding between the main ribs. Above the oriel window are 15C sculptures, with the Father blessing His dying Son, and angels with the instruments of the Passion, etc. Also notable are the recumbent funeral effigy (copper on wood) of Blanche of Champagne (died 1283), from the abbey of La Joie, near Hennebont (Morbihan); and the first part of a set of tapestries depicting the Life of St. Stephen, woven for Jean Baillet, Bp of Auxerre c 1490: the series is continued in the adjoining rooms.

R21 is devoted largely to metalwork, mainly of copper and bronze, including an eagle-lectern (1383) from Tournai; measures and weights; 'aquamaniles'; cauldrons, candlesticks and other implements; and oliphants or ivory hunting-horns (10C; from Southern Italy). **R22**. Iron-work, with fine examples of grilles (12C); a metal-plated chest; bolts, locks and keys; a small selection of arms and armour, spurs and knives; shields and targes or bucklers; coffers, etc. **R23** contains articles of pewter, tin and lead, including a collection of medallions, pilgrims' badges (and their moulds); guild counters, toys, etc.

Most of the later objects, from the era of the Renaissance but part of the collections of this museum, are now to be seen at Ecouen: see Rte 37.

6 South east of the 'Quartier Latin': The Institut du Monde Arabe; the Jardin des Plantes; the Bibliothèque de France; the Gobelins; St.-Médard

METROS: Monge, Gare d'Austerlitz, St.-Marcel, Gobelins, Censier-Daubenton.

At the east end of the Rue des Ecoles (conveniently approached from métros Maubert-Mutualité or Cardinal Lemoine) rises the extensive utilitarian block of buildings, with their obtrusive tower, housing departments of the

Faculty of Science of the Univerisity of Paris, to the north of which the Rue des Fossés-St.-Bernard descends towards the Seine and the Pont Sully. The mineralogical collections of the university are displayed at No. 5 in this street.

Here, until their transfer to Bercy, stood the huge bonded warehouses of the Halles aux Vins, itself on the site of the Abbaye de St.-Victor. This had been dispersed in 1790: here Thomas à Becket and Abélard resided and in its library Rabelais studied.

The **Institut du Monde Arabe** (open Tues.–Sun. 13.00–20.00), inaugurated in the autumn of 1987 at 23 Quai St. Bernard, was founded in 1980 in an attempt to further cultural and scientific relations between France and some 20 Arab countries. The building covers an area of $7250m^2$ and rises to a height of 32m. The public parts of the Institut include a library and documentation centre and museum. A curious feature of the exterior of the south façade are the shutters of the windows. They were intended to regulate the size of the window aperture by photo-electric cells reacting to the sun's intensity but in fact they are automatically moved every hour. A spiral of white marble is visible in the Book Tower.

The museum comprises $2800m^2$ with an additional $700m^2$ for temporary exhibitions. A proportion of the material in the museum—ceramics, MSS, metalwork, ivories, fabrics, etc.—has come from the Arab-Islamic collections of the Musée du Louvre, the Musée des Arts Africains et Océaniens and from the Union Central des Arts Décoratifs.

Between the Quai St.-Bernard and the Seine, among riverside gardens, extends the **Musée de Sculpture en Plein Air** (Pl. 15; 5), in which some 40 characteristic examples of contemporary sculpture, fabrications, etc., are exhibited. Few are notable; the most noticeable is Nicolas Schöffer's gyrating metallic tower, with its struts and discs, while among earlier works are some by Brancusi and Zadkine.

Bearing south from the Rue Jussieu, you ascend the Rue Linné, off which the Rue des Arènes climbs right to the remains of the 2–3C amphitheatre of Roman Paris, only discovered in 1869 and fully excavated since 1883. The **Arènes de Lutèce** are now surrounded by the gardens of the Sq. Capitan named after Dr Capitan, who restored the ruins in 1917–18.

At the junction of the Rue Linné with its continuation, the Rue Geoffroy-St.-Hilaire, stands the Fontaine Cuvier (1840), and the north-west entrance to the **JARDIN DES PLANTES** (known until 1793 as the Jardin du Roi), officially the **Musée National d'Histoire Naturelle** (Pl. 15; 7), 28 hectares in area and combining the attractions of a menagerie, botanical gardens and natural history galleries. Its collections of wild and herbaceous plants are unrivalled, and in May and June the peonies make a magnificent show. The library contains a remarkable collection of botanical MSS, including the '*Vélins du Roi*', illustrated by Nicolas Robert (1614–85) and others; also works by Redouté, etc.

The Jardin des Plantes is open Mon., Wed.–Fri. 10.00–17.00; Sat., Sun. 11.00–18.00. Zoo open 09.00–19.00.

There are other entrances in the Rue Geoffroy-St.-Hilaire and in the semicircular Pl. Valhubert to the east opposite the Gare d'Austerlitz. The nearest métro stations are Jussieu, Monge, Censier-Daubenton and Gare d'Austerlitz.

Founded in 1626 under Louis XIII as a 'physic garden' for medicinal herbs by the royal physician Guy de la Brosse, the garden was first opened to the public in 1650. In 1647–51 its keeper was William Davison, a Scotsman. Its present importance is mainly due to the great naturalist, the Comte de Buffon (1707–88), who was superintendent from 1739 and greatly enlarged the grounds. In 1793 it was reorganised by the Convention under its present official title and provided with 12 professorships. The animals from the royal collection at Versailles were brought to form the nucleus of a menagerie during Bernardin de Saint-Pierre's brief directorship. In 1792, Richard Twiss, the traveller, was told by the director that the names of some plants had been changed: 'We will not have any aristocratic plants!'

Many distinguished French naturalists have taught and studied here, and are commemorated by monuments in the garden or nearby. A statue of the naturalist J.-B. Lamarck (1744–1829) faces the east entrance. Among other scientists associated with the Jardin des Plantes are the zoologist Geoffroy Saint-Hilaire (1772–1844), Louis Daubenton (1706–99) who did the honours when visited by Joseph Townsend, traveller and geologist, in 1786, and the botanists Joseph de Tournefort (1656–1708) and Bernard de Jussieu (1690–1777).

Entering from the north west you pass (left) the Maison de Chevreul, named after the chemist Eugène Chevreul (1786–1889) and the Maison de Cuvier, where Georges Cuvier (1769–1832), zoologist and paleontologist, gave Saturday evening receptions during the 1820s and '30s, attended by Mérimée, Stendhal and Delacroix, among others. Here also are the Administrative Building, in a mansion of 1785, and the restored amphithéâtre or lecture hall of 1788. The menagerie occupies most of the northern side of the gardens. It is said that many of its earlier occupants were killed in 1870–71 to feed besieged Parisians during the Franco-Prussian War.

On the right of the entrance is the Butte, a hillock with a maze, with the first cedar of Lebanon (from Kew Gardens) to be planted in France, in 1734, and a belvedere on the summit. The sundial here bears the inscription *'Horas non numero nisi serenas'*: I only count the sunny hours. In the centre are the Jardin d'Hiver and Jardin Alpin.

Along the southern side of the gardens are ranged the Zoological Galleries, in the north vestibule of which is the tomb of Guy de la Brosse (died 1641); the Mineralogical Galleries, with the library (c 700,000 vols and 2500 MSS) and Buffon's House, which he occupied from 1773 to his death; the Botanical Gallery; and Paleontological Gallery. To the south, on the far side of the Rue Buffon, is an annexe to the museum.

To the west of the Rue Geoffroy-St.-Hilaire is a green-tiled mosque, complete with minaret, which has stood here since 1925.

Slightly further west (in the Rue Puits-de-l'Ermite) was the site of the Prison de Ste.-Pélagie, where Joséphine, the future empress, and Mme du Barry were confined during the Revolution, and where Mme Roland (1754–93) wrote her memoirs.

Not far to the south, the Blvd St.-Marcel is reached at a point near which lay the Cimetière Ste.-Catherine, where the bodies of Mirabeau and other revolutionaries were reburied after being ejected from the Panthéon. This thoroughfare leads north east to meet the Blvd de l'Hôpital.

To the right of this latter junction stands the huge **˚Hôpital de la Salpêtrière** (Pl. 15; 8), founded in 1656 on the site of a gunpowder factory as a home for aged or insane women.

In 1684 a criminal wing was built, in which 'Manon Lescaut' and Mme de la Motte were jailed, and which was notorious for its filth and vice. A house of correction for wayward wives and young girls was later added. In 1790 there were said to be 8000 females living there including, according to Townsend, 7000 foundlings and about 900 prostitutes (of the 28,000 then on the lists of the police). Part of the building contained political prisoners during the Revolution and some of the worst massacres of September 1792 took place here.

The main building, by Le Vau and Le Muet, dates from 1657–63; the domed church of **St.-Louis**, built in 1670–77, is by Libéral Bruant. Statues by Etex were added after 1832. As a whole, it is a notable example of the austere magnificence of the architecture of the period and may be compared in some ways to Les Invalides.

Dr Jean-Martin Charcot (1825–93), the hypnotist, is commemorated by a monument to the left of the gateway; his consulting-room, laboratory and library have been preserved intact.

Adjacent to the south is the Hôpital de la Pitié, transferred in 1911 from the Rue Lacépède, where it had been founded by Marie de Médicis in 1612.

To the north east is the **Gare d'Austerlitz** (at present being restored), the main railway terminus for Tours, Bordeaux, Bayonne, Toulouse, etc.; see Pl. 15; 6. Between 1870 and 1871 (during the Franco-Prussian War), the station, then known as the Gare d'Orléans, was turned into a balloon factory under the management of Eugene Godard. Some 65 manned balloons left besieged Paris carrying letters and dispatches. One was blown as far afield as Norway.

The area immediately south east of the station is undergoing drastic change as part of a larger, long-term project to renovate this district. The Blvd St.-Marcel will be extended north east across the Blvd de l'Hôpital and the station to the southern end of the new Pont Charles-de-Gaulle. This will provide direct access between the Gare d'Austerlitz and the Gare de Lyon.

The Quai d'Austerlitz (facing the new buildings of the Ministère des Finances and Palais Omnisport on the far bank of the Seine) will be cleared and an avenue, flanked by new buildings, will be driven south west from the station. A footbridge will span the river directly to the new Parc de Bercy; see Rte 31.

Beside the Seine, and half way between the Pont de Bercy and the Pont de Tolbiac, will be the site of the future Bibliothèque de France, which was at one time expected to be inaugurated in mid 1995, but in January 1992 widespread criticism of the plan caused it to be reconsidered.

The immense project, the design of Dominique Perrault, will consist of four L-shaped 96m-high towers, each of 20 storeys (to simulate books opened at right angles), which will stand at the corners of the 7.5 hectare site. In the centre will be an esplanade and sunken gardens. The upper parts of each tower-block and the wings surrounding the reading rooms, which flank the garden, will contain the book stacks ($71,000m^2$) which will have a storage capacity of over 15,000,000 volumes. The reading rooms themselves will have an area of $58,000m^2$ and seating for 5000.

The library will be provided with all the latest technology services and facilities, which will allow access to an extensive range of bibliographical information. It will also accommodate, an audio-visual department, conservation and restoration sections, and legal deposit offices.

The present Bibliothèque Nationale will probably retain the Departments of Maps and Plans, and Prints, among others, together with the Cabinet des Médailles et Antiques; see Rte 18.

The Blvd St.-Marcel runs south west of the Blvd de l'Hôpital to meet the Av. des Gobelins, beyond which it divides to be continued by the Blvd Arago (leading due west to the Pl. Denfert-Rochereau) and the Blvd de Port-Royal (eventually meeting the Blvd du Montparnasse).

A short distance south of this junction stands (right) **La Manufacture Nationale des Gobelins** (CNMH) (Pl. 14; 8; admission Tues.–Thurs. by guided tour only at 14.15 and 14.45), the famous tapestry factory which has been a state institution for over 300 years, and still retains some of its 17C buildings.

The original factory at Fontainebleau was moved to Paris during the reign of Henri II. Suspended during the 16C Religious Wars, the industry was revived by Henri IV and installed in 1601 in the buildings of the Gobelins, named after Jean Gobelin (died 1476), head of a family of dyers who made their reputation with the discovery of a scarlet dye, and who had set up their dye-works here on the banks of the Bièvre in 1443. In 1662, under Colbert, the royal carpet factory of the Savonnerie, established in 1604 in the galleries of the Louvre and subsequently moved to a 'savonnerie' (soap-factory) at Chaillot, was placed under the same management. It was not until 1768 that private individuals were allowed to buy Savonnerie carpets. The factory transferred its workshops to the Gobelins in 1825. In 1667 Louis XIV added the royal furniture factory and Charles le Brun and then Pierre Mignard (in 1690) were appointed directors. The Beauvais tapestry workshops, destroyed in 1940, were also moved here.

The tapestry is still woven by hand on high-warp looms, several of which date from the time of Louis XIV. The weaver works on the reverse side of the tapestry; the painting which he is copying is placed behind him and reflected in a mirror. The average amount of tapestry that a weaver can produce in a day is 15cm^2.

In the former chapel hang two tapestries specially made for it. The tour crosses the Rue Berbier-du-Mets, behind the factory, which now covers the non-calcareous waters of the Bièvre, which used to flow between the dye-works and workshops. Another new building contains workshops for the weaving of carpets, where the original methods are still followed.

Adjacent is the Mobilier National (or National Furniture Store), and beyond, where the allotments of tapestry workers stood, is the Sq. René-le-Gall (with the hunting lodge of M. de Julienne, the patron of Watteau).

The Av. des Gobelins ends to the south at the Pl. d'Italie, the hub of seven important thoroughfares.

Turning north down the Av. des Gobelins, you approach picturesque **St.-Médard** (Pl. 14; 8), dedicated to the St. Swithin of France. The nave and west front are of the late 15C; the choir, in construction from 1550 to 1632, was 'classicised' in 1784, when the Lady Chapel was added. The church was sacked by the Huguenots in 1561, and not much 16C glass survives. The churchyard was notorious for the hysterical orgies of the Jansenist fanatics, or *convulsionnaires*, at the tomb of the Abbé Pâris (died 1727).

The narrow, shabby but busy Rue Mouffetard, an ancient thoroughfare (the lower end is closed to traffic), climbs north through a squalid district (but with a good street market) past (left) the Rue de l'Arbalète, where at No. 3 Auguste Rodin was born in 1840. Eventually you pass (right) the Pl. de la Contrescarpe, where No. 1 has a tablet commemorating the 'Cabaret de la Pomme-de-Pin', immortalised by Rabelais and the 'Pléïade'. (There was another cabaret of the same name in the Rue de la Cité.)

You shortly enter the Rue Descartes where the poet Paul Verlaine (1844–96) died at No. 39, before reaching the Rue Clovis, see Rte 4.

Also in this district, but slightly to the west and best approached by the Rue d'Ulm (leading south from the Panthéon), is the Maronite church of N.-D. du Liban, facing Rue Lhomond. The Collége des Irlandais, founded in 1578 by John Lee and re-founded in 1687 by English Catholics as a seminary, stands at the corner of the adjacent Rue des Irlandais.

At 29 Rue Lhomond, leading south east, with an 18C façade seen from the Rue Amyot, Mme du Barry and Juliette Drouet were educated in the Couvent de Ste.-Aure. A short distance beyond, at the Ecole de Physique et de Chimie industrielles, in the Rue Pierre-Brossolette, Pierre and Marie Curie did their experimental work in 1883–1905.

At 45 Rue d'Ulm is the Ecole Normale Supérieure, established in 1794 for the training of teachers and sited here since 1843. Pasteur worked in laboratories here between 1864 and 1888. Among its pupils were Taine, Bergson, Péguy, Romain Rolland, Giraudoux, Jules Romains, Jean Jaurès and Edouard Herriot.

7 Val-de-Grâce; Observatoire; Montparnasse

METROS: Luxembourg, Port-Royal, Denfert-Rochereau, Cité-Universitaire, Vavin, Montparnasse-Bienvenue.

Turning south from the Rue Soufflot along the Rue St.-Jacques (Pl. 13; 8; see p 74) you pass No. 195, the Institut Océanographique, and No. 218, which occupies the site of the house of Jean de Meung, part-author of the 'Roman de la Rose' (c 1300).

On the right is **St.-Jacques-du-Haut-Pas**, a plain classical building (1630–88), replacing an earlier chapel, and the favourite church of the Jansenists. It was completed in 1712 with the help of the Duchesse de Longueville (1619–79; who is buried here), together with Jean Duvergier de Hauranne (1581–1643), the prominent Jansenist, and Jean-Dominique Cassini (1625–1712), the astronomer.

No. 254, at the corner of the Rue de l'Abbé-de-l'Epée, is the **Institut National des Sourds-Muets**, a deaf and dumb asylum founded by the Abbé de l'Epée (1712–89) about 1760 and taken over by the State in 1790; the building, once the Oratorian seminary of St.-Magloire, was reconstructed in 1823. In the courtyard is a statue of the Abbé by Félix Martin, a deaf and dumb sculptor (1789). Joseph II, when visiting his sister Marie-Antoinette, was taken over the asylum and, on his return to Vienna, established a similar institution there.

Further on, at No. 269 (left) is the **Schola Cantorum** (visitors admitted), a free conservatoire of music established in 1896 by three pupils of César Franck, including Vincent d'Indy. Among composers who studied here were Albéniz, De Falla, Granados, Roussel, Milhaud, Messiaen and Satie.

The buildings (1674; by Charles d'Avilère) are those of the English Benedictine monastery of St. Edmund, founded in France in 1615, which occupied this site from 1640 until the Revolution. The salon and staircase are good examples of the Louis XIV style; the lower part of the chapel is now a concert hall. The *chapelle ardente*, where James II's body lay in state in 1701, may also be seen.

What was left of his corpse, and those of his daughter Louise Maria-Theresa (1692–1712) and the Duke of Berwick (1670–1734), his son by Arabella Churchill, were also buried here. At the Revolution their remains were either dispersed or possibly hidden in the catacombs, which were once accessible from the house. The last burial here was that of Berwick's second son Charles (died 1787).

At No. 284 (left), the door between columns at the end of the courtyard was once the entrance to the distinguished Carmelite convent to which Louise de la Vallière, mistress of Louis XIV, retired in 1674. Another relic of the convent is a crypt beneath 25 Rue Henri-Barbusse, to the west.

Rue St.-Jacques widens opposite the impressive front of *VAL-DE-GRACE* (Pl. 13; 8), from 1624 the house of the Benedictine nuns of Val-Profond, whose patroness was N.-D. du Val-de-Grâce and a military hospital since 1790. The Army Medical School was added in 1850. The present more extensive buildings were erected by Anne of Austria in thanksgiving for the birth of Louis XIV in 1638 (she had been married 22 years without issue), and the first stone of the new works was laid by the young king in 1645. In the courtyard is a bronze statue of Napoléon's surgeon, Baron Larrey (1766–1842), by David d'Angers.

François Mansart was succeeded as architect before 1649 by Jacques Lemercier, and after 1654 the buildings were finished by Le Muet and Le Duc, the church being completed in 1667. The remains (often only their hearts) of royalty interred here, including Anne of Austria (wife of Louis XIII), Marie-Thérèse (wife of Louis XIV), La Grande Mademoiselle and the Regent Philippe II d'Orléans, were dispersed at the Revolution.

The façade of the church (by Mansart) is a notable example of the Jesuit style, and the lead and gilt *dome (by Le Duc) is one of the finest in France. The sculptures within are by François and Michel Anguier, Pierre Sarazin and others. The high-altar, with its six huge twisted marble columns, is inspired by Bernini's *baldacchino* or canopy over the Saint's tomb in St. Peter's, Rome; the sculptured Nativity on it is a copy of Anguier's original (now at St.-Roch). The painting in the dome is by Pierre Mignard. In the chapel on the right of the choir is a portrait of Anne of Austria borne by an angel; and in the Chapel of the Sacrament is the Communion of the Angels, by J.-B. de Champaigne. The imposing cloisters may be visited, and also, in the former refectory, a museum of military hygiene.

Val-de-Grâce was only one of the many religious houses which, until the Revolution, were established in this district. To the north are the Rue des Ursulines and Rue des Feuillantines (in which the young Victor Hugo spent the years 1808–13), whose names recall vanished convents; almost opposite were the Carmelites (see above); to the south stood Port-Royal (see below), beyond which, in the Blvd Arago, stood a 13C Franciscan nunnery.

To the right on the far side of the Blvd de Port-Royal, a maternity hospital has, since 1814, occupied the buildings of Port-Royal de Paris, a branch of the Jansenist abbey of Port-Royal-des-Champs (south west of Versailles; see Blue Guide France), destroyed at the instigation of the Jesuits and its site ploughed over in 1709. In the chapel, completed by Le Pautre in 1647, is the tomb of Angélique Arnauld (1591–1661), the reforming abbess.

The extensive buildings of the Hôpital Cochin lie to the left of the Rue Faubourg-St.-Jacques. Here, in February 1929, George Orwell was treated for pneumonia; Samuel Beckett was also treated here after being stabbed by a tramp. At No. 38 (right), is the Hôtel de Massa (1784), transferred here from the Champs-Elysées in 1927 and re-erected, and now occupied by the Société des Gens de Lettres.

Next turn right into the Rue Cassini, where at No. 2 Alain-Fournier lived in 1910–14 and wrote 'Le Grand Meaulnes' (1913). Balzac lived in 1829–34 at a house on the site of No. 1, where he wrote 'La Peau de Chagrin'.

On the left is the **OBSERVATOIRE** (Pl. 14; 7), founded by Louis XIV in

1667 and completed by Claude Perrault in 1672, the year of his death. It was visited in 1672 by John Locke, in 1680 by Edmund Halley and in 1698 by Dr Martin Lister, all of whom met its director Jean Dominique Cassini (1625–1712), the first of the family of astronomers and cartographers. The famous Danish astronomer Olaf Römer (1644–1710), was also working here from 1672.

The four sides of the building face the cardinal points of the compass, and the latitude of the southern side is the recognised latitude of Paris (48°50'11" north). A line bisecting the building from north to south is the meridian of Paris (2°20'14" east of Greenwich), which until 1912 was the basis for the calculation of longitude on French maps. The Observatoire is also the headquarters of the Bureau International de l'Heure, and a 'speaking' clock (tel. 46 99 84 00) is installed in its cellars.

Application to attend a guided tour should be made in advance to the Secrétariat at 61 Av. de l'Observatoire.

On the first floor of the main building is a Museum of Astronomical Instruments, and the contents of the Rotunda in the west tower illustrate the history of astronomy. On the floor of a room on the second storey, the Paris meridian is traced; it also contains older instruments. A shaft descending from the roof of the main building into the catacombs has been used for the study of falling bodies. In the east cupola is an equatorial telescope of 38cm aperture.

Turning north from the Observatoire, the Av. Denfert-Rochereau is crossed to reach the Carrefour de l'Observatoire.

To the north west is Rude's statue of Marshal Ney (1769–1815), who was shot close by, for ('traitorously') espousing Napoléon's cause on his return from Elba. Among those 'Royalists' who voted for his death were marshals Marmont and Victor. Behind it is the Closerie des Lilas, long a literary resort and frequented by Baudelaire, Verlaine, Gide, Jarry and Apollinaire, among others. To the north is the Fontaine de l'Observatoire (1875) by Davioud, Frémiet and Carpeaux.

Returning from the *carrefour*, the Av. Denfert-Rochereau, passes (right) the Hôpital St.-Vincent-de-Paul, with a chapel of 1650–55. Chateaubriand lived in 1826–38 in the grounds of the Infirmerie Marie-Thérèse, which occupied an adjacent site, and which was directed by his wife.

The Place was known as the Pl. d'Enfer until 1879, when it received its present name in honour of the defender of Belfort during the Franco-Prussian War. The earlier name originated as Via Inferior, the Roman road (now the Blvd St. Michel) leading south to it from the Ile de la Cité, parallel to and west of the Via Superior (now the Rue St.-Jacques).

In the centre of the Place is a copy, though smaller in size, of Bartholdi's sculpture of the 'Lion of Belfort'. On the south-west side is one of the octroi pavilions of the old Barrière d'Enfer (by Ledoux; 1784). Here is the main entrance to **Les Catacombes**. This labyrinthine series of underground quarries dates from Roman times and extends from the Jardin des Plantes to the Porte de Versailles and into the suburbs of Montrouge, Montsouris and Gentilly. In the 1780s they were converted into a charnel-house for bones removed from disused graveyards, and most of the victims of the massacres of the Terror were later transferred here. In 1944 they served as a headquarters of the Resistance Movement.

Guided tours take place Tues.–Fri. between 14.00–16.00, and Sat.–Sun. 09.00–11.00; 14.00–16.00. It is advisable to take a torch. The tour lasts over an hour, through a

Rodin's statue of Balzac, Montparnasse

macabre series of galleries lined with bones and skulls, to a huge ossuary containing the debris of over six million skeletons, and tends to be monotonous.

Leading south from the Pl. Denfert-Rochereau, the Av. René-Coty approaches the Parc de Montsouris, some 16 hectares in area and laid out in 1875–78. Near its north-east corner is a lake (which suddenly dried up on the day of inauguration, and the engineer responsible committed suicide).

Among artists who lived in this quarter was Braque (1882–1963), with a studio in the Rue du Douanier (Rousseau), to the west. Lenin lived at No. 4 Rue Marie-Rose in 1909–12, some minutes' walk further north west.

Facing the south side of the park, flanked by the Blvd Jourdan, is the Cité Universitaire, founded in 1922, accommodating c 7000 students in some 37 halls of residence, the individual style of each reflecting the characteristic national architecture. The US foundation dates from 1928; the British hostel from 1937; and the huge Maison Internationale from 1936. Few of these heterogeneous buildings are of any great interest, although those by Le Corbusier (the designer of the Swiss and Brazilian halls) are noteworthy.

Montparnasse. From the Carrefour de l'Observatoire the long Blvd du Montparnasse leads north west across the Blvd Raspail, where to the north stands Rodin's statue of Balzac. This junction may be regarded as the centre of a quarter which partly supplanted Montmartre as the principal artistic and bohemian rendezvous. Both Henry Miller and Hemingway have described the café life, disreputable and otherwise, of the district in its heyday, which was largely blighted by the mid 1930s.

Inexorably, the smaller intimate cafés were replaced by Le Dôme, La Coupole, La Rotonde, etc., and the district was invaded by hangers-on and pseudo-bohemians; the '*boîtes*' in the Rue de la Gaité and elsewhere still attract this polyglot crowd. Nevertheless, the neighbouring streets still retain (fast fading) associations with late-19C and early 20C artists and intellectuals. Gauguin had a studio at 8 Rue de la Grande-Chaumière, leading north east, on his return to Paris after his first visit to Tahiti. Trotsky and his fellow-revolutionaries frequented the Rotonde before 1917. Rilke and Modigliani lived in the Rue Campagne-Première, to the south east, as did Whistler, who, with Rodin, had studios at 132 Blvd du Montparnasse (demolished).Whistler later had a studio at 86 Rue N.-D. des Champs, to the north east, from 1892–1901. Carolus-Duran's studio was at No. 58. In earlier decades, Sainte-Beuve, the critic (1804–69), lived at No. 19 in that street, and died at No. 11 Rue du Montparnasse. Romain Rolland lived at No. 162 Blvd du Montparnasse in 1901–14. The area is now dominated by the obtrusive **Tour Montparnasse** (1973; 200m high), which has little to recommend it except for the impressive panoramic views (fee) from the 56th floor and its open-air terrace.

To the south west and parallel to the Blvd de Montparnasse, is the Blvd Edgar-Quinet, with the main entrance of the **Cimetière Montparnasse** (Pl. 13; 7), an 18-hectare site laid out in 1824. Buried here are: Maupassant, Louÿs, Banville, Baudelaire, J.-K. Huysmans, Leconte de Lisle and Sainte-Beuve, among writers; César Franck, D'Indy, Saint-Saëns, Chabrier, Jean de Reszké and Clara Haskil, among composers and musicians; Fantin-Latour, Gérard, Houdon, Rude, Soutine, Zadkine, Bourdelle, Bartholdi and Brancusi, among artists and sculptors; Pierre-Joseph Proudhon, the social reformer; Arago, the scientist and politician; Alfred Dreyfus; Charles Garnier, the architect; Augustin Thierry, the historian; André Citroën, the car manufacturer; and Pierre Laval, prime minister in the wartime Vichy régime.

From near the south-west corner of the cemetery the Rue Raymond-Losserand leads south west. Just south of its junction with the Rue du Château stood, until the turn of the century, the Château du Maine, a hunting-lodge of the Duc de Maine, on the road to Sceaux: see Rte 38.

Adjacent to the Tour, and forming part of the glass and concrete complex, is the **Gare Montparnasse** (Pl. 13; 7), 18 storeys high, surrounding the station platforms on three sides.

At 34 in the Blvd de Vaugirard, flanking the station to the north west, is the ***Musée de la Poste**, a well-displayed collection explaining the history of the French postal system from its earliest days, and laid out in some 15 rooms, descending in stages from the 5th floor (lift). Sections are devoted to methods of communication and transport; to postmen themselves, illustrated by old costumes and prints, etc.; to letter-boxes; to stamps and their printing; and to telecommunication and the mechanisation of the service. The catalogue is well-produced and informative.

Further to the west is the Blvd Pasteur, off which runs the Rue du Docteur-Roux, with (left) the Institut Pasteur, founded by Louis Pasteur (1822–95) in 1887 and built by private subscription. Pasteur is buried in the crypt; the tomb of Dr Emile Roux (1853–1933), inventor of the treatment of diphtheria by serum-injection, lies in the garden.

At 16 Rue Antoine-Bourdelle, north of and parallel to the Blvd de Vaugirard, is a museum devoted to the sculptor Bourdelle (1861–1929).

The métro at Montparnasse-Bienvenue is well-connected with lines returning to the centre.

8 Faubourg St.-Germain: Eastern Sector Institut de France; Hôtel des Monnaies; Palais du Luxembourg; St.-Sulpice; St.-Germain-des-Prés

METROS: Pont-Neuf, Odéon, Luxembourg, St.-Sulpice, St.-Germain-des-Prés, Mabillon.

The district known as the **Faubourg St.-Germain** stretches south from the Seine opposite the Louvre, from the Institut on the east to the Pont de la Concorde to the west. Until the end of the 16C, much of this area, the property of the Abbaye St.-Germain-des-Prés, was open country. In the following century, with the religious revival, several convents were built here and in 1670, the Hôtel des Invalides was constructed on the outskirts to the west. By 1685 the new Pont Royal provided easy access to the Palais des Tuileries, which became the home of the court during the Regency, and this, together with the creation of the Ecole Militaire, was the main reason for the building of this new aristocratic quarter, which gradually supplanted the Marais. About half the houses were built between 1690 and 1725, a quarter between 1725 and 1750, and most of the rest between 1750 and 1790. In style they are very similar; often the more handsome façade face the interior garden, and the gateway or 'Porte-cochère' from the street leads to the 'Cour d'Honneur'.

Today, the main thoroughfares are the Blvd St.-Germain and the Blvd Raspail, which have done much to alter the character of the quarter. The most characteristic streets of the once 'noble faubourg' are now the Rue de Lille, Rue de l'Université, Rue St.-Dominique and Rue de Grenelle. About 100 old mansions remain, many of them converted to house embassies or government offices, and the 6th and eastern half of the 7th arrondissements are still two of the more pleasant districts of Paris.

It is convenient to divide this large area into two sections: Rte 8 describes the Luxembourg and St.-Germain-des-Prés (from the Blvd St.-Michel to the Rue des Saints-Pères and Blvd Raspail): Rte 10 describes the rest of the 7th arrondissement.

The Pl. de l'Institut, on the south bank of the Seine, facing the Louvre, is flanked by the curved wings of the *INSTITUT DE FRANCE (Pl. 14; 1). Surmounted by a dome, the buildings are one of the more attractive features of this reach of the quais.

The building may be visited by prior arrangement with the Secrétariat, 23 Quai de Conti.

The east wing of the Institut and the adjacent Hôtel des Monnaies (see below) cover the site of the Hôtel de Nesle (13C), in which was incorporated the 12C Tour de Nesle or Tour Hamelin, the river bastion of Philippe Auguste's wall (which ran south east parallel to the Rue Mazarine). The tower was notorious in legend as the scene of the amours of Marguerite (c 1290–1315) and Jeanne of Burgundy (1292–1325/30), wives of Louis X and Philippe V respectively, who are said to have had their lovers thrown into the river. Later occupants were Isabeau de Bavière, Charles le Téméraire (the Bold) and Henry V of England.

The western part, known as the Petit-Nesle and the workshop of Benvenuto Cellini in 1540–45, was demolished in 1663. The eastern part, or Grand-Nesle, rebuilt in 1648 by François Mansart, became the Hôtel de Conti, and in 1770, the Mint.

The present building, with its conspicuous cupola, was erected in accordance with the will of Cardinal Mazarin, who bequeathed 2 million *livres* in silver and 45,000 *livres* a year for the establishment of a college for 60 gentlemen of the four provinces acquired by the Treaties of Münster and the Pyrenees: Flanders, Alsace, Roussillon and Piedmont (Pinerolo). It was popularly called the Collège des Quatre-Nations, although officially known as the Collège Mazarin. Designed by Louis le Vau, it was built in 1662–74, but Christopher Wren suggested that it was set 'ill-favouredly, that he [the architect] might shew his Wit in struggling with an inconvenient Situation'. The Institut, founded in 1795, and installed first in the Louvre, acquired the building in 1806.

The Institut de France comprises five academies: the exclusive Académie Française, founded by Richelieu in 1635 and restricted to 40 members (and already satirised by Saint-Evremond in 1643), whose particular task was the editing of the dictionary of the French language; the Académie des Beaux-Arts (1816), founded by Mazarin in 1648 as the Académie Royale de Peinture et de Sculpture; the Académie des Inscriptions et Belles-Lettres, founded by Colbert in 1663; the Académie des Sciences, also founded by Colbert, in 1666; and the Académie des Sciences Morales et Politiques, founded in 1795 and reconstituted in 1832. The Institut is also responsible for several collections, among them the Musée Marmottan, and the Musée Condé at Chantilly. An annual general meeting of all five academies is held on 25 October (restricted admission).

The Académie Française holds special receptions for newly elected members who are known, ironically, as 'Les Immortels' (cf. Daudet's novel of that title). Among the great figures of French literature who were not elected to the Académie were Pascal, Descartes, Molière, La Rochefoucauld, Diderot, Rousseau, Beaumarchais, Balzac, Flaubert, Baudelaire, Maupassant, Zola and Proust. It was not until 1980 that the first woman member was elected.

From the first octagonal courtyard (beyond which are two others, the third being the Kitchen Court of the former Collège Mazarin), the door on the left leads to the **Bibliothèque Mazarine,** containing c 350,000 vols, 5800 MSS and 1900 incunabula. Originally the Cardinal's personal library, opened to scholars in 1643, it became the first public library in France and was considerably augmented by other collections during the Revolutionary period.

The Institut library is also in this wing, together with several rooms decorated with academic statues and busts of eminent academicians. Among many of little merit, Pigalle's Voltaire is striking.

In the former chapel in the west wing is the Salle des Séances Solennelles. Restoration has undone the damage caused by Vaudoyer, and Mazarin's Tomb, by Coysevox, has been returned from the Louvre. His niece, Hortense Mancini, Duchesse de Mazarin (died 1699), the celebrated beauty of the court of Charles II, was also buried here. The room contains some 400 seats (green for members of the Académie Française; red for the others), and is used for receptions and general meetings.

At 13 Quai de Conti (the riverside embankment here, as elsewhere in this reach of the Seine, lined with the bookstalls of the *bouquinistes*) is the Hôtel Guénégaud or de Sillery-Genlis, by François Mansart (1659), often visited by Napoléon when on leave from the Ecole Militaire. Baron Larrey, Napoléon's surgeon, lived here from 1805 to 1832.

No. 11, the *****HOTEL DES MONNAIES**, the former Mint, is a dignified building by J.-D. Antoine (1771–75). The handsome doorway is ornamented with Louis XVI's monogram and elegant bronze knockers; above is the *fleur-de-lys* escutcheon with Mercury and Ceres as supporters. From the vestibule, a notable example of 18C architecture, a double staircase on the right ascends to Musée de la Monnaie (Tues., Thurs,–Sun. 13.00–18.00; Wed. 13.00–21.00), containing an impressive collection of stamping presses, punches, medals and coins. Medals are for sale in the far wing.

The Salle Guillaume Dupré, in the centre of the building, is (apart from the modern ceiling) representative of the best period of the Louis XVI style; showcases display medals from the Renaissance to the present. The Salle Sage contains new acquisitions; the Salle Jean Warin, portraits of the Walloon medallist Warin (1604–72) and directors of the Mint. The Salle Denon, named after Baron Denon (1747–1825), the engraver and director general of French museums under Napoléon (cf. Musée du Louvre), is devoted to medals of the Consulate and Empire period and the Salle Duvivier displays examples of coins illustrating the evolution of French currency from Merovingian times.

On the right of the second courtyard is the entrance to the *Ateliers* or workshops, where you can see the processes of coin and medal production. In 1973 the minting of French coins was transferred to a new establishment at Pessac, near Bordeaux.

At No. 5, on the corner of the Rue Guénégaud, Col de Marguerittes, of the Resistance, set up his headquarters while conducting operations for the liberation of Paris 19–28 August 1944.

At the end of the adjacent Rue de Nevers (entered below an arch), part of Philippe Auguste's wall is visible.

From the southern end of the Pont Neuf, the Rue Dauphine leads south, passing (left), at 9 Rue Mazet, the site of Chez Magny, a literary rendezvous in the 1860s, to the Carrefour de Buci with its street market. No. 5 Rue Mazet was until 1906 the site of the 'Cheval Blanc' coaching inn, terminus in the 17–18Cs of the diligence to Bourges, Bordeaux and La Rochelle, etc.

In parallel Rue des Grands-Augustins stands the Hôtel d'Hercule, dating from the 17C (Nos 3–7); No. 21 was the birthplace of the lexicographer Emile Littré (1801–81); the poet Heinrich Heine lived at No. 25 in 1841, as had the writer La Bruyére in 1676–91 and Augustin Thierry, the historian, in 1820–30.

At 35 Quai des Grands-Augustins (where a famous convent of that name stood from 1293 until its demolition in 1797) is another 17C mansion, at the corner of the Rue Séguier, which was the home of the printer François Didot in 1740, and of Laplace during the Directory. This street, lined with old houses, leads south to meet the Rue St.-André-des-Arts, also containing several notable 17–18C buildings (Nos 27, 28 and 52).

From the Pl. St.-André-des-Arts, to the east, where at No. 11 Gounod (1818–93) was born, the Rue Hautefeuille leads south; No. 5, the Hôtel des Abbés de Fécamp, has a pretty turret. Among its occupiers was Godin de Sainte-Croix, an accomplice of the Marquise de Brinvilliers. Baudelaire (1821–67) was born at No. 15 (demolished). The novelist J.-K. Huysmans (1848–1907) was born at 9 Rue Suger, leading west from the Pl. St.-André-des-Arts.

Leading south from the Rue St.-André-des-Arts, the Rue de l'Eperon shortly meets (right) the Rue du Jardinet, in which Saint-Saëns (1835–1921) was born. Further along the alley is the entrance to the Cour de Rohan (16–17C), originally part of the palace of the Archbishop of Rouen. Turning left on passing through an archway, at No. 4 in the characteristic Cour de Commerce-St.-André the basement of one of Philippe Auguste's towers can be seen. At No. 8, Marat's journal 'L'Ami du Peuple' was printed.

At No. 9, opposite, popular myth has it that Dr Joseph-Ignace Guillotin (1738–1814), a professor of anatomy, perfected his 'philanthropic beheading machine', although in fact he merely proposed to the *Assemblée constituante* that beheading should be the only method of capital punishment, preferably by a machine. A mechanic built one to the specifications of the secretary of the College of Surgeons, a certain Dr Louis, which was put into operation on 25 April 1792, at first being known as the 'Louisette'.

The Rue de l'Ancienne Comédie (the next street to the west) takes its name from the Comédie Française of 1689–1770, which occupied No. 14, while opposite, the Café Procope (after its founder, a Sicilian named Francesco Procopio dei Coltelli), of 17C origin, was a favourite haunt of Voltaire and the Encyclopédistes, Musset, George Sand, Balzac, Gautier, Gambetta, Verlaine, Huysmans and Wilde, among others.

To the north the Rue Mazarine (in which Smollett stayed in 1763, at the Hôtel de Montmorency) leads back to the Institut, passing the sites (at No. 42) of the *jeu de paume* 'de la Bouteille', where the Abbé Perrin established the Opéra in 1669–72; occupied by Molière's company in 1673–80, after his death in 1673; and by the Comédie-Française in 1680–89, and (at No. 12), another *jeu de paume*, where the 'Illustre Théâtre' was opened in December 1643 by Molière's company. No. 30, known as the Hôtel des Pompes, was until 1760 the headquarters of the *pompiers* or fire brigade of Paris, founded in 1722 by the actor François Dumouriez du Périer, *père*, who died here the following year.

In the mid-19C the Blvd St.-Germain was cut through this picturesque area of narrow lanes leading south from the river. Opposite the Rue de l'Ancienne Comédie, beyond the Pl. Henri-Mondor, is the Carrefour de l'Odéon (Pl. 14; 3), both busy crossroads. At the Café Voltaire, which stood there, a banquet was held in honour of Gauguin before he left for Tahiti in 1891.

To the east is a building of the **Faculty of Medicine**, erected by Gondouin in 1769–76 on the site of the Collège de Bourgogne and Collège des Prémontrés, and since enlarged. The older part, facing the Rue de l'Ecole-de-Médecine, is considered one of the most Classical works of the 18C. The façade facing the Blvd St.-Germain was added in 1878.

In the courtyard is a statue of the anatomist Xavier Bichat (1771–1802) by David d'Angers. The library contains c 600,000 vols and commentaries of the heads of the faculty from 1395 onwards. Also of interest are the lecture hall, the Musée d'Histoire de la Médecine, and the Salle du Conseil, hung with four Gobelins tapestries of the Louis XIV period, after Le Brun.

Opposite is the entrance to the former refectory of the Couvent des Cordeliers, a 15C Franciscan house, which during the Revolution was a meeting-place of the extremist Club des Cordeliers, the leaders of which were Marat (a doctor by profession), Camille Desmoulins and Danton. Marat was stabbed in his bath by Charlotte Corday in 1793 at No. 20 (demolished).

At No. 5, the Institut des Langues Modernes occupies the old Amphithéâtre du Jardin du Luxembourg St.-Côme (1691–94), with an attractive portal. This was originally the lecture-hall of the College of Surgery. A plaque commemorates the birth of the actress Sarah Bernhardt (1844–1923).

Further east (left) at the corner of the southern section of the Rue de Hautefeuille (No. 32), Gustave Courbet (1819–77) had his studio in the former chapel of the Collège des Prémontrés.

The Rue de l'École-de-Médecine narrows before meeting the Blvd St.-Michel.

From its western end, you may ascend steps before turning left along the Rue Monsieur-le-Prince (de Condé). At No. 10, Auguste Comte (1798–1857), the positivist philosopher, lived from 1841; Saint-Saëns at No. 14 in 1877–89, and Longfellow had lodgings at No. 49 in 1826 (and in a subsequent winter, at No. 5 in the adjacent Rue Racine). At No. 54 (altered) Pascal lived in 1654–62 and wrote his 'Pensées'. To the left, on meeting the Rue de Vaugirard, is the Lycée St.-Louis, built by Bailly on the site of the influential Collège d'Harcourt (1280), where Racine and Boileau studied. Its entrance faces the Pl. de la Sorbonne.

Adjacent to the south end of the Rue Monsieur-le-Prince is the Pl. Edmond-Rostand, with a good view of the Panthéon (see Rte 4). George Sand's last Paris home, in the 1870s, was at 5 Rue Gay-Lussac, to the south east. To the south, on the right of the Blvd St.-Michel, the Ecole Supérieure des Mines occupies the Hôtel de Vendôme, an 18C building enlarged after 1840, and having its principal façade facing the Luxembourg Gardens. It contains a Museum of Mineralogy and Geology. César Franck (1822–90) died at No. 95 in the boulevard. Leconte de Lisle, leader of the 'Parnassiens', a poetic coterie, lived at No. 64 in 1872–94.

One of many entrances to the ***Jardin du Luxembourg** (Pl. 14; 5) is a few paces south of the Pl. Edmond-Rostand. These extensive gardens (23 hectares), embellished by numerous statues, several of which are notable, form one of the more pleasant and colourful open spaces in central Paris and long a favourite with nannies. Laid out in the 17C, they were deplorably mutilated in 1782 and 1867, and little remains of the original garden as known by Marie de Médicis.

Steps descend from the east terrace to lawns surrounding an octagonal pond with a fountain. Beyond the formal west terrace is the Jardin Anglais;

A vista in the Jardin du Luxembourg

while to the south, beyond the Pl. André-Honnorat, gardens are continued between the two branches of the Av. de l'Observatoire, which were laid out under the First Empire on the site of a Carthusian monastery demolished at the Revolution.

North of the central octagonal pond, on the right, at the end of an oblong pool, is the Fontaine Médicis, attributed to Salomon de Brosse (c 1627), moved here in 1861.

In the central niche is Polyphemus about to crush Acis and Galatea; on either side are Pan and Diana, and at the back a bas-relief, the Fontaine de Léda, brought from the Rue du Regard in 1855.

André Gide (1869–1951) was born at 19 Rue de Médicis, flanking the gardens to the north east.

The ***PALAIS DU LUXEMBOURG** was once a royal residence. With its heavily rusticated masonry, it is more visually attractive externally than internally. The northern façade, where the main entrance is surmounted by an eight-sided dome, is original; the south façade, facing the gardens, is a 19C copy by Gisors. The two wings, terminating in steep-roofed pavilions, with three orders of columns superimposed, are connected by a single-storeyed gallery.

The Luxembourg was built by Salomon de Brosse in 1615–27 for Marie de Médicis, widow of Henri IV, who, it is said, wished to have a residence which reminded her of the Pitti Palace in Florence, her birthplace. She also acquired the adjacent mansion of the Duc de Tingry-Luxembourg (the Petit-Luxembourg; 1570–1612), which has retained its name. The building was altered in 1808 and enlarged in 1831–44.

After Louis XIII's death, the palace passed to her second son Gaston, Duc d'Orléans, and the 'Palais Médicis' became known as the 'Palais d'Orléans'. Subsequently, it belonged in succession to Mlle de Montpensier, the Duchesse de Guise (1672), Louis XIV (1694) and the Orléans family. Here, from 1724 until she retired to a convent, lived the obstreperous Louise-Elisabeth, the 15-year-old widow of Luis I of Spain. Among prisoners confined here during the Revolution were Marshal de Noailles (executed at the age of 79 with his wife, daughter and granddaughter); Hébert, Danton, Desmoulins, Fabre d'Eglantine, the painter David and Tom Paine (imprisoned here in 1793 for voting in the Assembly against the king's execution, and who escaped the guillotine only by an accident).

In 1794 the Directory transferred the seat of government from the Tuileries to the Luxembourg and here Général Bonaparte presented them with the Treaty of Campo Formio (1797). In 1800 the 'Palais Directorial' became the 'Palais du Consulat'. Under the Empire it was the 'Palais du Sénat' and later the 'Palais de la Pairie'. Marshal Ney was confined and tried here in 1815. The ministers of Charles X were tried here under Louis-Philippe in 1830, and Louis-Napoléon Bonaparte after landing at Boulogne in 1840. From 1852 to 1940 the Palais was the meeting-place of the Senate, the upper chamber of the French Republic, except in 1871–79, when it was the seat of the Préfecture de la Seine.

In 1940–44 it was occupied by Sperrle, commander-in-chief of the Luftwaffe on the Western Front. In 1946 it was the seat of the Conseil de la République, but in 1958 it reverted to the Senate.

The INTERIOR, drastically remodelled by Chalgrin under Napoléon I, is decorated in the sumptuous but decadent 19C manner, replete with statues and paintings, historical and allegorical, few of which are of any merit. (The series of paintings devoted to the Life of Marie de Médicis, by Rubens, which once hung in the palace, is now in the Louvre.)

Notable is the luxuriously gilt Cabinet Doré, Marie de Médicis's audience chamber. Other rooms (on the first floor) occasionally open to the public are the Salles des Conférences, the hemicycle of the Salle de Séances and the library, overlooking the gardens, which contains paintings by Delacroix, that in the cupola being the Limbo of Dante's Inferno.

The adjoining **Petit-Luxembourg** (now the residence of the President of the Senate) was presented to Richelieu by Marie de Médicis in 1626. It includes the cloisters and chapel of the Filles du Calvaire, for whom the queen built a convent; the chapel is a charming example of the Renaissance style; the cloister forms a winter-garden. To the west is the Orangery, once occupied by a museum, some of the former contents of which now embellish the Musée d'Orsay.

A few paces to the north east of the Palais stands the *Théâtre de l'Odéon, built in the form of a classical temple by Wailly and Peyre in the garden of the Hôtel de Condé, which was demolished by Louis XV to this end. This town house of the family from 1612–1764 stood on the site of Nos 5–9 in the Rue de Condé, parallel to the west. Here was born the Marquis de Sade (1740–1814), his mother being a lady-in-waiting to the Princess.

The Théâtre de l'Odéon was inaugurated in 1782 as the Théâtre-Français. It was rebuilt by Chalgrin after a fire in 1799 and re-opened in 1808.

From its north entrance, the Rue de l'Odéon, bordered by 18C houses, slopes downhill towards the Carrefour de l'Odéon. At No. 12 once stood the Librairie Shakespeare, founded by Sylvia Beach, where in 1922 the first edition of James Joyce's 'Ulysses' was published, in an edition of 1000 numbered copies. At No. 22 in this street lived Lucile Duplessis before her marriage to Camille Desmoulins; No. 26 was the home of Beaumarchais in 1763–76, whose 'Le Barbier de Séville' was produced in 1775.

From the main entrance of the Palais du Luxembourg, in the Rue de Vaugirard (the longest street in Paris, stretching from the Blvd St.-Michel to the Porte de Versailles), the wide and stately *Rue de Tournon leads gently down to the Blvd St.-Germain, north of which it is extended by the Rue de Seine, also flanked by number of attractive houses, to the Institut.

Balzac lived at 2 Rue de Tournon in 1827–30; Marie Lenormand, the fortune-teller consulted by Revolutionary celebrities, lived at No. 5 for over 50 years and died here in 1843; Hébert ('Père Duchesne'; 1755–94), the revolutionary journalist, lived here in 1793; and Charles Cros (1842–88), one of the pioneers of the phonograph, died here. No. 6, the Hôtel de Brancas, was reconstructed during the Regency by Bullet; Alphonse Daudet lived at No. 7, the Hôtel du Sénat, when he first came to Paris (1857); Gambetta lived here (on the top storey) in 1858–61. No. 10 (now barracks of the Garde Républicaine) was the Hôtel de Concini. Paul Jones (1747–92), the first admiral of the US navy, died at No. 19 in 1792; the actor Gérard Philipe (1922–59) died at No. 17.

At 20 Rue de Vaugirard stood the Café Tabourey, a famous literary rendezvous; while at No. 48 the composer Massenet (1842–1912) long resided, and died. Mme de la Fayette (1634–93), author of 'La Princesse de Clèves', died at No. 50, the Hôtel de la Vergne, her home since 1655.

The next street, turning right off the Rue de Vaugirard, the Rue Bonaparte (which narrows as it approaches the Seine), contains numerous antique shops and galleries, and is one of the more characteristic in the commercial part of the faubourg. It skirts the Pl. St.-Sulpice (Pl. 13; 6), in the centre of which is the Fontaine des Quatre-Evêques by Visconti, with statues of four famous preaching bishops: Bossuet, Fénelon, Massillon and Fléchier.

In 1843–45 Renan was a scholar at the seminary which stood on the south side; opposite, No. 6 is a dignified mansion by Servandoni (1754), the first of a range which never materialised. Many of the neighbouring shops display cloying modern ecclesiastical art and furniture.

ST.-SULPICE, the wealthiest church on the Left Bank, although described by Gibbon as 'one of the noblest structures in Paris', is a somewhat ponderous classical building, imposing mainly for its size. The west front consists of an Ionic colonnade over a Doric. The north tower is 73m high; the south tower is 5m lower.

It was begun in 1646 by Gamard on the site of an older church, and continued on a larger scale by Le Vau in 1655 and Gittard in 1670. After an interval from 1675 to 1719 work was resumed by Oppenordt. The building of the west front was entrusted to Servandoni, who failing to give satisfaction, was replaced in 1745 by Maclaurin. His successor, Chalgrin, rebuilt the north tower in 1777, since Maclaurin's design had also failed to please, but the south tower was left incomplete.

Camille Desmoulins married Lucile Duplessis here in 1790. Under the Convention St.-Sulpice became the 'Temple de la Victoire', and in 1799 a public banquet was given here by Général Bonaparte. Saint-Simon, writing earlier, was contemptuous of its clergy, with their 'barbes sales' (dirty beards).

The church is noted for its music and organ recitals.

The INTERIOR, a representative example of the 'Jesuit' style, is 110m long, 56m wide, and 33m high. In the nave are two huge *Tridacna gigas* shells serving as holy-water stoups, presented to François I by the Venetian Republic; the marble 'rocks' supporting them were sculpted by Pigalle. The late 18C pulpit, by Wailly, bears gilded figures of Faith and Hope by Guesdon, and Charity by Dumont.

The organ, one of the largest in existence (6588 pipes), was built in 1781 and remodelled in 1860–62; the case was designed by Chalgrin, and is adorned by statues by Clodion and decoration by Duret.

In the paving of the south transept is a bronze table connected by a meridian line with a marble obelisk in the north transept; at noon the sun's rays, passing through an aperture in a blind window in the south transept, strike the meridian at different points according to the time of year.

The encircling CHAPELS are decorated with frescoes: in the 1st (right) are late works by Delacroix (1853–63). In the 5th is the tomb, by Slodtz, of the *curé* Languet de Gergy (1674–1750), founder of the Enfants Malades, and responsible for the completion of the church. In the choir are works by Bouchardon. The Lady Chapel was designed by Servandoni. In a niche behind the altar is a marble Virgin by Pigalle, with angels by Mouchy. The wall-paintings are by Carle van Loo; those in the dome are by Lemoyne. Remains of the 16C church may be seen in the crypt.

The next cross street to the north is the Rue du Four. The artist Chardin lived from 1720–44 at 1 Rue Princesse, leading south from the Rue du Four, and at No. 13 from 1744–57.

Beyond is the busy intersection of the Pl. St.-Germain-des-Prés (Pl. 13; 4). Diagonally opposite, at Nos 170 and 172 are the Café des Deux Magots (grotesque Chinese figures) and the Café de Flore, respectively; while at No. 151 in the boulevard is the Brasserie Lipp. All were once known for the artists, writers and existentialists who patronised them.

Restored *ST.-GERMAIN-DES-PRES*, the oldest church in Paris and the only one retaining any considerable remains of Romanesque work, dominates the north east of the square.

A part of the great Benedictine abbey founded in 558 by Childebert I, who was buried there, as was St. Germanus, Bishop of Paris (died 576), it was rebuilt at the beginning of the 11C, and consecrated by Pope Alexander III in 1163. In the 17C it was the chief house of the reformed Congregation de St.-Maur, and numbered the scholars Jean Mabillon (1632–1707) and Bernard de Montfaucon (1655–1741) among its members.

The massive flying buttresses of the choir are among the earliest in France. The west porch dates from 1607, but retains the jambs of a 12C door and a battered lintel depicting the Last Supper. The transepts were remodelled c 1644. The bell-chamber of the tower was added in the 17C. Flanking the choir are the bases of two towers pulled down in 1822, when the church was drastically restored after its partial destruction following an explosion and fire in 1794, just prior to which its refectory had been used as a saltpetre store.

The INTERIOR (65m by 21m, and 19m high) is interesting architecturally for the combination of Romanesque in the nave with the earliest Gothic in the choir. The vault of the nave and the aisles date from 1644–46. The pillars are flanked by four columns, the sculptured capitals of which in 1848–53 were either re-cut or removed to the Musée de Cluny and replaced by copies, with the exception of one remaining in the north west corner. Both nave and choir were painted with murals by Hippolyte Flandrin (1842–64), among others.

To the right in the south aisle is a marble image of N.-D. de Consolation, presented to the Abbey of St. Denis by Queen Jeanne d'Evreux in 1340. In the south transept is the tomb, by Girardon, of Olivier and Louis de Castellan, killed in the king's service in 1644 and 1669. In the 1st ambulatory-chapel is the tomb of Lord James Douglas (1617–45; son of the first Marquess of Douglas), commander of Louis XIII's Scots regiment, killed near Arras; 2nd chapel: tombstones of Descartes (1596–1650; removed from Ste.-Geneviève in 1819) and of Mabillon (see above); 4th chapel: fragments of mid 13C stained glass.

Choir: the small marble columns in the triforium are re-used material from the 6C abbey of St. Vincent; their bases and capitals are of the 12C. The Lady Chapel was rebuilt at the beginning of the 19C.

In the northern aisle is the tombstone of Nicolas Boileau (1636–1711; removed from the Ste.-Chapelle) and the tomb of William Douglas, 10th Earl of Angus (1554–1611), who died in the service of Henri IV. In the north transept are a statue of St. Francisco Xavier, by G. Coustou; and the theatrical tomb, by G. and B. Marsy, of John Casimir V, King of Poland, who became abbot of St.-Germain in 1669 and died in 1672.

In the garden to the north are fragments of sculptures from the Lady Chapel built in 1212–55 by Pierre de Montreuil within the precincts of the abbey. In the Rue de l'Abbaye, but further east, is the Abbot's Palace, erected c 1586 by Cardinal de Bourbon, behind which was the Prison de l'Abbaye (its site crossed by the present boulevard), where Jacques-Pierre Brissot wrote his memoirs and Charlotte Corday spent her last days. Both were guillotined in 1793. It had also been the scene of a beastly massacre of 'suspects' in September 1792.

In 1857, six years before he died at 6 Rue de Furstenberg (or Fürstemberg) Delacroix built a studio in the adjoining Pl. de Fürstemberg, which with its four Paulownias, is now less of a back-water than it once was. This was later shared by Monet and Bazille, and now contains the **Musée Delacroix** (open Wed.–Mon. 09.45–12.30, 14.00–17.15).

A few paces east, 1 Rue Bourbon-le-Château was Whistler's first home in Paris (1855–56), while the Pré-aux-Clercs, which lay to the north (now crossed by the Rue Jacob), was once a favourite promenade and scene of medieval student brawls.

For streets radiating south west and west of the Pl. St.-Germain-des-Prés, see below.

The Rue Bonaparte continues north, crossing the Rue Jacob. At No. 18 in the former street the Czech government was formed in 1916; No. 14 is the main entrance to the Ecole des Beaux-Arts (see below), while the Hôtel du

Marquis de Persan (Nos 7–9) was the home of Monge in 1803, and the birthplace of Manet (1832–83).

The Rue Jacob and the two streets diverging right off the Rue Bonaparte have interesting associations. Laurence Sterne put up in the **Rue Jacob** on his arrival in Paris in 1762 (at the 'Hôtel de Modène'; as did Philip Thicknesse in 1791), and was later a guest of Mme de Rambouillet at No. 46. Wagner lodged at No. 14 in 1841–42, working on 'The Flying Dutchman'; it was later the home of the social reformer Pierre-Joseph Proudhon (1809–65). In 1848 Mérimée lived at No. 18 (rebuilt); No. 32 belonged to Baptiste du Cerceau, architect of the Pont Neuf; Stendhal stayed at both Nos 28 and 52 in 1808–10. At No. 56 a provisional treaty was signed recognising the independence of the United States (3 September 1783); and after 1810 it became the offices of the printer Didot. In 1765 Horace Walpole lived in the Rue de Colombier near the eastern part of the street.

To the north in the parallel Rue Visconti (then the Rue des Marais St.-Germain) Racine (1639–99) lived from 1693 until his death (house demolished); at No. 16 the actress Adrienne Lecouvreur (1692–1730) died in the arms of Marshal Saxe; at No. 17 Balzac had a printing business, liquidated in 1828, and on the 2nd floor is a studio once occupied by Delaroche (1827–34) and Delacroix (1838–43).

At No. 10 in the next street to the right, the Rue des Beaux-Arts, lived the novelist Mérimée (1803–70) and later Corot; Fantin-Latour lived at No. 8 in 1868. At No. 13 Oscar Wilde, who called himself 'Sebastian Melmoth' when on the Continent, died in debt in 1900; his drama *'Salomé'* had been first produced in French in Paris in 1896, while he was in Reading Gaol.

The **Ecole des Beaux-Arts** (Pl. 13; 4), begun in 1820 by Debret and finished in 1862 by Duban, replaced the convent of the Petits-Augustins, founded in 1608, of which certain relics remain. It was here that Alexandre Lenoir (1762–1839) collected together numerous pieces of sculpture, saving them from destruction during the Revolutionary period (cf. St.-Denis). The building, with its main entrance at 14 Rue Bonaparte, was further enlarged in 1885 on the acquisition of the Hôtel de Chimay (see below). The library contains c 80,000 volumes and one million engravings and drawings.

The main points of interest are the former convent chapel (c 1600), with the central part of the façade of the Château d'Anet (by Philibert Delorme) built against the south wall; in the adjoining Chapel of Marguerite de Valois, the small domed hexagon has claims to be the first dome built in Paris. Part of a Renaissance façade from the Château de Gaillon (1500–10) in Normandy separates the first courtyard from the second. An arcade from the Hôtel de Torpane (c 1570) and the façade from the Hôtel de Chimay are also preserved. Both in the courtyards and inside the buildings are many sculptured fragments, antique marbles, etc., while the Salle de Melpomène is used for the display of students' work when competing for the Grands Prix de Rome. Rodin was rejected three times by the Ecole des Beaux-Arts.

Leading south west from the Pl. St.-Germain-des-Prés is the Rue de Rennes, at the far end of which obtrudes the Tour Montparnasse (see Rte 7). A short distance down the street to the left is the Rue Cassette, diverging left, in which the writer Alfred Jarry (1873–1907) died at No. 20. No. 27 was the family home of the poet and dramatist Alfred de Musset in 1818–32; the German poet Rainer Maria Rilke lived at No. 29 in 1906.

Turning right at the end of this street into the Rue de Vaugirard, you pass domed St.-Joseph-des-Carmes, once the chapel of a Carmelite convent, dating from 1613–20, and containing several 17C canvases. In the crypt are the bones of some 120 priests massacred in the convent garden in September 1792. Prisoners held here but later released included Général Hoche, Joséphine de Beauharnais and Mme Tallien.

Adjacent are the buildings of the Institut Catholique, where, in 1890, radio waves were discovered by Edouard Branly (1844–1940).

Some distance south in the next crossroad, the Rue d'Assas, is No. 62, where Strindberg lived in 1895–96, while Auguste Bartholdi (1834–1904), sculptor of the Statue of Liberty (New York), died at No. 82. At 100 bis is the studio from 1928 of the sculptor Ossip Zadkine (1890–1967), with a small museum devoted to his work.

Turning right into the Rue d'Assas, and recrossing the Rue de Rennes, you reach the Rue du Cherche-Midi (deriving its name from an 18C sign on No. 19 representing an astronomer tracing a sundial), containing several attractive 17–18C houses. For its western section, beyond the Blvd Raspail.

From the busy Carrefour de la Croix-Rouge (Pl. 13; 5) the Rue de Sèvres leads south west. J.-K. Huysmans lived at No. 11 from 1872 to 1898. Off the north side of the street, the Rue Récamier recalls the Abbaye aux Bois, the home of Mme Récamier, where the most frequent visitor to her salon was Chateaubriand, from 1819 to her death, when totally blind, in 1849. Here also, from 1831–38 lived Mary Clarke, once mistress of Frederick, Duke of York, who had resided in Paris since c 1816 (see p 110).

For the west section of the Rue de Sèvres and the Rue de Grenelle, which also starts at the Carrefour de la Croix-Rouge, see Rte 10. Across this junction is the Rue du Dragon, the possible site of the pottery workshop of Bernard Palissy (1510–89). Hugo lived at No. 30 in 1821, before his marriage to Adèle Foucher.

The poet Rémy de Gourmont (1858–1915) died at No. 71 in the parallel Rue des Saints-Pères, to the west.

At the junction of the Rue des Saints-Pères and the Blvd St.-Germain stood the Hôtel de Selvois, where the Duc de Saint-Simon (1675–1755) lived until 1714. At No. 184 in the boulevard is the Hôtel de la Société de Géographie, founded in 1821.

On the east side of the Rue des Saints-Pères, after crossing the boulevard, is the Chapelle St.-Pierre, rebuilt in 1611, the sole relic of the Hôpital de la Charité, which stood on this site from 1605 to 1937. It is now the church of the Ukrainian Catholic community in Paris (St.-Vladimir-le-Grand). Adjacent are buildings of the Faculty of Medicine (1936–53), while opposite, in the 18C Hôtel de Fleury, by Antoine, is the Ecole des Ponts et Chaussées, a civil engineering school founded in 1747.

Further north, at the corner of the Rue de Lille, is the Ecole des Langues Orientales, founded by the Convention in 1795. Manet died at 5 Rue des Saints-Pères, and the organist Widor (1844–1937) lived at No. 7, the Hôtel de Falconet (c 1650). From the Hôtel Tessé, on the corner of the Quai Voltaire, the Marquis de Becqueville attempted to glide with wings, Icarus-like, across the Seine in 1742.

The Quai Malaquais, leading east to the Institut, contains a number of 17–18C mansions. The writer Anatole France (1844–1924) was born at No. 19 (the home of George Sand in 1832–36), but until 1853 he lived at No. 15. In 1662, Henrietta Maria (the widow of Charles I) lived at No. 17, part of the Hôtel de Chimay, built by François Mansart c 1640, and altered in the 18C for the Duchesse de Bouillon (died 1714), the friend of La Fontaine.

No. 9, at the corner of the Rue Bonaparte, the Hôtel de Transylvanie, is a good example of Louis-XIII architecture (1622–28). No. 5 was occupied by Marshal de Saxe (1696–1750) from 1744 until his death; and No. 3 was the residence of the naturalist Alexander Humboldt during the Restoration.

9   Musée d'Orsay

METROS: Musée d'Orsay, Solférino.

The Quai d'Orsay is dominated by the huge and ornate bulk of the *MUSEE D'ORSAY*, inaugurated in December 1986 (Pl. 13; 1).

The address of the museum is 62 Rue de Lille, 75007, but the main entrance is at No. 1 Rue Bellechasse, at its west end. Open Tues.–Sun. 09.00/10.00–18.00.

The building was originally the Gare d'Orsay, erected in 1898–1900 by Victor Laloux (1850–1937) on the site of the ancient Cours des Comptes, set ablaze in 1871 during the Commune. Edouard Detaille, the artist, remarked ironically at the time that the railway station looked exactly like a Palais des Beaux-Arts, but 86 years were to elapse before the transformation took place. By 1939 the station had virtually outlived its usefulness because of its comparatively short platforms. During the Second World War it became a depot for parcels destined for prisoners of war, and was later used as a reception centre for those liberated. It then served in part to house a theatre, and became the temporary home of the Hôtel Drouot (the auction house). But the building progressively deteriorated, and its demolition was planned—after all, Baltard's pavilions at Les Halles had gone—and there was a project to replace it with a large hotel. However, with the belated revival of interest in the conservation of 19C industrial architecture it was decided to convert the building into a museum rather than attempt to demolish it.

220m long and 75m wide, it now contains a vast museum. The coffered vault of its central hall alone—with its 1600 rosettes—which once spanned the platforms (where a snorting engine would still not appear out of place) is 138m in length, 40m wide and 32m high. For those fascinated by such technical details, the structure contains 12,000 tonnes of metal (compared to the mere 7000 of the Eiffel Tower); 40,000 acoustic resonators; 350 surveillance cameras; 500 radar detectors; and 6500 sensors connected to a central control unit. Some 16,000 square metres are devoted to permanent exhibitions, the space being divided into some 80 separate sections or galleries.

The architects of the new museum were Messieurs Renaud Bardou, Pierre Colboc and Jean-Paul Philippon of ACT; the architect/designer responsible for the interior was Gae Aulenti. Certain rooms retain their 1900s decoration.

The permanent collections are mainly French works of art dating from 1848 until 1914, although there are certain overlaps, with particular emphasis on the works of artists, sculptors, photographers and designers born between 1820 and 1870. It is also the venue of numerous temporary exhibitions and occasional concerts, films and of lectures, etc. Brochures detailing forthcoming events are available. The building also has a restaurant (in the former hotel restaurant), a rooftop café, bookshop, library and postcard shop (with access from the exterior); postal and exchange facilities are also available.

While a knowledge of the 'Style Pompier' may be useful to appreciate the art of the epoch in its historical perspective, it must be admitted that the quantity and mediocrity of the works on view are apt to swamp the more important masterpieces of the period. Numerous canvases from the 'romantic era' to that of the Art Nouveau, many extracted from the '*réserves*' of museums, where they have long slumbered, now again see the light, and many visitors have wondered to whose advantage. The remarkable collec-

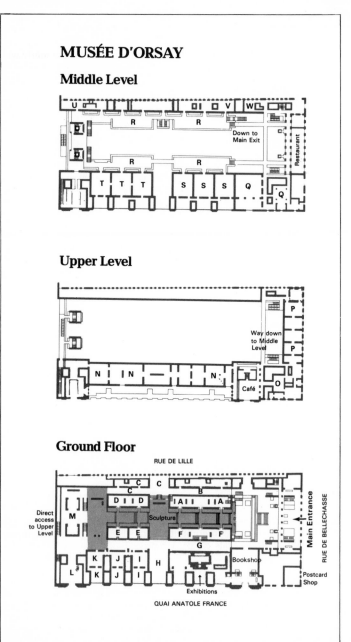

tion of Impressionists, many of them formerly in the Jeu de Paume (and some remain in the Orangerie; see Rte 13) have been relegated to a series of rooms on an upper level, which, with certain other important sections, can easily be overlooked by the unwary, and they are not particularly well displayed. The layout is confusing, and the collection very extensive: both patience and time are required to cover the ground.

The main permanent collection—approximately 2300 paintings, 250 pastels, 1500 sculptures, 1100 objets d'art and 13,000 photographs (exhibited in rotation)—is shown on three floors. Separate sections are devoted to individual collections, including the collections of Chauchard, Gachet, Kaganovitch, Mollard, Personnaz, and Moreau-Nélaton (which may be moved be the the Louvre).

On the GROUND FLOOR, with its entrance below the great clock of the central aisle, are displayed some of the more important sculptures; among them: *Jean-Baptiste Carpeaux* (1827–75), Ugolin group (1862), the Four Quarters of the World bearing the celestial sphere (1867–72) and La Danse (1869), commissioned for the façade of the Opéra.

Visitors are advised, however, to follow the route indicated below, first entering the section to the right of the aisle, marked **(A)** on our plan, displaying *Ingres* (1780–1867), La Source (completed 1856); *Delacroix* (1798–1863), The Lion Hunt, among other characteristic works by the artist; and *Winterhalter* (1806–73), Portrait of Mme Rimsky-Korsakov. Also to be seen here, and in the passage adjacent **(B)** are *Auguste Clésinger* (1814–83), Woman bitten by a snake (marble; 1847; Mme Sabatier being the model); and Henri Regnault (1843–71), Général Prim on horseback.

The section immediately to the east **(C)** is devoted to the decorative arts of the period 1850–80. Facing the main aisle is a huge canvas by *Thomas Couture* (1815–79), Roman Decadence (1847). The following section **(D)** contains *Puvis de Chavannes* (1824–98), The poor Fisherman (1881), among other works by the artist, whose Summer is displayed near the museum entrance. Among more recent acquisitions are The Pigeon and The Balloon, painted by Puvis de Chavannes during the period of the Siege of Paris (1870–71). Close by are representative paintings by *Gustave Moreau* (1826–98), and early works by *Degas* (1834–1917), including The Bellelli Family (1858/60), Portraits of Hilaire De Gas, the artist's grandfather (painted on a visit to Italy in 1857) and of Thérèse De Gas, The Opéra orchestra, Before the race, and the unfinished Semiramis watching the construction of Babylon.

Crossing the central aisle, enter the section opposite **(E)** to view *Monet* (1840–1926), two sections from Le Déjeuner sur l'herbe (1865/6), Women in a garden and The Magpie (a snow scene); *Manet* (1832–83), The balcony (with Berthe Morisot in the foreground), Portrait of Zola (1868), Olympia, The fife-player and Portraits of his parents; *Renoir* (1841–1919), Bazille painting; *Bazille* (1841–70), Portrait of Renoir, The improvised ambulance, The Meeting, and Family reunion.

In section **(F)** are displayed *Millet* (1814–75), The gleaners (1857), The Angelus (1858/9) and several portraits and landscapes; also works by *Théodore Rousseau* (1812–67), *Charles Daubigny* (1817–78), *Corot* (1796–1875) and Diaz de la Peña (1807–76); and works by members of the Barbizon *School* in general. Adjacent is a room devoted to paintings by *Daumier* (1808–79), but also including a remarkable series of 26 painted clay caricature busts of Parliamentarians, modelled from 1831.

The ground floor of the Musée d'Òrsay

In the adjoining passage **(G)** are a number of realistic paintings of the period, among them *Meissonier* (1815–91), Napoléon at the head of his troops. Off this passage opens a section **(H)** largely devoted to *Courbet* (1819–77), including Stags by a stream, Cliffs at Etretat, Burial at Ornans, and The artist's studio (in which Baudelaire is shown on the right, reading).

The passage is continued, with several more works by *Monet*, including his Portrait of Mme Gaudibert.

Off this are six rooms **(I, J, K)** displaying *Fantin-Latour* (1836–1904), The studio in the Batignolles (1870), in which Manet is shown painting, while standing (from right to left of the canvas) are Monet, Bazille and—beyond another figure—Zola and Renoir (with a picture-frame behind him). Close by is *Whistler* (1834–1903), Portrait of his mother, and several characteristic works by *Boudin* (1824–98), *Lépine* (1836–92) and *Jongkind* (1819–91). In section **(J)** are displayed *Manet*, Le déjeuner sur l'herbe (1863) and Blonde with bared breasts; also *Monet*, The poppies, Lilacs, and The railway-bridge at Argenteuil; and *Sisley* (1839–99), The footbridge at Argenteuil. In the adjacent room are the Eduardo Mollard collection of paintings by *Jongkind* (including The Seine at Notre-Dame), *Boudin* (including The beach at Trouville), several remarkable works by *Pissarro* (1830–1903) and *Sisley*, The bridge at Moret-sur-Loing.

Section **(K)** contains representative canvases by *Adolphe Monticelli* (1824–86), among other artists.

On leaving this section turn left to reach the east end of the museum. To the left, is a section **(L)** devoted to architectural and decorative features of the period 1850–1900, including furniture and other objects produced by members of the British Arts and Crafts Movement and the Century Guild, etc.

Below the main vault of the building is another section **(M)** concerned with *Charles Garnier* (1825–98) and the construction of the Paris Opéra, commenced in 1862. This contains a maquette of the entire Opéra quarter at 1:100 as it was in 1914; a model of the Opéra shown as a cross-section; and a maquette of the Stage of the Opéra built for the Universal Exhibition of 1900.

A bank of escalators ascends to the UPPER LEVEL and a series of rooms devoted to the **Impressionists (N)**, the majority moved here from their former home in the Jeu de Paume. They are displayed in roughly chronological order. Among them are *Monet*, Fête in the Rue Montorgueil (1878); several Landscapes by *Pissarro*, including Red Roofs; *Caillebotte* (1848–94), Planing the floor; *Renoir*, Portraits of Monet, of Mme Charpentier, and Richard Wagner, among others, his Dancing at the Moulin de la Galette, Nude in sunlight, The swing, and The path through long grass; and his sculpted Bust of Mme Renoir. Also in this first section are *Sisley*, Snow at Louveciennes, and Flooding at Port-Marly; and *Berthe Morisot* (1841–95), The cradle.

You pass on to *Degas*, The absinthe drinkers (1876), The Bourse, Women ironing and several Horse-racing scenes, and of Ballet-dancers, together with examples of his sculptures, including the realistic 14-year-old Dancer wearing her tutu; also *Manet*, The beach at Berck-sur-Mer, and Portraits of Mallarmé and of Clemenceau. The following section contains *Renoir*, Dance in the country, and Dance in the town, and Girls playing the piano; and *Monet*, Ice thawing on the Seine, The church at Vetheuil, Woman with an umbrella, Blue waterlilies, and the series of five views of the cathedral at Rouen painted in 1892–93. The next section contains part of the Personnaz collection, including *Pissarro*, Winter at Louveciennes; *Guillaumin* (1841–1927), The Place Valhubert; *Mary Cassat* (1844–1926), Woman sewing. This is followed by the Gachet collection, with a number of paintings by *Van Gogh* (1855–90), among them a Portrait of Dr Paul Gachet, Self-portraits, The church at Auvers, The restaurant de la Sirène, L'Arlésienne, His bedroom at Arles, The siesta; and *Cézanne* (1839–1906), The card-players, L'Estaque, Woman with a coffee-pot, and Still lifes; also *Toulouse-Lautrec* (1864–1901), Panels for La Goulue's booth at the Foire du Trône.

In the next two rooms are displayed a number of pastels by *Degas*, including The tub; and Manet, Mme Manet on a blue couch.

Adjacent is the Rooftop Café, providing a curious view of Paris through the hands of the huge clock, and also from the terrace.

The next series of rooms **(O)** contain several Neo-Impressionist paintings by *Seurat* (1859–91), including The circus; *Paul Signac* (1863–1935), Henri Cross (1856–1910); and *Odilon Redon* (1840–1916), including several pastels by the last.

Rooms **(P)** on the west end of the museum contain *Toulouse-Lautrec*, Jan Avril dancing, La toilette, and Cha-U-Kao (the female clown), among others; *Henri Rousseau* (Le Douanier; 1844–1910), Female portrait and War; *Gauguin* (1845–1905), La belle Angèle, Tahitian women on the beach, Haymaking in Brittany, The white horse, Les Alyscamps, The meal, Arearea, and also several carvings and other souvenirs from Tahiti. Other sections are devoted to the Nabis, including representative examples of the work of *Pierre Bonnard* (1867–1947), among them The croquet party, and Nude; *Paul Sérusier* (1863–1927); *Maurice Denis* (1870–1943); *Félix Vallotton* (1865–1925), The ball; *Edouard Vuillard* (1868–1940), Au lit; and paintings by *Aristide Maillol* (1861–1944).

The last section on this upper level displays the Kaganovitch collection, including *Gauguin*, Breton peasant women, and works by Monet, Sisley, Renoir, Pissarro, Van Gogh, among others.

Passing along a passage-way displaying material concerning the Press during the epoch, you reach escalators descending to the MIDDLE LEVEL of the museum and to a section displaying the Decorative Arts of the Third Republic **(Q)**. Here, among paintings, are such representative canvases as William Bouguereau (1825–1905), The birth of Venus, and Alphonse de Neuville (1835–85), The cemetery at St.-Privat. Notable is the decoration of the former ballroom of the station hotel, and the restaurant.

Another passage leads to a landing **(R)** overlooking the Ground Floor, displaying a collection of Monumental Sculpture of the period, off which are rooms **(S)** containing a collection of naturalistic paintings and sculptures, among which are *Bastien-Lépage* (1848–84), Haymaking; *Léon Bonnat* (1833–1922), Portrait of Mme Pasca; *Max Liebermann* (1847–1935), Brewery at Brannenburg; *Valentin Serov* (1864–1955), Mme Lwoff; *Jacques-Emile Blanche* (1861–1942), The Thaulow family; *Giovanni Boldini* (1842–1931), Portrait of Robert de Montesquiou (on whom Proust based his 'Baron Charlus'), together with Paul Troubetzkoy (1866–1938), Statuette of Montesquiou seated; also *Boldini*, Mme Max; *Eugène Carrière* (1849–1906), Portrait of Verlaine; and *Burne-Jones* (1833–98), The Wheel of Fortune.

Turning left on regaining the landing you reach an important collection of sculpture by *Rodin* (1840–1917), including a plaster cast of The Gate of Hell, The Baptist, The Bronze Age and numerous busts, including the marble Head of Camille Claudel (1864–1943), whose impressive bronze group entitled L'Age mûr (Maturity) is also in this section.

Adjacent is a further series of rooms **(T)** containing a collection of Art Nouveau material, including jewellery by *René Lalique* (1860–1945); furniture and woodwork by *Hector Guimard* (1867–1942), *Alexandre Charpentier* (1856–1909), *Jean Dampt* (1854–1945) and *F.-R. Carabin* (1862–1932); and glass, ceramics and enamel work by *Emile Gallé* (1846–1904) and the School of Nancy. More work by Guimard may be seen in a room to the left as you cross to the south side of the museum, while other rooms **(U)** contain bentwood furniture by *Michael Thonet* and his brothers (from 1853), and work by *Adolf Loos* (1870–1933), *Charles Rennie Mackintosh* (1868–1928), *Otto Wagner* (1841–1918) and *Josef Hoffmann* (1870–1956); and also examples of the productions of the Wiener Werkstatte, including designs by *Koloman Moser* (1868–1918).

The south landing displays more sculpture, among them *Bourdelle* (1861–1929), Hercules drawing his bow, and several works by *Maillol*. Passing a section devoted to temporary exhibitions (often of old photographs; see below), you reach to the left **(V)**, the last series of rooms containing paintings, largely post 1900, among them further examples of the work of *Bonnard* (Woman with a cat); Vuillard, Portrait of Mme de Polignac; Matisse (1861–1954), Luxe, calme et volupté; Gustav Klimt (1862–1918), Roses under trees; Edvard Munch (1863–1944) Summer night at Aasgaarstrand; and lastly, Henri Rousseau's, The snake-charmer.

Also reached from the landing is a section **(W)** devoted to the early days of the cinema.

Among collections of early photographs are representative examples of the art of Eugène Atget, Edouard Baldus, L.-A. Humbert de Molard, Félix Nadar, Charles Nègre, Pierre Petit, George Charles Beresford, Julia Margaret Cameron, Lewis Carroll, Roger Fenton and George Shaw.

Also of interest are a collection of drawings from the Gustave Eiffel archive.

10 Faubourg St.-Germain: Western Sector Palais de la Légion d'Honneur; Palais Bourbon; Musée Rodin

METROS: Solférino, Musée d'Orsay, Assemblée Nationale, Invalides, Varenne, Sèvres-Babylone, Rue du Bac (RER).

From the Louvre, the Pont du Carrousel crosses the Seine to the Quai Voltaire (Pl. 13; 3), which continues the Quai Malaquais to the W, (see p $$$), and was formerly the Quai des Théatins. Voltaire (1694–1778) died at No. 27, the home of the Marquis de Villette; St.-Sulpice refused to accept his corpse, which was rushed by his nephew to the Abbaye de Sellières, near Troyes, to save it from a common grave.

Louise de Kéroualle, Charles II's mistress *en titre*, and created Duchess of Portsmouth in 1673, occupied Nos 3–5 in 1695–1701. Ingres died at No. 11 in 1867. At No. 13 was installed the 'Moniteur Universel', an influential newspaper during the Revolution. Here as a tenant in 1829–36, Delacroix was preceded by the artist Horace Vernet and followed by Corot. At No. 19 Baudelaire lived in 1856–58, while writing 'Les Fleurs du Mal', while Wagner completed the libretto of 'Die Meistersinger' there in 1861–62; Sibelius and Oscar Wilde, were later tenants, the poet and dramatist Alfred de Musset lived at No. 25 in 1841–49; it was later the home of the novelist and playwright Henri de Montherlant (1896–1972).

To the west extends the Quai Anatole-France and the Quai d'Orsay (the latter, beyond the Pont de la Concorde, being a focus of 'foreign affairs'). The former is dominated by the new Musée d'Orsay; see Rte 9.

Opposite the west end of the museum is the ***Palais de la Légion d'Honneur**, flanked by a colonnade with bas-reliefs by Roland on the attic storey. The Corinthian portico in the courtyard is adorned with a frieze of arabesques with the motto 'Honneur et Patrie'. Facing the quay is a rotunda with Corinthian columns and symbolic busts, etc.

Built by Rousseau in 1782–86 for the Prince de Salm-Kyrbourg, at the Revolution it was raffled and won by a former wig-maker's apprentice who had made a fortune. He was later imprisoned for forgery. The house became the Swedish Embassy in 1797. Mme de Staël, the ambassador's wife, gave her famous receptions here under the Directory but in 1804 it was bought by the government for the grand chancellory of the Legion of Honour. It was restored in 1878, being severely damaged by fire during the Commune.

The entrance to the Musée National de la Légion d'Honneur et des Ordres de Chevalerie, exhibiting medals, decorations, etc., relating to the history of the Order, together with foreign heraldic trappings, is at No. 2 in the adjoining Rue de Bellechasse. This non-hereditary order, instituted in May 1802, comprises five classes (in ascending order): Chevalier, Officier, Commandeur, Grand-Officier and Grand-Croix. It is open Tues.–Sun. 14.00–17.00.

At 80 Rue de Lille (to the south) is the Hôtel de Seignelay by Boffrand, also architect of the adjacent Hôtel de Beauharnais (1713). It was acquired by Eugène de Beauharnais in 1803 and soon became the occasional home of his sister Queen Hortense. In 1814 it became the Prussian legation and in 1871 the German Embassy (now the ambassador's residence). Note the curious neo-Egyptian peristyle. Mérimée lived at 52 Rue de Lille for the last 18 years of his life, but his library was burnt out during the Commune a few weeks before his death at Cannes. Mme de Tencin held an important literary salon from 1726–40 at her home (from 1715) on the site of No. 75, visited by Marmontel, Fontenelle and Helvétius, among others.

A few minutes' walk to the west is the west end of the Blvd St.-Germain and the **Palais Bourbon**, seat of the Assemblée Nationale (Pl. 12; 2), facing the Pont de la Concorde (see Rte 13).

In 1722 a mansion was erected on this site for the Dowager Duchess of Bourbon (legitimised daughter of Louis XIV and the Marquise de Montespan), of which only the inner courtyard and main entrance (at 128 Rue de l'Université) have survived. The Prince de Condé, forced to leave his home because of the construction of the Théâtre de l'Odéon, bought the palace from Louis XV and enlarged it between 1764 and 1789, incorporating the Hôtel de Lassay, in which he lived after the Revolution. The Palais became national property under the name of Maison de la Révolution, the meeting-place of the Council of Five Hundred, and was later occupied by the Archives (1799–1808). Since 1815 it has been used by the Chambre des Députés, the French equivalent to the House of Commons, its name being changed to the Assemblée Nationale in 1946.

In 1940–44 the Palais Bourbon was the headquarters of the German military administration of the Paris region. At the time of the Liberation considerable fighting took place in the neighbourhood, causing some damage to the building and the destruction of over 30,000 volumes in the library.

The north façade (1804–07), a neo-Hellenistic piece of imperial bombast designed principally to balance the Madeleine when seen from the Pl. de la Concorde, is entirely decorative and consists of a portico of twelve Corinthian columns, with statues of statesmen, allegorical bas-reliefs, etc.

by Poyet. The decoration of the interior is of slight artistic merit; certain rooms contain historical paintings by Horace Vernet and Ary Scheffer, and by Delacroix (in the Salon du Roi and library); the Salle des Séances retains bas-reliefs by Lemot (1798).

The Galerie des Fêtes (1848) connects the building to the Hôtel de Lassay (1724), the official residence of the President of the Assembly.

Further along the Quai d'Orsay (with which it is synonymous) stands the Ministère des Affaires Etrangères (Foreign Office), built by Lacornée in 1845. Adjacent, on the Esplanade des Invalides, is the Gare des Invalides and Aérogare (or Air Terminus).

For the Hôtel des Invalides and Musée de l'Armée, see Rte 11.

Turning east along the Rue de l'Université, you shortly reach the Pl. du Palais Bourbon, an elegant ensemble of Louis XVI mansions built to the same pattern after 1776. Maria Edgeworth lived here in 1820.

At 108 Rue de l'Université (entrance at 121 Rue de Lille, parallel to the north) is the Institut Néerlandais, with a good collection of Dutch and German paintings. Jacques Turgot (1727–81), the economist, died here; La Fayette lived at No. 123, adjacent, in 1799.

Further east (on the far side of the Blvd St.-Germain), at 51 Rue de l'Université, is the Hôtel de Soyécourt (1707, by Lassurance); No. 24, the Hôtel de Senneterre, has a notable façade in the courtyard, perhaps by Servandoni (1700). Benjamin Franklin's first lodging on his arrival in Paris in 1776 was at the Hôtel de Hambourg in this street. The writer Alphonse Daudet (1840–97) died at No. 41; from 1885 he had lived in the neighbouring Rue de Bellechasse. This leads south to regain the Blvd St.-Germain, flanked to the west, at this point, by the extensive buildings of the Ministère de la Défense (by Bouchot; 1867–77), with a clock-tower at the corner of the Rue de Solférino.

Nos 1, 3 and 5 Rue St.-Dominique, running west from the Blvd St.-Germain, date from c 1710; No. 5 was the home of Gustave Doré (1832–83) from 1849 until his death. Nos 10–12 (since 1804 part of the Ministère de la Défense) occupy the former Couvent des Filles de St.-Joseph (1641), established for orphaned girls.

It was generously supported by Mme de Montespan (1640–1707), who retired here in 1687 after being supplanted in royal favour by Mme de Maintenon (c 1674). Mme du Deffand (1697–1780) held her literary salons here from 1755 until 1764 when her companion Mlle de Lespinasse left. The latter held her own salon from 1764 to 1776 at the Hôtel de Hautefort, formerly at No. 6 in the same street.

Nos 14–16, in the same block of buildings, the Hôtel de Brienne (1714 and 1730), was acquired by Lucien Bonaparte in 1802 and from 1806 to 1817 was the home of Letizia Bonaparte (Mme Mère). No. 28 was the Hôtel Rochefoucauld-d'Estissac (1710), while further west, the Hôtel de Sagan (No. 57), built by Brongniart in 1784 for the Princess of Monaco, is now the Polish Embassy, and was the British Embassy prior to the purchase of the Hôtel de Charost: see Rte 26. It was during this period that David Hume (who had lived in France in 1734–37) was secretary to the embassy (1763–65) and briefly chargé d'affaires. He was an intimate of Mme Geoffrin, D'Alembert and Turgot.

South of the Rue St.-Dominique rises the uninspired Gothic-revival church of Ste.-Clotilde, built in 1846–56 by Gau and Ballu, where César Franck was organist from 1858 until his death in 1890; a commemorative monument, by Lenoir, stands opposite.

The Rue de Grenelle, flanked by a number of embassies and ministries, may be conveniently approached by following the Rue de Bellechasse south. At No. 41, the Conseil de la Résistance and the Comité Parisien de la Libération organised operations for the rising of 19 August 1944.

Turning left into the Rue de Grenelle, you pass, at No. 106, the Temple de Panthemont (by Constant d'Ivry; 1747–56), once the chapel of a convent where Joséphine de Beauharnais lived for several years. Its main buildings (now Nos 37–39 in the Rue de Bellechasse) housed an aristocratic school for girls, where Thomas Jefferson's daughter was a pupil during her father's embassy (1785–89).

No. 102, the Hôtel de Maillebois, built early in the 18C by Deslisle-Mansart, was the home of the Duc de Saint-Simon (1675–1755) from 1738, when he was working on his 'Mémoires', until his death in 1755. No. 87 is the Hôtel de Bauffremont (1721–36), with a curved façade; No. 85, the Hotel d'Avaray (1718; by Leroux), home of Horace Walpole (1678–1757) during his Paris embassy (1727–30), is now the Netherlands Embassy. No. 79, the Hôtel d'Estrées, the Soviet Embassy, was built by Robert de Cotte in 1713.

Retracing your steps towards the west, you pass No. 110, the Hôtel de Courteilles (1778); No. 116, the old Hôtel de Brissac, was rebuilt in 1709 for Marshal de Villars by Boffrand. No. 101, opposite, the former Hôtel Rothelin (or de Charolais), built by Lassurance in 1700; Nos 138 and 140 were built by Jean Courtonne in 1722 and decorated by Lassurance in 1735 for Mlle de Sens. Marshal Foch (1851–1929) died in the former; the latter is occupied by the Institut Géographique National (cf. Rue de la Boétie). No. 127, the Hôtel du Châtelet, and one of the finest examples of the Louis-XV style. It was at one time used as the Archbishop's Palace in 1849–1906. The Hôtel de Chanac, at No. 142, opposite (by Delamair; 1750), is now the Swiss Embassy.

By turning left along the Blvd des Invalides, you pass the north east corner of the Hôtel des Invalides (see Rte 11), and turn back into the Rue de Varenne. At No. 77, the *'Hôtel Biron (Pl. 12; 4), on the corner, is the *MUSEE RODIN (métro: Varenne), containing an important and impressive collection of sculpture by Auguste Rodin (1840–1917), which he left to the State, many being the originals of works executed in marble or bronze, and also a fine selection of drawings.

The mansion, built in 1728–30 by Aubert and Gabriel, was occupied by the Duc de Biron in 1753, after the death there of Louise de Bourbon, widow of the Duc de Maine, and in 1820 by the aristocratic convent of the Sacré-Coeur. The State bought the house in 1901. In 1910 two ground-floor rooms were used as a studio by Rodin, who lived here from 1907 until his death, while Rainer Maria Rilke, at one time his secretary, also had lodgings here (1908–09). Much of the painted and gilt panelling, which had been removed by the superior of the convent as being mere ostentation, has been recovered and replaced.

Of the many outstanding examples of Rodin's work displayed here, a few only are listed. Grand Salon: St. John the Baptist; 'L'Homme qui marche'; the Kiss; the Hand of God; Iris; and two studies of hands. In a room to the left: 'L'Age d'Airain'; busts of Carrier-Belleuse, Mahler and Puvis de Chavannes. In rooms to the right of the Grand Salon: the Thinker; Orpheus; Eve; bust of Lady Sackville-West; of Eve Fairfax, the suffragette; Rodin's father. On the Staircase: Three Shades (from the Gate of Hell).

FIRST FLOOR. Case of models for the Gate of Hell; two busts of Victor Hugo; four nude studies of Balzac; Man with a broken nose; the Good Genius; Eternal Spring; Triton and Nereid on a dolphin; Water-fairy; Young Mother. Also shown are dance studies by Renoir and paintings by Renoir, Monet and Van Gogh, including the latter's Le Père Tanguy.

The gardens are embellished by numerous bronzes and marbles, including: the

Rodin's The Thinker in the gardens of the Hôtel Biron

Thinker; Hugo at Guernsey, formerly in the gardens of the Palais-Royal; Balzac; and the Gate of Hell; also, near the entrance, and seen from the street, the Burghers of Calais.

There is an annexe to the museum at Meudon, see Rte 33.

No. 72 in the Rue de Varenne is the Hôtel de Castries (1700), sacked by the mob in 1790 after the duel between the reactionary Duc de Castries and the radical Comte Charles de Lameth. No. 69 is the Hôtel de Clermont by Leblond (1708). At 1 bis in Rue Vaneau (right) André Gide (1869–1951) died.

Just beyond is the ***Hôtel de Matignon** (No. 57), built by Courtonne in 1721 and altered in the 19C. The Austro-Hungarian Embassy from 1888 to 1914, since 1935 it has been the residence of the Présidence du Conseil (or Prime Minister). One of the most beautiful mansions in the faubourg, it has an unusually large garden. Talleyrand lived here in 1808–11.

No. 50, the handsome Hôtel de Gallifet, with an Ionic peristyle built by Legrand in 1775–96, is now the Italian Institute; their embassy is at No. 47. (See below for the continuation of the route north from the Rue du Bac.)

To the south, 98 Rue de Bac, with gilt angels above the door, and good iron balconies, was the Café des Deux-Anges, the secret rendezvous of the

Chouans (c 1800), and here Georges Cadoudal hatched the conspiracy of 1804. Laplace (1749–1827), the astronomer and mathematician, died at No. 108 bis. At No. 110 Whistler (from 1892) was visited by Beardsley and Mallarmé, and scandalised his landlord by letting his child-models run naked in the garden. Nos 118–120, with doors designed by Toro, are the Hôtel de Clermont-Tonnerre, where Chateaubriand (1768–1848) lived from 1838 until his death. Here Mary Clarke (1793–1883; Mme Jules Mohl after 1847) had her salon from 1838–76, and was visited by Dean Stanley, Ticknor, Thackeray, Mrs Gaskell and Florence Nightingale. No. 128 is the Séminaire des Missions Etrangères, founded in 1663, with relics of martyred missionaries. Nos 136–140 are the Hôtel de la Vallière, with handsome portals, occupied by the Soeurs de Charité.

To the left is the Grands Magasins du Bon Marché, built on the site of an asylum, the Petites Maisons, to the east of which is the Sq. Boucicaut (Pl. 13; 5; named after the foundress of the Bon Marché).

A short distance to the south west, in the Rue de Sèvres, No. 42 is the Hôpital Laënnec, formerly a home for incurable women, founded by Cardinal de la Rochefoucauld c 1635, which retains its original courtyard and chapel. At No. 95 is the Eglise des Lazaristes, with a silver shrine containing the body of Vincent de Paul (1576–1660), canonised in 1737. Barbey d'Aurevilly (1808–89), the Romantic writer, lived for 30 years and died close by at No. 25 in the adjacent Rue Rousselet.

At 31 Rue St.-Placide, the southern extension of the Rue du Bac, the novelist J.-K. Huysmans (1848–1907) died; David d'Angers and Michelet, the historian, lived in the same street, while Parmentier resided in the parallel Rue de l'Abbé-Grégoire.

No. 40 in the Rue du Cherche-Midi, near the Blvd Raspail, belonged to Rochambeau (1725–1807), who fought for the Americans in the War of Independence, notably at Yorktown. At No. 38, the Maison des Sciences de l'Homme, has been built on the site of the Prison Militaire du Cherche-Midi, where many French patriots were imprisoned between 1940 and 1944.

The Rue du Bac leads north from the Rue de Varenne, shortly crossing the Rue de Grenelle, where to the right (Nos 57 and 59) is the *Fontaine des Quatre-Saisons, designed by Bouchardon in 1739, with sculptures of the City of Paris with the Seine and Marne at her feet, and with bas-reliefs of the Seasons. Alfred de Musset (1810–57) lived at No. 59 from 1824 to 1840.

Half-left across the Blvd St.-Germain, government offices occupy Nos 244–248, two early-18C houses. No. 246, the Hôtel de Roquelaure (1722), by Lassurance and Leroux, has a fine courtyard. Cambacérès, Second Consul in 1799, lived here in 1808.

Guillaume Apollinaire (1880–1918) lived and died at No. 202 Blvd St.-Germain; off which, to the right, leads the Rue St.-Guillaume, where the 16C Hôtel de Mesmes (No. 27), enlarged in 1933, is the Institut National des Sciences Politiques; No. 16, the Hôtel de Créqui, built in 1660–64, and extended in 1772, was for a time the home of poet, statesman and historian Lamartine, and later of Renan, the philologist and historian.

Crossing the Boulevard, the Rue du Bac leads north to the Seine, and is named after the ferry operating there before the construction of the Pont Royal. No. 46 Rue du Bac, the former Hôtel de Boulogne, with its courtyard, was built in 1744 by Boffrand for Jacques Bernard, who died after a scandalous bankruptcy in 1753; it was the lodging of Chateaubriand in 1815–18.

To the east is St.-Thomas-d'Aquin, begun in 1682 by Pierre Bullet in the Jesuit style, and completed, with the construction of the façade, in 1787. The ceiling-painting in the Lady Chapel is by Lemoyne.

11 Les Invalides and le Musée de l'Armée

METROS: Invalides, Varenne, La Tour-Maubourg, St.-François-Xavier.

The districts to the west of the Faubourg St.-Germain are overshadowed by the Dôme of Les Invalides, the Tour Eiffel to the west and the Tour Montparnasse (cf.) not far to the south east.

From the Right Bank, the best approach is by the Pont Alexandre-III (cf.), which provides an impressive vista of Les Invalides at the end of its esplanade. This walk can be conveniently combined with a return via the Palais de Chaillot.

The Esplanade des Invalides, 487m by 250m, was laid out in 1704–20 by Robert de Cotte and planted with trees along the sides. At its north-east corner is the Aérogare.

The north front of the Hôtel des Invalides

To the west, the Quai d'Orsay extends as far as the Pont de l'Alma. At No. 63 on the Quai is the American Church, built in a Gothic style in 1927–31; the playwright Jean Giraudoux (1882–1944) died at No. 89. For the adjacent public entry to the sewers of Paris, At 7 Rue Edmond-Valentin, a short distance south west, off the Av. Bosquet, James Joyce lived from 1935 to 1939.

From the Pl. des Invalides, south of the Esplanade, the Av. de la Motte-Picquet leads south west past the front of the Ecole Militaire (see Rte 12); the Blvd des Invalides skirts the east side of the Hôtel des Invalides, the formal façade of which contrasts with the domestic architecture opposite. To the left runs the Rue de Grenelle and the Rue de Varenne; near the corner of the latter is the Musée Rodin (see Rte 10).

The **∗∗HOTEL DES INVALIDES** (Pl. 12; 4; headquarters of the military governor of Paris) was founded by Louis XIV in 1671 as a home for disabled soldiers, the first enduring institution of its kind; at one time it housed between 4000 and 6000 pensioners or *invalides*. At present about 70 wounded live here. The infirmaries were on the ground floor of the east wing; workshops in part of the west wing. Most of the dormitories were on the second and third floors, while attics contained corn-lofts.

The buildings, which form a majestic ensemble, were erected from the designs of Libéral Bruant (died 1697), and J. Hardouin-Mansart continued the work. Antoine Parmentier (1737–1813) was chemist here (c 1775), where he carried out researches into the properties of the potato and the processes of baking bread. The Marquis de Sombeuil, governor of Les Invalides from 1786, on 14 July 1789, was forced by the mob to hand over arms stored here, including 20,000 firearms. During the Revolution it was known both as the 'Temple de l'Humanite' and 'Temple de Mars'. It was restored under Napoléon I, who was later buried beneath its Dôme. Part of the building now houses the Musée de l'Armée; see below. Among its governors have been Latour-Maubourg, Jourdan and Jérome Bonaparte.

Tickets, which may be used on two consecutive days, cover both the museums and entry to Napoléon's Tomb (the main entrance to which is in the Pl. Vauban). Open daily 10.00–17.000/18.00; Musée des Plans-Reliefs 10.00–16.45/17.45.

Facing the Esplanade are two artillery batteries: the unmounted Batterie Trophée, and the Batterie Triomphale, whose salvoes announcing victory were last heard at the end of the First World War. The Batterie Triomphale were removed by the Germans in 1940. Made for Frederick the Great in 1708, these eight pieces were captured by Napoléon at Vienna in 1805.

From the entrance gate you see the dignified façade, over 200m long. The dormer windows, both here and elsewhere, take the form of trophies, each different, and deserve attention. Flanking the main entrance are copies of the original statues of Mars and Minerva by Guillaume Coustou (1735). The equestrian bas-reliefs above the central door, of Louis XIV accompanied by Justice and Prudence, by Pierre Cartellier, replaced (in 1815) the original design by Coustou, destroyed during the Revolution.

Opposite the entrance to the Cour d'Honneur (102m by 64m) is the door of the church of St.-Louis, above which are Seurre's original bronze statue of Napoléon, formerly surmounting the Vendôme Column (see Rte 17), and an astronomical clock (1781).

On the east side of the courtyard is the main entrance to the Musée de l'Armée; see below. At the foot of the staircase to the right of the entrance to the church, is one of the Renault cars (the Marne taxis), which, commandeered by Général Gallieni, carried troops to the Front in September 1914.

∗**St.-Louis** (the chapel of Les Invalides) was built by Bruant and Mansart. The imposing interior, decorated with captured regimental colours, has a gallery built at the same level as the dormitories of the disabled. In 1837 it resounded to the first performance of Berlioz's 'Grande Messe des Morts', the orchestra being reinforced by a battery of artillery on the esplanade. The organ (1679–87), by Alexandre Thierry, with a case originally by Germain Pilon, has been rebuilt several times. Concerts still take place here. A sheet of plain glass behind the high altar separates the chapel from the Dôme des Invalides.

In vaults below (no adm.) are the graves of numerous French marshals and generals, among them Jourdan, Bertrand, Grouchy and Oudinot, and, more recently, Leclerc de Hautecloque and Juin.

On leaving the chapel, turn left along the Corridor de Nîmes to reach the entrance of the Dôme. Visitors approaching from the Pl. Vauban, to the south, will find a ticket-office near the main entrance (Pl. 12; 4).

The *Dôme des Invalides, begun by J. Hardouin-Mansart in 1675 and finished in 1706, was added to the church of St.-Louis as a chapel royal. In the niches on either side of the entrance are statues of Charlemagne and St. Louis by Coysevox and Nicolas Coustou. The ribbed dome is roofed with lead, adorned with regilt trophies, and crowned with a short spire reaching to a height of 107m.

The admirably proportioned interior, 56m square, is in the form of a Greek cross. The focus of attention is the sumptuous *Tomb of Napoléon, designed by Visconti, in which the Emperor was placed in April 1861, 40 years after his death at St. Helena (see Château de Bois-Préau, Rte 35). His remains were brought to Les Invalides in December 1840 (see Arc de Triomphe). His body lay in the Chapel St.-Jérome while the sarcophagus of dark red porphyry (from Finland), resting on a pedestal of green Vosges granite, was being prepared.

The tomb, 4m by 2m and 4.5m high, is surrounded by a gallery with ten bas-reliefs after Simart representing the 'benefits' conferred on France by the Emperor. Facing the sarcophagus are 12 figures by Pradier symbolising his greater victories, between which are six trophies of 54 colours taken at Austerlitz. The statue of Napoléon in his coronation robes is also by Simart.

The error of placing the tomb in an inappropriately inferior position as seen from the circular gallery is now generally recognised. An imposing view is gained by descending to the Crypt, the inscription at the entrance to which, taken from Napoléon's will, 'Je désire que mes cendres reposent sur les bords de la Seine, au milieu de ce peuple français que j'ai tant aimé', translates as: 'I desire that my mortal remains rest on the banks of the Seine, in the midst of the French people whom I have loved so dearly'.

On re-ascending, you can visit the surrounding chapels, passing (in an anti-clockwise direction from the south east) the tombs (some enshrining only hearts) of Joseph Bonaparte (died 1844), Vauban (died 1707; tomb of 1847 by Antoine Etex), Foch (died 1929; tomb by Landowski); Lyautey (died 1934; tomb by Albert Laprade); La Tour d'Auvergne (died 1800; 'the first grenadier of the Republic'); and Turenne (died 1675, first buried at St.-Denis, his remains were saved from destruction; tomb by Le Brun, Tuby and Marsy). The last chapel, St.-Jérome, stands empty. Relics of the Roi de Rome (1811–32), Bonaparte's only son, who died prematurely of phthisis and was originally buried in Vienna, were brought here by the Germans in 1940, but since 1969 have lain in the vaults of the crypt (see above).

The * *MUSEE DE L'ARMEE comprises one of the world's most interesting, extensive and well-displayed collections of arms and armour, weapons, uniforms, military souvenirs, etc., and without an excessive display of chauvinism. The building also houses the Musée des Plans-Reliefs (see below), a library and a small cinema.

From the main entrance (east side of the Cour d'Honneur), you can first visit the restored Salle Turenne (right), in which colours of French regiments from the First Republic to the present have been re-hung, and the fine frescoes, variously attributed to J.-B. Martin 'des Batailles' (1659–1735) or pupils of Van de Meulen, are now seen to advantage. The maquette of Les Invalides (made before 1757) is also of interest. To the left is the Salle Vauban, containing cavalry uniforms and equipment, and similar frescoes.

From the Vestibule, stairs ascend to the SECOND FLOOR. To the right is the entrance to a series of rooms devoted to the military exploits of the Ancienne Monarchie (1618–1792), set out in chronological order. Most figures are displayed in such a way that they can be seen in the round: this also applies to the suits of armour to be seen in the west wings. Among the numerous plans, engravings, prints and portraits, those individual objects which may be pointed out are the cannon-ball that killed Turenne and the perforated back plate of his cuirass, his marshal's baton and his portrait attributed to Le Brun. Note also the colours of the Irish Clancarty regiment (1642).

Another room contains souvenirs of Général la Fayette (1757–1834). You next enter compartments concentrating on the Revolutionary, Directory and Consulate periods, with numerous Napoleonic souvenirs, including one of Bonaparte's grey coats; his tent and furniture; and the stuffed skin of his white horse, 'Vizier', which outlived the Emperor by eight years. Among portraits of his marshals, that of Ney, by Gérard, is notable. A further series of cabinets devoted to Napoléon at St. Helena, and the period 1830–52, bring you back to the stairs. See also Malmaison and Bois-Préau, Rte 35.

On the THIRD FLOOR are sections devoted to the Second Empire, Crimean War and Franco-Prussian War of 1870, additionally illustrated by early photographs, and paintings by Alphonse de Neuville and Edouard Detaille.

On the ATTIC FLOOR of the east wing are housed the important collections of the autonomous *MUSEE DES PLANS-RELIEFS**, recently reorganised after the roof had been restored, although the political scandal about their partial dispersal has not died down; some 19 models of fortresses near what is now the Belgian border still remain at Lille.

The surviving collection consists of some 120 relief models (apart from those dismounted or in *réserve*), and it is known that another 41 existed in 1697. The majority were built to the scale 1:600 and, together with maquettes, maps and plans, represent the form of fortresses—both in France and near her frontiers—since the time of Vauban. They are of very considerable military, historical, architectural and topographical interest.

The idea of their construction is attributed to Louvois (1641–91), Louis XIV's minister of war. Until 1776 they remained secreted in the Louvre, and were only shown to such important visitors as Peter the Great (1717), who could be trusted. They were then moved to Les Invalides, where—although evacuated to Chambord during the Second World War—they have for the most part remained. The models were made during the period 1668–1870, although many of them have since been restored, and occasionally some-what over-restored. The new distribution displays the following models, apart from sections devoted to military cartography and descriptions of their construction: La Kenoque, no longer existing, being built over by the Belgian town of Knokke-le-Zoute; Fort Quarré, Antibes; Constantine, Tunisia; Antwerp; Metz; Berg-op-Zoom; Landrecies; Auxonne; Brest; Marsal (Moselle); Perpignan (restored 1986); Strasbourg; Château-Trompette (the former citadel at Bordeaux); and Briançon.

On the west side of the Cour d'Honneur are the **Collections of Arms and Armour**, extraordinarily rich in weapons of all periods, many exhibits being of great artistic interest and masterpieces of damascening and chasing. To the right, the Salle François I, retaining the original frescoes (restored) of the dining-rooms and a painting of the Founding of Les Invalides by Pierre Dulin, contains suits of armour (including parade armour) and the horse armour of François I, his sword, and plaques from his tomb. Note the heavy armour of the Elector Palatine Otto Henry.

A small room near the entrance, containing arms dating from before the 9C, may be visited on request.

To the left of the entrance to this wing is the Salle Henri IV, with frescoes by Martin 'des Batailles', concentrating on jousting armour. Note the diminutive 'sample' suits made by the armourer to obtain orders. Straight ahead of the vestibule are galleries containing the important **Collection Pauilhac**. Among the numerous medieval and Renaissance pieces are suits belonging to Louis XIII, Henri III, Henri IV and Louis XIV. The *Collection of Firearms, showing the evolution of such weapons, is outstanding.

Another section is devoted to collections of **'Oriental'** arms and armour from the Balkans, Turkey, Persia, India and China, etc. Among individual helmets of interest are those of Voivode (Russia; 16C) and of the Ottoman sultan Bajazet II (1447–1512). On the far side of the adjacent courtyard is a wing containing some thousands of *figurines* of soldiers.

From these galleries there is a view into adjacent courtyards, in which stand a number of artillery pieces, while the walls of the Cour d'Angoulême (north) are embellished by the 'Danube Chain', with which the Turks held their vessels in position during the Siege of Vienna in 1683. Other pieces, usually unmounted, are arranged around the main courtyard.

On the SECOND FLOOR are galleries devoted to the 1914–18 War and France's participation in the 1939–45 War, while 'animated' maps describe graphically the movements of troops during the various campaigns. Occupied France, France Liberated and the sad history of deportations are also covered, as are the Normandy Landings.

Further rooms on the THIRD FLOOR are devoted to France's Allies during the Second World War war, while displayed in the Gribeauval Hall is an extensive collection of scale models of French and foreign artillery of all periods.

12 Ecole Militaire; Tour Eiffel

METROS: Ecole Militaire, Cambronne, Bir. Hakeim, Champ-de-Mars, La Motte Picquet-Grenelle.

From the Pl. Vauban (Pl. 12; 4), to the south of the Les Invalides, the Av. de Tourville leads west towards the Ecole Militaire, and the Av. de Villars leads south east, shortly meeting the southern section of the Blvd des Invalides (by the church of St.-François-Xavier; 1875). This continues as far as the Rue de Sèvres, beyond which it is extended by the Blvd de Montparnasse.

At this latter junction are the buildings of the Institut National des Jeunes Aveugles (Blind), founded in 1793 by Valentin Haüy. Vincent d'Indy (1851–1931) lived for 70 years and died at 7 Av. de Villars.

South of the Rue de Sèvres are the Hôpital des Enfants-Malades (founded 1724) and Hôpital Necker, once a Benedictine nunnery, founded in 1779 by Louis XVI, directed at one time by Mme Necker, and rebuilt in 1840.

Also radiating from the Pl. Vauban are the wide tree-lined Av. de Breteuil; and to the south west, the Av. de Ségur, which leads towards (right) the controversial buildings of the UNESCO headquarters, perhaps best approached by the Av. de Lowendal.

The main **UNESCO Building** (by Breuer, Zehrfuss and Nervi; 1958), flanking the semicircular Pl. de Fontenoy, consists in fact of three buildings: one for the permanent delegation; a Conference Building, with its accordion-pleated concrete roof covered in copper, and containing murals by Picasso and Rufino Tamayo; and the dominating Y-shaped Secretariat of seven floors supported by 72 pylons. In the Piazza are 'decorative works' by Henry Moore, Alexander Calder, Jean Arp and Miró, and a Japanese Garden has been designed by Noguchi. An annexe, to house even more functionaries, lies a short distance due south. The main building was the object of arson in March 1984.

To the north is the *Ecole Militaire (Pl. 12; 3–5), a handsome structure covering part of the former 'ferme' and 'château' of Grenelle, built by J.-A. Gabriel, and enlarged in 1856.

18C railings separate the Cour d'Honneur from the Pl. de Fontenoy, which has lost its 18C character. On the entablature of the entrance façade, the figure representing Victory is in fact Louis XV, a likeness that escaped destruction during the Revolution.

The school was founded in 1751 by Louis XV (influenced by Mme de Pompadour) for the training of noblemen as army officers. It was opened in 1756 and completed in 1770. In 1777 its rigid rules for entry were modified so that it could take in the élite of provincial military academies; thus in 1784 Bonaparte (who was confirmed in the chapel during his training) was chosen from the Collège de Brienne. It was closed in 1787 and used as a depot and barracks. It is now occupied by the Ecole Supérieure de Guerre, or staff college.

On written application to the Commandant, 1 Pl. Joffre, a guided tour of the interior can be arranged. The most impressive room is the Salon des Maréchaux, with its fine *boiseries*. The chapel is open to the public daily.

A short distance south west is the Pl. Cambronne. It was Général Cambronne (1770–1842) who made the famous and defiant expletive—'*Merde!*'—when the Imperial Guard was summoned to surrender at Waterloo, since known as 'le mot de Cambronne'. The Rue Frémicourt and its extension, the Av. Emile-Zola, lead due west to the Pont Mirabeau: see below.

Between the Ecole Militaire and the Seine lies the **Champ-de-Mars**, almost 1km long, laid out in 1765–67 as a parade ground on the old Plaine de Grenelle, with its market-gardens; it was used as a racecourse after the Restoration, and converted into a park after 1913.

The ground was the scene of several early aeronautical experiments by Joseph and Jacques Montgolfier, by Charles and Robert, and by Blanchard (1783–84). Numerous revolutionary festivals were held here, the most famous of which was the Fête de la Fédération on 14 July 1790, when the king, the Assembly, the delegates from the provinces and the army, took the oath at the Autel de la Patrie to observe the new Constitution; the 'Champ de Mai', held by Napoléon on his return from Elba; and several international exhibitions.
  Bailly, president of the Constituent Assembly, was brutally executed here in 1793; and Capitaine Alfred Dreyfus was publicly degraded here in December 1894.

The **Tour Eiffel** (Pl. 11; 7), at the river end of the Champ-de-Mars, is still one of the tallest structures in the world (300m high, or 320m including the television installation). An inseparable part of the Paris landscape, it continues to dominate this quarter, although the equally obtrusive Tour Montparnasse threatens to divide your attention.

Tour Eiffel, Champs-de-Mars

Built in 1889 for the important Paris Exhibition, the Tour Eiffel was originally granted only 20 years of life but its use in radio-telegraphy in 1904 saved it from demolition. Constructed by the engineer Gustave Eiffel (1832–1923), the tapering lattice-work tower weighs over 7000 tonnes, and is composed of 15,000 pieces of metal, fastened by 2,500,000 rivets, while its four feet are supported by masonry piers sunk 9–14m into the ground.

It was at the Paris Exhibition that the sound of a gamelin orchestra from Jakarta was heard which introduced oriental music to Debussy, Ravel (aged 14), Satie and Rimsky-Korsakov, among other composers.

The first, second and third platforms, the latter 274m from the ground, are reached by lift/elevator. On a clear day, particularly about one hour before sunset, the extensive *views are remarkable.

The Pont d'Iéna spans the Seine to the Palais de Chaillot: see Rte 27.

Further south west is the Pont de Bir Hakeim, from which the Blvd de Grenelle leads south east, on No. 8 of which a plaque records the round-up of some thousands of Parisian Jews in the vélodrome (or cycling-track) here in July 1942 before their deportation.

The Quai de Grenelle leads south west, with a view across the Allée des Cygnes (an island used as a charnel-house for dead horses in the 18C) to the Maison de la Radio (see Rte 27), passing (left) a concrete-jungle area of tower blocks flanking the Seine. It is joined to the far bank by the Pont de Grenelle and Pont Mirabeau (1895–97), leading to Auteuil.

To the south east, facing the Rue de la Convention, in this not very interesting 15th arrondissement, are the buildings of the Imprimerie Nationale (founded 1640), moved here in 1925 from the Hôtel de Rohan.

The riverside beyond the Pont Mirabeau, until recently the site of a large Citroën factory, is at present being radically developed. Beyond the Blvd Victor and the Pont du Garigliano, is the Blvd Périphérique (Quai d'Issy; with the Porte de Sévres further east), on the far side of which is the Héliport de Paris, while adjacent to the east are various buildings of the Armée de l'Air and other Service departments, exhibition areas and Palais des Sports.

THE NORTH OR RIGHT BANK:
LA RIVE DROITE

13 From Pl. de la Concorde to Pl. du Carrousel

METROS: Concorde, Tuileries, Palais-Royal.

The *PL. DE LA CONCORDE (Pl. 7; 7), occupying a central position by the Seine, and midway between the Etoile and the Ile de la Cité, is still—in spite of the traffic swirling round it—one of the world's most impressive squares. Its perspectives were a design of the First Empire but its present appearance dates from 1852, when the surrounding ditch was filled in.

The site, then a vacant space to the west of the main built-up area of the city (but within the enceinte of the Fermiers-Généraux raised some 30 years later), was chosen in 1757 to receive a bronze statue of Louis XV commissioned by the 'échevins' (or magistrates, see Hôtel de Ville, Rte 19), and unveiled in 1763. The surrounding square was named after the king. In 1770 panic during a firework display celebrating the marriage of the dauphin Louis and Marie-Antoinette provided its first holocaust (133 dead).

In 1792 the statue was replaced by a huge figure of Liberty, designed by Lemot (the object of Mme Roland's famous apostrophe: 'O liberté, que de crimes on commet en ton nom'; Oh Liberty, what crimes are committed in your name!), and the square was re-named Pl. de la Révolution. In the same year a guillotine was erected here for the execution of the robbers of the crown jewels (cf. below).

Louis XVI was guillotined on 21 January 1793 on the site now occupied by the fountain nearest the river, and between May 1793 and May 1795 the blade claimed among its 1119 victims: Charlotte Corday (17 July 1793), Marie-Antoinette (16 October), the Girondins (31 October), Philippe-Egalité (6 November), Mme Roland (10 November), Hébert (24 March 1794), Danton (5 April), Lavoisier (8 May), Mme Elisabeth (9 May) and Robespierre (28 July). The square received its present name in 1795 at the end of the Reign of Terror.

On the north side of the square are two handsome mansions designed by Gabriel in 1763–72 (with pediment sculptures by M.-A. Slodtz and G. Coustou the younger) and originally intended as official residences. That to the right, from which the crown jewels were stolen in 1792, is now the Hôtel de la Marine; that to the left has long been shared between the Automobile Club and the Hôtel Crillon.

Between these buildings leads the Rue Royale, at the end of which stands the Madeleine (see Rte 22), while in the opposite direction the southern perspective is completed by the assertive Classical façade of the Palais-Bourbon, see Rte 10.

To the west of the Pl. de la Concorde, the Av. des Champs-Elysées (see Rte 25) rises gently towards the Arc de Triomphe, the vista framed by replicas of the *Marly Horses, two groups by G. Coustou, which were brought from the Château de Marly in 1794 and now mirror to the winged horses at the west entrance of the Tuileries. In the opposite direction the view extends to the Louvre.

On the south side of the Place, the Pont de la Concorde, with magnificent perspectives, was built by Perronet in 1788–90 and widened in 1932. Stone from the Bastille was used in the construction of the upper part; one reason

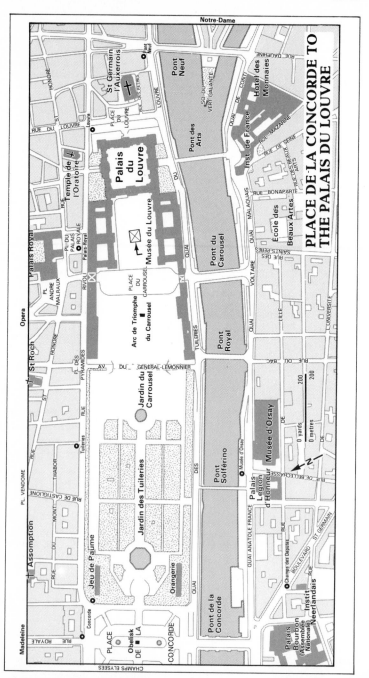

PLACE DE LA CONCORDE TO THE PALAIS DU LOUVRE

for this is said to be that the Parisians would be able to tread under foot that symbol of royal despotism.

In the centre of the Place rises the **Obelisk of Luxor**, a monolith of pink syenite, almost 23m high and c 230 tonnes in weight. It originally stood before a temple at Thebes in Upper Egypt and commemorates in its hieroglyphics the deeds of Rameses II (13C BC).

The obelisk was presented to Louis-Philippe in 1831 by Mohammed Ali (the donor of Cleopatra's Needle in London). The pedestal, of Breton granite, bears representations of the apparatus used in its erection in 1836 (see also Musée de Marine, Rte 27). The two fountains, by Hittorf, copies of those in the piazza of St. Peter's at Rome, are embellished with figures emblematic of inland (north) and marine navigation.

The eight stone pavilions round the Square, built by Gabriel in the 18C, support statues personifying the great provincial capitals. Strasbourg (as capital of Alsace, lost to France in 1871) was hung with crêpe and wreaths until 1918. Pradier's model for Strasbourg was Juliette Drouet (1806–83), Victor Hugo's mistress.

The **Jardin des Tuileries**, the tree-lined formal garden of 25.5 hectares, adorned with statues, extends eastwards to the Pl. du Carrousel and is crossed by the Av. du Gén.-Lemonnier, now partly subterranean and which will provide access to underground parking for the Louvre. The west section was the private garden of the Tuileries and has been little altered since it was laid out by Le Nôtre in 1664.

The earlier gardens, in the Italian style, had been designed by his grandfather. It became the favourite promenade of the fashionable nobility until superseded by the Palais-Royal just before the Revolution.

Here, on 1 December 1783, the scientists Charles and Robert made an ascent in a gas-filled balloon, watched by a vast crowd. The first such ascent had been made some 40 days previously: cf. La Muette, see Rte 27.

The gateway opening from the Pl. de la Concorde has pillars crowned by replicas of equestrian statues of Fame and Mercury, by Coysevox (brought from Marly in 1719).

The large octagonal pond is surrounded by statuary of the 17–18C by N. and G. Coustou and Van Cleve; on the steps to the south is 'Hommage à Cézanne' by Maillol; to the north, a copy of Coysevox's bust of Le Nôtre (original in St.-Roch).

Terraces extend along both sides of the gardens. On the south, overlooking the Quai des Tuileries (from which the Pont Solférino, demolished in 1963 and replaced by a footbridge, crosses to the Quai Anatole-France), is the Terrasse du Bord-de-l'Eau. A new road bridge is projected. From beneath this terrace, a passage led from the palace cellars to the Pl. de la Concorde, providing Louis-Philippe with an escape route in 1848. At the west end of the terrace is the Orangerie (1853), see below.

On the north side, the Terrasse des Feuillants, skirting the Rue de Rivoli, is named after a Benedictine monastery which in 1791 was the meeting-place of the 'Club des Feuillants' (moderate republicans, among whom were Lavoisier and André Chénier).

Below the east side of the terrace are fragments of the Palais des Tuileries, though not *in situ*. Further east, nearly opposite the Rue de Castiglione, was the site of the Manège, the riding-school of the palace, where the National Assembly met from 1789 to 1793, and where Louis XVI was condemned to death.

Here, until its contents were transferred to the Musée d'Orsay, stood the

Musée du Jeu-de-Paume, so-named because it was accommodated in a real tennis-court built in 1851. The restored building is now the venue of temporary exhibitions of 20C art. On the terrace on its south side is a monument to Charles Perrault (1628–1703), the writer of fairy tales, at whose suggestion the gardens were thrown open to the public by Colbert.

In the **Orangerie**, three minutes' walk to the south across the Tuileries gardens, are displayed Monet's series of mural paintings, 'Les Nymphéas' (see also Musée Marmottan, Rte 27).

Since 1984 the upper gallery has been the permanent home of the works of art acquired by Jean Walter and Paul Guillaume, and donated to the State on the condition that they remained a separate collection. It comprises some 144 paintings, not many of which are of the first quality, including 28 examples of the work of Derain, 24 by Renoir, 22 by Soutine, 14 by Cézanne, 12 by Picasso, 11 by Matisse, 10 by Utrillo and 9 by Henri Rousseau (le Douanier), together with representative works by Sisley, Monet, Modigliani, Marie Laurencin and Van Dongen. Among the more notable canvases are: Cézanne, Portrait of his wife, c 1885; Renoir, Gabrielle and Jean, Young girls at the piano, Claude playing and Dressed as a clown, and Snowscape, and several lush nudes; Derain, The artist's niece, and Portrait of Mme Guillaume; Picasso, The embrace, and Nude on a red background; Henri Rousseau, The wedding, and Père Junier's cart; and Modigliani, The young apprentice, and Portrait of Paul Guillaume.

The central avenue of the **Jardin des Tuileries**, of chestnuts and plane trees, leads to the Round Pond, between which and the Av. du Gén.-Lemonnier survive the railings put up by Louis-Philippe to isolate the 'private garden'. Galignani's 'New Paris Guide' (1841 ed.) stated that 'Great care is taken in keeping the garden clean; persons in working habits or carrying any parcels, except books, are not allowed to enter it'! Among the flower-beds are groups of sculpture, notably by G. and N. Coustou, Coysevox and Le Pautre.

The main west wing of the former **Palais des Tuileries** no longer exists, except for the Pavillons de Flore and de Marsan (to the south and north respectively), both of which have been restored or rebuilt, and which now form the western extremities of the wings of the Palais du Louvre; see below. The Pavillon de Marsan accommodates the Musée de la Mode (see Rte 15).

The Palais des Tuileries was begun in 1564 by Philibert Delorme (c 1515–70) for Catherine de Médicis, who left the Hôtel des Tournelles after Henri II's lingering death in 1559. The site, beyond the city walls, was known as the 'Sablonnière' and occupied by tile-kilns (*tuileries*). Delorme was succeeded by Jean Bullant and then, in 1595, by Jacques du Cerceau, responsible for the Pavillon de Flore. The Pavillon de Marsan was built in 1660–65 by Louis le Vau and his son-in-law François d'Orbay. Both pavilions were rebuilt where necessary and restored in 1875–78 by Lefuel.

Louis XVI was confined here after being brought from Versailles (except during his ineffectual attempt to escape in 1791) until the riot of 10 August 1792, when his Swiss Guards were massacred. In 1793–96 it was the headquarters of the Convention. Pope Pius VII was lodged in the Pavillon de Flore for four months in 1804–05.

The Tuileries became the main residence of Napoléon I, Louis XVIII (who died here), Charles X, Louis-Philippe and Napoléon III. Eugénie escaped from the palace in September 1870 to the house of Dr Thomas Evans, her American dentist, who cleverly extracted her from Paris. Sir John Burgoyne's yacht awaited the Empress at Deauville. In May 1871 the Communards set fire to the building which, like the Hôtel de Ville, was completely gutted. Its charred remains stood until 1884, when the main wing was razed, and the site was converted into a garden in 1889. This is at present embellished by statues in bronze by Aristide Maillol (1861–1944) and Rodin, but it is likely that the whole area will be radically restored during the next few years.

The restored and regilt **Arc de Triomphe du Carrousel**, a copy on a reduced scale of the Arch of Septimius Severus at Rome (14.60m high instead of 23m), was begun in 1806 from the designs of Fontaine and Percier to commemorate the victories of Napoléon I in 1805. It then constituted the main entrance to the courtyard of the Tuileries from the Cour du Carrousel.

It is surmounted by figures of Soldiers of the Empire and a bronze chariot-group by Bosio (1828) representing the Restoration of the Bourbons. The original group incorporated (at the suggestion of Baron Denon) the antique horses looted by Napoléon from St. Mark's, Venice, in 1797 and replaced there in 1815 (the sculptor Canova being instrumental in their return). The four sides are decorated with marble bas-reliefs: the Battle of Austerlitz; the Capitulation of Ulm; the Meeting between Napoléon and Alexander at Tilsit; the Entry into Munich; the Entry into Vienna; and the Peace of Pressburg.

The Pl. du Carrousel, which derives its name from an equestrian fête given here in 1662 by Louis XIV, lies to the east of the arch. Until the middle of the 19C a small square surrounded by a labyrinth of narrow and noisome alleys, which for centuries had remained almost encircled by the royal palaces; see the rooms devoted to the history of the Louvre, p 128.

The archways to the north lead to the Rue de Rivoli and beyond to the south end of the Av. de l'Opéra; those on the south give onto the Quai des Tuileries opposite the Pont du Carrousel.

To the east lies the Cour Napoléon, and the main entrance to the **Musée du Louvre**, below its glass pyramid; (see Rtes 14 and 15); westwards the Place commands a distant view towards the Arc de Triomphe and the towers of La Défense beyond.

14 Palais du Louvre

METROS: Tuileries, Palais-Royal, Louvre, Pont-Neuf.

The ***PALAIS DU LOUVRE** (Pl. 13; 2), occupying an extensive site between the Rue de Rivoli and the Seine, was one of the most magnificent of the world's palaces, and remains the most majestic public building in Paris.

The Musée du Louvre is described in Rte 15, and the Musée des Arts Décoratifs in Rte 16.

Its name is derived either from an early wolf-hunter's rendezvous known as '*Lupara*' or '*Louverie*', or from a '*Louver*', a blockhouse. It first appears in history as one of Philippe Auguste's fortresses (1190–1202), which stood at the south-west corner of the Cour Carrée, the remains of which may now be seen to advantage in the basement; see Rte 15. Charles V made it the official royal residence and surrounded it with a moat. The west and south sides were rebuilt under François I (1515–47) and extended by Henri II. Catherine de Médicis, Henri II's widow, began the LONG GALLERY, flanking the river, to connect the Louvre with her new palace at the Tuileries (see above).

It was here that she extorted from her son Charles IX the order for the

Massacre of St. Bartholomew (24 August 1572). In 1591, during the Wars of the League, the Duc de Mayenne hanged three members of the 'Council of Sixteen' in the Salle des Gardes (now the Salle des Cariatides). In 1648, Henrietta Maria, later the widow of Charles I of England, found refuge in the Louvre. In 1658 Corneille's 'Nicomède' was performed in the Salle des Gardes.

The building was further extended during the reigns of Henri IV and Louis XIII, and the quadrangle was completed, on Colbert's orders, during the minority of Louis XIV.

When Christopher Wren visited Paris in 1665, he observed that 'The Louvre for a while was my daily Object; where no less than a thousand Hands are constantly employ'd in the Works; some in laying mighty Foundations; some in raising the Stories, Columns, Entablements, &c. with vast Stones, by great and useful Engines; others in Carving, Inlaying of Marbles, Plaistering, Painting, Gilding, &c.... Mons. Colbert...comes to the Works of the Louvre, every Wednesday, and, if Business hinders not, Thursday'. Wren met Bernini, and remarked 'I would have given my Skin' for his design of the Louvre, 'but the old reserv'd Italian gave me but a few Minutes View'.

But the king, preoccupied with his new palace at Versailles, soon lost interest in the new buildings, which were left in a state of disrepair and were occupied by squatters. It was not until 1754 that Louis XV commissioned Gabriel to renovate and restore the palace. Under Napoléon I the west part of the northern gallery was erected, and under Napoléon III the main wings were completed.

In 1793 the Musée de la République was opened in the Louvre, which, with a change of name, has remained the national art gallery and museum ever since. In 1810 the wedding feast of Napoléon and Marie-Louise was celebrated in the Salon Carrée. The building was attacked during the revolutions of 1830 and 1848, and in 1871 it was set on fire by the Communards, though serious damage was limited to the library: but see Palais des Tuileries, p 122.

The Louvre's history is well illustrated and explained in several rooms devoted to the subject, which lie just east of the Hall Napoléon (mezzanine level) below the Pyramid entrance; see Rte 15.

The Louvre consists of two main divisions: the Old Louvre, comprising the buildings surrounding the Cour du Louvre (or Cour Carrée); and the New Louvre, the 19C buildings north and south of the Cour Napoléon, together with their extensions to the west. It is proposed to call the whole, entirely renovated, the Grand Louvre.

By 1981 the museum was extremely short of space, for both visitors and workshops, and so the north wing, occupied by the Ministry of Finance since 1871, was handed back. An ambitious project has been under way since February 1983, when M. Mitterrand approved the plan proposed by Ieoh Ming Pei (a Chinese-born American architect). To overcome the problems of light and space (being so close to the Seine it was impractical to excavate more than 8m below ground, so giving insufficient height for such a huge area), Pei designed the glass pyramid because it takes up less space than conventional building shapes and the glass reflects and refracts the light. Apart from continuing restoration of the fabric and façades of the Palais du Louvre itself, which is expected to be completed by late 1996, and with the redesigning of the Jardin des Tuileries in due course, it comprises the following transformations.

Firstly, the Cour Carrée has been excavated, to expose the foundations of the medieval fortress and the palace of Charles V, now called the 'Crypte Philippe Auguste'; see p 129.

In a central position in the Cour Napoléon, further west, between the Pavillon Denon and the Pavillon Richelieu, rises a glass **Pyramid**, 30m square and 20m high, beyond a lead equestrian statue of Louis XIV (1988; after Bernini). (There has been some criticism that the pyramid incon-

Looking into the pyramidal entrance to the Musée du Louvre

trovertibly interrupts the Classical proportions and profile of the palace.) It is flanked by three subsidiary pyramids and seven fountains with basins of Brittany granite. From an entrance on its west side, steps and an escalator descend into a large well or Entrance Vestibule; see Rte 15. From here passages lead to the basements to the Cour Carrée, to the South Wing of the Louvre, and similarly to the North Wing, into which the museum will expand. Direct access will be provided between the adjacent métro station (Palais-Royale) and the Louvre. From the west side of the vestibule a passage will lead to extensive underground car and coach parks beyond the foundations of the Arc de Triomphe du Carrousel, entered from the now subterranean Av. du Gén. Lemonnier. Below the Pl. du Carrousel and Cour Napoléon will be a complex providing space for the '*reserves*' of the Louvre, studios for the restoration of works of art, service areas and other facilities. A section of the fortifications of Charles V, which came to light during excavations, will be preserved. An inverted glass pyramid—in the form of a suspended prism—will provide daylight for this area.

Further information on work in progress, or completed, will be given in the next edition of this Guide. Meanwhile, until the contents of each department of the Louvre have been redistributed—which may take several years—the visitor must expect a certain amount of confusion, nor should you be surprised at the unkempt condition of most of its rooms awaiting restoration.

On the west side of the restored and cleaned Cour Carrée, to the south of the Pavillon Sully, is the oldest visible part of the early 16C Palace, by Lescot, with sculptural decorations by Jean Goujon and Paul Ponce. The north half of the west façade, and part of the north façade, were designed by Lemercier in imitation of Lescot; the caryatids on the Pavillon Sully are after Sarazin. The remainder of the court was built by Le Vau after 1660.

The top storeys on the north, east and south sides, out of keeping with Lescot's attic, were added in the 17–18C, to bring them up to the height of the great Colonnade of 52 Corinthian columns and pilasters that now forms the exterior east façade (facing St.-Germain l'Auxerrois; see Rte 19). The work of Claude Perrault (1667–70), it was designed without due regard to former dimensions, and to give this east façade its correct proportions, a moat was excavated in 1966–67, and the terreplein previously envisaged was added. During these works the base was of an earlier façade, begun by Le Vau (in collaboration with Perrault), was uncovered and abandoned when Colbert became superintendent of the building.

The Galerie du Bord de l'Eau, the long south façade flanking the Seine, was the work of Pierre Chambiges, architect to Catherine de Médicis, and Thibaut Métezeau, as far as the Pavillon de Lesdiguières. Jacques du Cerceau was responsible for the prolongation of this wing, largely rebuilt in 1863–68.

The building of the New Louvre (north and south of the Cour Napoléon) was undertaken by Visconti in 1852, who soon after died of apoplexy, and the work was carried on by Lefuel (who made several radical modifications in its decoration), and completed in 1871. The north side, known as the Aile Richelieu, had until 1989 been occupied by the intrusive Ministère des Finance, whose functionaries have now been transferred to a new building at Bercy. This long overdue move has enabled the wing to be extensively rebuilt, renovated and adapted to accommodate the enlarged Musée du Louvre; see Rte 15.

Three bridges cross the Seine from the Louvre to the Quai Voltaire. To the west is the Pont Royal, a five-arched bridge by Père F. Romain and Gabriel (1685–89); the last pillar on either bank has a hydrographic scale indicating the low-water mark (zero; only 24m above sea-level), besides various flood-marks.

The Pont du Carrousel (1834; rebuilt in 1939) retains four seated figures by Petitot and Pradier from the original structure.

The pedestrian Pont des Arts was built of cast iron by Cessart and Dillon in 1801–03, deriving its name from the 'Palais des Arts' as the Louvre was then called. It was rebuilt in a similar style to the original in 1983–84, having been dismantled for several years.

15   The Musée du Louvre

METROS: Tuileries, Palais-Royal, Louvre, Pont-Neuf.

The exterior of the Palais du Louvre, and its architectural history, is described in Rte 14.

The galleries of the Musée du Louvre are open Wed.–Mon. 09.00–18.00; until 21.45 on Mon. and Wed.

The main entrance of the ****MUSEE DU LOUVRE** is now situated on the west side of the glass Pyramid sited in the centre of the Cour Napoléon. This courtyard is flanked by three blocks of buildings which are named on the orientation plaques within the museum: SULLY (the four sides of the Cour Carrée), to the east; DENON (to the south); and RICHELIEU (to the north); see plan.

The Pyramid is reached at street level from the west, from the Cour Carrée and from the Passage Richelieu (between the Cour Marly and Cour Puget). A spiral stair, an escalator and a lift (for the handicapped) descend from the entrance below the Pyramid to the **Hall Napoléon**, the main reception area, which may be entered also from an escalator descending from the Passage Richelieu (and in due course directly from the métro Palais-Royale), and from the parking area below the Jardins du Carrousel.

The reception area is on the lower level, with an information desk giving details of times of lectures, guided tours (in English), etc. There are also cloakrooms, a restaurant and a café, a post office, exchange facilities and an auditorium.

At the south-west corner is the museum bookshop where catalogues and books—not necessarily concerned with the collections of the Louvre—may be bought. Adjacent is a section selling postcards and slides of objects in the Musées Nationaux. Close by is the Chalcographie du Musée, where an extensive range of prints, many of them from the original plates, is for sale.

On an upper mezzanine level are displayed *moulages* or casts—in bronze, resin or plaster—which may be bought, together with replicas of jewellery (of very fine quality, and priced accordingly), and copies of other objects from the national collections.

This upper level, reached also by escalators, provides direct access to the departments of the Louvres in the sections Sully, Denon and, in due course, Richelieu.

Hand cameras are admitted without charge but a special ticket is required for those with tripods. The use of flash is prohibited.

In outline, the seven departments of the museum are or will be distributed as follows:

A. Paintings: French School on the second floor of SULLY; Dutch, Flemish, English Schools and some early French paintings will be transferred to the second floor of RICHELIEU; Italian and Spanish Schools will remain on the first floor of DENON, together with a few of the very large French paintings of the Renaissance.

To give some indication of the amount of space which will be available once the reorganisation has taken place, the number of paintings on display will be 4100, compared with 2050 in1988. Those of the French Schools will be 1830 (previously 984); Italian Schools 780 (380); Dutch and Flemish 1200 (540); Spanish 85 (60); German 85 (45); and English and others 120 (40).

B. Cabinet des Dessins (drawings) will remain on the first floor of the Aile de Flore, extending west from DENON.

C. Greek, Etruscan and **Roman Antiquities:** the larger sculptures will remain in the Cour du Sphinx (east end of DENON), and in the south-west corner of the ground floor of SULLY. Roman copies of Greek sculpture will probably be moved to the Salle des Cariatids on the ground floor of DENON. Smaller objects and ceramics will be displayed in the Campana Gallery (south wing of SULLY) and in the Clarac Gallery (south end of west wing).

D. Egyptian Antiquities: larger objects will be in the east wing and south east corner of the ground floor of SULLY, with smaller objects on the first floor.

E. Oriental Antiquities: on the north wing of the north west-corner of the ground floor of SULLY, with the Assyrian and Mesopotamian sections on the ground floor of the Cour Khorsabad, at the east end of RICHELIEU, together with collections from Persia, and probably Islamic collections on the basement of the Pavillon Marengo (SULLY).

F. Objets d'Art: in the northern half of the first floor of SULLY, extending into the first floor of RICHELIEU. The ostentatiously decorated Second Empire salons, known as those of the Duc de Morny, on the first floor of this wing and which miraculously escaped the fire in May 1871, have been restored. Several huge Renaissance tapestries will also be displayed on this floor.

G. Sculptures: the larger French sculptures will be moved to the ground floor of RICHELIEU, including the Cours Marly and Puget, which will be glazed over. Italian sculptures will be displayed in the ground and mezzanine floors at the north-west corner of DENON.

Of particular interest are the two galleries on either side of the passage leading east from the mezzanine floor of the Pyramid entrance devoted to the *History of the Louvre, entering the right-hand rooms first. The passage (at a central point in which are re-sited reliefs of 1559–65, attributed to Jean Goujon) continues towards the **Crypte Philippe Auguste**; see below.

Notable are the ten maquettes made by Remi Munier and Sophie

Polonovsky, which explain the growth of the fortress and palace, and the paintings (some imaginary, of the palace in ruins) by Hubert Robert.

Passing below the west wing of the Pavillon Sully, you enter the Fossé Charles V, a moat surrounding the foundations of the two surviving walls of the medieval fortress, forming its north and east sides, which now stand below the south-west corner of the Cour Carrée. This outer moat was filled in by Lemercier in 1624 and by Le Vau in 1660. The Tour du Milieu is seen first, which like the other, shows considerable batter. Beyond is the Tour de la Taillerie and the basements of the twin towers forming the eastern entrance of the former Louvre, and the support for its drawbridge. These are part of the castle extended by Charles V (1364–80), as depicted in the miniature of 'October' in the 'Trés Riches Heures' of the Duc de Berry (c 1415) reproduced, together with a maquette, in an adjoining room. The circular keep of the earlier fort, established at the turn of the 13C by Philippe Auguste, which formed a quadrilateral 70m x 77m, was razed, and the moat surrounding it was filled in in 1528. Skirting the foundations of this keep (15m in diameter and 7m high and formerly 30m high), you enter a vaulted basement room below the present Salle des Cariatides, once the Salle des Gardes. Some of the extensive archaeological finds (c 25,000) extracted from this site and from the Cour Napoléon, are displayed. The area was excavated and the walls strengthened in 1984–87, and the moats given ceilings to sustain this south-west corner of the Cour Carrée.

At the far end of the moat is the entrance to the Crypte du Sphinx, in the basement of the Pavillon des Arts, giving access to parts of the Egyptian, and Greek and Roman Antiquities; see pp 142 and 140.

The approximate position of each department is indicated on the Plan of the Louvre (p 131) by the letters A, B, C, etc.

History of the collections. The nucleus of the royal art collection was formed by François I. At his request Leonardo da Vinci spent the last few years of his life in France (dying at Amboise in 1519). Henri II and Catherine de Médicis carried on the tradition; Louis XIV made some notable additions to his collection of Old Masters, and Louis XVI acquired some important paintings of the Spanish and Dutch Schools. During the 18C the Academie de Peinture et de Sculpture (founded in 1648) had a permanent exhibition in six salons of the Louvre, and also held annual exhibitions of the works of its members here. These, during the years 1759–81, were the subject of Diderot's 'Salons' (written at the suggestion of Baron Grimm), which set a standard for all subsequent art criticism. William Hazlitt spent four months in Paris during the winter of 1802–03 copying paintings in the Louvre.

In 1793 the Musée de la République was opened to the public, and during the next few years a large number of the most famous paintings of Europe—spoils of conquest by the victorious Republican and Napoleonic armies—were exhibited here; although after 1815 the French government was obliged to restore some works of art to their former owners. Under Louis XVIII, the Vénus de Milo and over a hundred pictures were acquired.

In 1848 the museum became the property of the State and an annual grant was made for the purchase of works of art, and these have been supplemented subsequently by private bequests. During the years 1939–45 the collections were dispersed throughout the country, for the sake of security. There have been a number of changes in layout during post-war decades, and the long drawn-out process of reorganisation continues: see below.

It is very easy to underestimate the size of the Musée du Louvre, and only the most indefatigable will even attempt to visit all departments at any one time. Most visitors will have their own priorities and should plan accordingly. The picture galleries themselves are enough for one day.

MUSÉE DU LOUVRE

Historical

Parts constructed under

- François I -Henri II
- Charles IX-Henri III
- Henri IV
- Louis XIII
- Louis XIV
- 19th Century

Departments of the Louvre

- **A** Paintings
- **B** Drawings
- **C** Greek & Roman Antiquities
- **D** Egyptian Antiquities
- **E** Oriental Antiquities
- **F** Objets d'Art
- **G** Sculpture

▶ Entrances

Historical

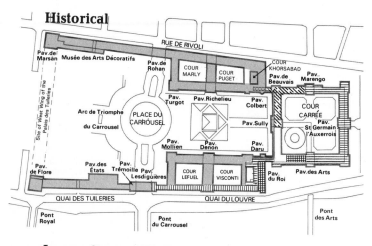

Lower Ground Floor

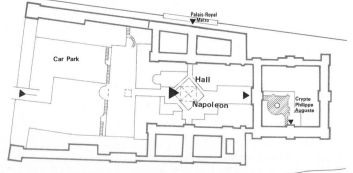

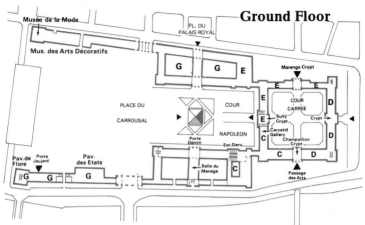

Ground Floor

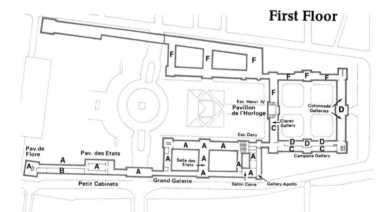

First Floor

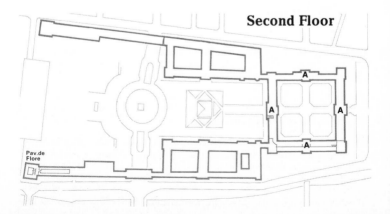

Second Floor

It is perhaps worth mentioning here the more important analogous or supplementary collections in Paris, which will interest the visitor to the Departments of the Louvre itself: the Musée d'Orsay; Petit-Palais; the Cabinet des Médailles of the Bibliothéque Nationale; Musée des Arts Décoratifs; the Musées Guimet, Cernuschi and d'Ennery (for Oriental Antiquities); the Musée de Cluny; and the Musées Carnavalet, Nissim de Camondo and Cognacq-Jay.

Among the more important collections in the immediate environs of Paris are those at Versailles, St.-Germain-en-Laye and Ecouen; and further afield, Chantilly and Fontainebleau, see Rtes 34, 35, 37, 39 and 40 respectively.

Note. Work is in progress on perhaps the most drastic reorganisation the Musée du Louvre has yet experienced. Many departments, or large sections of them, are likely to be closed for months at a time, as 80 per cent of the objects have been or will be moved from their previous positions.

In view of this general upheaval, it has been decided, reluctantly—with certain exceptions—not to attempt to describe the contents of each room, but rather to give some idea of the range of works which may be seen by listing representative items of outstanding quality or interest in each department and, in the section devoted to paintings, to sub-divide them into their various Schools. However unsatisfactory this may be, there appears to be little alternative at present, but it is hoped that by the time the next edition of this Blue Guide is published, the dust might have settled and a more detailed description can again be given. Many of the 19C canvases have been transferred to the Musée d'Orsay (see Rte 9) and replaced by others at present out on loan to other museums, by new acquisitions or by those in '*rèserve*'. Meanwhile, the visitor will be directed to those Departments, or parts of them, open to the public.

The plan is to separate the various disparate departments, which at present too often impinge on each other, and in the case of the paintings, to distribute them in chronological order, divided into Schools, which may then be studied without the intrusion of works of other Schools or periods.

Certain rooms, such as the Chambre à Alcôve and Chambre de Parade, retain restored panelling originally in Henri II's apartments in the Louvre; the vestibule adjacent to the former contains 17C *boiseries* from the Queen's Pavilion of the Château de Vincennes.

A. Paintings

The new rooms devoted to the **French School** of painting—displayed in roughly historical order—are on the second floor of the Cour Carrée (SULLY) and are reached from the Escalier Henri II in its west wing.

R1. Anon. (c 1350), Portrait of Jean I (Le Bon; 1319–64); grisaille of Le Parement de Narbonne (c 1375); and two sections of the Retable de Thouzon (School of Avignon, c 1410).

R2. *Henri Bellechose*, Retable of St. Denis (1415–16); *Jean Hey* (the Maître de Moulins), Portraits of Pierre II, Duc de Bourbon, Anne of Beaujeu, his wife, and their daughter Suzanne, and of Madeleine de Bourgogne; *Josse Lieferinxe* (fl. 1493–1505), Calvary, and Adoration of the Child; *Jean Fouquet* (c 1420–81), Portraits of Guillaume Juvenel des Ursins and of Charles VII of France; *Nicolas Froment* (fl. 1461–83), The Matheron

Diptych, with portraits of King René of Anjou and his wife Jeanne de Laval; *Enguerrand Quarton* (fl. 1444–66), The Pietà of Villeneuve-lès-Avignon; late 15C School of Avignon, Three Prophets; *anon.*, Retable of the Parlement of Paris (c 1455; note background); the *Maître de Coëtuvy* (fl. 1450–75), The raising of Lazarus.

R3. *Jean Cousin the Elder* (c 1490–c 1560), Eva Prima Pandora; *First School of Fontainebleau*, Diana the huntress (c 1550–60), and Toilet of Venus; *Jean Clouet* (c 1485–c 1540) and ? François Clouet, Portrait of François I (c 1530); *François Clouet* (c 1543–72), Portrait of Pierre Quthe, apothecary (1562); *attrib. François Quesnel* (c 1543–1616), Portrait of Henri III; *Nicolò dell'Abbate*, Harvest scene; *anon.*, One-eyed flautist (1566).

R4, a room devoted to a remarkable collection of small portraits, largely anon., and many from the collection of Roger de Gaignières (1642–1715), which included 1096 items. Among them are portraits of Jean Babou de la Bourdasière, Michel de l'Hospital, Catherine de Médicis, and also The ball at the wedding of Anne, Duc de Joyeuse; Pourbus the Younger (1569/70–1622), Henri IV; *François Clouet*, Elisabeth of Austria (wife of Charles IX, painted in 1571), Charlotte de Roye, and an Unknown woman; attrib. to Clouet, Claude de Beaune de Seblençay; and several by *Corneille de Lyon* (1505–74) or his school, among them of Pierre Aymeric.

R5. Second School of Fontainebleau (late 16C), a Portrait of Gabrielle d'Estrées and one of her sisters (? the Duchesse de Villers); and adjacent, anon., Double portrait (c 1610); *attrib. Daniel Dumonstier* (1574–1646), Portrait of a lady.

R6. *Nicolas Tournier* (1590–1639), Crucifixion, with the Virgin, Mary Magdalen, St. John and St. Francis de Paule; *Valentin de Boulogne* (1591–1632), Tavern scene, The Innocence of Suzanne, The Judgement of Solomon, The fortune-teller, and Concert scenes; *Nicolas Regnier* (1591–1667), The fortune-teller; *Simon Vouet* (1590–1649), Louis XIII between France and Navarre, and St. Guillaume d'Aquitaine; *Eustache le Sueur* (1616–55), Reunion of friends; *Philippe de Champaigne* (1602–74). Portraits of Louis XIII, and of Richelieu.

R7 is devoted to *Nicolas Poussin* (1594–1665), Self-portrait (1650), and numerous Arcadian scenes, more notable among which are Orpheus and Eurydice, and Rebecca at the well.

R8. *Georges de la Tour* (1593–1652), The Card-sharper, Joseph the carpenter, St. Irene nursing St. Sebastian, The Adoration of the shepherds, Mary Magdalen watching a candle, St. Thomas.

Still lifes by *Sébastien Stoskopff* (1597–1657), *Jacques Linard* (c 1600–45), *Pierre Dupui* (1610–82), *Lubin Baugin* (1612–62), and *Louise Moillon* (1610–96), also her The fruit and vegetable sellers.

Louis Nain (c 1600–48), or possibly his brother Antoine, the Peasants' meal, The Forge, The hay-wain, The Corps de Garde, and others; *anon.* Reunion of amateurs; *Sébastein Bourdon* (1616–71), The soldiers' halt, Beggars, Interior scene; and four small scenes by *Claude Gellée*, better known as Claude Lorrain (c 1602–82).

R9. *Claude Lorrain*, View of the Campo Vaccion, Rome, and several landscapes and luminous mythological port scenes; *Poussin*, Summer, and

Winter; *Pierre Patel the Elder* (c 1605–76) Landscape with ruins, etc.

R10. Huge religious paintings by *Le Sueur, Poussin, Laurent de la Hyre* (1606–56) and *Charles le Brun* (1619); and *Philippe de Champaigne*, The Prévôt des Marchands, Male portrait, Jean-Antoine de Mesme, Robert Arnauld d'Andilly, Crucifixion, and The artist's daughter with Mère Catherine-Agnès Arnauld, Ex voto of 1662; *Sébastien Bourdon*, Portrait of Descartes?

R11. Four huge paintings (each 12m x 5m) by *Le Brun* of the Battles of Alexander, Equestrian portrait of Chancellor Séguier escorted by pages, Meleager and Atalanta; *Nicolas de Largilllierre* (1656–1746), Portrait of Le Brun in his studio.

R12. Huge paintings by *Jean Jouvenet* (1644–1717), including The Miracle of the Fishes, and The Descent from the Cross; *Largillierre*, Male portrait, perhaps of Jacques de Laage; *Hyacinthe Rigaud* (1659–1743), Portrait of Louis XIV in 1701; *François de Troy* (1645–1730), Charles Mouton playing the lute.

At the time of printing, the eastern and southern wings of SULLY had not yet been prepared for the hanging of the rest of the paintings of the French school, but many, if not all, of the paintings listed below will be displayed in the following rooms, together with a number of others, which it is not at this stage possible to specify. A few of the larger canvases may remain in the north side of the first floor of DENON.

Among the paintings on view may be: *Joseph Parrocel* (1646–1704), Louis XIV's army crossing the Rhine; *Hyacinthe Rigaud*, The sculptor Martin Desjardins, Portrait of the artist's mother; *Nicolas de Largillierre*, Self-portrait, with his wife and daughter; *François Desportes* (1661–1743), Self-portrait 'en chasseur'; *Jean-Baptiste-Siméon Chardin* (1699–1779), The skate, 'Le souffleur', Boy with a teetotum, Man with a violin, and still-lifes, including Hare and powder-flask, and genre scenes; *Antoine Watteau* (1684–1721), Gilles, the clown; *Jean-Honoré Fragonard* (1732–1806), Two figures: Inspiration and Study, Portrait of Marie-Madeleine Guimard; *Jean-Baptiste Oudry* (1686–1755), Bittern and partridge watched by a white dog; *Louis Tocqué* (1696–1772), The painter Louis Galloche; *Joseph Silfrein-Duplessis* (1725–1802), Allegrain, the sculptor; *Pierre Subleyras* (1699–1749), The Abbé Cesare Benvenuti, Portrait presumed to be of Joseph Baretti.

It is likely that a selection of pastel portraits will be displayed in the central section of this wing.

Joseph Duplessis (1725–1802), Portrait of Joseph-Marie Vien, the artist; *Hubert Robert* (1733–1808), The Pont du Gard, The Triumphal Arch at Orange, The Maison Carrée, and Temple of Diana (Nîmes); *Elisabeth Vigée-Lebrun* (1755–1842), Portrait of Hubert Robert; and examples of the work of *François Boucher* (1703–70), *Nicolas Lancret* (1690–1743) and *Jean-Baptiste Greuze* (1725–1805), including his Broken pitcher, and Portrait of Claude Henri Watelet.

Claude-Joseph Vernet (1714–89), The Ponte Rotto; *Jean-Baptiste Perronneau* (1715–83), Mme de Sorquainville; *Jacques-Louis David* (1748–1825), M. Sériziat, His wife and son, Mme Trudaine, The Marquise d'Orvilliers, Alexandre Lenoir, Mme Récamier in a familiar pose, Pope Pius VII, Coronation of Napoléon I (by Pope Pius VII in Notre-Dame, 2 December 1804); *Baron Antoine-Jean Gros* (1771–1835), Portrait of Madeleine Pasteur, Bonaparte at the bridge of Arcole (1796), Christine Boyer, first wife of Lucien

Bonaparte, Bonaparte visiting the plague-striken at Jaffa, and at Eylau (with portraits of Berthier, Murat, Soult and Davoust); *Baron François Gérard* (1770–1837), Portraits of his wife, of Comtesse Regnauld de Saint-Jean d'Angély, and of J.-B. Isabey; *Jean-Auguste-Dominique Ingres* (1780–1867), Portraits of the Rivière family, and of L.-F. Bertin, senior, of C.-J.-L. Cordier, The Turkish bath, 'La grande odalisque', 'La baigneuse', and the composer Cherubini; *Pierre-Paul Prud'hon* (1758–1823), The Empress Joséphine at Malmaison; *Théodore Géricault* (1791–1824), Officer of the Chasseurs de la Garde, The raft of the 'Medusa', The Vendéen, Equestrian portraits, including horses at Epsom; *Eugène Delacroix* (1789–1863), Self-portrait, Hamlet and Horatio, The orphan at the cemetery, Portrait of Chopin, Liberty leading the people (or 'Les Barricades'), Scenes of the massacre of Chios, Algerian women at home; *Alexandre Decamps* (1803–60), Defeat of the Cimbri; *Gustave Courbet* (1819–77), The wave, Portrait of Pierre-Joseph Proudhon; *Joseph Berger* (1798–1870), Male portrait; *Marie-Guillemine Benoist* (1768–1826), A black woman; *Henri-François Riesener* (1767–1828), Portrait of Maurice Quay; Martin Drölling (1752–1817), Kitchen interior; *A.-L.-C. Pagnest* (1790–1819), Portrait of Nanteuil-Lanorville; *P.-H. Valenciennes* (1750–1819), Views of Rome and the Campagna; *Louis Boilly* (1761–1845), Genre scenes; *A.-E. Michallon* (1796–1822), Landscapes; *Eugène Isabey* (1803–86), The wooden bridge.

It is possible that the paintings in the Moreau-Nélaton Donation (at present in the Musée d'Orsay) may be hung in the southern part of the west wing of SULLY. For later paintings of the French School, see Musée d'Orsay, Rte 9.

Some of the more important works from other schools of paintings are listed below as it not possible to describe them room by room at present.

Flemish and Dutch Schools

Frans Hals, Portraits of Paulus van Berestyn, and of his third wife, Catherine Both van der Eem; The van Berestyn family, now attributed to Pierre Soutman; also by Hals, The gipsy girl; *Johannes Cornelisz Verspronck*, Portrait of Anna van Schoonhoven; *Salomon van Ruysdael*, The landing-stage, Still life with a turkey; *Jan van Goyen*, View of Dordrecht. *Rembrandt*: Self-portrait, bareheaded; another wearing a toque and with an architectural background; and a third with a toque and gold chain; a fourth self-portrait is of the artist in his old age (1660) at his easel; Christ at Emmaus, Portrait of Hendrikje Stoffels, Bathsheba bathing, St. Matthew inspired by an angel, The meditating philosopher, and Carcase of an ox.

Albert Cuyp, Cavaliers; *Allart van Everdingen*, Landscape with hunters and fishermen; *Paul Potter*, Horses at a cottage door; *Jacob van Ruysdael*, The bush; *Philips Wouwerman*, Landscape with a cart; *Karel Dujardin*, Italian charlatans; *Jan van der Heyden*, The Town Hall, Amsterdam; Ferdinand Bol, The mathematician; *Frans Post*, Tropical landscapes painted in Brazil; *Cornelis van Poelenburgh*, Orpheus charming the beasts, Ruins of Rome with the Castel Sant'Angelo, etc.; *Willem Claesz Heda*, The dessert; *Willem Cornelisz Duyster*, Robbers; *Pieter Codde*, Dancing-lesson; *Hendrik Pot*, Copy of Daniel Mytens' portrait of Charles I of England; *David Teniers*, The Seven Works of Mercy, 'Les joueurs de Hoquet', Winter scene, Tavern interior; *Frans Francken the Younger*, The Prodigal Son; *Adrien Brouwer*, The inn, Landscape at dusk; *Joos van Craesbeek*, The smoker (? self-portrait); *Denis van Alsloot*, Winter landscape; *Paul Bril*, Landscape with a pond, Fishing; *Gotthard de Wedig*, Still-life; *Roelant Savery*, Polish mercenaries in the forest; *Adriaen Pietersz van de Venne*, Celebrating the truce of 1609; *Jan Brueghel the Younger* (Velours), The battle of Arbela, Virgin and Child with a garland of flowers, Air and Earth (part of a series of the four Elements: Fire and Water are in the Ambrosiana Museum, Milan), and Landscapes.

Joos van Cleve, Triptych of the Descent from the Cross, St. Francis of Assisi receiving the stigmata, A Dominican offering his heart to the Virgin and Child, and The Last Supper; *Master of the St. Bartholomew Altarpiece*, Descent from the Cross; *Master of the View of St. Gudule*, Pastoral instruction; *Thierry Bouts*, Descent from the Cross, Virgin and Child; *Gérard de Saint-Jean*, Raising of Lazarus; *Jan van Eyck*, Chancellor Nicolas Rolin before the Virgin; *Rogier van der Weyden*, Salvator Mundi, triptych of the Braque family; *Petrus Christus*, Pietà; *Memling*, The Mystic Marriage of St. Catherine, with the donor praying under the protection of St. John the Baptist, Portrait of an old lady, The martyrdom of St. Sebastian, Resurrection of Christ, Ascension, The Virgin of Jacques Floreins; *Gérard David*, Triptych of Mary, Marriage at Cana; *Cornelis van Dalem*, Farmyard in winter; *Brueghel the Elder*, Beggars; the Brunswick Monogramist, Sacrifice of Abraham; *Lucas van Leyden*, The card-dealer, Lot and his daughters; Mabuse, Diptych of Jean Carondelet (Chancellor of Flanders) and the Virgin; *Quentin Metsys*, Moneylender and his wife, The dead Christ; *Van Orley*, Portrait of an old man; *Joachim Patinir* (or Patenier), St. Jerome in the desert; *Hieronymus Bosch*, The Ship of Fools; *Lucas van Valckenborgh*, The Tower of Babel; *Brueghel the Elder*, contemporary copy of The blind men; *Antonio Moro* (Anthonis Mor van Dashorst), Cardinal de Granvella's dwarf, A nobleman in the Cardinal's entourage; *anon*. Portrait of a lady of quality; *Nicolaes Berchem*, Landscape with animals; *Gérard Dou*, Woman with dropsy; *Gabriel Metsu*, The female toper, Soldier and young girl, The grass-market at Amsterdam; *Nicolaes Maes*, Bathing scene; *Gerard Ter Borch*, The military gallant, Reading lesson, The concert, Portrait of a man in black; *Pieter de Hooch*, Card-players, 'La Buveuse'; *Jan van der Heyden*, The Herengracht in Amsterdam; Adriaen Coorte, Shells; Vermeer, The lacemaker; *Adriaen van Ostade*, The schoolmaster; *Michiel Sweerts*, Young man and matchmaker.

Van Dyck, Portraits of the Marchesa Spinola Doria, Francisco de Moncada, Conde de Osuna and Gov.-Gen. of the Spanish Netherlands, the Duke of Richmond, Charles Louis, Elector Palatine, and his brother Prince Rupert, later Duke of Cumberland, Charles I of England, A gentleman with his sword, A lady of quality with her daughter, and A gentleman with his daughter.

Rubens, Kermesse (the village fair), Portraits of his wife Hélène Fourment with two of her children, her sister Suzanne, and Hélène Fourment descending from her coach, Baron Henri de Vicq—a portrait of the ambassador who obtained for the artist the commission to paint the Medici canvases (see below), The Adoration of the Magi; Jan Fyt, Still life with game; Victor Boucquet, Standard-bearer; Jordaens, The king drinks; David Teniers the Younger, Riverside tavern.

Also by Rubens, the 21 large allegorical paintings depicting the Life of Marie de Médicis, designed in 1622–25 to decorate the Luxembourg Palace, and executed with the aid of his pupils. The paintings follow a chronological sequence, from Marie's birth in April 1575 to the reconciliation with her son, Louis XIII, in 1619. These will be placed in a new room on the second floor of Richelieu.

Paintings from the De Croy Bequest include *Gerrit van Honthorst*, The dentist, and (after Van Honthorst) Portrait of Frédéric-Henri of Nassau; *Samuel van Hoogstraten*, The slippers; *Jan Verspronck*, Young woman from Haarlem; *Joos van Craesbeek*, Spring; *Barent Avercamp* and *Jan van Goyen*, Skating scenes.

German School

Hans Baldung, A knight, a young woman and Death; *Master of the Legend of St. Ursula*, Ambassadors at the court of St. Ursula; *anon.* painter from Cologne, Pietà of St. Germain-des-Prés; *Luger Tom Ring the Elder*, Sybil; also a fine anon. (L.C.Z.) Flagellation; *Hans Holbein the Younger*, Portraits of Sir Henry Wyatt, Anne of Cleves, Erasmus (painted for Sir Thomas More), Nicolas Kratzer (Henry VIII's astronomer), and William Warham, Archbishop of Canterbury; *Dürer*, Self-Portrait (1493); *Wolf Huber*, The grieving Christ; Lucas Cranach the Elder, Venus in a landscape, A young girl (?Magdalena Luther); *Hans Maler*, Mathäus Schwartz. Also studies for the decoration of the Ducal Palace at Urbino by Just de Gand (Justus of Ghent) and Pedro Berruguete.

Spanish School

Jaime Huguet, The Flagellation, and The Entombment; *Barnat Martorell*, Four episodes from the life of St. George; *El Greco*, Crucifixion with two donors (signed in Greek characters), St. Louis of France; *Ribera*, St. Paul the hermit, The Entombment, Adoration of the shepherds, and Club-footed boy; *Zurbaran*, St. Bonaventura at the Council of Lyon, The saint's corpse exposed, and Sta. Apollina; *Murillo*, Legend of San Diego, known as 'the angels' kitchen' (one of a series of 16 painted for the Franciscan convent at Seville, another of which has been acquired by the Louvre); *Carreño*, Foundation of the Trinitarian Order; *Velázquez*, Mariana of Austria, her daughter the Infanta Margarita, and the Infanta María Teresa; *Francisco Collantes*, The Burning Bush; *Murillo*, Young beggar; *Luis Eugenio Meléndez*, Self-portrait, and Still-life; Goya, The unequal wedding, Christ in the Garden of Olives, Woman with a fan, portraits of Ferdinand Guillemardet, Mariana Waldstein, Marquesa de Santa Cruz, and Evaristo Pérez de Castro.

Portuguese School

Anon., Man with a glass of wine.

Italian Schools

14–15C. *Cimabue*, Madonna with angels; Giotto, St. Francis receiving the stigmata; an anon. 14C Florentine Calvary; *Bernardo Daddi*, Annunciation; *Bartola di Maestro Fredi*, Presentation in the Temple; Barnaba da Modena, Madonna and Child; *Lorenzo Veneziano*, The Madonna enthroned; 12 *anon.* Venetian scenes from the Life of the Virgin; *Simone Martini*, Christ bearing the Cross; *Guido da Siena*, Nativity, and Presentation in the Temple; *Pisanello*, A princess of the House of Este; *Gentile da Fabriano*, Presentation; Jacopo Bellini, Madonna and Child with donor; *Benozzo Gozzoli*, The triumph of St. Thomas Aquinas; *Alessio Baldovinetti*, Madonna adoring the Child; *Paolo Uccello*, Battle of San Romano, 1432; *Fra Angelico*, Coronation of the Virgin, The martyrdom of St. Cosmas and St. Damian; *Sano di Pietro*, Five episodes from the dream of St. Jerome; the

Master of the Observance, St. Anthony; *Sassetta*, Madonna and Child with angels, St. Anthony of Padua and St. John the Evangelist, and The miraculous deliverance of the poor incarcerated in the prisons of Florence; *School of Fra Filippo Lippi*, Nativity; *Botticelli*, Madonna and Child surrounded by angels, Portrait of a young man, 'The Madonna of the Guidi of Faenza', Madonna and Child with St. John the Baptists; *Mantegna*, St. Sebastian, and Calvary; *Antonello da Messina*, The condottiere; *Catena*, Portrait of Giangiorgio Trissino; *Piero della Francesca*, Portrait of Sigismondo Malatesta; *Bernardo Parentino*, Adoration of the Magi; *School of Fra Angelico*, Herod's banquet; *Pesellino*, St. Francis of Assisi receiving the Stigmata, and St. Cosmas and St. Damien nursing the sick; *Signorelli*, Birth of St. John the Baptist; *Bartolomeo di Giovanni*, Marriage of Thetis and Peleus, and Wedding procession; *Ghirlandaio*, The bottlenosed old man and his grandson, The Visitation; *Piero di Cosimo*, Madonna and dove; Perugino, Madonna with saints and angels, and Tondo showing the Madonna and Child with St. Catherine and St John the Baptist; *Giovanni Bellini*, Crucifixion, Resurrection, and Blessing, Portrait of two men, Male portrait; *Carpaccio*, St. Stephen preaching; *Venetian School*, Reception of a Venetian ambassador in an oriental town; *Cima da Conegliano*, Madonna and Child with St. John the Baptist and the Magdalen; *Jacopo de Barbieri*, Madonna at the fountain; *Marco Palmezzano*, Christ supported by angels.

16C. *Veronese's* huge Marriage at Cana; others by Veronese are the so-called 'La belle Nani', a Calvary, and Supper at Emmaus; *Titian*, Lady at her toilet (called 'Alfonso da Ferrara and Laura de' Dianti'), St. Jerome in the desert, Man with a glove, and another Male portrait, Supper at Emmaus, The Entombment, Allegory representing the wife of Alfonso d'Avalos being entrusted to Chastity and Cupid, François I (painted from a medal of the kind the artist never saw), Jupiter and Antiope, known as 'the Venus of the Pardo', and Pastoral concert (once attributed to Giorgione); *Tintoretto*, Susanna and the elders, and Self-portrait (1590); Palma Vecchio, Adoration of the shepherds; *Giulio Romano*, Portrait of Joanna d'Aragón (the face by Raphael); *Andrea del Sarto*, Charity; *Correggio*, The Mystic Marriage of St. Catherine of Alexandria, Jupiter and Antiope; *Lotto*, The woman taken in adultery, Christ bearing the Cross; *Raphael*, St. George, and St. Michael, Portrait of Baldassare Castiglione (author of 'The Courtier'), 'La belle Jardinière', Self-portrait with a friend; *Leonardo da Vinci*, Annunciation, Madonna and Child with St. Anne, The Virgin of the Rocks (1482; probably earlier than the similar composition in London), St. John the Baptist (apparently painted from a female model or worked on later by another hand); School of Leonardo, Bacchus, and the so-called 'La belle ferronnière' (from the chain around her forehead).

A portrait by Leonardo da Vinci, traditionally assumed to be of Mona Lisa Gherardini, third wife of Francesco di Zanobi del Giocondo, hence also 'La Gioconda', or in French, 'La Joconde'.

Leonardo worked intermittently on this portrait between 1503–06. In spite of drastic restoration at different periods, this remains one of the outstanding achievements of the Italian Renaissance. In August 1911 it was stolen from the Salon Carré by a thief disguised as a workman, but was recovered in Florence in December 1913. It has also been claimed that the sitter was Costanza d'Avalos, mistress of Giuliano de' Medici, and that another somewhat similar portrait in a private collection represents Mona Lisa; correctly Monna, the Italian for lady or dame.

17–19Cs. *Caravaggio*, Portrait of Alof de Wignacourt, and The fortune-teller; *Bartolomeo Schedone*, Entombment; *Guido Reni*, St. Sebastian, Ecco Homo; *Domenichino*, Herminia among the shepherds, St. Cecilia; *Pietro da Cortona*, Venus as a huntress appearing to Aeneas; *Carlo Maratta*, Maria-Magdalena Rospigliosi, niece of Pope Clement IX; Lionello Spada, Return of the Prodigal Son; *Bernardo Strozzi*, Holy Family; *Salvator Rosa*, Landscape with hunters; *Paolo Porpora*, Still life; *Aniello Falcone*, Battle scene; Giuseppe Angeli, The little drummer; *Giuseppe-Maria Crespi*, Woman with flea; *Guardi*, eight of 12 scenes depicting festivities organised for the coronation of the Doge Alvise IV Mocenigo, View of the church of SS. Giovanni e Paolo; *Longhi*, The Presentation; *Giovanni Paolo Panini*, Concert in Rome (26 November 1729) to celebrate the birth of the Dauphin Louis to Marie Leczinska and Louis XV, Preparations for festivities in the Piazza Navona; *Michele Marieschi*, View of Santa Maria della Salute, Venice; *Batoni*, Portrait of Charles John Crowle; *Giovanni Battista Lampi*, Count Stanislas Félix Potocki and his sons; *G.-B. Tiepolo*, The Last Supper; *Domenico Tiepolo*, Carnival Scene, and The charlatan.

Among the larger 17–18C canvases are *Annibale Carracci*, The Virgin appearing to St. Luke and St. Catherine, Hunting, and Fishing; *Caravaggio*, Death of the Virgin; *Louis Bréa*, Pietà; and *Guercino*, The raising of Lazarus.

The undispersed Beistégui Collection contains an *anon.* Franco-Flemish Virgin and Child; and *Master of Moulins*, Portrait of the Dauphin Charles Orlando (1494; son of Charles VIII and Anne of Brittany). Among portraits are *François-Hubert Drouais* (1727–75), Anne-Françoise Doré, his wife; *Van Dyck*, A Genoese gentleman (not Livio Odescalchi); *Lawrence*, Mrs Cuthbert; *Zuloaga*, Carlos de Beistégui; *David*, Gén. Bonaparte, sketched near Rivoli (c 1797), M. Mayer, envoy from the Batavian Republic; *Gérard*, Mme Lecref, his cousin; *Ingres*, Mme Panckoucke; and Goya, The Condesa del Carpio, and The Marquesa de Solana.

English School

Ramsay, Lord Elcho; *Gainsborough*, Conversation in the park, Lady Gertrude Alston; *Reynolds*, Master Hare; *Romney*, Sir John Stanley; *Wright of Derby*, The Lake of Nemi; *John Linnell*, Hampstead Heath; *Lawrence*, Charles William Bell, John Julius Angerstein and his wife; *Raeburn*, Capt. Robert Hay of Spott; *Bonington*, The Adriatic; and examples of the work of *John Hamilton Mortimer, Fuseli, Constable, Turner* (including watercolour view of St.-Germain-en-Laye), and *Angelika Kauffmann*.

B. Cabinet de Dessins

The **Cabinet de Dessins** itself is not open to the public, but researchers and connoisseurs (who need a letter of introduction on their first visit) are allowed to study its superb collections, which include some 1200 miniatures, 30,000 engravings and 90,000 drawings.

Although drawings had already existed in the Bibliothèque du Roi, it was not until 1671, when Louis XIV acquired the 5542 drawings (in addition to important paintings) collected by Everard Jabach (died 1695) that the main nucleus of the Royal Collection was formed. To this were added drawings by Le Brun, Mignard and Coypel. By 1730 an inventory included some 8593 works, to which were added some 1300 drawings collected by the great connoisseur Pierre-Jean Mariette. By 1792 some 11,000 drawings were listed, and in the following decades the figure almost doubled (including the Saint Maurice collection, the collection of the Dukes of Modena and of Filippo Baldinucci.

The Codex Vallardi (including a number of drawings by Pisanello) was acquired in 1856 and Jacopo Bellini's sketchbook in 1884. The collection was further enriched by a number of important donations in succeeding years. Among more recent collections acquired by the Cabinet des Dessins have been those of Gustave Caillebotte, Isaac de Camondo, Etienne Moreau-Nélaton, Walter Gay, D. David-Weill, Carle Dreyfus and Baroness Gourgaud.

Approximately 100 pastel portraits are exhibited in rotation, among them: *Leonardo da Vinci*, Isabella d'Este, Duchess of Mantua; *Charles le Brun* (1619–90), Three portraits of Louis XIV; several by *Robert Nanteuil* (c 1623–78); *Joseph Vivien* (1657–1734), the sculptor François Girardon, and the architect Robert de Cotte, among others. *Rosalba Carriera* (1657–1757; who did much to popularise the technique in France), Young girl with a monkey (the model may have been the daughter of financier John Law); *Maurice-Quentin Delatour* (1704–88), Hermann-Maurice, Comte de Saxe, Philibert Orry, Jacques Dimont, and the Marquise de Pompadour; *Perronneau*, Abraham van Robais, The engraver Laurent Cars; *Chardin*, His second wife, Self-portraits, with spectacles, with a green eye-shade, and at his easel.

Other portraits by *Gustav Lundberg, Adélaïde Labille Guiard* (1749–1803), *Joseph Boze* and *John Russell* (1745–1806) may be displayed, together with a representative selection of 19C pastels; later examples may be seen in the Musée d'Orsay; see Rte 9.

C. Greek and Roman Antiquities

The larger objects are now displayed in a series of rooms on the GROUND FLOOR, extending east from the Galerie Denon-Daru; around the Cour du Sphinx and at the south-west corner of the Cour Carrée. The first section is devoted to 7–6 BC sculpture, including the so-called *Dame d'Auxerre* (c 630 BC), of Cretan origin; the *Hera of Samos* (c 570–550 BC), one of the oldest and best authenticated works of island sculpture, inscribed *Cheramues*; the *'Rampin Head'* (6C BC), with a plaster cast of the equestrian figure (in the Acropolis Museum, Athens); bas-reliefs from the architrave of the Temple of Assos (near Troy, Turkey) representing Hercules battling against the Triton, a banquet, a procession of animals and centaurs, etc.

The *'Apollo of Piombino'*, a 5C bronze figure, with copper encrustations—lips and nipples—which was retrieved from the sea near Piombino, Italy, and perhaps a replica of a work by Kanachos; the upper part of the stele *'Exaltation of the Flower'*, from Pharsalus; the torso of *Apollo* (Miletus, Turkey; 5C BC). Fragments of the E frieze of the Parthenon at Athens (5C BC)—the greater part of the frieze, which represents the Panathenaic procession, is in the British Museum; the *'Laborde Head'*, from the pediments of the Parthenon. The so-called *'Kaufmann Head'*, after Praxiteles; the *Venus 'de Milo'*, found in five fragments by a peasant in 1820 on the island of Melos in the Greek archipelago and now regarded as a 2C BC copy after a 4C BC original. The late Hellenistic *'Borghese Warrior'*, signed on the tree-trunk by Agasias (c 100 BC), found at Anzio, Italy, in the 17C. Apollo Sauroktonos (about to kill a lizard), after Praxiteles; the *Aphrodite of Cnidos*; the *'Venus of Arles'*.

Salles des Cariatides, the oldest surviving room in the palace, was built by Pierre Lescot for Henri II, who commissioned Jean Goujon to execute the caryatids supporting the gallery at the far end. Other decoration and the chimney-piece at the near end are by Percier and Fontaine (c 1806). Mary Stuart married François II in this room in 1558, and here Louis XIV washed the feet of 13 poor men on Maundy Thursdays. It contains *Hermes fastening his sandal*, and *Artemis, the huntress*, known as the 'Diana of Versailles', acquired from Rome by François I.

R15. Etruscan antiquities, including five terracotta plaques from Cerveteri, Italy, (c 530 BC); the imposing terracotta *sarcophagus* (also discovered at Cerveteri, by Campana, in 1850), on which, as if on a funeral couch, recline the lifelike figures of a man and his wife represented as if still alive and conversing. The woman wears a cap (tutulus) and a small gorget; the man, bare-footed, is draped. Further examples of Etruscan antiquities, including cinerary urns, bronze figurines, mirrors, jewellery and ceramics, are also displayed.

Roman portraits and reliefs, and busts—among which those of *Agrippa* and *Livia* (in black basalt) are outstanding—frescoes, mosaics, cameos, sarcophagi, etc., are shown adjacent.

On the floor of the **Cour du Sphinx**, with a façade by Le Vau, is a huge mosaic of *The Seasons* (c AD 325) from a villa near Antioch. On the walls, a frieze from the temple of Artemis at Magnesia on the Maeander, depicting a battle between Greeks and Amazons (2C BC); also the *God of the Tiber*, a colossal group found in the 16C.

On the landing of the monumental Escalier Daru stands the **Nike of Samothrace**, or 'Winged Victory'. This imposing statue of Parian marble, the centrepiece of a fountain, was found in the Sanctuary of the Great Gods, on the island of Samothrace, in 1863. Further excavations in 1950 led to the discovery of the mutilated right hand (in a case to the right), and established the probable date of the statue as c 200 BC. The breast and left wing are of plaster.

FIRST FLOOR. Passing through an upper rotunda, you see (right) the wrought-iron gates of c 1650, brought from the Château de Maisons (see Rte 35), which close the Galerie d'Apollon. The gallery, built during the reign of Henri IV, was burnt in 1661 and rebuilt by Le Brun. It is admirably decorated; the central ceiling painting, by Delacroix, depicts Apollo's victory over the Python.

The first room you enter contains the '*Treasure of Boscoreale*', a collection of superbly decorated silver objects discovered in 1895 in a fine state of preservation in a villa overwhelmed by the eruption of Vesuvius in AD 79; two silver masks from the Gallo-Roman '*Treasure of N.-D. d'Allençon*'; and the silver '*Treasure of Graincourt-lès-Havrincourt*'.

Among exhibits of the pre-Hellenic civilisations: pithoi from Knossos (Crete; 1700–1600 BC) and from Thera and Rhodes (14C BC); marble idols from the Cyclades (2500–2000 BC); terracotta and bronze figurines and painted ceramics (Minoan) from Crete (14–12C BC); and funerary objects.

Other impressive collections of Greek and Roman bronzes, jewellery, arms, utensils, etc. are arranged in chronological and geographical groups, outstanding among which are ARCHAIC GREEK ART: a *minotaur*; statuette of *Athene*; a *warrior*; a javelin thrower; and *Silenus* dancing (all 6C BC). Pan and his syrinx. Mirrors, including one in its box decorated with scenes in relief. CLASSICAL GREEK statuettes (5C BC): group of *Lycurgus and the Maenads*; a stag; *Hercules fighting*; *Zeus*; Athlete's head (Greek; 5C BC), found at Benevento, Italy. HELLENISTIC ART: a *crouching Aphrodite*; an hermaphrodite figure; 'Napoléon's cist' (a cylindrical box in which jewels and toilet accessories were kept). ROMAN GAUL: Statuettes and busts: note eyes; bull; boar; a cock found at Lyon. A winged helmet encircled by a gold crown; gladiator's armour; and a collection of jewellery and goldsmiths' work from all the periods and regions covered by other exhibits.

Among the superlative collection a **Antique Pottery** from the 10C BC to the 4C BC, are examples of the Geometric style; Boeotian figurines, etc.; Attic vases found in the Dipylon cemetery (c 800 BC); pottery from the Greek islands; vessels in the 'orientalised' style; pottery from Corinth; Tyrrhenian amphorae, kraters and other vessels; black-figure Attic ceramics; oenochoai and vases in the Attic style, including both black and red figures; coloured terracottas; Attic red-figure pottery (c 500 BC) including a large krater depicting the combat of Hercules and Antaeus, a kylix on which are Eros and Memnon, and an amphora showing Croesus on a pyre; terracotta figurines and statuettes from Tanagra; figurines of the Hellenistic period; and antique glassware.

D. Egyptian Antiquities

The first curator of this department was the great Egyptologist Jean-François Champollion (1790–1832), who in 1826 had acquired the collection of the British Consul-General Henry Salt (1780–1827), to which other collections were added in subsequent decades.

You enter the Crypt du Sphinx first, passing the stele of Antef, first herald in the service of King Thothmes III (1504–1450 BC), and other steles of the 12th Dynasty; the crypt itself contains a stele dedicated by Queen Hatshepsout to her father Thothmes (1530–20 BC); a colossal sphinx in pink granite, from Tanis (Lower Egypt; Old Kingdom).

Among remarkable objects in the collection are a colossal statue of Seti II (19th Dynasty) in red sandstone; the limestone cult chamber of the 'mastaba' or tomb of Akhouthotep, an Egyptian dignitary (c 2500 BC; 5th Dynasty), found at Sakkara: inscribed in the architrave above the door are the occupants' name and titles. Within, the walls are covered with vivid scenes in bas-relief of contemporary life in the Old Kingdom, as well as depicting the funeral of the deceased, some of them among the finest extant examples of the art. The offerings of food and drink were placed on the adjacent table of pink granite.

Among smaller objects from the Egyptian collection are, from the PREHISTORIC AND THINITE PERIODS (4000–2800 BC): schist palettes, for grinding and mixing paints, one decorated with a bull—symbolising the king—pinning an enemy to the ground, and another depicting both imaginary and real animals (giraffes, etc.); a knife from Gebel-el-Arak (c 3400 BC), and small ivory nudes, known as 'concubines of the dead'.

THINITE EPOCH (c 3100–2700 BC). Stele of King Zet, known as the Serpent King, his name being represented here as a serpent; the falcon above symbolises Horus, the god of kingship: it was found near the king's tomb at Abydos (c 3000 BC).

OLD KINGDOM (c 2700–2200 BC). Stele of Nefertiabet (4th Dynasty), in painted stone: she is seated before a table of offerings, dressed in a leopard's skin; three fine columns of pink granite with palm-leaf capitals, one being marked with the name of King Uni (5th Dynasty); the other two, which were taken by Rameses II, are of the same period. Sarcophagus in the 'palace façade' style, found at Abu Roash (5th Dynasty): note the charming low relief in limestone of a girl smelling a flower; finds from the pyramid of Didoufri, son of Cheops, including a red quartzite head of King Didoufri. Small limestone figure of a scribe seated cross-legged, known as the 'Scribe accroupi', remarkable for its lifelike appearance, with eyes of white quartz and rock crystal. Limestone group of the official Raherka, and his wife Merseankh (5th Dynasty); alabaster and hard-stone vessels dating from pre-dynastic times to the 6th Dynasty (c 3400–2300 BC).

MIDDLE KINGDOM (2200–1750 BC). Limestone lintel of Sesostris III (1887–1850 BC): the king is shown making an offering of bread to the hawkheaded god Montou; sandstone statue of the scribe Mentuhotep; statuette of Sesostris III in green schist, and part of the head of the same king in grey granite; statues in black granite of Sesostris III in his youth, and as an old man. Silver and lapis lazuli treasure discovered in four bronze caskets, marked Amenemhat II (1938–1904 BC), in the foundations of the temple of Tod; a portico with papyrus-like columns (13th Dynasty).

ARCHITECTURAL and colossal stone pieces, including black granite statue of the god Amon protecting King Tutankhamun (18th Dynasty); the head (the right half eroded by sand and wind) and feet of a huge pink granite statue of Amenophis III (18th Dynasty), with a list of the peoples he subdued inscribed on the base; the sarcophagus of Rameses III (20th Dynasty), the lid of which is in the Fitzwilliam Museum at Cambridge; painted bas-relief of Seti I and the goddess Hathor, from the tomb of the former (19th Dynasty); a red granite fragment from the base of the Obelisk of Luxor (see Rte 13), with four cynocephali (dog-faced baboons) adoring the rising sun, and cartouches of Rameses II; also several statues of Sekhmet, the lion-headed goddess; Hathor capital of pink granite, from Bubastis, where Sekhmet was especially worshipped; limestone statue of a dog; a statue of a Nubian woman from Korosko; and mummy-shaped sarcophagi, including that of Tenthapi.

The **Crypt** contains a number of imposing funerary monuments of the late period, among them a wooden statue of Osiris; also smaller funerary objects and statues—many zoomorphic—of the Ptolemaic and Roman periods. On the ceiling, the large circular sandstone zodiac is from the temple of Hathor at Dendera.

Antiquities: painted cloths used as shrouds, showing masks of the deceased, outstanding among which is the Fayoum portrait, and the mummy of a woman showing the form of its wrapping, and how the mask was mounted; plaster mask of a child; and colourful Coptic woven fabrics; fragments of mural-paintings from one of the first monasteries, and a collection of bronze statuettes, crosses, lamps, candlesticks, etc.; reconstructed part of the nave of the monastery of Bawit (5–9C AD): note the Coptic icon, painted on wood, of Christ protecting Apa Mena, superior of the monastery.

On the staircase leading up to the first floor are displayed objects discovered by François-Auguste-Ferdinand Mariette (1821–81) in 1850–53 at the Serapeum at Memphis, including the limestone sphinxes which bordered its approach. (Mariette provided the librettist of Verdi's 'Aida' with the plot.) The serapeum itself was the underground burial-chamber of the sacred bulls, and canopic jars held the entrails of two Apis bulls (18th Dynasty). Note also a limestone statue of the god Bes from the temple of Nectanebo and a limestone statue of the bull of Apis, of the 30th Dynasty (378–341 BC).

FIRST FLOOR. Note the sphinx from Medamoud, and a huge bust of Amenophis IV (who adopted the name Akhnaton), from Karnak.

MIDDLE KINGDOM (continued): models of granaries; funerary furniture from the tomb of Chancellor Nakhti and a wooden statue of the same, one of the largest wooden funerary effigies known of this period; statue of stucco and painted wood known as the 'Porteuse d'Auge', a young girl, clothed in a tunic of netted pearls, carrying on her head a trough containing a joint of an ox, an essential of the funerary offering; statuette of a concubine (nude), her thumbs having been intentionally cut off; five wooden figures of girls carrying offerings; the inner case of the coffin of Chancellor Nakhti (note the two mystical eyes painted on the outside); models of funerary boats for transporting the dead down the Nile; examples of blue-glaze ware, including several hippopotami.

BEGINNING OF THE 18TH DYNASTY (c 1555–1365 BC): Prince Ahmosis, a seated statue of painted limestone; a wooden one of the priestess Toui (1200 BC); life-size statues of Seny Nefer and his wife Hatchepsout; two statuettes of the scribe Nebmertuf writing to the dictation of the cynocephalic god Thot.

NEW KINGDOM: household objects; furniture; musical instruments; games; the toilet, etc.

AMARNA PERIOD: limestone bust of Akhnaton, and statuette of the young king with his wife Nefertiti, also a bas-relief of the royal couple; painted limestone head of a princess of El-Amarna; quartzite female torso; objects from the time of Tutankhamun, and Horemheb, and reliefs from the tomb of the latter; a royal head in blue glass paste; and fragments of reliefs of this period.

RAMESSIDE PERIOD: (1320–1086 BC): green enamelled schist statuette of the priestess Nacha. Note the wooden statues, among them that of Piay; statue of the scribe Sethi, kneeling, and holding a naos containing a figure of Osiris (19th Dynasty). Note, in the showcase containing jewellery, the gold shell of the Middle Kingdom; a bracelet of sphinxes of King Ahmosis (New Kingdom); a collar with gold pendant fishes; General Djchouty's gold and silver bowl; jewels from the tomb of Prince Khaemouaset, son of Rameses II; the triad of Osorkon II, in gold and lapis lazuli, with the deities Osiris, Isis and their son Horus; necklace of Pinedjem I, of gold and lapis lazuli; and Roman jewellery from Egypt.

THIRD INTERMEDIATE PERIOD (1085–663 BC): large bronze statues: note that of Horus, the falcon-god, making a libation; bronze sistrum; bronze tablet-cover, decorated in silver, gold and electrum; bronze figures of kings and priests; a damascened bronze statue of queen Keramana, wife of Takelot II (847–823 BC); bronze statuette of King Taharqa on a silver-plated wooden stand, kneeling before the falcon-god Hemen, of gold-plated schist. A showcase displays 'Shawabty' figures, placed in tombs to serve the dead; sarcophagi and other funerary objects of the 21st Dynasty.

SAITE PERIOD (663–525 BC), and the last native dynasties (525–333 BC): Portrait reliefs; bronzes representing Bastet, the cat-faced goddess of Bubastis; images of Bes, god of recreation, and other deities in the form of animals; protective steles, amulets, and other objects associated with magic and superstitious beliefs, and a black basalt 'healing statue' representing Horus on the crocodiles, covered with magical signs.

PTOLEMAIC AND ROMAN PERIOD (332 BC–AD 337): Ptolemaic and Roman sculpture; highly decorated 'Mit-Rehineh' faïence objects; a section devoted to mummification; portrait masks, which covered the deceased; and papyrus Book of the Dead, etc.

E. Oriental Antiquities

This department contains objects from the Middle East, apart from Egypt; antiquities from the Far East may be seen in the Musée Guimet (Rte 27). See p 128 concerning the redistribution of certain sections.

The Crypte Sully at present contains antiquities from Palestine, including an ossuary in the form of a house, from Azor (4th millennium), and one of the jars in which were preserved the Dead Sea Scrolls (2C BC and 1C AD), found by Bedouin in 1947; jewellery, glass and metal objects; the Moabite Stone, or stele of Mesha, king of Moab (842 BC), discovered in 1868 in a remote village east of the Dead Sea.

The 34-line inscription, recording victories over the Israelites in the reigns of Omri, Ahab and Ahaziah, is one of the most important, if not the earliest, examples of the alphabetic writing which has come down to us from the Phoenicians through Greek and Latin.

SUMERIAN ANTIQUITIES: objects from Lagash (Mesopotamia), and Semitic reliefs and sculptures of the Akkadian Dynasty (2340–2190 BC) from Susa; bas-reliefs of a 'plumed figure' from Girsu (Sumer; 3rd millennium) and of Ur-Nanshe, prince of Lagash, carrying a basket of bricks on his head, with his sons; bronze bull's head, etc.; stele of the Vultures, commemorating the victory of Eannadu, king of Lagash, over a rival city, Umma; silver vase of Entemena, with a frieze of incised animals and the Lagash 'crest', a lion-headed eagle; stele of the victorious Naram-Sin, king of Akkad.

NEO-SUMERIAN ANTIQUITIES of c 2150 BC: eleven diorite statues of Gudea, ruler of Lagash; a large clay cylinder recording, in cuneiform, Gudea's achievements as a builder; 'turbaned' head (Gudea); goblet belonging to Gudea, decorated with serpents and winged dragons with scorpion tails; alabaster statuette of Ur-Ningirsu, son of Gudea; woman with a scarf, from Girsu; the dog of Sumu-ilu; terracotta figurines (one strangling a bird); late cuneiform documents (3–2C BC); seals and cylinders.

MARI AND LARSA: objects from the temple of the goddess Ishtar (c 2500 BC) at Mari, including an alabaster statue of the intendant of Mari, Ebih-II, and head of Ishtar; mosaic panel showing a scene of war; two murals from the 2nd millennium palace, depicting Ishtar investing King Zimrilim with regal powers, and a sacrificial scene; two bronzes, one of Hammurabi on bended knee, his face and hands covered in gold leaf: the other of a group of three rampant ibex, with horns interlaced, from Larsa; ceremonial vase from Larsa, with Ishtar and figures of animals; relief of a goddess smelling a flower; statuette of Idi Ilum, prince of Mari; a bronze lion from the temple of Dagon.

BABYLON: alabaster statuettes, including reclining female figures, some with jewelled eyes and navels; bronze horned dragon (6C BC), symbol of Marduk, terracottas (c 2000–1700 BC); the **Codex of Hammurabi**, a block of black basalt, covered with the closely written text of 282 laws embracing practically every aspect of Babylonian life of c 1800 BC, at the top of which the god Shamash dictates the law to the king; 'Kudurrus' or boundary-stones, with inscriptions; statues of the princes of Ashnunnak, a rival state, captured by Shutruk-Nakhunté, an Elamite prince, who erased the original inscriptions and substituted his own (c 1100 BC).

SUSA: pottery and the first attempts at metallurgy from Susa (Mesopotamia; 4th millennium), northern Iran (3–2nd millennia), Tepe Giyan and Tepe Sialk; silverware and jewellery (12–5C BC): note the ornamental vase-handle in the form of a winged ibex (6C BC); brick reliefs from Achemenian times, of lions, winged bulls and griffins.

Susa (3–2nd millennia): vase 'à la cachette', with treasure hidden inside it; headless bronze statue of Queen Napir Asu, and ritual scene celebrating the sunrise, known as the Sit Shamshi; vessels in bitumen and terracotta; votive offerings and toys; monumental capital in grey marble from the palace of Darius I at Susa (521–486 BC); lion in enamelled terracotta (700 BC); reliefs in enamelled brick of a winged bull and a lion, and two warriors; two rhytons (silver and bronze); bronze fibula; alabaster vase; a bronze cup decorated with an ostrich hunt, etc.; *Charter of Darius*, reporting how he had the raw materials required for building his palace brought from distant lands; friezes of enamelled brick with royal archers in relief; also lions, griffins and winged sphinxes, from the palace of Darius; sculpted head in stone; bronze lamp with a monkey on the lid, etc.; Luristan bronzes; four large earthenware pots from Susa (3–2C BC); funerary lions; cast of a mural niche from the palace of Shapur (3–4C AD), and Parthian and Sassanid antiquities (3–9C AD).

The Crypte Marengo contains lead Phoenician sarcophagi, and the black sarcophagus of Eshmunazar, king of Sidon (5C BC), which although Egyptian in style, has an inscription in Phoenician (cursing the eventual violator of the tomb); also statues from the sanctuary of the god Mithra.

Busts and funerary reliefs from tombs found at Palmyra in Syria, and three divinities in military attire (2–3C AD); PHOENICIAN sculptures and collections of objects from their great cities of Baalbek (Heliopolis), Sidon, Tyre, Byblos and Rase-Shamra (Ugarit); bust of the pharaoh Osorkon (924–895 BC); the 'Lady of Byblos' stele (5–4C BC), and an unusual three-sided stele in relief; woman's head in marble (3C BC); statuettes of Jupiter of Heliopolis, flanked by bulls (3–2C); votive hand and other examples of the same cult; head of a sphinx (Roman; Baalbek); terracotta figurines; gold plaquettes; Syrian glass, etc.; a headless Aphrodite from Dura-Europos; wall-painting of a wild-ass hunt (194 BC); gilded bronze figurines of the god Reshef, from Byblos; sphinx dedicated by princess Itar, daughter of pharaoh Amenemhat II, found at Qatna.

Antiquities from excavations at Ugarit; Cypriot, Mycenaean and Canaanite pottery; ivory pyxis depicting a goddess of fertility in Minoan style; gold cup with hunting scene; bronze and gold figurines of the god Ba'al; alphabetic tables describing Canaanite epics.

Reliefs from the great ASSYRIAN palaces of Nimrud, Khorsabad and

Nineveh (9–7C BC); carved ivories from Arslan-Tash; a bronze lion, and winged bulls from Khorsabad (7C BC), each with an extra leg, for the sake of symmetry; note the reliefs of Kings Assurnasirpal, Tiglathpileser III and Sargon with his ministers; reliefs from the palace of Assurbanipal at Nineveh; two bulls from the temple of Arslan-Tash (8C BC).

These reliefs are being moved to a new position in the Cour Khorsabad, at the east end of the ground floor of Richelieu.

CYPRUS: 'Vase of Amathus', a huge monolithic cistern (5C BC); statues of the 'King of Cyprus' (5C BC); sculptured heads in the Greek style; a bronze charioteer with silver inlay; gold jewellery and repoussé work from Enkomi; Bronze Age ceramics; Mycenaean kraters, terracotta and painted stone figurines, etc.

The HITTITE, CAPPADOCIAN and ISLAMIC antiquities are not at present on display.

F.   Objets d'Art

The collections of this department may—for the time being—be conveniently divided into the art of the Gold and Silversmith, some examples of which may be displayed in other sections; Medieval and Renaissance Objets d'Art; and French Furniture and Objets d'Art or de Vertu, mostly 16–early 19C.

The display of MEDIEVAL AND RENAISSANCE GOLDSMITHS' WORK may also contain some furniture and furnishings, including a Florentine mosaic table from the Château de Richelieu, a coloured marble table-top dating from the reign of Louis XIV, and one of 13 Savonnerie carpets (1667; usually rolled).

A number of items were originally part of the collection of the French royal house, including semi-precious vessels of lapis lazuli, jade, amethyst, amber, red and green jasper, agate, sardonyx, basalt, etc. Individual objects include: the crowns of Louis IX (c 1255) and of Louis XV (1722; after his coronation the gems were replaced by coloured stones, according to custom); crown of Napoléon I (after Charlemagne's), never placed on his head; the Crown Jewels retained when the rest were sold in 1887, including the Regent diamond (137 carats), discovered in India, and bought by the Regent in 1717; the 'Côte de Bretagne' ruby, once owned by Marguerite de Foix, Anne of Brittany, Claude de France and François I, and later cut into the shape of a dragon as a decoration of the Order of the Golden Fleece; the 'Hortensia' diamond, acquired in 1691; reliquary brooch of the Empress Eugénie (1855); and plaque of the Order of St.-Esprit.

Ecclesiastical ornaments from the Abbey of St.-Denis, presented by Abbot Suger; antique porphyry vase mounted in silver gilt as an eagle; rock-crystal vase given by Eleanor of Aquitaine to Louis VII, who gave it to Suger; rock-crystal vase with decorations illustrating Noah in his vineyard, and other vessels; antique sardonyx ewer, mounted c 1150; crystal ewer of the 10C (Islamic); serpentine paten inlaid with gold dolphins (5–6C) set in an 8–9C border; lapis lazuli plaque with figures of Christ and the Virgin (Byzantine; 11–12C); two Byzantine reliquary plaques from the Ste.-Chapelle and the so-called 'Ring of St. Louis' (14–15C) from St.-Denis; silver-gilt statuette of the Virgin (14C), presented in 1339 to St.-Denis by

Jeanne d'Evreux; gold sceptre of Charles V; gold coronation spurs, set with garnets and fleurs-de-lys (12C; restored); coronation sword 'of Charlemagne' (? 11C); enamelled gold shield and morion (a type of helmet) of Charles IX; sword of Charles X; candlestick and rock-crystal mirror presented to Marie de Médicis on her marriage to Henri IV (1600); sword and dagger of the Grand Master of the Knights of Malta (Augsburg; 16C), given to Napoléon in 1797; reliquaries and plate from the chapel of the St.-Esprit, founded by Henri III in 1578.

MEDIEVAL AND RENAISSANCE OBJETS D'ART: four ceremonial mantles of the Order of St.-Esprit; tapestry of the Battle of Jarnac, from the workshop of *Claude de Lapierre*; a chest belonging to Marie de Médicis, with her monogram; a richly decorated late 17C altarpiece; a Mortlake tapestry (1630–35) and 17C wall-hangings in silver thread; the shrine of St. Potentin, in copper gilt, from Steinfeld, near Trèves (13C); other tapestries include an Adoration of the Magi (15C Flemish); St. Luke painting the Virgin (Brussels; 16C), the Virgin in Glory (Flanders; 1485); three hangings illustrating the life of St. Anatole de Salins (Bruges; early 16C); an embroidered cross from a chasuble (Bohemia; early 15C); two porphyry columns from the 4C basilica of St. Peter at Rome.

A beautiful and extensive collection of **ivories**, including the Harbaville triptych (Byzantine; 10C); triptych of the Nativity (Byzantine; 11C); caskets with scenes from the Life of Christ (Metz; 10C), and with mythological scenes (Byzantine; 10C); plaques, including Christ and St. Peter (5–6C), Miracle of the Loaves (Ottoman; 10C), and the Rout of Silenus (Alexandria; 3C); two 6C pyxes; Virgin (English?; 11C); liturgical comb depicting Samson and the lion (Metz; 10–11C); 12C chessmen; a huge ivory altarpiece by the *Embriachi* (c 1400), presented to the abbey of Poissy by Jean, Duc de Berri; 13–14C ivories from Paris workshops, some with distinctive decoration (c 1320–40); and of Spanish and Italian origin.

Among **enamels**: the reliquary of the arm of Charlemagne (Mosan; c 1170) from Aix-la-Chapelle; cross-reliquary given to the abbey of St.-Vincent at Laon (1174–1205); champlevé work from Cologne and the Moselle (12–13C); chalice and paten (Spanish; c 1200); Limoges and other enamels of the 12–13C, including a small shrine, a Crucifixion, and a Eucharistic dove; the casket of St. Louis, a wooden box with enamel and metal decoration (Limoges; late 13C); enamelled ciborium, signed 'G. Alpais of Limoges' (mid 13C); Limoges enamels with repoussé and champlevé work; and Spanish and Italian enamels, notably a Spanish 14C communion cup.

Reliquaries, including that of the arm of St. Louis of Toulouse (Italian; 1337), of St. Martin (14C), and of Jaucourt (Byzantine 11–12C work with French 14C supporters); a ring containing a portrait of Jean sans Peur and a ring of the Black Prince; a bronze equestrian statue of Charlemagne (9C); 12–15C metalwork and 'dinanderie'; and fragments of 13C stained-glass from Reims.

Renaissance **bronzes** of the Florentine and Paduan Schools (15–16C), including a Flagellation attributed to *Donatello*, Gnome with a snail (Paduan; 15C), and eight bronze reliefs from the tomb of Marcantonio della Torre, in San Fermo, Verona, by *Andrea Riccio* (1470–1532), and examples by Bellano; a collection of French and Italian **medals** by *Pisanello, Matteo de'Pasti, Germain Pilon* and *G. Dupré*; 16C engraved Italian crystals, including work by Valerio Belli; twelve small busts of Caesars (16C); the 'Spinario', a Renaissance cast of the antique original (c 1541); 16C Florentine table, with a bronze fountain (Spanish).

Later Italian and Limoges enamels (15–16C), including superb examples from the workshops of Poillevé, Jean and Pierre Pénicaud, Jacques and Pierre Nouailher, Jean and Suzanne de Court, Pierre Courteys, J. Pierre and Martial Reymond, Jacques I and Jacques II Laudin, and Jean and Léonard Limousin, including a Portrait of the Constable Anne de Montmorency by the latter (1556); also a medallion with a self-portrait by Jean Fouquet.

An impressive collection of Hispano-Moresque, French and Italian **ceramics** of the 15–17C, with fine examples of the art of *Bernard Palissy* (c 1510–89) and from the St.-Porchaire workshop. Notable are three intarsia panels attributed to *Fra Vicenzo da Verona* (c 1500), and four ceramic medallions attributed to *Girolamo della Robbia*, from the Château of St.-Germain-en-Laye (16C). Also a series of twelve tapestries of the months, 'Les Chasses de Maximilien', *after Van Orley* (Brussels; c 1530).

FRENCH FURNITURE AND OBJETS D'ART: among tapestries, etc., the Martyrdom of St.-Mammès, by *Jean Cousin the Elder*, and another of an Elephant Hunt (mid 16C); pre-Gobelins tapestries *after Simon Vouet*, including Moses in the bulrushes; a Gobelins tapestry of the Life of Scipio, from designs by *Giulio Romano* (1689); Gobelins tapestry of Sheepshearing (1735); Gobelins tapestries and bed-hangings from the Chambre Rose, woven for the Condé family at the workshop of *Neilson*, c 1775; Gobelins tapestries representing the story of Don Quixote, *after Tessier* and *Coypel* (c 1785); and 'Chinese' hangings *after Blain de Fontenay* and *Vernansal* (Beauvais; early 18C); also a screen woven in the Savonnerie after a design by *Desportes*.

Notable examples of furniture include a walnut coffer from the Château of Azay-le-Rideau, in the Italian manner; an inlaid desk belonging to Marie de Médicis; the *nécessaire* of Marie Leczinska (1729); examples of the ornate style of *André-Charles Boulle* (1642–1732), and other furniture of the period, including a pair of ebony cupboards once owned by the writer and collector William Beckford (1760–1844); French Regency furniture by *Charles Cressent* (1685–1768); a bureau by *Mignon* and *Dubois*; four armchairs by *Nicolas Heurtaut* (c 1755–75); works by the *ébéniste* Jean-*François Oeben* (c 1720–63); roll-top desk 'of the King of Sardinia' (c 1770), by *Mathieu-Guillaume Cramer* (died 1794); a flat-topped bureau by *Hauré* and *G. Beneman* (1787) made for Louis XVI's library at Fontainebleau; roll-topped secretaire in mottled mahogany (1784) by *Jean-Henri Riesener* (1734–1806); a large commode by *Beneman*, from Compiègne; armchairs by *J.-B. Sené* (1748–1803); lacquered corner-pieces and commodes by *Martin Carlin* (c 1730–85), in the Chinese taste; Marie-Antoinette's travelling-case, made in Paris c 1787; chairs by *Rode* and *Georges Jacob* (1739–1814).

The latter, who usually signed his work 'G. Jacob', had two sons, and their furniture was often marked 'Jacob Frères' until 1804, after which François-Honoré-Georges Jacob—'Desmalter'—worked on his own for another decade. The latter's son—Alphonse Jacob—signing his work 'Jacob', flourished in the 1840s.

Napoléon's throne from St.-Cloud, by *Jacob Desmalter*, and a cradle for his son, by the same *ébéniste* and *Pierre-Philippe Thomire* (1751–1843) after a design by Proudhon (1811); the 'Grand Ecrin' jewellery-case by *Jacob Desmalter* and *Thomire* after a design by Percier (1809); a commode decorated with Wedgwood plaques (1790); and a *nécessaire* by *M.-G. Biennais* (1764–1843) and *Lorillon*, offered by Napoléon to Tsar Alexander

I in 1808; a bed belonging to Louis XVIII at the Tuileries, by *Jacob Desmalter*. Also panels of Chinese papers of the late 18C, and gilt and white panelling from the Hôtel de Luynes.

Sections are devoted to the display of a magnificent collection of **silverware** (16–18C), including work by *Thomas Germain* (1674–1745), among them a series made for José of Portugal, and a *surtout* by *Jacques Roettiers*, made for the Prince of Condé, depicting a stag hunt; a silver-gilt tea-service by *Biennais* ordered by Napoléon for his marriage with Marie-Louise, and a Sèvres porcelain coffee-service decorated with views of Egypt, made for the wedding, and which the Emperor took with him to St. Helena. Also notable are bronzes from the workshops of *Jean de Bologne* (Giambologna) and Pietro Tacca; and a superb collection of snuffboxes and watches of the 17–18C, with examples dating from 1746–59, by *Moynat, Noël Hardivilliers* (1752–79), *J.-J. Barrière* (1765–76), the *Drais family* (1769–82), and *P.-J. Menière* (1773–82), as well as representative works from other countries, notably Switzerland, together with more silverware, jewellery, clocks, 15–16C ivories, a Delft *tulipière* (17C), etc.

Individual donations are displayed in separate rooms, among them that of Adolphe de Rothschild, containing a 15C Flemish tapestry of the Miracle of the Loaves; a bas-relief of the Madonna and Child by Agostino di Duccio, and a remarkable late 13C polyptych-reliquary from the abbey of Floreffe, Flanders.

The COLLECTION CAMONDO contains four armchairs by *S. Brizard* (c 1775), a *chaise-longue* by *Delanois* (c 1765); a bed, signed G. Jacob, covered with Genoa velvet; six chairs by *Tilliard* (c 1755); a marble clock, 'the Three Graces', attributed to *Falconet* (c 1770), and a collection of Meissen porcelain, etc.

The COLLECTION SCHLICHTING: a roll-top desk (c 1780) attributed to *David Roentgen* (1743–1807), once the property of the Tsarina Catherine II; a child's armchair (? the Dauphin's) by *Gay* (1780); and a portrait of Louis-Elisabeth de Maillé by *Drouais*.

The COLLECTION THIERS includes a number of Italian Renaissance bronzes, ivory carvings, etc., collected by the statesman, together with examples of Sèvres and Vincennes porcelain (18C), among others.

G. Sculpture

French. 11–12C: two capitals from Moutiers-St.-Jean, one depicting the vintage, rare at this period; a marble Merovingian capital recarved in the 11C of Daniel in the lions' den, from the former abbey of Ste.-Geneviève, Paris; a relief of St. Michael and the Dragon, from Nevers; a Descent from the Cross (painted wood), probably Burgundian (early 12C); a carved wooden seated Virgin and Child (from the Forez; 12C); doorway from the priory of Estagel (Gard) and a remarkable head of St. Peter (1170–89), with eyes lined with lead, from Autun.

Early Gothic sculpture: fragments of a frieze from N.-D-en-Vaux (Châlons-sur-Marne); column-statues of Solomon and the Queen of Sheba from N.-D. de Corbeil (c 1180–90); two historiated spiral columns from the abbey of Coulombs (mid-12C).

13–14C. The Virgin 'de la Celle' (Ile de France; 14C); tomb statues of

Charles IV (le Bel) and Jeanne d'Evreux, from the abbey of Maubuisson (1372), by *Jean de Liège*; statues of Charles V and Jeanne de Bourbon, from the Palais du Louvre; two *pleureurs* (weepers or mourners) from the tomb of Jean, duc de Berry (died 1416) by *Etienne Bobillet* and *Paul Mosselman*.

15–early 16C. Tomb of Philippe Pot, Grand Seneschal of Burgundy (died 1493), formerly in the abbey of Cîteaux; marble high relief of St. George and the Dragon, by *Michel Colombe* (c 1508); marble tomb (1515–24) of Renée d'Orléans-Longueville, from the Célestins church, Paris; tomb of Louis de Poncher and his wife, from St.-Germain-l'Auxerrois.

Renaissance period. The Three Graces, *Germain Pilon* (c 1535–90); a funeral monument for the heart of Henri II; Diana leaning on a stag, an early garden figure, from the Château of Anet; tomb-statue of Admiral Philippe Chabot in armour, *attributed to Pierre Bontemps* (1505–68); Deposition and the Evangelists (reliefs, c 1545), *Jean Goujon*; effigies of the Constable Anne de Montmorency and his wife, *Barthélemy Prieur* (c 1540–1611); and tomb of Valentine Balbiani, by *Pilon*.

17–19C: representative works by Antoine Coysevox (1640–1720), Sébastien Slodtz (1655–1726), Nicolas and Guillaume Coustou (1658–1733 and 1677–1746 respectively), J.-L. and J.-B. Lemoyne (1665–1755 and 1704–78), René Fremin (1672–1744), Edme Bouchardon(1698–1762), Christophe-Gabriel Allegrain (1710–95), J.-B. Pigalle (1714–85) and Etienne-Maurice Falconet (1716–91).

Pierre Julien (1731–1804), sculptures of Poussin and La Fontaine; *Jean-Jacques Caffieri* (1725–92), Corneille; *Augustin Pajou* (1730–1809), Pascal, Mme du Barry, and Mme Vigée-Lebrun; a bronze bust of Lemoyne, his master, and a bust of Pajou by his pupil Roland (1746–1816). Among works by *Jean-Antoine Houdon* (1741–1828), a bronze Diana (1790), and busts of his contemporaries, including Voltaire, the singer Sophie Arnould, Rousseau, Houdon's smiling wife (original plaster), Diderot, Washington, Franklin, the Brongniart children, and Mme Adelaïde.

Among other notable sculptures are *F.-N. Delaistre* (1746–1832), Cupid and Psyche; *Claude Ramey* (1754–1838), Sappho; *Claude Michallon* (1751–99), Alexandre Lenoir; Antonio Canova (1757–1822), Psyche revived by the kiss of Cupid, and Cupid and Psyche standing; *Charles-Louis Corbet* (1758–1808), La Tour d'Auvergne; *Jacques-Edme Dumont* (1761–1844), Gén. Marceau; *Joseph Chinard* (1756–1813), bust of a young woman; James Pradier (1790–1852), Niobe wounded; *François Rude* (1784–1855), Mercury, and Louis David, showing the deformation of his mouth; works by Antoine-Louis Barye (1795–1875); and other early 19C French sculptors of varying merit.

Italian: a collection of enamelled earthenware from the Florentine workshop of *Della Robbia*; Madonna and Child surrounded by angels (marble bas-relief), by *Agostino di Duccio*; Dietisalvi Neroni (marble), by *Mino da Fiesole* (1418–81); Madonna and Child, by *Donatello* (1386–1468); Bust of a Woman, in painted and gilded wood, and St. John the Baptist as a youth, attributed to the workshop of *Desiderio da Settignano*; Mercury, by *Giambologna* (1529–1608); monumental portal of the Palazzo Straga at Cremona, attributed to *Pietro da Rho*; the Nymph of Fontainebleau, a bronze bas-relief by *Benvenuto Cellini* (1500–72); the Two Slaves, by *Michelangelo Buonarotti* (1475–1564), intended for the tomb of Pope Julius II, but given to Henri II in 1550 by Robert Strozzi; and a bronze bust of Michelangelo by one of his pupils.

German. Virgin of the Annunciation, kneeling, by *Tilman Riemenschneider* (1468–1531), of painted and gilded marble; a naked Magdalen, 'the beautiful German girl', by *Gregor Erhardt* (1470–1541), of painted wood. See also Musée d'Orsay, Rte 9.

16 Musée des Arts Décoratifs; Musée des Arts de la Mode

METROS: Tuileries, Palais-Royal.

The autonomous ****MUSEE DES ARTS DECORATIFS**, with its main entrance at Palais du Louvre, 107 Rue de Rivoli, in the north-west wing of the Palais du Louvre (Pl. 8; 7). It contains an outstanding collection of French decorative and ornamental art from medieval times to the present, and is one of the most rewarding museums to visit in Paris.

Its history is bound up with the Union Centrale des Beaux-Arts appliqués à l'Industrie and the Société du Musée des Arts Décoratifs (founded in 1864 and 1877 respectively), which in 1882 merged to become the Union Centrale des Arts Décoratifs. In 1901 work commenced on the rehabilitation of the interior of the Pavillon de Marsan, then ceiling-high with archives and dossiers from the Cours des Comptes, and the Musée des Arts Décoratifs was inaugurated in May 1905. Today, its inventory lists over 80,000 items.

It is affiliated with the Musée des Arts de la Mode (see below), and the Musée Nissim de Camondo, 63 Rue de Monceau, 8e; see Rte 26.

It also houses the Centre National des Métiers d'Art Contemporains, and an important specialised library (over 100,000 volumes and 1500 periodicals) with a Photographic Service; and also the Musée de la Publicité (posters).

A new and enterprising departure is the department selling replicas of choice objects from the collections themselves, or of contemporary design, their reproduction being undertaken in collaboration with French manufacturers and craftsmen of quality.

Temporary exhibitions, usually in the fields of design and decoration, are held here throughout the year.

Among sections which may be visited by appointment are the Cabinet des Dessins (containing some 15,000 drawings), the Departments of Textiles, and of Wallpapers (among the latter are the series depicting Views of Naples, and the 'Inca' series of wallpapers manufactured by Dufour, Leroy, Zuber and others, in the 1820s).

The six main floors of the wing are arranged as follows: GROUND FLOOR: entrance hall, information desk, shop, bookshop, etc. FIRST FLOOR: Late 19C, 20C and Contemporary collections. Notable is the Salle 1900, with Art Nouveau woodwork by Georges Hoentschell (1855–1915), and furniture by Hector Guimard.

The SECOND FLOOR is devoted to collections of the Gothic and Renaissance periods, with 13–16C tapestries—among them the 'Woodcutters'

(Tournai; 15C)—among other hangings and furniture; also representative examples of German woodcarving; medieval metal work and Renaissance bronzes; a richly carved retable (Brussels; early 16C); an anon. Portrait of a young girl (Bruges; c 1550), and a Portrait of Madeleine de France, Queen of Scotland, by the 'Maître de Marie Tudor'.

Another section illustrates the arts of Spain, including Catalan paintings by Jaume and Pere Serra, and the Retable of the Baptist (c 1415–20) by Luis Borrassa; also stalls from Rueda (Valladolid; early 16C); and stamped leather panels or *guadameciles*.

The THIRD and FOURTH FLOORS are mainly devoted to collections from the time of Louis XIII to the Second Empire period (17–early 19C), including examples of panelling of c 1707 from 7 Pl. Vendôme, and oak-panelling of c 1735; a ceiling of c 1710 by Claude Audran (1658–1734) from the Hôtel Bertier de Flesselles, Rue de Sévigné, and another of c 1715 from the Hôtel de la Comtesse de Verrie in the Rue du Cherche-Midi; also decorative panels by N. Coypel and by Hubert Robert; painted panels in the Etruscan style (c 1780); and a number of carved wood brackets, panels, picture-frames, mirrors, etc.

The furniture includes a collection of 17–18C chairs arranged to show their evolution in style; a fine marquetry cabinet of c 1670; a marquetry *armoire* attributed to Boulle of c 1680 and another by Charles Cressent (c 1725); and examples in the Chinese taste, together with other Chinoiserie objects. Also chairs by members of the Jacob family; a boat-shaped bed by F. Baudry (1827).

Among the paintings are a Portrait of the Chancellor d'Anguesseau by Robert Tournières; a pastel of Molière; Venetian scenes by Michele Marieschi; and monastic scenes by Alessandro Magnasco; garden scenes by Pillement; flower studies (1614–15) by G. Pini; watercolours by Lavreince, J.-B. Huet, Debucourt and Mallet; an early work (c 1806) by Ingres, The Casino de Raphael at Rome; and Houdon's Studio, and the Gohin family, both by Louis Boilly. Note also a series of wax-portrait moulds, some by G.-B. Nini (c 1717–80), and a collection of portrait-miniatures.

Among the extensive ceramic collections are examples from St.-Cloud, Moustiers, Strasbourg, Rouen (some exhibiting strong Chinese influence—Oriental works of art at that time entering France at Dieppe), Sceaux, Sinceny, Marseille; faïences 'en trompe-l'oeil' and 'fine blanches'; ware from Vincennes, Sèvres, Mennecy and Chantilly; biscuit figures, and a curious terracotta of a girl playing with her pet dog, by Clodion (1738–1814); an important collection of Chinese cloisonné; and Delft and Meissen porcelain, etc.

Complementary collections, which may be shown with other displays of their period, or 'thematically' and separately, are such diverse objects—usually of very fine quality—as door furniture; bronze appliqués, and ornaments (and also a 'coiffeuse' used by Joséphine at the Tuileries); silverware; mathematical instruments; pewter; clocks and watches; ivory boxes; snuff grinders; rings; cutlery; '*nécessaires*'; embroidered purses; shuttles; walking-sticks; paperweights; pipes; plaster plaques; statuettes; glass ornaments; decorative embossed leather cases; and book-bindings.

The third floor also contains space for temporary exhibitions, and a section devoted to toys; the fourth floor displays furniture and furnishings in the Louis-Philippe taste, and in the style of the Second Empire (Napoléon III). Charles le Brun's projects for tapestries of The Months, and certain other sections, are not at present on display.

The Salon Barriol contains collections of 18C furniture.

Important temporary exhibitions are held in the adjacent **Musée des Arts de la Mode**, with its entrance at 109 Rue de Rivoli, in the Pavillon de Marsan, the north-west extremity of the Palais du Louvre; see Rte 14 for its history. It had its origins in the Union Française des Arts du Costume, established in 1901, since when its collections of costumes and accessories have been very considerably increased, partly due to donations. A proportion has been acquired with the participation of several famous fashion houses—among the more notable names being Balenciaga, Chanel, Dior, Fath, Givenchy, Lanvin, Patou, Ricci, Rochas, Saint-Laurent, Schiaparelli, Ungaro and Worth. The growth of the industry was spectacular during the latter half of the 19C; the Bottin directory of 1850 listed some 158 couturiers in Paris. By 1872 this had risen to 684 and in 1895 to 1636 (six of whom employed 400–600 workers each), not including small independent dressmakers.

Its *réserves* at present contain over 9000 costumes and over 32,000 accessories of all types (including a rare collection of umbrellas, Second Empire hats, costume jewellery, fans, shoes, handbags, gloves, and what not) apart from collections of materials, prints, tapestries, laces, embroideries, braids, patterns and pattern-books, etc. And these holdings are being increased continually. The specialised library contains an extensive collection of books on European costume, fashion magazines, photographs, prints, designs, catalogues, slides, etc., and the building also contains a laboratory for the restoration of fabrics.

17 North of the Rue de Rivoli
Pl. Vendôme; Palais-Royal; Banque de France

METROS: Concorde, Tuileries, Pyramides, Palais-Royal.

The **Rue de Rivoli**, constructed in 1811–56 and named in honour of Bonaparte's victory over the Austrians in 1797, runs east from the Pl. de la Concorde (Pl. 7; 7; see Rte 13). It skirts the Tuileries Gardens and the Louvre, and in its western half, is flanked by uniform ranges of buildings above an arcade. No. 107 is the entrance of the Musée des Arts Décoratifs and adjacent, at 109, that of the Musée de la Mode; see Rte 16.

Oscar and Constance Wilde stayed at the Hôtel Wagram, which was at 208 Rue de Rivoli, on their honeymoon in 1884. No. 220 was the home of Léo Delibes. No. 224 is Galignani's Bookshop, established here since 1855.

The first English bookshop and circulating library had been opened c 1800 at 18 Rue Vivienne by Anne Parsons, who had married M. Galignani when he worked in London some five years earlier. In 1815 they were publishing 'Galignani's Messenger', a newspaper for the English community, a Guide to Paris with English and German descriptions on opposite pages for the use of the occupying troops, and—until 1852—reprints of English books. The house in Rue Vivienne soon became a club and reading-room for English residents.

At the west end, at the corner of the Rue St.-Florentin, stands the 18C Hôtel de la Vrillière, or de Talleyrand, built to designs by Chalgrin, where Talleyrand (1754–1838) died, and where the Princesse de Lieven held her salon in 1846–57. The design of the American Embassy (see Rte 25) was inspired by this building, and completes the symmetry of the north side of the Pl. de la Concorde. At 228 Rue de Rivoli, the Hôtel Meurice, General Von Choltitz, commander of the German forces in Paris, allowed himself to be captured (25 August 1944), having refused orders to destroy the capital's principal buildings. No. 374 was the home of Mme Geoffrin (1699–1777) from 1750, where she entertained many of the artists, writers and intellectuals of the day, among them Marivaux, Helvétius, Saint-Lambert, Diderot, d'Alembert, Falconet, Boucher and Delatour.

On the left is the Rue Cambon, where at 5 (previously No. 3) Stendhal lived from 1810–14, and where Hubert Robert died in 1808 (at No. 21), the birthplace of novelist Eugène Sue (1804–75). In the Rue du Mont-Thabor, which it crosses, Alfred du Musset (1810–57) died at No. 6; Washington Irving lodged at No. 4 in 1821. The Rue Cambon continues north to the Rue St.-Honoré, leading east, parallel to the Rue de Rivoli.

At its junction with the Rue Cambon stands the Church of the Assumption, built in 1670 as the chapel of the convent of the Haudriettes and now used by the Polish community. Funeral services for La Fayette and Stendhal were held here. At No. 398 (opposite) stood the house where Robespierre lodged with the cabinet-maker Duplay from July 1791 until his arrest in 1794.

Turning east, you shortly cross the Rue de Castiglione, where in the Hôtel Lotti (No. 7) George Orwell was employed as a *plongeur*, as described in 'Down and out in London and Paris' (1933).

The street leads north into the octagonal *Place Vendôme (Pl. 7; 8),—in fact a rectangle of 213m by 124m with canted corners—a superb example of the Louis XIV style, surrounded by mansions designed by Hardouin-Mansart. Many of the buildings were built after his death but the façades of all conformed to the original design. Originally called Pl. des Conquêtes, it owes its present name to a mansion built here in 1603 by César, Duc de Vendôme, son of Henri IV and Gabrielle d'Estrées. A number are now luxury hotels (the Bristol at No. 3; the Ritz at No. 15), or shops. Nos 5, 22 and 28 were built for John Law (who also lived at No. 23 as controller-general of finance); Chopin died at No. 12 (1849); Nos 11–13 are the Ministère de la Justice (since 1815); No. 16 was let to Dr Mesmer, the quack, in 1778; the composer Piccinni lived at No. 17 in 1787.

The centre of the Place is dominated by the *Vendôme Column, constructed by Denon, Gondouin and Lepère in 1806–10 in the style of Trajan's Column in Rome. It replaced an equestrian statue of Louis XIV by Girardon.

Encircling the column (43.50m high) is a spiral band of bronze bas-reliefs, designed by Bergeret and made of the metal of some 250 Russian and Austrian cannon, in which the principal feats of arms in the campaigns of 1805–07 are glorified. The statue of Napoléon surmounting it is a copy (1863) of the original by Chaudet torn down by the royalists in 1814 and replaced at the Restoration by a fleur-de-lys. In 1833 Louis-Philippe put up a statue of Napoléon, which is now at Les Invalides. The present statue narrowly escaped destruction in 1871, when a group of Communards led by Gustave Courbet, the artist, brought the whole column—which was felled like a tree—crashing to the ground. Courbet preferred exile in Switzerland, where he died in 1877, rather than ruin himself by paying—as he was ordered—for its re-erection (in 1873–74).

The once fashionable Rue de la Paix (now lined with travel agencies and airline offices) leads north to the Pl. de l'Opéra (see Rte 22), crossing the Rue Danielle-Casanova (named after a Resistance heroine; previously Rue des Petits-Champs), with 17–18C houses, where at No. 22 Stendhal (1783–1842) died of apoplexy.

You may return to the Rue St.-Honoré via the Rue du Marché-St.-Honoré, passing the site of a Dominican convent where the Jacobin Club met in 1789–94.

To the east, steps climb up to baroque **ST.-ROCH** (Pl. 7; 8), begun by Jacques Lemercier in 1653. Work was abandoned in 1660, but a donation by John Law on his conversion to Rome in 1719 enabled the nave to be completed; Robert de Cotte was responsible for the façade (1735). The church was consecrated in 1740.

The unkempt INTERIOR (126m long) contains monuments of interest. To the left of the entrance is a medallion of Corneille (1606–84), who died in the neighbouring Rue d'Argenteuil (plaque on No. 6), and is buried in the church. In the 1st bay (right) are a bust of François de Créquy (died 1687) by Coysevox and the tomb of the Comte d'Harcourt (died 1666) by Renard. 2nd bay: statue of Cardinal Dubois (died 1723) by G. Coustou and a monument to the astronomer Maupertuis (1698–1759; the first Frenchman to be made a member of the Royal Society, London) by Huez. In the Lady Chapel, by Hardouin-Mansart, is a marble group of the Nativity by François and Michel Anguier, from Val-de-Grâce.

WEST AISLE. On the last pillar of the ambulatory (right) is a bust of Le Nôtre (died 1707) by Coysevox. The 3rd chapel (beyond the transept) contains a mourning figure, by J.-B. Lemoyne the Elder, of Catherine, Comtesse de Feuquières (c 1700) incorporated in a monument, the central feature of which is the bust of her father, Pierre Mignard (1610–95) by Girardon. Diderot, Holbach (1723–89, whose hospitable home from 1759 was 8 Rue des Moulins, a few minutes walk to the north), Mme Geoffrin, Le Nôtre, Cherubini and the Abbé de l'Epée (see beginning of Rte 7) are also buried in St.-Roch. The organ-case dates from 1755.

The adjoining Rue St.-Roch, where Vauban (1633–1707) died, rejoins the Rue de Rivoli just west of the Pl. des Pyramides, with a bronze-gilt statue of Joan of Arc by Frémiet.

Continuing east along the Rue St.-Honoré, the scene both here and in neighbouring streets of Bonaparte's suppression of the royalist rising of 5 October 1795 (some marks of his 'whiff of grape-shot' may be detected on the front of St.-Roch), you shortly enter the Pl. André-Malraux (Pl. 8; 7; formerly Pl. du Théâtre-Français), with a view north west towards the Opéra. The two fountains are by Davioud. To the south the short Rue de Rohan reaches the Rue de Rivoli opposite the arch leading to the Pl. du Carrousel.

On the east of the Place stands the restored **Théâtre Français**, built in 1786–90 by Victor Louis, but largely remodelled after a fire in 1900.

As an institution the Théâtre-Français (or Comédie-Française) dates from the amalgamation in 1680 of the Hôtel de Bourgogne actors with Molière's old company, which had already absorbed the Théâtre du Marais. In 1812 Napoléon signed a decree (at Moscow) reorganising the Comédie-Française, which is still a private company although controlled by a director nominated by the government and enjoying a state subsidy.

The vestibule contains, among other statues of actors, Talma by David d'Angers; the staircase and foyer display busts of eminent dramatists including Dumas *fils* by Carpeaux, and Mirabeau by Rodin, a statue of George Sand by Clésinger (her son-in-law), and a *seated statue of Voltaire by Houdon. The chair in which Molière was sitting when acting in 'Le Malade Imaginaire' and taken fatally ill, is also preserved. The library may be consulted.

An inscription at the corner of the Rue de Valois (on the eastern side of the

Palais-Royal) marks the site of the 'Salle de Spectacle du Palais-Cardinal', occupied by Molière's company from 1661 to 1673, and by the 'Académie Royale de Musique' from 1673 until a fire in 1763.

Abutting the Théâtre Français, the ***PALAIS-ROYAL** and its surroundings constitute one of the most attractive and interesting areas of Paris. (It is hoped, however, that the black and white truncated columns by Daniel Buren misguidedly placed there under the aegis of M. Lang, will be removed.) The name Palais-Royal is now applied not only to the original palace but also to the extensive range of buildings and galleries surrounding the gardens to the north. This pedestrian thoroughfare, entered from neighbouring streets by several passages, is now a delightful backwater and haunt of the philatelist.

It played an important role in the Revolutionary period, and among the profligate society of the late 18C and early 19C, was the scene of unbridled licence and revelry, packed with '*tripots*' or gaming-houses, cafés, restaurants and numerous haunts of lesser repute.

The Palais-Royal proper was originally known as the 'Palais-Cardinal', having been built by Jacques Lemercier in 1634–39 for Richelieu, who, as chief minister, wished to be near the Louvre. He died there in 1642. (It contained a *salle de spectacle*, later used for operas.) Bequeathed to Louis XIII, it was first called 'Palais-Royal' during the residence of Anne of Austria (died 1666), then regent, and her sons Louis XIV and Philippe d'Orléans. Richelieu's apartments were then occupied by Cardinal Mazarin. During the Fronde they all had to escape to St.-Germain-en-Laye; Louis XIV therefore disliked the palace and it was Philippe and his wife Henriette d'Angleterre who returned to live there, although the king housed the Royal Academy of painting and sculpture in the west wing, and also his mistress Louise de la Vallière. This was the period of Mansart's alterations.

In 1692 the palace was given by Louis to his brother and his heirs. It acquired an equivocal reputation from the dissolute '*petits soupers*' given by the Regent, Philippe, Duc d'Orléans (1715–23). Changes were made for his son, Louis, by Constant d'Ivry and Jean-Silvain Cartaud. In 1763 a fire destroyed the east wing and the theatre. The houses and galleries around the gardens were built as a speculation in 1781–86 by Philippe-Egalité, the Regent's great-grandson, under pressure of debt, and let out as shops and cafés, etc. He also built the Théâtre-Français. The Théâtre du Palais-Royal, in the north-west corner, dates from the same period.

The cafés became a rendezvous for malcontents, since the police were excluded from entry, and on 13 July 1789 Camille Desmoulins delivered in the gardens the fiery harangue which precipitated the fall of the Bastille the following day.

The name Palais-Royal was changed to the 'Palais-Egalité', and it was used as government offices. In 1814 it was returned to the Orléans family and reverted to its earlier name. It was residence of Louis-Philippe until 1832. In 1848 it was plundered by the revolutionaries and occupied for a time by the 'Rights of Man' club. During the Second Empire it was the residence of Jérôme Bonaparte; Taine, Flaubert, Sainte-Beuve and the brothers Goncourt were often entertained here. The palace was rebuilt by Chabrol in 1872–76 after damage during the Commune. It is now occupied by the Conseil d'Etat and the Ministère de la Culturel.

The **Hôtel de Rambouillet**, built on part of the site of the Palais-Royal, and the town house of Catherine de Vivonne, Marquise de Rambouillet (1588?–1665; known in her refining circle as 'Arthénice'), was, during c 1618–50, a famous intellectual centre, Vincent Voiture, Saint-Evremond, Malherbe, Godeau, La Rochefoucauld, the Scudérys, Bossuet and the Duchesse de Longueville being among its *habitués*.

The buildings in the Cour de l'Horloge, facing the Pl. du Palais-Royal, were erected by Constant d'Ivry (1763–70), with sculptures by Pajou (left wing) and Franceschi (right; 1875). The façade on the north side, overlooking the Cour d'Honneur, was begun by D'Ivry, continued by Louis, and completed by Fontaine, who also restored the east and west wings. The so-called 'Galerie des Proues', on the east side of the court, is the only relic of Lemercier's 17C building. To the north, the Cour d'Honneur is separated from the gardens by the Galerie d'Orléans, a double Doric colonnade by Fontaine (1829–31), which was restored and cleared of its shops in 1935.

The *Gardens* of the Palais-Royal are surrounded on three sides by arcades and buildings (by Louis; 1781–86), still occupied by shops and dwellings, altogether a charming and harmonious ensemble. Among residents in recent decades were poet, playwright and film director Jean Cocteau and the actor Jean Marais. Colette (1873–1954) lived from 1938 until her death at 9 Rue de Beaujolais, beyond the Galerie Beaujolais to the north. On the west side is the Galerie de Montpensier, and opposite is the Galerie de Valois, where at No. 113 Le Peletier de Saint-Fargeau was assassinated in 1793. Nos 79–82 Galerie de Beaujolais, the Grand Vefour, was the fashionable rendezvous of writers in the Second Empire. Earlier, in the same house, Mlle de Montansier entertained the leaders of the Revolution in 1789. In 1785, 17 Galerie de Montpensier was a museum of waxworks, founded by Curtius, the uncle of Mme Tussaud. Here at Nos 83–86, Fragonard died in 1806. The Café du Caveau (Nos 89–92) was the rendezvous of the partisans of Gluck and his rival Piccinni; other *habitués* were Méhul and Boïeldieu.

Immediately east of the Palais-Royal is the Rue de Valois, with (Nos 1–3) the Pavillon du Palais-Royal (1766, by D'Ivry and Moreau); at Nos 6–8, once the Hôtel Melusine, the first meetings of the French Academy took place in 1638–43. The ox sculptured above the door recalls its period as the restaurant 'Boeuf à la Mode' from 1792 to 1936.

In the parallel street to the east, the Rue Croix-des-Petits-Champs, is the entrance to the **Banque de France** (Pl. 8;7), founded in 1800 and accommodated here in 1811.

The buildings incorporate the former Hôtel de la Vrillière, built by Mansart in 1635–38 and restored by Robert de Cotte in 1719. Later known as the Hôtel de Toulouse from its occupancy by the Comte de Toulouse, son of Louis XIV and Mme de Montespan, it became the residence of the Princess de Lamballe, murdered in the prison of La Force in 1792.

The profusely decorated *Galerie Dorée, within the bank, may be visited by those providing suitable *bona fides*.

The Hôtel Portalis (by Ledais; 1750) stands at the corner of the Rue de la Vrillière and the Rue Croix-des-Petits-Champs, No. 13 in which is the site of a house occupied by Malherbe from 1606–27. Vincent de Paul lived in the street in 1613–16, and Bossuet in 1699–1702, at No. 52. Another resident was Mme de Pompadour (1721–64), from 1725 to 1745, before her introduction to Versailles; she was born (as Jeanne Antoinette Poisson) in the Rue de Cléry, a short distance to the north east. Richelieu is believed to have been born (in 1585) in a house on the corner of the Rue du Bouloi, just to the east. Corneille lived in this street from 1665–81; La Rochefoucauld also resided here in his youth.

33 Rue Radziwill, on the north side of the Banque de France, has an unusual double staircase; while Mansart's projecting angle here, supported by a bracket, is a masterpiece of stonework.

To the north east of the Bank lies the circular *Pl. des Victoires**, laid out by Jules Hardouin-Mansart in 1685; the surrounding houses were designed by Pradot. The equestrian statue of Louis XIV by Bosio (1822) replaces the original, destroyed in 1792; the bas-reliefs on the pedestal depict the Passage of the Rhine, and Louis XIV distributing decorations.

The Rue Hérold, to the south east, is named after the composer Louis-Joseph-Ferdinand Hérold (1791–1833), born at No. 10.

Immediately north west is the Pl. des Petits-Pères, with a surprisingly provincial appearance, off which the Rue du Mail leads north east, where Colbert lived (at No. 5, richly decorated), and Mme Recamier resided (No. 12), while Liszt was a frequent visitor at No. 13 between 1823 and 1878. The composer Gasparo Spontini (1774–1851) also lived in this street in 1803.

On the north side of the Place stands **N.-D.-des-Victoires**, or the church of the Petits-Pères, dedicated in 1629 by Louis XIII to commemorate the capture of La Rochelle from the Huguenots in the previous year. Replacing a chapel, it was not actually begun until 1666, and only finished in 1740. Every interior wall is plastered with ex-voto tablets. In the 2nd chapel on the left is the tomb of the composer Jean-Baptiste Lully (1633–87) by Pierre Cotton, with a bust by Gaspard Collignon; in the choir are elaborately carved stalls, and seven paintings by Carle van Loo.

The adjoining street leads north to the **Bourse des Valeurs** or Stock Exchange, built by Brongniart and Labarre in 1808–27, and resembling the Temple of Vespasian in Rome. The north and south wings were added in 1903.

The Rue Feydeau, to the north, built on Louis-XIII fortifications, and the Rue des Colonnes, to the west, retain some interesting houses in an old district through which the Rue du Quatre-Septembre was driven in 1864, before being renamed on the proclamation of the Third Republic.

The Rue Vivienne leads south from the Bourse along the east side (right) of the Bibliothèque Nationale (see Rte 18), and retains several 17–18C houses; Simón Bolívar lived at 2 bis in 1804.

Of more interest is the parallel Rue de Richelieu, to the west, laid out by the cardinal, running south to the Pl. André Malraux. Rossini and Meyerbeer lived in its north half; Grétry resided at No. 52, further south, in 1780. No. 101, with decorative masks in the courtyard, was the home of the Abbé Barthélemy (1716–95), the antiquary, author of the 'Voyage du jeune Anacharsis', and curator of the royal collection of medals, then housed in the Hôtel de Nevers (see below). Anthelme Brillat-Savarin (1755–1826), author of the 'Physiologie du goût', died at No. 66; Ninon de Lenclos (1620–1705) had lived there in 1653–59.

On the left, at the corner of the Rue Colbert, stands part of the Hôtel de Nevers, built by Mazarin in 1649 to house his library (see below). As the home of the Marquise de Lambert (1647–1733) it was a famous literary salon from 1710, where Montesquieu and Marivaux met.

Further on is a fountain of 1708, and beyond (right) in the Sq. Louvois (Pl. 8; 5–7), the Fontaine Louvois, by the younger Visconti (1844).

The Square was laid out in 1839 on the site of a theatre (the Salle Louvois) built in 1794, which housed the Opéra until 1820. On 13 February 1820 the Archbishop of Paris was called here to administer the last sacraments to the Duc de Berry (assassinated here—by Louis Pierre Louvel—while on his way to watch the dancing of his mistress, Virginie Oreiller), consenting to do so on such unholy ground on condition that the theatre was afterwards pulled down (see Rue le Peletier).

Donizetti lived at No. 5 Rue de Louvois in 1840. Bossuet (1627–1704) died at 46 Rue Ste.-Anne, the street to the west.

For the **Bibliothèque Nationale**, on the east side of the square, see Rte 18.

Immediately south of the Bibliothèque Nationale is the Rue des Petits-Champs; No. 45 was the residence of Lully, built with financial help from Molière until 1683; the garret of No. 57 was the home of Rousseau and Thérèse Levasseur c 1754; Mme Récamier (1777–1849) died at No. 8.

Chamfort (1741–94), the author of posthumously published 'Maximes', attempted suicide in 1793 at No. 10 Rue Chabanais, immediately to the west. No. 12 in this street had an equivocal reputation in the late 19C. Its interior was also the setting of Toulouse-Lautrec's painting 'Au Salon' (1894). Holbach entertained Diderot, Marmontel, Grimm, Helvétius and Saint-Lambert during the years 1759–89 at 6 Rue des Moulins, further west.

Continuing south, at the corner of the Rue Molière (where Voltaire lived at No. 37 with Mme du Châtelet) is the Fontaine Molière by Visconti (1844; the dramatist is by Seurre, and the figures of Comedy by Pradier).

Molière (1622–73) died in a house on the site of 40 Rue de Richelieu. Denis Diderot (1713–84) died at No. 39; and Pierre Mignard (1610–95) at No. 23. No. 21, formerly the Hôtel Dodun, by Bullet (1715), retains some of its 18C grandeur; the composer Maria Gasparo Sacchini (1730–86) died at No. 14.

The street ends at the Pl. Andre-Malraux (see p 156).

18 Bibliothèque Nationale; Cabinet des Médailles et Antiques

METROS: Bourse; Pyramides, 4 Septembre.

On the east side of the Sq. Louvois (with its entrance at 58 Rue de Richelieu) rises the western façade of the **Bibliothèque Nationale**.

By mid 1995 it is expected that a high proportion of the contents of this library, which, with the British Library, is one of the two largest in Europe, will be moved to the new Bibiothèque de France, now under construction east of the Gare d'Austerlitz; see Rte 6. However, it will retain several departments, to be reorganised, among them that of maps and plans, and of prints. The important Cabinet des Médailles et Antiques will also remain here; see below.

The buildings of the Bibliothèque Nationale were erected at various times on the site of the 17C Hôtel Mazarin, and include the Hôtel Tubeuf, whose brick and stone façade, set back in the Rue des Petits-Champs, was built by Le Muet in 1635.

Formerly known as the Bibliothèque Royale and the Bibliothèque Impériale, it originated in the private collections of the French kings. Largely dispersed at the end of the Hundred Years' War, the Library was refounded by Louis XII and moved to Blois. During the next two centuries it was at Fontainebleau, and then Paris, before finding its present home in the Rue de Richelieu in 1721. Guillaume Budé (c 1468–1540) had earlier been appointed the first Royal Librarian. It was enriched by purchase or by gift of many famous private libraries and smaller collections (including that of Colbert), and at the Revolution its range was further increased with the confiscation of books from numerous convents and châteaux. In 1793 it was enacted that a copy of every book, newspaper, etc. printed in France should be deposited by the publishers in the Bibliothèque Nationale.

The main entrance vestibule is on the right of the Cour d'Honneur. The Reading Room (seen through glass doors opposite), roofed by nine faïence domes, seats 360 readers (as against the 5000 which the new Bibliothèque de France will accommodate). The Galerie Mansart, to the right at the foot of the stairs, was formerly Mazarin's sculpture gallery; note his arms above the door, and the carved foliage and paintings by Grimaldi. The Cabinet des Estampes, beyond, contains over five million prints. The Department of Music contains over 300,000 works including collections of musical scores, books on music, and MSS (among them Mozart's 'Don Giovanni') previously in the Library of the Conservatoire de Musique.

The *Musée du Cabinet des Medailles et Antiques, beyond the iron gates on the first floor landing reached by stairs to the left of the main entrance, is of exceptional interest to the connoisseur and should not be overlooked. The collection, founded in the 16C, but containing objects known to be in royal hands some time before that date, contains c 250,000 coins and medals, in addition to antiquities of outstanding quality, only a small proportion of which are on display.

Near the entrance is a Parian marble torso of Aphrodite (Hellenistic period), while in a series of showcases on this and on the mezzanine floor are selected examples of French and foreign coins and medals, engraved cameos, jewels, etc. Notable is the 'Grand Camée', from the Ste.-Chapelle, representing the Apotheosis of Germanicus, with Tiberius and Livia—the largest antique cameo known; the aquamarine intaglio of Julia, daughter of Titus, one of the best glyptic portraits extant; an engraved Chaldaean stone (1100 BC), found near Baghdad; the agate nef (incense boat) from St.-Denis; the Dish of Chosroes II, king of Persia (c 600 AD); the sardonyx Cup of Ptolemy; the 'Patère de Rennes' (a Roman gold dish found in 1774); a Merovingian chalice and oblong paten (6C), from Gourdon, in the Charollais; a bust of Constantine the Great, once the head of the cantor's wand at the Ste.-Chapelle; and a series of ivory chessmen (11–12C), which were once reputed to have belonged to Charlemagne (died 814).

Other cases contain Renaissance medals and bronzes; Egyptian terracottas and painted limestone statuettes; Roman bronze statuettes; ancient arms and armour, and domestic utensils; Greek and Etruscan vases, etc., including a red-figured amphora, signed Amasis; cyclix of Arcesilaus, king of Cyrene; vase of Berenice (239–227 BC), from Bengazi, and other ceramics; gold objects from the tomb of Childeric I, at Tournai; ivory consular diptychs, and Byzantine diptychs; gold bullae of Charles II of Anjou, king of Naples (1285–1309), of Baldwin I, Emperor of Constantinople in 1204–06, and of Edmund, Earl of Lancaster, titular king of Sicily, 1255–63; gold coins found at Chécy (Loiret); a Celtic bracelet (Aurillac; 5–6C); a silver hoard from the temple of Mercurius Canetonensis (Berthouville, Eure), including silver figurines and vessels of the 2C BC and others of the best Greek period.

Also displayed is the so-called Throne of Dagobert, on which the kings of France were crowned: a Roman curule chair of bronze, with arms and back added in the 12C by Suger.

The restored Salon Louis XV, decorated by Van Loo and Natoire, with *dessus de portes* by Boucher, has its original coin cabinets.

On the floor above, is (right) the **Manuscript Room** (with more than 130,000 MSS, of which some 10,000 are illuminated); and left, the Galerie Mazarine, by Mansart (1645), with a ceiling by Romanelli. Beyond is the Department of Maps and Plans.

19   From Pl. du Palais-Royal to Pl. de la Bastille
St.-Germain l'Auxerrois; the Bourse du Commerce; St.-Eustache; Forum des Halles; St.-Merri; Hôtel de Ville; St.-Gervais-St.-Protais; St.-Paul-St.-Louis; Hôtel de Sully

METROS: Palais-Royal, Louvre, Les Halles, Etienne-Marcel, Châtelet, Rambuteau, St.-Paul, Sully-Morland, Bastille, Châtelet-les Halles (RER).

Walking east from the Pl. du Palais-Royal, with the façade of the Palais-Royal on your left (see Rte 17), follow the Rue St.-Honoré, skirting the north side of the **Louvre des Antiquaires**.

The building, of 1852, formerly the department store of the Grands Magasins du Louvre, was acquired in 1975 by the British Post Office Staff Superannuation Fund as an investment, and gutted. Since 1978 it has tastefully accommodated, on three floors, some 250 professional antique-dealers' stalls, open to the public daily from 11.00–19.00, except Monday (also closed on Sunday from mid July–mid September). They can also organise transport, settle customs formalities and provide certificates of authenticity, etc. Lectures and exhibitions are frequently held here.

A short distance to the east is (right) the **Temple de l'Oratoire**, designed by Clément Métezeau the younger and Jacques Lemercier, and built in 1621–30 for Cardinal Bérulle as the mother church in France for his Congregation of the Oratory. In 1811, Napoléon assigned it to the Calvinists. The portal was added in 1845.

Against the apse is a monument to Admiral Coligny (1519–72), the chief victim of the massacre of St. Bartholomew, who was wounded in a house now replaced by 144 Rue de Rivoli, and murdered in the Louvre, where the king had given him sanctuary. Here stood the Hôtel de Ponthieu, where the actress and singer Sophie Arnould (1764–1804) was born.

Further east in the Rue-St.-Honoré, in which are several well-preserved 17C houses, Molière was born on the site of No. 96 in 1622; opposite is the Fontaine du Trahoir (rebuilt by Soufflot in 1778, replacing an earlier fountain by Goujon), with its stalactites and shells. The chemist Lavoisier (1743–94) owned No. 47; and Riesener (1734–1806), the cabinet-maker, died at No. 2.

Gallows stood at the point where the street is intersected by the Rue de l'Arbre-Sec, and nearby Cardinal de Retz was attacked during the Fronde (1648). Gabrielle d'Estrées (1573–99) died at the Hôtel de Sourdis (21 Rue de l'Arbre-Sec) a few days before she was to have married Henri IV.

A short distance east of the Oratoire, the Rue-St.-Honoré is intersected by the Rue du Louvre. By turning right here, and—crossing the Rue de Rivoli, with a view of the east façade of the Palais du Louvre—you reach the Pl. du Louvre, which claims to be the area where Caesar's legions encamped in 52 BC. Opposite stands the Mairie of the 1st Arrondissement (1859), which, according to Viollet-le-Duc, seems to have been intended as a caricature of the adjoining church, to which the conspicuous north tower was added in the following year.

*ST.-GERMAIN-L'AUXERROIS (Pl. 14; 1), a Gothic church of the 13–16C, was itself drastically restored in the 18–19C. The most striking exterior feature is the porch, by Jean Gaussel (1435–39), with a rose window, and above it, a balustrade which encircles the building. The transeptal doorways (15C) and Renaissance doorway (1570), north of the choir, are noteworthy. Nothing remains of the cloister.

In 885, the Norman invaders turned the church, dedicated to the 5C St. Germanus, Bp of Auxerre, into a fortress. A second church was built on the site in the 11C, which, in the following century, being the parish church of the adjacent palace, was found to be too small and was replaced by the present building in the 13C. The ringing of its bells for matins on 24 August 1572 was the signal for the slaughter of Huguenots to commence, known as the Massacre of St. Bartholomew.

Molière was married and his first son baptised here, and Danton was also married here. During the Revolution, having first served as a granary and then as a printing-works, it became the 'Temple of Gratitude'. It was sacked by a mob in 1831 during a mass celebrated on the eleventh anniversary of the death of the Duc de Berry (cf. Sq. Louvois), and poorly restored after 1838.

Among those buried in St.-Germain are the poets Jodelle and Malherbe; the architects Lemercier, De Cotte, Gabriel and Le Vau; the artists Coypel, Boucher and Chardin; the sculptors Coysevox, N. and G. Coustou; and the engraver Israël Silvestre.

The INTERIOR (78m by 39m) is double-aisled. The 'restoration' of 1745, mingling the classicism of the 18C with 14–15C architecture, mangled the choir-arches, converted the piers into fluted columns and heightened their capitals. Fragments of the destroyed rood-screen are preserved in the Louvre. The pulpit and royal pew are fine examples of late 17C woodwork by François Mercier (designed by Le Brun). Behind the latter is a sculptured triptych with painted wings (16C; Flemish), and in the aisle-chapel opposite is another altarpiece (1519; from Antwerp) in carved wood. The wrought-iron choir-railings date from 1767. On the left at the choir entrance is a wooden statue of St. Germanus; on the right a stone figure of St. Vincent (both 15C).

The outer south aisle is occupied by the Chapelle de la Vierge (late 13C), containing a 14C Virgin of the Champagne School, a 15C St. Mary of Egypt, a 13C St. Germanus (of the Paris School), and a 13C wooden Crucifixion. Only the transepts have their original 15–16C stained-glass. Above a small door in the ambulatory (south side) is a late-15C polychrome Virgin. The first inner bay is the base of the 12C belfry. In the 4th chapel are marble statues of Etienne d'Aligre and his son, both Chancellors of France (died 1635; 1677); 6th chapel, a relic of a Pietà by Jean Soulas (1505); and in the 7th chapel, effigies from the tomb of the Rostaing family (1582 and 1645).

Immediately to the south is the Rue des Prêtres; No. 17 was the site of the Café Momus from 1841 to 1861.

At 11 Rue du Louvre, leading north from the Rue-St.-Honoré to the small Pl. des Deux-Ecus, are slight remains of Philippe Auguste's fortifications. Off the Rue Jean-Jacques-Rousseau (leading south west from here) is the once fashionable Véro-Dodat arcade (1822), named in fact after two characters—M. Véro and M. Dodat.

To the east of the Pl. des Deux-Ecus stands the refurbished **Bourse du Commerce** (Pl. 8; 8), formerly the Corn Exchange, a circular mid-18C building; it was remodelled in 1888.

A fluted Doric column abutting its south-east side is the only relic of the Hôtel de la Reine (later Hôtel de Soissons, in the garden of which stock-jobbing took place from 1720), built for Catherine de Médicis in 1572 on the site of the earlier Hôtel d'Orléans which had belonged to Blanche of Castile (died 1252). The column may have been used as an astrologer's tower.

Bourse du Commerce

This building is now the only remaining relic in Paris of the Halles Centrales, which by mid 1969 had been moved to extensive modern markets at Rungis (c 11km south of Paris and a short distance north of Orly airport). Markets had stood here since the early 12C, but the ten huge pavilions constructed by Victor Baltard (1805–74) in the 1850s immediately to the east, together with two additional market halls completed in 1936, were needlessly demolished by 1974 (with the exception of No. 8, which was re-erected at Nogent-sur-Marne).

What Zola called 'Le ventre de Paris' is no more, although the excavated site some distance further east was for a decade known as the '*trou*' or hole; and more recently gratuitously endowed with the epithet '*cul*' de Paris. For the area immediately to the north, see below.

The radical redevelopment of the whole area of **Les Halles**, now completed, has been much criticised, not only for the overall design, which had been subject to numerous changes and compromises, too involved to detail here. A number of architects took part in the project, among them Ricardo Bofill, who later left the scene.

The technical problems posed and resolved were prodigious. These included the siting of the important underground railway-station at the intersection of the north–south and east–west lines of the RER system at the bottom of the '*trou*'; the provision of road tunnels and underground parking facilities; air-conditioning plants, skilfully disguised behind the façades of houses; and the erection of new blocks of buildings, which to some extent harmonise with the old.

Certainly St.-Eustache (see below) comes into its own (as does the Bourse du Commerce), while the restored Fontaine des Innocents (see below) is also now seen to advantage. Large areas have been designated a pedestrian precinct—indeed the Pl. Ste.-Opportune has already been styled Ste.-Importune—both in streets to the east and west of the transverse Blvd de Sébastopol, and there has been a notable revival of trade in the district, which has, with the improvements in communication, become a hub of activity of all kinds.

The much-vaunted **Forum des Halles**, its ribbed and glazed courtyard forming the sunken lid to the '*trou*', and embellished by curious pink marble statuary entitled 'Pyègemalion' (sic), by the Argentinian sculptor Julio Silva, has been the object of considerable critical comment since it was inaugurated in September 1979. Most of the building is on three subterranean floors, and although partially lit from the central square and supplied with numerous escalators and lifts, the feeling experienced by many visitors is of claustrophobia combined with agoraphobia. Certain walls, ceilings and pillars in passages—when not defaced by graffiti—are decorated with examples of pop art; the various levels contain eight cinemas, and some 200 shops.

To the north and east of the Forum are terraces on which mirrored mushroom-shaped pavilions have sprung up. Gardens have been laid out further west, and near St.-Eustache, together with an open-air auditorium with a covered swimming-pool below; the waterless Parc Océanique Cousteau; conservatories and hanging-gardens, etc., all of which should be seen to be believed.

From the western side of the Bourse du Commerce, the Rue du Louvre continues north, on the right of which is the **Hôtel des Postes** (1880–84), the main Post Office of Paris: opposite, in the elegant Hôtel d'Ollone (built in 1639 and altered in 1730), the Caisse d'Epargne (or Savings Bank) is installed.

From the 13C to the 18C the University of Paris was responsible for the postal service for private citizens, while from 1461 the royal mail was carried by relays of post riders. In 1719 the University lost its privilege and all mail was controlled by the royal service. In 1757 the postal headquarters was in the Hôtel d'Hervart.

On the east façade of the Hôtel des Postes, facing the northern extension of the Rue Jean-Jacques-Rousseau (where Rousseau lived at No. 52 in 1776), is an inscription marking the site of the hôtel which had been occupied by La Fontaine (1621–95) at the time of his death. Nos 64 and 68 in the street are worth noting.

From just north of the Bourse du Commerce, the Rue Coquillière (with a remarkable shop selling kitchen utensils) leads east.
  *ST.-EUSTACHE (Pl. 8; 8), just beyond, in detail and decoration a Renaissance building, but in plan and in its general lay-out of medieval design, dominates the area.

Begun in 1532, perhaps by Pierre Lemercier, it was consecrated in 1637. The main west doorway was rebuilt in 1754–88 in a completely inharmonious Classical style. Both transepts have handsome round-headed doorways (c 1638–40). The north transept is approached by a passage from the Rue Montmartre. The open-work bell-tower ('Plomb de St.-Eustache') above the crossing, has lost its spire. Above the Lady Chapel in the apse is a small tower built in 1640 and restored in 1875.
  The church was the scene of the riotous Festival of Reason in 1793, and in 1795 became the 'Temple of Agriculture'. Molière was baptised here in 1622, and Antoinette Poisson (Mme de Pompadour) in 1721; Lully was married here in 1662. In 1791 the body of Mirabeau lay in state here before its removal to the Panthéon. Among those buried here are Colbert (1619–83), Admiral de Tourville (died 1701) and Rameau (1683–1764). St.-Eustache has always been noted for its music. It was here that Berlioz conducted the first performance of his 'Te Deum' (1855) and Liszt his 'Messe Solenelle' (1866). It is the venue of frequent organ recitals.

The INTERIOR is unusual in its striking combination of Classical forms with a Gothic plan. The double aisles and chapels of the nave are continued round the choir. The square piers are flanked by three storeys of columns in Renaissance variants of the Classical orders. The chapels are decorated with paintings from the time of Louis XIII, but restored. The 11 lofty windows of the apse were executed by Soulignac (1631), possibly from cartoons of Philippe de Champaigne. The churchwardens' pew by Pierre le Pautre dates from c 1720. The stalls come from the convent of Picpus.
  South aisle. The 2nd chapel commemorates Rameau; by the transept doorway is a 15C statue of St. John the Evangelist; the 2nd choir chapel has a Pietà attributed to Luca Giordano. In the Lady Chapel, on the altar, is a Virgin by Pigalle; the murals are by Thomas Couture.
  North aisle. In the 1st choir chapel as you return is the tomb of Colbert, designed by Le Brun, with statues of Colbert and Fidelity by Coysevox, and of Abundance by Tuby. Above the west door is the Martyrdom of St.-Eustache by Simon Vouet.

The Rue de Turbigo leads north east from St.-Eustache towards the Pl. de la République, soon reaching the Rue Etienne-Marcel, in which, to the left (at No. 20), rises the Tour de Jean-sans-Peur, a graceful defensive tower of c 1400 once incorporated in the Hôtel de Bourgogne. Part of this mansion (see No. 29) was used from 1548 until the turn of the 18C as a theatre, where Corneille's 'Le Cid' and Racine's 'Andromaque' and 'Phèdre' were performed.
  The next street to the east is the old Rue St.-Denis. At No. 135, in its north section, an inscription indicates the former position of the Porte St.-Denis or Porte aux Peintres, a gateway in the walls of Philippe Auguste. At the corner of the Rue Tiquetonne (then the Rue du Petit-Lion), stood the shop bearing the sign of the 'Cat and Racket', referred to in Balzac's story 'La Maison du Chat qui Pelote'. On No. 142 is the Fontaine de la Reine (1730).

Walking south down the street, where at No. 133 are some statues from the medieval Hôpital de St.-Jacques (on this site), you reach (left) **St.-Leu-St.-Gilles**, built in 1235, the nave reconstructed after 1319. The aisles were added in the 16C; the choir, still partly Gothic, in 1611 (and reconstructed in 1858–61 to make way for the adjacent boulevard). The façade and windows were remodelled in 1727 and a crypt excavated in 1780. The church contains three Nottingham alabaster reliefs (in the sacristy entrance) and a sculptured group of St. Anne and the Virgin, perhaps from Ecouen, by Jean Bullant (2nd south chapel). The organ gallery is by Nicolas Raimbert (1659).

Marivaux (1688–1763) was born on the site of 106 Rue Rambuteau, two streets further south.

Continuing south in the Rue St.-Denis, you reach the small Sq. des Innocents, on part of the site of the medieval Cimetière des Innocents, the main burial ground of Paris until 1785, when the remains, probably including those of La Fontaine, were transferred to the catacombs (see Rte 7). According to Pantagruel, 'the grave-digging rogues of St. Innocent used in frostie nights to warme their bums with dead mens bones'. Traces of the arches of the cemetery galleries are still to be seen on Nos 11 and 13 in the Rue des Innocents.

The restored Renaissance *** Fontaine des Innocents** was originally erected in 1548 in the neighbouring Rue St.-Denis by Pierre Lescot, with bas-reliefs by Jean Goujon (now in the Louvre). It was remodelled and set up here by Payet c 1788, the south side (for it had earlier abutted a building) being decorated by Pajou.

To the south is the Rue de la Ferronnerie, where, in front of No. 11, Henri IV was assassinated by Ravaillac in 1610.

33 Rue St.-Denis has an 18C sign, 'Au Mortier d'Argent'. The playwright and librettist Eugène Scribe (1791–1861) was born at No. 32.

Across the ugly Blvd de Sébastopol (left) is the narrow Rue Quincampoix (parallel to the east), one of the oldest streets in Paris, although most of the houses date from the 17–18C. At No. 43 John Law (1671–1729 in Venice), the Scottish financier, established his Mississippi bank in 1716, which, after frenzied speculation, obstructed by jealous rivals, ended in a bankruptcy (1720) even more catastrophic than the 'South Sea Bubble'. No. 54 stood on the site of the Cabaret de l'Epee de Bois, where the Royal Academy of the Dance had its origins in 1658. After the creation of Law's bank the wealthy 'Mississipiens' made it their club, when it was frequented by Louis Racine and Marivaux. Nos 10, 12, and 14 (further south) have rococo façades: No. 36 is also worth noting.

To the east opens the Pl. Edmond-Michelet (or Sq. de la Reynie), diagonally across which there is a view of the Centre Beaubourg on approaching the Piazza Beaubourg, flanked to the west by the Rue St.-Martin.

Gérard de Nerval (1808–55) was born at No. 168 in this street. At the junction of the Rue Bernard-de-Clairvaux, leading east into this redeveloped Quartier de l'Horloge, and the Rue Brantôme, is an imaginative modern clock, with automata, by Jacques Monestier (1979). For the Centre Beaubourg or Pompidou, see Rte 20.

Immediately south of the Centre, is the Pl. Igor-Stravinsky, flanked by relics of the Rue Brisemiche, in which Pascal's family once lived.

Here rises **ST.-MERRI**, built in the Flamboyant style (1515–52) on the site of at least two older churches, which covered the grave of St. Médéric of Autun (died c 700). In 1796–1801 it was called the 'Temple of Commerce' (much of which in this area, from the 14C at least, was of the carnal kind). The west front is notable for its rich decoration, but the statues are mostly poor replacements of 1842. The north-west turret contains the oldest bell in Paris (1331); the south-west tower lost its top storey in a fire. The nave has a double aisle on the right; a single on the left. The pulpit was designed by Michel-Ange Slodtz (1753), who also altered the choir. The organ dates from 1567; Saint-Saëns was organist here. The remaining stained-glass windows, contemporary with the church, are good.

In the right aisle, the 1st outer chapel has remains of the 13C church; further on is a large chapel by Boffrand (1743–44), with decorations by Paul-Ambroise Slodtz. In the left aisle, the 1st chapel contains a 15C tabernacle; the 3rd a Pietà attributed to Nicolas Legendre (c 1670); the 4th, a painting by Coypel (1661). From the 5th, a staircase descends to the crypt (1515), which has grotesque corbels and the tombstone of Guillaume le Sueur (died 1530). In the north transept is St. Merri delivering prisoners by Simon Vouet. Among other paintings are a late-16C work of the Fontaine-bleau School (south of the Lady Chapel) of St. Geneviève guarding her flocks, with Paris in the background.

The quarter around St.-Merri, with its narrow and picturesque alleys, retains several characteristic old houses which have survived the rage for demolition during the Halles-Beaubourg redevelopment scheme.

According to tradition, Boccaccio (1313–75), whose mother was French, was born near the junction of the adjacent Rue des Lombards and the Rue St.-Martin (in which note the 17C bas-relief of the Annunciation on No. 89). In the basement of 14 Rue des Lombards (now a restaurant) is the vaulted chapel of the former women's prison of St.-Merri. This ancient street is continued to the east by the Rue de la Verrerie, in which both Boucher and Bossuet were born, in 1703 and 1727 respectively, on the sites of Nos 60 and 83.

You regain the Rue de Rivoli just south of St.-Merri. This eastern section of the street was laid out under Napoléon III to allow rapid access for troops to the Hôtel de Ville in case of emergency.

In the centre of the Sq. St.-Jacques rises the flamboyant Gothic **Tour St.-Jacques,** dating from 1508–22, since 1797 the only relic of the church of St. Jacques-la-Boucherie. It was used as a shot-tower after 1836, until 'restored' in 1858 by Ballu, and later as a meteorological station.

Among its 19C statues is one of Pascal, who in 1642 verified here (or on the tower of St.-Jacques-du-Haut-Pas) the barometric experiments he had set up on the Puy de Dôme.

Adjoining to the south west is the Pl. du Châtelet (Pl. 14; 2), bounded by the Seine, here crossed by the Pont au Change: see Rte 1.

The Place is named after the vanished Grand Châtelet, a fortress gateway leading to the Cité, once the headquarters of the Provost of Paris and the Guild of Notaries. It was begun in 1130, and demolished between 1802–10. Both François Villon and Clément Marot—in 1448 and 1526 respectively—were confined here. There is a plan of the fort on the front of the Chambres des Notaires on the north side of the square.

On the east side is the Théâtre de la Ville, restored after a fashion and reopened in 1980, only to be severely damaged by fire in 1982. To the west is the Théâtre du Châtelet (1862), in which the Communards were court-martialled in 1871. Jacques-Louis David (1748–1825), the artist, was born in a house which stood on the south side of this site. In the centre is the Fontaine du Châtelet (or de la Victoire or du Palmier) dating from 1808 and 1858. An inscription indicates the position of the 'Parloir aux Bourgeois', the seat of the municipality of Paris from the 13C until 1357 (see below).

From the north side of the Place, the Av. Victoria (named in honour of Queen Victoria's visit to Paris in 1855) leads east to the **Pl. de l'Hôtel-de-Ville** (Pl. 14; 2), known until the Revolution of 1830 as the Pl. de Grève, for here, since the 11C, ships had moored on the strand or grève.

This square was the usual site for public executions: among the more famous of which (many incredibly barbarous) were those of the Comte de St.-Pol (1475), Constable of France, on the orders of Louis XI; Briquemont and Cavagnes, the Huguenot leaders (1572; among many other Protestants); the Comte de Montgomery (1574), captured at the siege of Domfront and formerly captain in the Scottish Guard; François Ravaillac, the assassin of Henri IV (1610); Eléonore Galigaï (the favourite of Marie de Médicis), executed for sorcery in 1617; the Marquise de Brinvilliers (1676), poisoner; the highwayman Cartouche (1721); and Damiens (1757), for attempting to murder Louis XV. In 1789, Foullon (controller-general of finance) and his son-in-law Bertier were hanged here by the Revolutionary mob. In 1795 Fouquier-Tinville suffered the same fate as his countless victims. Louvel, who assassinated the Duc de Berry, was executed here in 1820.

It was often a rendezvous for unemployed or dissatisfied workers, who were said to 'faire grève', which came to mean 'to go on strike'.

The **Hôtel de Ville**, on the eastern side of the square, stands on the site of its historic predecessor, begun c 1532, and burnt down by the Communards in 1871. This caricature replica, in the style of the French Renaissance, was built (on a larger scale) in 1874–84 from the plans of Ballu and Deperthes.

Its over-decorated façades are embellished with statues of eminent Frenchmen: its interior is also lavishly adorned in the official taste in architecture of the period, with sculpture, elaborate carvings, mural paintings, etc., including Puvis de Chavannes' The Seasons.

At 29 Rue de Rivoli, on the north side of the building, is the Municipal Tourist Office.

In 1264 Louis IX created the first municipal authority in Paris by allowing the merchants to elect magistrates ('échevins'), led by the 'prévôt des marchands', who was also head of the 'Hanse des marchands de l'eau'. This merchant guild, which had the monopoly of the traffic on the Seine, Marne, Oise and Yonne, took as their emblem a ship, a device which still graces the arms of the city. Their first meeting-place was known simply as the 'Parlouer aux Bourgeois'; later they met at the Grand-Châtelet itself; and finally, in 1357, the Provost Etienne Marcel bought the 'Maison aux Piliers' or 'Maison du Dauphin', a mansion in the Pl. de Grève, for their assemblies. In 1532 plans for an imposing new building were adopted but work was stopped at the second floor, and the new designs approved by Henri II in 1549 were not completed until 1628.

In 1789, the 300 electors nominated by the districts of Paris met there. On 17 July, Louis XVI received the tricolour cockade from the hands of Jean Sylvain Bailly, the Mayor. On 10 August 1792, the 172 commissaries elected by Paris gave the signal for a general insurrection. In 1794 Robespierre took refuge here, but was arrested on 27 July and, his jaw smashed by a bullet, dragged to the Conciergerie. In 1805 it became the seat of the Préfet de la Seine and his council, and was the scene of numerous official celebrations (including Napoléon's marriage to Marie-Louise).

The Swiss Guards put up a stout defence of the building during the stormy days of 1830. In 1848 it became the seat of Louis Blanc's provisional government and witnessed the arrest of the revolutionary agitators Armand Barbès and Louis-Auguste Blanqui. Verlaine was employed here in the mid 1860s. The Third Republic was proclaimed here in 1870 (4 September) and, in the following March, the Commune. On 24 May 1871 the building was evacuated before being set ablaze by its defenders.

In 1944 the Hôtel de Ville was a focus of opposition to the occupying forces by the Resistance movement, who by 19 August had established themselves in the building, repelling German counter-attacks until relieved by the arrival of Général Leclerc's division five days later.

From the north-east corner of the Hôtel de Ville, you may cross the Rue de Rivoli to the **Temple des Billettes**, at 22 Rue des Archives, which is conveniently approached from here. It was built in 1756 for the Carmelites, but since 1812 has been used as a Lutheran church. Abutting it to the north, the cloister, the only medieval example in Paris, is a relic of an older convent (1427).

The Rue de Rivoli, and its eastern extension, the Rue St.-Antoine, split the ancient **Marais** district into two unequal sections; the smaller, to the south, is described below; for the area to the north, see Rte 21.

To the east of the Hôtel de Ville, between two of its annexes, lies the Pl. St.-Gervais, with its elm tree, a reminder of the famous elm of St.-Gervais, beneath which justice used to be administered; the proverbial expression for waiting for Doomsday is, ironically, 'Attendre sous l'orme' (the elm). This was one of the first inhabited areas on the Right Bank, and the Rue François-Miron follows the course of a Roman road which led from Lutetia to Senlis.

To the east it is dominated by *****ST.-GERVAIS-ST.-PROTAIS** (Pl. 15; 1–3); founded in the 6C, its present form dates from the rebuildings of 1494–1578 (choir and transepts) and 1600–57 (nave, chapels and tower).

The original plans are attributed to Martin Chambiges, whose work was continued by his son Pierre. The lower stages of the tower are an early 15C survival. The façade (1616–21), by Clément Métezeau and (probably) Salomon de Brosse, is thought to be the earliest example in France of the superimposition of the three Classic orders—Doric, Ionic and Corinthian. In 1795 the church was converted into a 'Temple of Youth'. Bossuet preached here; Mme de Sévigné was married here (1644); and Philippe de Champaigne (1602–74), Scarron (1610–60) and Crébillon the Elder (1674–1762) are buried here.

François Couperin (1668–1733) and seven members of his family served as organists here from 1653 to 1830, and their organ, restored, survives. Couperin 'le Grand' was born in a house on the site of 4 Rue François-Miron.

The INTERIOR, impressive for its loftiness and unity of style, is remarkably rich in works of art. The high windows of both nave and choir contain much stained-glass of c 1610–20 by Robert Pinaigrier and Nicolas Chaumet. The nave was completed in flamboyant Gothic at a time when Renaissance influence was strongest.

South aisle. The 2nd chapel has an altar commemorating some 50 victims of the bombardment of Good Friday 1918, when a German shell struck the church. In the 3rd, seven low 17C painted panels of the Life of Christ; 5th and 6th, stained-glass of 1531. In the 8th chapel, the tomb of Michel le Tellier (died 1685), by Mazeline and Hurtrelle; the bearded heads supporting the Chancellor's sarcophagus are from the tomb of Jacques de Souvré (died 1670), by François Anguier, the rest of which are in the Louvre. The Lady Chapel, an overdecorated example of flamboyant Gothic (1517), retains fine contemporary glass.

The sacristy, in the north choir aisle, retains a good iron grille of 1741. In the north transept is a restored mid 16C Flemish painting of the Passion. From the next chapel you can enter the well-restored Chapelle Dorée (1628); in the adjacent chapel are a 13C high relief of the Dormition of the Virgin (below the altar), and a portrait by Pajou (1782) of Mme Palerme de Savy.

In the choir, the stalls are of the 17C (west end) and mid 16C, the latter with curious misericords. Against the north entry-pillar is a 14C Virgin, known as N.-D. de Bonne-Délivrance; and on either side of the altar, wooden statues of the patron saints, by Michel Bourdin (1625). The 18C bronze-gilt candelabra are by Soufflot.

The south façade of the church can now be seen since the area has been the subject of clearance and restoration. Note the façades of some houses in the Rue des Barres, behind the building.

The stepped Rue François-Miron, leading north east from St.-Gervais, is one of the more imposing streets in the district. Nos 2–14, built c 1735, are adorned with wrought-iron work displaying the famous elm (see above); Nos 30, 36 and 42 all have good features.

No. 26 Rue Geoffroy-l'Asnier (right) is the Hôtel de Chalons-Luxembourg (1608), with a magnificent doorway (1659) and an attractive Louis XIII pavilion in the courtyard. No. 22 also retains a handsome 17C façade. No. 17 is a Jewish Study Centre, with a memorial.

Further east in the Rue François-Miron (off which is the Rue de Jouy; see below) is the mutilated **Hôtel de Beauvais** (No. 68; by Le Pautre), with an interior courtyard, ornate circular vestibule and carved staircase. From its balcony Anne of Austria and Cardinal Mazarin watched the entry of Louis XIV and Marie-Thérèse into Paris in 1660.

It was built in 1655 for Pierre Beauvais, on the proceeds gained from having ignored the fact that his 40-year-old wife Catherine-Henriette Bellier, a 'lady-in-waiting' to the queen-mother (and known as 'Cateau-la-Borgnesse', for she had only one eye), had taught the 14-year-old king certain essential facts of life.

Christina of Sweden was a later tenant, and here in 1763 Mozart (aged 7) was the guest of the Bavarian ambassador.

The balcony of the Hôtel du Président Hénault (No. 82) should be noted.

To the right in the Rue de Jouy, No. 7, the Hôtel d'Aumont, by Le Vau (1648) and François Mansart (1656), retains some of its original decoration, including work by Le Brun.

Beyond, the Rue du Figuier leads right to the **Hôtel de Sens** (Pl. 15; 3), built c 1474–1519 for the archbishops of Sens, at a time when the bishopric of Paris was suffragan to the metropolitan see of Sens (before 1623); it is older than the Hôtel de Cluny (cf.), the only other important example of 15C domestic architecture in Paris. Unfortunately it has suffered a long period of neglect, and has been poorly restored. It now houses the Bibliothèque Forney, a reference library devoted to the fine arts.

Marguerite de Valois (1553–1615), whose memoirs may have assisted Brantôme in the composition of his 'Dames illustres', passed sinful years here with her younger lovers. In 1605, she had executed one of them for the jealous murder of another on her doorstep.

To the east, the Quai des Célestins, commanding attractive views of the Ile St.-Louis, passes (left, at No. 32) the site of the Tour Barbeau. This completed, on the river bank, the northern perimeter of Philippe Auguste's defensive wall, a section of which may be seen from the adjacent Rue des Jardins-St.-Paul.

Here also stood the tennis-court of the Croix-Noire, where Molière performed in 1645 until his arrest for debt. Rabelais (1494?–1553) died in the Rue des Jardins-St.-Paul, and was buried in the vanished church of St.-Paul-des-Champs (see below), as were the Mansarts (1666 and 1708) and the 'Man in the Iron Mask', who had died in the Bastille (1703).

The neighbouring Rue St.-Paul had acquired its name before 1350; at No. 32, part of the church belfry survives. See below for the eastern end of the Quai des Célestins.

Turning right at the north end of the Rue des Jardins-St.-Paul and then left brings you to the Rue St.-Antoine, an ancient thoroughfare retaining several elegant façades.

A few paces to the west is **St.-Paul-St.-Louis** (Pl. 15; 3), or the Grands-Jé-suites, built for that Society by Louis XIII in 1627–41 to replace a chapel of 1582. St.-Paul was added to the original name in 1796 to commemorate the demolished St.-Paul-des-Champs.

Designed by François Derrand, its florid style, founded on 16C Italian churches, is the earliest example of the Jesuit school of architecture in France. Richelieu said the first mass here. The handsome Baroque portal is by Martellange. The interior is over-decorated but imposing, and contains, in the left transept, a Christ in the Garden by Delacroix; and in the right, Louis XIII offering a model of the church to St. Louis by Simon Vouet. Bp. Huet (died 1721), the original editor of the Delphin classics, is buried here, and so is Louis Bourdaloue, who made most of his famous orations here: 'he preached like an angel', commented Mme de Sévigné.

Gérard de Nerval, who was educated at the adjacent Lycée Charlemagne, occupying a 17C Jesuit house, was found hanged in the old Rue de la Vieille Lanterne, near the Sq. St.-Jacques (see above) in 1855.

Turning east along the Rue St.-Antoine, you shortly reach (left; No. 62) the ***Hôtel de Sully** (CNMH) (or de Béthune-Sully), now occupied by offices of the Caisse Nationales des Monuments Historiques, who can give information about guided tours to the sites and monuments of Paris; they also publish 'Monuments Historiques', a review devoted to the restoration of architecturally important buildings; and have a bookstall. Their publications are also available at Porte F of the Grand Palais, facing the Cours-la-Reine.

The mansion, by Jean du Cerceau (1624–30), was acquired by Sully, the minister of Henri IV, in 1634. The courtyard, a particularly fine example of the Louis-XIII style, the entrance pavilions, and the interior, retaining 17C ceilings and panelling, have been extensively restored. The Hôtel de la Mouffle had previously stood on this site, from 1407.

The Photographic Archives of the Caisse Nationale, invaluable to the student of French art and architecture, are at 4 Rue de Turenne, adjacent to the west.

From just east of the Hôtel de Sully, the short Rue de Birague approaches the southern entrance of the Pl. des Vosges (see Rte 21); Nos 12 and 14 have elegant features.

Opposite, from the south side of the Rue St.-Antoine, leads the Rue Beautreillis. Beneath the carriage-entrance of No. 22, the Grand Hôtel de Charny (where Baudelaire lodged in 1858–59), are some woodcarvings in the purest Louis XIII style. No. 16, the Petit Hôtel de Charny, was the birthplace of the dramatist Victorien Sardou (1831–1908). To the right in the Rue Charles V is the imposing Hôtel d'Aubray (No. 12; 1620), residence of the notorious Marquise de Brinvilliers (1630–76), the poisoner. No. 10, the Hôtel de Maillé, retains its Louis XIII façade and No. 15, opposite, dates from 1642.

10 Rue Beautreillis was the Hôtel des Princes de Monaco, built c 1650,

but altered in the 18th and 19Cs; No. 7, with a wooden staircase and wrought-iron balcony, is one of the finest bourgeois houses of its period in Paris (late 16C).

On reaching the Rue des Lions, with a number of 17–18C mansions, including No. 10 (the passage in the modern façade leads to a courtyard of 1642) and No. 11, in which Mme de Sévigné lived in 1645–50, turn left and then right to regain the Quai des Célestins.

4 Quai des Célestins, the stately Hôtel de Fieubet, with an interesting courtyard, was built by Jules Hardouin-Mansart (1676–81) for Gaspard de Fieubet, chancellor to Anne of Austria; unfortunately it was badly disfigured in 1857. It now accommodates the Ecole Massillon. The Hôtel de Nicolai, No. 4, is also of the late 17C.

At No. 1 Rue de Sully, on the far side of the Blvd Henri-IV, in the Quartier de l'Arsenal (named after the arsenal established here by Henri IV), stands the **Bibliothèque de l'Arsenal** (Pl. 15; 4).

The library, opened to the public in 1797, was founded in 1757 by Antoine-René d'Argenson, Marquis de Paulmy (1722–87), and sold by him to the Comte d'Artois in 1785. It is partly installed in the former residence of the Grand Master of Artillery, built in 1594 for Sully. The façade in the parallel Blvd Morland (facing the starkly functional Préfecture de Paris) is by Boffrand (c 1723). Noteworthy are the Salon de Musique, by Boffrand, with superb Louis-XV woodwork, and the Apartment of the Duchesse de La Meilleraie, with a ceiling by Simon Vouet.

The library possesses some 15,000 MSS, one million printed volumes and 120,000 engravings. It is known particularly for its incomparable series of illuminated MSS, and its almost complete collection of French dramatic works. The Gordon Craig collection was acquired in 1957. Among its archives are the papers of the Bastille; documents relating to the 'Man in the Iron Mask', and the 'Affair of the Diamond Necklace'; letters of Henri IV to the Marquise de Verneuil, etc.; also Louis IX's Book of Hours and Charles V's Bible, among others. Nodier, Hérédia, Mérimée and Anatole France were librarians here.

Turning north east (right) past the Caserne des Célestins (barracks of the Gendarmerie Mobile, built on part of the site of the famous Celestine monastery founded in 1362, but suppressed in 1779), you shortly bear left off the Blvd Henri-IV, to regain the Rue St.-Antoine (via the Rue Castex). On the corner is the circular Temple de Ste.-Marie, originally the chapel of the Convent of the Visitation, and now a Protestant church. It was built by François Mansart in 1632–34.

The unscrupulous Surintendant des Finances, Nícolas Fouquet (1615–80) and Henri de Sévigné (Mme de Sévigné's husband, killed in a duel in 1651) were buried here. Vincent de Paul was almoner of the convent for 28 years.

A few paces to the west, at No. 21, is the Hôtel de Mayenne (or d'Ormesson), retaining a turret and charming staircase. Now the Ecole des Francs-Bourgeois, it was built by Jean du Cerceau in 1613–17. It is flanked by the Rue du Petit-Musc, a corruption of its 14C name, which was either 'La pute y Muse' or 'La Pute qui muse'.

Turning east you pass (right) the Rue de Lesdiguières, where at No. 9 was Balzac's first Paris lodging, in a garret at three *sous* a day. A tablet on 5 Rue St.-Antoine marks the position of the court of the Bastille (see Rte 21), by which the Revolutionary mob gained access to the fortress. Near the junction of this street and the Pl. de la Bastille was the site of the great barricade of 1848, and also the last stronghold of the Communards in 1871. See also Rte 21.

20 Centre Beaubourg (Centre Pompidou)

METROS: Rambuteau, Hôtel de Ville, Châtelet.

The **CENTRE BEAUBOURG** is officially called the **Centre National d'Art et de Culture Georges-Pompidou,** named after the well-meaning Président, who in 1969 conceived the idea of a form of cultural centre. It is also known by the initials CNAC, or merely as the Centre Pompidou (Pl. 14; 2).

The building—selected from 681 projects received—designed by the Anglo-Italian team, Richard Rogers and Renzo Piano, in association with G. Franchini, and the Ove Arup group, was inaugurated early in 1977, and already looks very much the worse for wear. The superstructure is 166m long from north to south, 60m wide, and 42m in height. Its superficial area is 103,300m^2 with a floor area on eight open-plan levels comprising 60,000m^2, of which 19,000m^2 is available for exhibitions, semi-permanent and temporary. The glazed surface is 11,000m^2; the *'ossature métallique'* weighs 15,000 tonnes, 3000 more than that of the Musée d'Orsay.

West side of the Centre Beaubourg

On its west side the lively 'Piazza Beaubourg' slopes down from the Rue St.-Martin to the main entrance on the ground floor of the Centre. Here a variety of 'manifestations' and exhibitions—both impromptu and organised—take place (beware of pick-pockets).

To the north is a reconstruction of a studio, once at 11 Impasse Ronsin, which belonged to Constantin Brancusi (1876–1904).

Stairs and escalators (left) rise to a mezzanine floor on a level with the Rue Beaubourg to the east. Turning left again you reach an 'external' escalator running up a glazed intestine-like tube, which writhes up to connect a series of platforms, each providing access to the upper five floors. On the first three are sections of the library (Bibliothéque Publique d'Information; BPI), containing over 350,000 volumes (less quantities 'missing' shortly after its opening); 250,000 transparencies; 12,000 records; reference material; films; video-cassettes, etc.

These levels are also partly occupied by the Centre de Création Industrielle (CCI), and the sonorous-sounding Institut de Recherche et de Coordination Acoustique/Musique (IRCA/M; director Pierre Boulez), happily muffled in sound-proof bunkers (below the Pl. Igor-Stravinsky, between the Centre and St.-Merri). (The institute may be moved to the projected Cité de Musique at La Villette; see Rte 29.)

On the THIRD LEVEL is the entrance to the *Musée National d'Art Moderne; see below. It extends to the floor above, reached by an interior escalator. On the top floor, devoted to temporary exhibitions (and occasional 'animations') is a Cinémathèque, a restaurant and a terrace (in addition to others on a lower level) providing some unusual views over Paris.

If the success of a museum or monument is to be gauged by the number of people whose curiosity has provoked them to enter it, then the Centre Georges-Pompidou has been a spectacular success, even if only a comparatively small proportion visit the permanent exhibition of modern art. Some have asserted that it is 'a remarkable achievement': others have been less kind. There have been varied reactions to the ungainly and incongruous physical appearance of what has been well-described as a 'culture factory' in the midst of the staid Marais, with its dignified 17–18C architecture.

Neither the canvases nor the dividing screens are adequately labelled and there is no recommended route for the visitor, but by following a vaguely clockwise direction after turning half-right on entering the museum you can at least see everything.

Among individual works to be seen are *Bacon*, Three people in a room; *Balthus*, Cathy's toilet; *Bonnard*, En barque, The toilet, and Landscapes; Braque, Girl playing a mandolin; *Camoin*, Portrait of Marquet; *Chagall*, Double portrait with a glass of wine, The acrobat, Guerre (1943); Robert *Delauny*, Portrait of Henri Carlier, Le manège de cochons, La Ville de Paris, Eiffel Tower, Towers of Laon, Self-portrait, La verseuse, and others; *Sonia Delaunay*, Prismes électriques, Marchè au Minho, and others; *Otto Dix*, Portrait of Sylvia von Harden; *Derain*, Nude against green curtains; *Dufy*, Bathers; *Roger de la Fresnaye*, La Ferté-sous-Jouarre, The cuirassier; *Gargallo*, Statue of the Prophet; *George Grosz*, Remember uncle August, the unhappy inventor; *Kisling*, Woman with a Polish shawl; *Marie Laurencin*, Apollinaire and his friends; *Lipchitz*, Head of Gertrude Stein (1920); *Magritte*, Le modèle rouge; *Manguin*, Portrait of Ravel; *Marquet*, Seated nude, Bassin du Havre; *Matisse*, L'Odalesque à la culotte rouge, La blouse roumaine, La ciel; *Modigliani*, Portrait of Dédié; *Picabia*, Young girl (1912); *Picasso*, Recumbant nude (1901), Seated nude (1905), Tête de femme rouge (1906), La Liseuse (1920), Minotaure (1927), Confidences (1934), Nature morte à la tête antique, Portraits of Mme Paul Eluard, and of Dora Maar, Two women on a beach, and others; *Rouault*, The wounded clown; *Soutine*, The groom, and Portrait of Miestchanioff; *Utrillo*, L'Impasse Cottin, Jardin de Montmagny; *Suzanne Valadon*, The blue room; *Felix Vallatton*, Romanian woman in red dress.

You can also see representative works by Brancusi, Dubuffet, Dali, Ernst, Alberto Giacometti, Julio Gonzalez, Gris, Kandinsky, Kemeny, Klee,

Kupka, Léger, Masson, Miró, Pevsner, Peyronnet, Schwitters, De Staël, Villon and Vlaminck, amongst others.

These are merely a selection of the modern or contemporary works of art held by the museum, only a proportion of which are regularly on display and which are likely to be changed without notice.

The collection is continued in the north part of the building with sections devoted to 'abstraction lyrique', 'nouveau réalisme', 'abstraction géométrique', 'art cinétique', 'Pop art' and 'Hyperréalisme et la nouvelle figuration'.

21 The Marais

METROS: Bastille, St.-Paul, Hôtel-de-Ville, Rambuteau, Temple, Arts-et-Métiers, Réamur-Sébastopol.

The *Marais, one of the more interesting districts of old Paris, is bounded by the Grands Boulevards on the north and east, by the Blvd de Sébastopol to the west, and by the Seine to the south, and it includes the greater part of the 3rd and 4th arrondissements. In spite of past neglect, demolition and some rebuilding, it remains substantially as developed in the 17C, and contains numerous buildings of outstanding architectural interest, many of them restored in recent years, and provides a fascinating and unique reminder of the elegance of this period.

The southern sector of the Marais and the Centre Beaubourg are described in Rtes 19 and 20.

So called from the marshy land ('marais', marsh or morass), the district only became habitable with the arrival of the Knights Templar and other religious houses, who settled here in the 13C, and slowly converted the marshes into arable land. Royal patronage began with Charles V, who, anxious to forget the associations of the Palais de la Cité with the rebellion of Etienne Marcel in 1358, built the Hôtel St.-Paul here. In the 16C, the Hôtel de Lamoignon and Hôtel Carnavalet were built, but the seal of royal approval came with the construction of the Pl. Royale (1605; later known as the Pl. des Vosges, see below).

Courtiers built themselves houses as near to the Pl. Royale as possible, and the Marais remained the most fashionable residential area of Paris until the creation of the Faubourg St.-Germain in the early 18C. The Revolution ended its long reign of splendour. The nobles had to flee; the State confiscated their property and sold it to the craftsmen, mechanics and merchants who flooded into the area, who appeared to take a brutish pleasure in disfiguring as much as possible. Much of the Marais continues to be a commercial district, even if its architectural merits are more appreciated as the value of its properties has increased.

Immediately east of the Marais lies the **Pl. de la Bastille** (Pl. 15; 4), laid out in 1803.

The ground plan of the famous fortress prison is marked by a line of paving-stones in the Place, beneath which some of its cellars are said to survive.

Its keep (a model of which may be seen in the Musée Carnavalet) stood on the west side, across the end of the Rue St.-Antoine, and the main drawbridge was slightly north of the junction with the Blvd Henri-IV. The July Column (see below) stands approximately in the centre of what was the east bastion. The Canal St.-Martin now runs beneath the Place, appearing to the south in the Gare d'eau de l'Arsenal, which flows into the Seine.

The **Bastille** (more correctly the Bastille St.-Antoine) originated as a bastion-tower defending the eastern entrance to Paris. It was developed under Charles V into a fortress with eight massive towers, immensely thick walls, and a wide moat. Nevertheless, in October 1559 Edward Grimston, who had been taken prisoner at the fall of Calais, escaped from here. By the reign of Louis XIII, the Bastille had become almost exclusively a state prison for political offenders, among whom were the mysterious 'Man in the Iron Mask' (1698–1703) and Voltaire (twice). The arbitrary arrest by *'lettre de cachet'* of persons obnoxious to the Court, and their protracted imprisonment without trial, made the Bastille a popular synonym for oppression. The soldier and statesman, Bassompierre, was imprisoned in 1629 for twelve years by Richelieu, 'not that he had done wrong, but for fear he might be led into mischief'. Bernard Palissy, the potter, was incarcerated here in 1588, at the age of 78; and among other notable temporary residents were Cagliostro, Marmontel, the Duchesse du Maine and Mme de Tencin. In 1657 John Harwood, one of the first Quakers to visit France, was briefly incarcerated here. A certain 'Dr Du Moulin of Aberdeen', with whom John Ray, Sir Philip Skippon and Martin Lister had travelled to Paris in 1666, was held here for ten months, arrested on suspicion of being an English agent among the Huguenots of Languedoc. Vanbrugh enjoyed Louis XIV's hospitality (for obscure reasons) for most of 1692; and Colonel John Parker, in 1702, for offending Maria of Modena. Linguet's 'Memoires' (1783, published in London) describe his own experiences when confined here in 1780–82. Another inmate was the notorious Marquis de Sade, who wrote 'Justine' and other lubricious works here. Mirabeau the Younger was also imprisoned here, another victim of the practice of arrest by *'lettre de cachet'*, albeit at his father's instigation. (Malsherbes reported to Walpole that the mistress of a former administrator, 'Madame Sabatin, had a bureau of printed *lettres de cachet* with blanks, which she sold for twenty-five louis apiece'.)

On 14 July 1789, the Revolutionary mob, aided by a few troops, attacked and overwhelmed its defenders, murdered the governor, the Marquis de Launay, and freed a handful of prisoners. Work on its demolition was immediately put in hand.

The **July Column** (*Colonne de Juillet*) is not connected with the storming of the Bastille, but was erected by Louis-Philippe in 1840–41 to commemorate the 504 victims of the three days' street-fighting of July 1830, who are buried in vaults beneath the circular base of the column. The

The new opera house at the Pl. de la Bastille

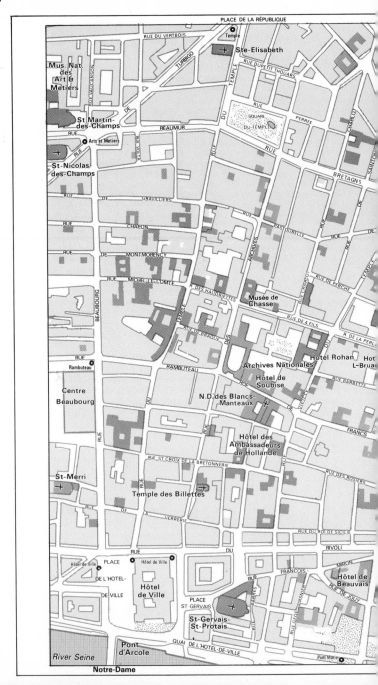

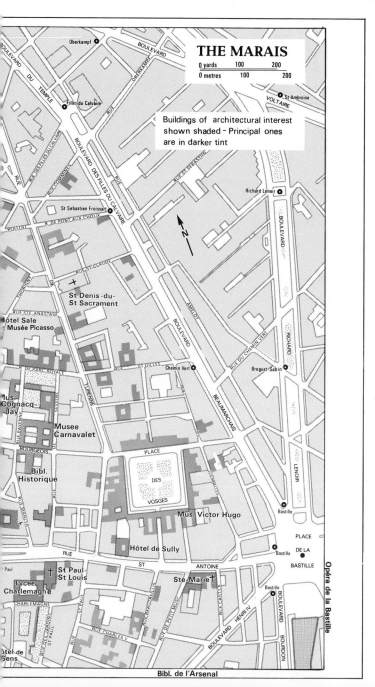

THE MARAIS

0 yards	100	200
0 metres	100	200

Buildings of architectural interest shown shaded – Principal ones are in darker tint

Oberkampf

BOULEVARD DU TEMPLE

Filles du Calvaire

St-Ambroise

VOLTAIRE

BOULEVARD OBERKAMPF

RUE DES FILLES DU CALVAIRE

RUE

BOULEVARD DES FILLES DU CALVAIRE

RUE ST-SEBASTIEN

Richard Lenoir

St Sebastien Froissart

R. DE PONT AUX CHOUX

POITOU

BOULEVARD

RICHARD LENOIR

RUE ST-CLAUDE

RUE AMELOT

St Denis-du-St Sacrament

THORIGNY

RUE STE-ANASTASE

Hôtel Sale
Musée Picasso

RUE DE PARC ROYALE

RUE DU CHEMIN VERT

BOULEVARD BEAUMARCHAIS

RUE DE SEVIGNE

Chemin Vert

RUE ST-GILLES

Breguet-Sabin

TURENNE

Mus. Cognacq-Jay

RUE DE BRAYE

Musee Carnavalet

BOURGEOIS

RICHARD LENOIR

Bibl. Historique

RUE MARIE

PLACE DES VOSGES

Mus. Victor Hugo

Bastille

PLACE DE LA BASTILLE

Bastille

Hôtel de Sully

RUE

ST

ANTOINE

Ste-Marie

St Paul

St Paul-St Louis

Lycée Charlemagne

CHARLEMAGNE

RUE ST-PAUL

RUE DE FOURCY ST-PAUL

RUE CHARLES V

RUE BEAUTREILLIS

RUE DE PETIT MUSC

RUE CASTEX

Bastille

BOULEVARD HENRI IV

BOULEVARD BOURDON

Opéra de la Bastille

Hôtel de Sens

Bibl. de l'Arsenal

victims of the Revolution of February 1848 were subsequently interred here, and their names added to the inscription. The bronze-faced column, 51.5m high, is surmounted by a bronze-gilt figure of Liberty.

To the south east of the Place, on the site of the former Gare de la Bastille, is the **Opéra de la Bastille**, a sophisticated, expensive but unalluring functional structure with a convex façade, built to celebrate the bicentenary of the Revolution. Its design, by Carlos Ott, a Uraguayan-born Canadian, was chosen from 744 projects: that of the Centre Pompidou was one of 681. Ostensibly erected with the intention of 'bringing opera within the reach of the masses', this has not proved economically viable in practice.

Incorporating the latest if not revolutionary technical equipment, the opera-house is reputed for its good acoustics. The building covers a large area and comprises a main auditorium with seating for 2700, a so-called 'Salle modulable' for from 600 to 1000, and a studio seating 280. In addition, there are several rehearsal rooms for the orchestra, chorus and ballet, apart from numerous studios, extensive workshops and store rooms for scenery, costumes, etc., and two restaurants. The scene changes are made by bringing into position any of six separate platforms, including the stage, without needing to make any specific, and often noisy, scene shifting behind the scenes.

For the Faubourg St.-Antoine, to the east, see Rte 31.

Nos 2–20 in the Blvd Beaumarchais, leading north from the Pl. de la Bastille, are built on the site of a luxurious mansion and garden belonging to the dramatist Caron de Beaumarchais (1732–99). The Hôtel de Mansart-Sagonne (see below) is well seen from Nos 21–23 in the boulevard which, with its continuation, the Blvd des Filles-du-Calvaire (recalling the site of a former convent; 1633–1790) and Blvd du Temple (see p 201), leads to the Pl. de la République.

The Rue de la Bastille leads north west from the Pl. de la Bastille, north of and parallel to the Rue St.-Antoine, to the Rue des Tournelles, No. 28 in which is the Hôtel de Mansart-Sagonne, built for himself in 1674–85 by Jules Hardouin-Mansart (1646–1708) and decorated by Le Brun and Mignard. The Rue du Pas-de-la-Mule leads left to the Pl. des Vosges; beyond, No. 50 has a splendid façade. The cultured courtesan Ninon de Lenclos (1620–1705) lived here from 1644, and died at No. 56.

The restored ***PLACE DES VOSGES** (Pl. 15; 2–4), the heart of the Marais, a large quadrangle surrounded by 39 houses in red brick with stone facings, was built on a uniform plan with arcaded ground floors (1606–11), and is one of the most attractive squares in Paris. Trees were not planted in the central gardens until 1783, and although they provide welcome shade, they spoil the effect of harmonious symmetry.

The main approach to the Pl. des Vosges, from the Rue St.-Antoine, is by the Rue de Birague (see p 172), passing through the Pavillon du Roi (see below).

It occupies the site of the royal Palais des Tournelles, the residence of the Duke of Bedford, regent of France in 1422, after the death of Henry V; in 1559 this was the scene of the fatal tournament when Henri II was accidentally killed by Montgomery, and it was in consequence abandoned by his widow, Catherine de Médicis. The square in its present form was laid out for Henri IV, probably by Baptiste du Cerceau, as the Place Royale and opened in 1605; the king's pavilion was above the gateway in the centre of the south side, while the queen's was the corresponding building on the north (No. 28). In the earlier part of the reign of Louis XIV this was one of the most fashionable addresses in Paris, and the centre of the 'Nouvelles Précieuses' satirised by Molière.

It only acquired its present name in 1799, the department of the Vosges having been the first to discharge its liabilities for the Revolutionary Wars.

At the corners of the square are fountains (1816), and in the centre a poor equestrian statue of Louis XIII (1825) set up to replace one destroyed in 1792. Mme de Sévigné (1626–96) was born in the Hôtel de Coulanges (No. 1 bis; built 1606), next to the Pavillon du Roi; No. 3 is the Hôtel d'Estrades.

No. 6 is the **Maison Victor Hugo**, in which Victor Hugo (1802–85) lived in 1832–48 (2nd floor), perhaps of more interest for his numerous pen and wash *drawings (c 350) displayed there than for the family souvenirs.

Note the bust of Hugo by Rodin; Portrait of Juliette Drouet by Bastien-Lepage; The Première of Hernani by Besnard; Portrait of Adèle Foucher, the poet's wife, by Louis Boulanger; Hugo on his death-bed by Bonnat; and works by Célestin Nanteuil and Delacroix. Note also the furniture and woodwork, designed or carved by Hugo.

No. 7, the Petit-Hôtel de Sully, was built by Jean Androuet du Cerceau. Both Gautier (in 1831–34) and Daudet lived at No. 8, the Hôtel de Fourcy (1605). No. 9, the Hôtel de Chaulnes, was from 1856 the residence of Rachel, the tragedienne (died 1858). No. 11 was occupied by Marion Delorme, the courtesan, in 1639–48. No. 21 was the mansion of Cardinal de Richelieu (1615), in front of which, on the day after his edict against duelling, the duel took place between François, Comte de Montmorency-Bouteville against the Marquis de Beuvron (1627). No. 12 occupies part of the Hôtel Dangeau, the home of Philippe, Marquis de Dangeau (1638–1720), the memorialist.

From the north-west corner of the Pl. des Vosges you cross the Rue de Turenne (where to the left, in the court of No. 23, is the Hôtel de Villacerf, of c 1660, with a fountain), and enter the Rue des Francs-Bourgeois. One of the principal streets of the Marais, it takes its name from the citizens who, being vassals to a feudal lord, were exempt from municipal taxes. For the north part of the Rue de Turenne.

The * *MUSEE CARNAVALET, or Musée Historique de la Ville de Paris (Pl. 15; 1; métro: St.-Paul), at the corner of the Rue des Francs-Bourgeois and the Rue de Sévigné, is an important collection illustrating the history of Paris from the 16C to the early 20C.

The museum is housed in the *Hôtel Carnavalet, an imposing mansion begun in 1548 for Jacques de Ligneris, President of the Parlement, and adorned with sculptures by Jean Goujon. It was altered in 1660 by François Mansart, who built the present façade, but retained the 16C gateway with its Goujon sculptures (on the keystone, a winged figure of Abundance standing on a globe which was later carved into a carnival mask, in punning allusion to Carnavalet, the nickname of a Breton gentleman called Kernevenoc'h or Kernevenoy, whose widow had acquired the mansion in 1578. Further alterations were made in 1876–90 and earlier this century).

In 1989 the museum was extended into the Hôtel le Peletier de St.-Fargeau, built by Pierre Bullet for Michel de Peletier in c 1687–90.

Mme de Sévigné lived here from 1677 until her death in 1696; her apartments, which were shared by her daughter, Mme de Grignan, and her uncle, the Abbé de Coulanges, were in the south-east corner of the first floor. The building was acquired by the municipality in 1866 and the museum was inaugurated in 1880.

The bronze statue of Louis XIV in the centre of the courtyard is by Coysevox. Of the sculptures in the courtyard, the best are those by Jean Goujon on the entrance arch and above the door on the left. The reliefs of The Seasons, on the side opposite the entrance, were probably done under his direction. On the right, the relief above the door is a 19C copy of the one opposite; those on the first storey are by Van Obstal (1660).

Bronze statue of Louis XIV by Coysevox in the entrance courtyard of the Musée Carnavalet

Several rooms are being rearranged and others are temporarily closed, but the following itinerary will take the visitor round the building in an approximate chronological progression, with one or two slight breaks in continuity.

The new entrance to the museum is to the right of the courtyard. Pass through a vestibule, off which is a bookshop, turn left into the Salle des Enseignes, displaying a collection of shop and tavern signs of the 15–19Cs. Beyond this you reach the foot of the Escalier de Luynes and turn left through RR31 and 30; see below.

Turning right beyond these rooms, you walk down the colonnaded Pavillon de Choiseul, between the Cour de la Victoire (right) and Cour des Drapiers, to enter **RR1–4**, devoted to the early history of Paris, displaying maquettes of Gallo-Roman Lutetia, and its extent during the Merovingian period. **R2** contains part of an architrave excavated when building the old Hôtel-Dieu; parts of a monument to Mars; and collections of glass, terracottas, bronze figurines, coins, etc. Other bronze objects, jewellery, ceramics, buckles and arms are displayed adjacent, together with parts of a sarcophagus, etc.

Returning through the colonnade, you enter **R7**, with a maquette of the Cité in the medieval period; an anon. mid 16C Flemish painting of the Prodigal Son in the company of courtesans, with a view of Paris in the background; a Portrait of Mary Stuart in 1561, wearing a white mourning veil (School of Clouet); and an anon. 16C View of the Cimetière des Innocents. **R8** contains a Portrait of the Duc de Guise (known as Le Balafré from his scar) attributed to François Quesnel, and of Catherine de Médicis (School of Clouet). **R9**, with an anon. Portrait of Henri III, and an anon. late 16C View of the Porcession of the League in the Pl. de Grève. **R10**, the Salle Bleu, with early views of Paris, including a Dutch painting of skaters on the Seine and 16C prints.

At the head of the Escalier Sévigné (**R11**) turn right.

RR12–23 describe Paris during the reigns of Louis XIII and Louis XIV, the first containing a view of the Pont Neuf in c 1633; **R13**, with Views of the Place Royale (now Pl. des Vosges), and of the Cité from the Quai de la Tournelle c 1646, and several views of Abraham de Verwer. **R14**, with engravings of buildings; and **R15**, with further views depicting the transformation of Paris at this period, including the Observatoire by Pierre-Denis Martin and also his View from the Quai de Bercy. **R16** contains early 18C panelling from the Hôpital de la Pitié, and views of popular scenes. **R17** displays richly painted and gilded *boisseries* of c 1656 from the Hôtel Colbert de Villacerf at 23 Rue de Turenne; in **R19** is panelling from the 'grand cabinet doré' by Le Vau from the Hôtel de la Rivière, 14 Pl. des Vosges, with ceiling-painting by Le Brun. **R20** contains another ceiling painting (1651), also by Le Brun, from the same mansion, together with views of royal palaces, among them Adam-Frans van der Meulen's Château Neuf de St.-Germain-en-Laye.

Returning through these rooms you regain R11 and enter **R21**, devoted to Mme de Sévigné, with a pastel portrait of her by Nanteuil, and a portrait by Mignard of her daughter, Mme de Grignan. Among souvenirs is the japanned desk she brought from the Château des Rochers near Vitré. **R22**, retaining its 17C panelling, describes the Regency period; **R23**, adjacent, contains a collection of faïence.

Return to R11, turn right and pass through **RR24–26**, the Salles des Echevins (the first of which contains a monumental chimneypiece of the Louis-XIII period), devoted to the Municipality of Paris. There are several portraits of aldermen by De Troy and Duplessis, and notably that by Largillierre of Françoise Boucher d'Orsay in 1702.

RR27–29 contain views of Paris between 1720 and 1760, notably those by Charles-Léopold de Grevenbroeck, and Nicolas Raguenet (1715–93).

MUSÉE CARNAVALET

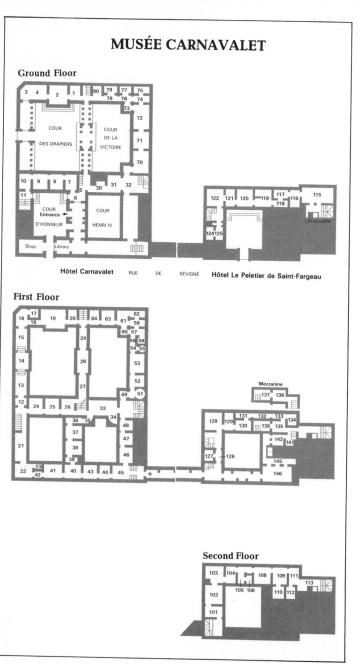

Ground Floor

Hôtel Carnavalet RUE DE SÉVIGNÉ **Hôtel Le Peletier de Saint-Fargeau**

First Floor

Second Floor

Picturesque among those by the latter is The regatta near the Pont Notre-Dame, showing the houses that formerly flanked the bridge.

To continue in historical order, descend the stairs beyond **R29**, walk down the colonnaded gallery again and turn left into **R30**, with panelling of 1762, designed by Claude-Nicolas Ledoux (1736–1809), saved from the Café Militaire (formerly in the Rue St.-Honoré). Here also are Martin Drolling's Portrait of Ledoux, attrib. Callet, Portraits of Ledoux and his daughter, and an anon. portrait of Ledoux's wife. **R31** contains some magnificent gilt panelling of 1767 from the Hôtel d'Uzès, Rue Montmartre, also from designs by Ledoux. Note the bust of Gluck by François Martin.

RR69–80, to the left of R32, are now devoted to temporary exhibitions.

In **R32** is a reconstruction of a stairway from the Hôtel de Luynes, decorated with trompe-l'oeil paintings of people on balconies, by P.A. Brunetti (1748). Ascending this, you enter **R33**, the first of a series of rooms containing the important collection of furniture donated in 1965 by Henriette Bouvier; several contain panelling taken from destroyed mansions. In **R39** is a collection of wax portraits; **R41** contains a portrait of the engraver Jean Mariette by Antoine Pesne, Chardin's Game of billiards, and Etienne Jeaurat (1699–1789), The transport of 'filles de joie' to La Salpêtrière, among others. These roooms also display Parisian scenes by Pierre-Denis Martin (1663–1742), De Machy, J.-B. Oudry, L.-P. Debucourt (1755–1832), and others. **R46** contains a portrait of the Abbé Tournus praying by Restout. **R47** is devoted to the theatre during the reign of Louis XV. **R48** contains a portrait of D'Alembert by Catherine Lusurier and Jean Huber, Voltaire dictating while dressing.

RR49–64 (beyond the Escalier de Luynes) also depict aspects of Paris during the latter years of the reign of Louis XV and that of Louis XVI. **R53** contains two genre paintings by Michel Garnier (1753–1819), of interest for their depiction of costume; **RR56–57** display several more topographical and architectural paintings, while **R58**, painted by Boucher and Fragonard c 1765, comes from the house of the engraver Gilles Demarteau in the Rue de la Pelleterie. **RR59–64** contain more paintings by De Machy, Hubert Robert (including his Demolition of the houses on the Pont Notre-Dame in 1786 and on the Pont au Change in 1788), J.-B. Lallemand, Debucourt, Alexandre Noël and others.

Stairs ascend to **RR65–68**, containing models of the Galeries du Palais-Royal, but may be closed. Temporary exhibitions are also held here.

Making your way back to R45, you pass along a passage (**R148** containing Foujita's painting of a bistro and St.-Pierre-de-Montmartre by Utrillo) to approach the **Hôtel le Peletier de St.-Fargeau**, and then ascend the staircase. This brings you to the first of a dozen rooms devoted to the French Revolution but which glosses over the bloody period when the Terror was in full action. It is a strange coincidence that the building, once the home of Michel Etienne le Peletier de St.-Fargeau, great-grandson of the founder, and who was assassinated on the some day as a member of the Convention, should now be devoted to this era.

R101 contains an anon. Portrait of Mirabeau, and a view of the revolutionaries in the Jeu de Paume, Versailles, 20 June 1789, attributed to David. **R102** displays the keys of the Bastille; a Portrait of Latude (who escaped from the Bastille in 1764) by Vestier; Harry Singleton, The Storming of the Bastille, and its destruction by Hubert Robert; also a model of the prison cut from one of its stones under the direction of Palloy, the demolition contractor, and other souvenirs of the event; views by J.-B. Lallemand; a Self-portrait bust, attributed to Curtius, the father of Mme Tussauds. **R104**

Portraits of Jean-Sylvain Bailly by J. L. Mosnier; of Dr John Moore (1729–1802), author of descriptions of Paris during this disturbed time, by Vestier; and an anon. Portrait of Dr Guillotin.

RR105–6 depict life in the Prison du Temple from 10 August 1792, with Joseph Ducreux's drawing of Louis XVI made a few days before his decapitation on 21 January 1793, and a Portrait of young Louis XVII painted there in 1793 by J.-M. Vien le fils. **RR107–8** are devoted to the Convention and the Terror, with prison scenes by Hubert Robert; anon. portraits of Robespierre, Danton, Camille Desmoulins and Condorcet; Joshep Boze (1744–1826), Portrait of Marat; C. Charpentier, Portrait of Danton; portrait busts of Marat and of Michel le Peletier de St.-Fargeau; scenes by De Machy and Hubert Robert (the Prison of St.-Lazare). **RR109–13** are concerned with the Directoire and the period of the Revolutionary wars, with Hubert Robert, the provisional mausoleum of Rousseau in the garden of the Tuileries, The violation of the royal tombs in St.-Denis, and The demolition of the churches of the Feuillants and of St.-Jean-en-Grève; The interior of the Panthéon, and Portrait of Gén. Kléber, both attributed to Boilly; Portraits of Gén. Augereau by Hensius, and of Alexandre Lenoir (largely responsible for saving artistic material from destruction) and his wife, both by Geneviève Bouliard. **R113** contains numerous colourful gouches by Pierre-Etienne le Sueur, and **R114** a collection of Sèvres porcelain depicting revolutionary emblems, etc. and a portrait of the composer Méhul by Gros.

Stairs and a lift descend to the GROUND FLOOR and **R115**, devoted to the Consulate and First Empire, with Gérard, portraits of Mme Récamier seated and of the actress Mlle Duchesnois; Pierre-Paul Prud'hon, Portrait of Talleyrand in 1807; Robert Lefèvre, Portrait of Napoléon in 1809; the Death-mask of Napoléon and his 'Nécessaire de Campagne', among other souvenirs; Etienne Bouhot, The Pl. Vendôme and Pl. du Châtelet; Boilly, Conscripts at the Porte St.-Denis and the Galeries du Palais Royal.

R116. Restoration period: Boilly, Distributing food and wine in the Champs-Elysées in 1822; Charles Remond, The Pavilion de Bagatelle; anon. Portrait of Benjamin Constant; Gérard, Portrait of Charles X.

RR117–18 contain paintings of Paris, notably by E. Bouhot, View of the Palais des Tuileries seen from the Quai d'Orsay; Hippolyte Adam, The Hôpital St.-Louis; James Chalon, The market and fountain 'des Innocents'; View of St.-Eustache seen from the artist's studio, attributed to Martin Drolling; Isidore Dagnan, The Blvd Poissonière in 1834; Corot, The Pont St.-Michel and Quai des Orfèvres; views by Giuseppe Canella, J.A. Regnier and other artists of the era.

RR119–20 are devoted to the Revolution of July and the July Monarchy, with a maquette depicting the arrival of the Duc d'Orléans at the Hôtel de Ville, 31 July 1830; L.-A. Peron, The Morgue, July 1830; François Scheffer, Portrait of Armand Carel; Rude, plaster model of the Departure of the Volunteers, for his relief on the Arc de Triomphe; François Dubois, The erection of the Obelisk of Luxor in the Pl. de la Concorde, together with a painting of the scene by Geslin; Portrait of Louis Philippe attributed to P. Vigneron; Amélie Serre, Portrait of Eugène Blanqui.

R121. The Second Republic. Horace Vernet, Portrait of Arago; anon., Portrait of Pierre-Joseph Proudhon and several paintings by H.-V. Sebron and J.J. Champin.

RR122, 124–25 concern the Romantic period, with portraits by Henri Lehmann of Liszt, and of Marie d'Agoult; of the divas Marietta Alboni and Malibran by A.-J. Péignon and Henri Decaisne respectively; an anon. Portrait of Mlle Mars; and Couture's Portrait of Michelet; together with a collection of miniature caricature sculptured busts in bronze or plaster of famous artists, musicians, etc. by Jean-Pierre Dantan. Notable are those of Berlioz, Verdi, Liszt, Rossini, Thalberg, the Duke of Wellington, Lord Grey and Lord Brougham.

Ascending the adjacent stairs, designed by Pierre Bullet, turn right into **RR126–127,** displaying a number of views of Paris, including Robert Stanley, The Blvd des Capucines; William Parrott, The Quai Conti; A. Dauzats, The Palais de Justice; and by J.-T. Meunier, Charles Mozin, et al.

Retracing your steps, from the landing you have a view of two huge bird's-eye Panoramas of Paris c 1852 by Victor Navlet, before entering **RR128–29**, devoted to the Second Empire, with the Prince Imperial's cradle (1856); a Portrait of Baron Haussmann attributed to Henri Lehmann; a pastel Portrait of Mérimée by Simon Rochard; T.-A. Vauchelet, Portrait of Visconti, the architect; anon. Portrait of Orsini; anon. Arrival of Queen Victoria at the Gare de l'Est to attend the Universal Exhibition of 1855; maquette of the Defile of the Army through the Pl. Vendôme; View of the levelling of the Colline de Chaillot in 1867 for the Exhibition, and a panoramic view of that exhibition.

R130 depicts the Siege of Paris in 1871, with a view of the artillery in the Jardin des Tuileries in late September 1870; The Red Cross flag on the Palais des Tuileries; Gambetta leaving Paris by balloon; sketches by Puvis de Chavannes for his The Pigeon, and The Balloon; and Corot, Paris burning.

R131. The Commune: Louis Tinayre, Portrait of Louise Michel; Courbet, Portrait of Jules Vallès; several scenes by G. Boulanger.

Passing through R132 you enter **R133**, with a Portrait of Blanqui by Eugène Carriere; and views by Victor Dargaud and E.-M. Lansyer. **R135** contains several views of Paris, among them Lépine, The Seine at Passy; Jongkind, The Rue St.-Séverin at night; Guillaumin, the Seine at Bercy; Lebourg, Notre-Dame under snow; and works by Signac, Ziem and Frank Boggs.

R136 is devoted to portraits of literary figures, among them, P.L. Mita, Nadar; Carriere, Edmond de Goncourt; L. Montegut, Daudet writing; Boldini, a pastel of 'Gyp'; Doré, Charles Philipon. **RR137–38** depict the Belle Epoque, with several works by Jean Béraud (1849–1935).

R141 contains the Art Nouveau decoration of a private room from the Café de Paris, which stood at 39 Av. de l'Opera (1899; by Henri Sauvage), until demolished in 1954. In adjoining **RR142–43** is the re-assembled decoration of 1900 for the jewellery shop of Fouquet, in the Rue Royale, designed by Alphonse Mucha.

You pass into **R146**, with the re-assembled baroque decoration of the ballroom of the Hôtel de Wendel, designed in 1924 by the Catalan artist Josep Maria Sert (1876–1945), the theme of which is the Procession of the Queen of Sheba.

R147 contains sections displaying furniture and mementoes from the homes of Paul Léataud, Marcel Proust, and Anna de Noailles, all of whom had the habit of writing in bed. Among portraits here are Countess Greffulhe, the Abbé Mugnier; J.-E. Blanche, Princesse Jean de Broglie, Cocteau in 1913, and René Crevel; Foujita, Jean Rostand (the biologist son of Edmond); and Romaine Brooks, Natalie Barney.

On leaving this room, turn to look at the caryatids from the Café de Paris (see R141 above) and the Portrait of André Wormser by Albert Besnard.

By continuing ahead along the passage (R148) and descending the stairs you return to the entrance vestibule.

A Library of Prints, Drawings and Photographs is open to researchers and professionals by appointment. The Photothèque of the Musées de la Ville de Paris is at 29 Rue de Sévigné, where reproductions of works of art in the municipal museums of Paris can be ordered.

No. 48 Rue de Sévigné, the Hôtel de Jonquières, retains the relief (1810) from an old fountain; No. 52, built by Pierre Delisle-Mansart for himself, has been much altered.

In the Rue Payenne, immediately west of the Hôtel Carnavalet, No. 11, the Hôtel de Polastron-Polignac, now houses the Swedish Cultural Centre and Musée Tessim, containing paintings by Alexander Roslin (1718–93), among others. No. 13, the Hôtel de Lude, is another good example of an early 18C mansion. There is a small lapidary collection in the Sq. Georges-Cain opposite.

South of the Hôtel Carnavalet, on the corner of the Rue Pavée, No. 24 is the **Hôtel Lamoignon**, built in 1584 for Diane de France, the legitimised daughter of Henri II, but named after Lamoignon, President of the Parle-ment of Paris (1658), a later occupant, and enlarged in the 17C. Daudet set up house here on his marriage in 1867.

It now houses the Bibliothèque Historique de la Ville de Paris, containing over 400,000 vols and 100,000 MSS relating to the history of the city, and to the Revolution. Adjacent are traces of the notorious prison of La Force (demolished 1850), where some 170 victims of the Revolution were massacred in September 1792.

On the south side of the Rue des Francs-Bourgeois, No. 31 is the Hôtel d'Albret, built c 1640 by François Mansart, with an 18C street façade. At the end of the courtyard of No. 33 is a fragment of the walls of Philippe Auguste. The Hôtel de Guillaume Barbès (No. 35) was built in the second half of the 17C.

At 8 Rue Elzévir, leading north, parallel to the Rue Payenne, is the Hôtel de Donon, since 1990 the new home of the *Musée Cognacq-Jay (Pl. 15; 1), formerly in the Blvd des Capucines. The restored mansion, dating from 1575, was built for Médéric de Donon, but several alterations were made in the mid 17C. The museum was originated by Ernest Cognacq (1835–1928), founder of the Magasins de la Samaritaine, advised by Camille Gronkowski, then conservateur of the Musée du Petit Palais, and was inaugurated in 1929.

The collections are well displayed in some 20 rooms on four floors and in an impressively beamed attic, but there has been some criticism that the elegance and intimacy of its former home has been lost.

Many of the rooms contain notable panelling, some removed from the Château d'Eu (Normandy), in **R1**, while **R3** retains its original 17C panel-ling. The Beauvais tapestry covered set of chairs by J.-B. Lelarge are remarkable; in general the furniture—much of it marquetry—is of good quality. Note the Louis XVI bed 'à la polonaise'. Among the objects d'arts, the colourful pair of 'Kien-Lung' porcelain cranes are notable; also ter-racotta busts by J.-B. Lemoyne of the Maréchal de Saxe and the Maréchal de Lowendal. Likewise, a collection of Meissen porcelain and French terracotta figures, including Clodion, Project for the tomb of Mme Dubarry's dog; and another collection of enamelled and jewelled boxes.

Outstanding among the portraits are: *Boucher*, Mme Baudouin, his daughter; *Francis Cotes*, Charles Colmore; *Drouais*, Alexanderine Lenor-mant d'Etioles (daughter of Mme de Pompadour); *Daniel Gardner*, Lady

Auckland and her daughter, Eleanor Agnes, and Lady Albinia Hobart; *Baron Gérard*, Mme Bauquin du Boulay and her niece; *Marguerite Gérard*, Claude-Nicolas Ledoux, the architect; *Hugh Douglas Hamilton*, Lady Carhampton (?); Adélaïde Labille Guiard, Comtesse de Maussion; *Largillierre*, The Duchess of Beaufort (?); *Maurice Quentin Delatour*, Mme la Présidente de Rieux, Self-portrait, Man in a blue waistcoat, and The Marquis de Bérenger; *Lawrence*, Princess Clémentine de Metternich, and a copy of the Calmady children; Lépicié, La Coiffe blanche; *Nattier*, Madame Henriette, Maria Leczinska; *Perronneau*, Charles Lenormant du Coudrey; *Reynolds*, Lord Northington (once in an oval frame), and a copy of his Portrait of Joanna Lloyd; *attributed to Romney*, Female portrait; *John Russell*, Miss Power; *Mme Vigée-Lebrun*, The Vicomtesse de Mirabeau playing a guitar, and A Dancer; *anon.*, Portrait of the Marquise de Sassenage.

Other works include *Boucher*, La belle cuisière, and attributed to him, The Music Lesson; *Canaletto*, two Venetian scenes; *Chardin*, Still life with a copper cauldron; *Morland*, The first steps; *Wright of Derby*, The young bird-catchers; *Rembrandt*, Balaam's ass (1626; an early work); *Ruisdael*, The old oak; *G.-B. Tiepolo*, Cleopatra's banquet; *Watteau*, Assembly in the park; and representative works by Boucher, Fragonard, Greuze, Guardi and Hubert Robert. The collector appears to have had a penchant for 'galante' scenes, of which there are a number by Boilly, Pierre-Antoine Baudouin (1733–69), Nicolas-René Jollain (1732–1804), Nicolas Lavreince (1737–1807) and J.-B. Mallet (1759–1835), among others.

Returning to the Rue des Francs-Bourgeois, you pass at No. 26 the Hôtel de Sandreville (late 16–18C); No. 30, the Hôtel d'Alméras, a red-brick mansion of the Henri IV period, is also noteworthy. The Allée des Arbalétriers (No. 38) was one of the entrances to the Hôtel Barbette (see below), and led to the field alongside the walls, once a practice ground for crossbowmen.

On the corner of the transverse Rue Vieille-du-Temple (right; No. 54) survives the pretty turret (c 1510; restored) of the Hôtel Hérouët.

A short distance south is the **Hôtel des Ambassadeurs de Hollande** (No. 47), built by Cottard in 1657–60. On this site stood the house of the Maréchal de Rieux, in front of which, returning from Isabeau de Bavière's residence (see below), the Duc d'Orléans was assassinated in 1407 by the hired bravos of Jean sans Peur (Duke of Burgundy).

The building was never in fact the property of the Dutch ambassadors, but in 1720–27 belonged to the chaplain of their Embassy, and its chapel was used several times for Protestant ceremonies. Mlle Necker (later Mme de Staël) was baptised here in 1766, and Franklin's daughter was married here. Beaumarchais also lived here, where he wrote his 'Mariage de Figaro' (accepted in 1781 by the Comédie-Française but, owing to the royal veto, not publicly produced until 1784); in 1788 he turned the house into a provident institution for poor nursing mothers.

Nos 36, 24 and 15 (the Hôtel de Vibraye) further south, are of some interest. For the north half of the Rue Vielle-du-Temple, see below.

On the left you pass **N.-D. des Blancs-Manteaux** (deriving its name from the white habits of an order of mendicant monks established here in 1285 by Louis IX); the 18C door came from St.-Barthélemy in the Ile de la Cité, demolished in 1863. The church contains a rococo pulpit in the Flemish style (1749) and a good organ (restored).

At 55 Rue des Francs-Bourgeois are the offices of the Crédit Municipal, formerly the Mont-de-Piété (a government pawnbroking establishment), founded by Louis XVI in 1777. Architecturally notable are Nos 54, the Hôtel de Camus; 56, the Hôtel de Fontenoy (early 18C); 58, which belonged to Louis le Tonnelier, Baron de Breteuil, minister of Louis XVI; and 58 bis, the Hôtel d'Assy (early 17C).

Beyond is the imposing portal of the *Hôtel de Soubise (No. 60; Pl. 15;1), the greater part of which was built by Delamair in 1706–12 on the site of the mansion of the Duc de Guise. The Archives Nationales have been housed here since 1808, ensuring the survival of the interior decoration (1712–45) by Natoire, Boucher, Van Loo, Restout, Lemoyne and others. The splendid Cour d'Honneur, with its colonnade, has copies of The Four Seasons by Robert le Lorrain on the façade.

The earlier entrance, the turreted Gothic gateway of 1380 (at 58 Rue des Archives), was part of the Hôtel de Clisson, built in 1372–75 by the Constable Olivier de Clisson, a supporter of Charles V against the English. Bolingbroke (later Henry IV) gave a farewell banquet here in 1399 before setting out for England. During the English occupation of Paris (1420–35), Thomas, Duke of Clarence (died 1421) and later the Duke of Bedford, lived here. With its purchase in 1553 by Anna d'Este, wife of François de Lorraine, Duc de Guise, it became the Hôtel de Guise, remaining in the family until 1696, when Anne de Soubise bought it. Another occupant during this period was Henri II de Lorraine, who killed the last of the Colignys in a duel in the Pl. des Vosges in 1643: his grandfather had instigated the murder of Admiral Coligny in the massacre of St. Bartholomew. Here he entertained lavishly and gave hospitality to Corneille.

The chapel bears traces of the Chapelle de Clisson of 1375 transformed in 1533 for the Guise by Primaticcio. The Oval Room is a masterpiece of the style of transition from Louis XIV to Louis XV. Here and elsewhere are exhibited some outstanding documents arranged to show the development of French institutions, etc.

Among the earliest is a will of 627; others concern Clovis and Charlemagne. Among letters from foreign potentates and statesmen are some from the Emperor Charles V, Christina of Sweden, Tamerlane, Franklin and Washington; among treaties displayed are those of Brétigny, Westphalia and the Pyrenees; the Edict of Nantes (with the signature of Henri IV) and its Revocation; the Oath of the Jeu de Paume; Marie-Antoinette's last letter and Louis XVI's will; also his diary with 'rien' written against the date 14 July 1789. The Orléans archives were donated to the Archives Nationales in 1969.

From the Rue des Archives, skirting the west side of the Hôtel de Soubise, leads the Rue de Braque, in which Nos 4–6, the Hôtel Le Lièvre de la Grange, is a fine late-17C mansion; No. 7 belonged to the Comte de Vergennes (1717–87), foreign minister to Louis XVI and supporter of American Independence.

At the corner of the Rue des Archives and the Rue des Haudriettes, further north, is a fountain, with a naiad sculpted by Mignot (1765).

Diagonally opposite is the Hôtel de Guénégaud (60 Rue des Archives) by François Mansart (c 1650), containing a **Musée de la Chasse**, and an exclusive Hunting Club (with an annexe at Chambord).

The first room displays a portrait, in falconer's costume, of Philip the Handsome (Felipe I of Castile; the father of the Emperor Charles V), and 'La Chasse de Diane' by Brueghel le Velours and Van Balen. Stairs ascend to rooms containing hunting weapons, powder flasks, daggers, crossbows, etc., and to the second floor. Here are collections of stuffed big game, swords, porcelain decorated with hunting scenes, and paintings by François Desportes (1661–1743), Chardin, Oudry, Carle Vernet and others.

No. 62, adjacent, the Hôtel de Montgelas (1709), is noteworthy.

22 Rue des Quatre-Fils, leading south east, was the home, until 1755, of the Marquise du Deffand (1697–1780), where her first salon was frequented by Voltaire, Montesquieu, D'Alembert, Condorcet, Turgot and Hénault. She then, when going blind, moved with Mlle de Lespinasse, her companion, to the Couvent des Filles de St.-Joseph in the Rue St.-Dominique (cf.).

No. 20, retaining a fine doorway, was the residence, after 1800, of Romain, Comte de Sèze (1748–1828), Louis XVI's lawyer.

In the Rue Charlot, leading north east from the Rue des Quatre-Fils, is St.-Jean-St.-François, built as a Capuchin chapel on the site of a *jeu de paume,* and completed in 1715. No. 7, opposite, the Hôtel de Brévannes, is partly 17C.

Further along the Rue des Quatre-Fils you regain the Rue Vieille-du-Temple, in which, at No. 87, a few paces to the right, stands the **Hôtel de Rohan**. It was known also as the Hôtel de Strasbourg, and was begun in 1704 by Delamair.

It was successively inhabited by four cardinals of the Rohan family, all of whom were bishops of Strasbourg. From 1808 to 1925 the mansion was occupied by the Imprimerie Nationale (cf.), after which it was thoroughly restored to house certain departments of the Archives Nationales not accommodated in the neighbouring Hôtel de Soubise (see above). In the second courtyard is a fine relief of the Horses of Apollo by Robert le Lorrain; the *'Cabinet des Singes' contains paintings by Christophe Huet (1745–50). It was here that Cardinal Edouard de Rohan was arrested during the 'Affaire du Collier' (1783–84; see p 260).

Slightly to the south, 17 Rue Barbette (recalling the name of the Hôtel Barbette, the favourite residence from 1403, of Isabeau de Bavière, which stood on this site) retains a door, badly damaged, with two medallions.

From the intersection of the Rues Vieille-du-Temple (in which No. 90 was the site of the Jeu de Paume des Marais, used as a theatre from 1634–73) and des Quatre-Fils, you can make a detour towards the north-eastern section of the Marais via the Hôtel Salé (see below). Its garden façade is approached by turning right off the former street along the Rue des Coutures-St.-Gervais, flanked by several 17C houses. Alternatively, you can follow the Rue de la Perle south east to the tastefully redeveloped Pl. de Thorigny, passing (right; No. 1) the restored *Hôtel Libéral-Bruant, built in 1685 for his personal use by the architect of Les Invalides. The pedimented façade, decorated with four busts in niches, is notable. The building now houses the *Musée de la Serrure (or Musée Bricard, after Eugène Bricard, the 19C collector of this splendid decorative door-furniture, including locks, keys, handles and plaques of all periods).

A few paces to the south east bring you to the Rue du Parc-Royal, in which Gautier lived from 1822–31 at No. 4, built c 1620. No. 10, the restored Hôtel de Vigny, of the same date, is now the offices of the Centre National de Documentation du Patrimoine—Inventaire Général. The Rue Payenne (cf.) leads back towards the Hôtel Carnavalet.

By turning north east up the Rue de Thorigny, you reach at No. 5 (left) the *Hôtel Salé (Pl. 15; 1) an impressive mansion also known as the Hôtel Aubert de Fontenay, after the financier for whom it was built in 1656–60 by Jean Boullier de Bourges. It was once called the Hôtel de Juigné, but became known as the Hôtel Salé on account of the huge profits its owner had made out of the salt tax. The decoration of the staircase is superb. The whole fabric has undergone a thorough and well-deserved restoration since being put to commercial use in the 19C, and now houses a museum devoted to the work of Pablo Ruiz Picasso (1881–1973).

The *MUSEE PICASSO comprises an extensive collection of works of art by that prolific artist, acquired by the State in lieu of death duties, together with a number of canvases by other artists once owned by Picasso. It includes among works by Picasso, some 230 paintings, 140 sculptures, 45 ceramics, almost 1500 drawings and over 1650 prints (displayed in rotation), apart from several 'constructions', etc. They are displayed in approximately chronological order, and are representative of most of his 'periods', although weak in youthful works.

Notable among the comparatively few works of outstanding importance are his Self-portrait (with a blue background; 1901); Self-portrait unshaven; The two brothers; Les demoiselles d'Avignon (1907); Sculpted female head (Fernande); Still-life with a cane chair (1912); Portrait of Olga Khoklova seated (1917); Bathers (Biarritz, 1918); Jug and apples; Women running along a beach (1922); Paul 'en arlequin' and 'en pierrot'; Female bust (1932); Corrida (1933); Portrait of Marie-Thérèse Walter (1937); Portraits of Dora Maar (1937); Maya and her doll (1938); Cat with a bird (1938); Massacre in Korea (1951); The picnic (after Manet; 1960); The young artist (1972); sculpted Nanny-goats; and among drawings, The frugal meal (1904), Young girl wearing a hat (c 1920), and Minotaur (1936).

Also Balthus, The children; Cézanne, The Château Noir; Corot, Little Jeannette; Miró, Self-portrait; Modigliani, Seated girl; Henri Rousseau, Self-portrait with lamp, The artist's wife, and The sovereigns; Renoir, Seated bather; and works by Braque, Matisse and René-Hilaire de Gas (1770–1858; grandfather of Edgar Degas).

It is likely that Marion Delorme died in a house on the site of No. 2 in 1650. Nos 6, 8 and 10 were built together as the Hôtel de Percey; No. 8 belonged to Mme de Sévigné in 1669–72.

The Rue Ste.-Anastase leads right off the Rue de Thorigny into the Rue de Turenne, where (right) Nos 52–54 form the 17C Hôtel de Montrésor. No. 56 was once the home of Scarron (1610–60; who died here) and his wife Françoise d'Aubigné (1635–1719; grand-daughter of the poet Agrippa d'Aubigné), later Mme de Maintenon. Crebillon the Elder died here in 1762; and Le Sage was a later occupier. No. 60 is the Hôtel du Grand-Veneur, with a boar's head on the façade, while No. 66 retains traces of the Hôtel de Turenne, built for the great marshal's father. On the site of the chapel of the convent later installed here, the church of **St.-Denis-du-St.-Sacrement** was built in 1835 in the Grecian style, by Godde. No. 80, a short distance north, belonged to the Marquis de Launay, the last governor of the Bastille.

The nearby Rue Debelleyme, leading north west, crosses the Rue Vieille-du-Temple. At their junction is the Hôtel d'Espinay (No. 110; which belonged to a favourite of Henri III), with a remarkable staircase. Nos 106–100 (to the left) all preserve features of the early 17C. Just to the north, the Rue de Poitou leads back across the Rue de Saintonge, retaining some attractive façades, to the Rue Charlot (in which No. 28, a short distance to the right, is the Hôtel de Béramcourt; 1690). Straight across is the Rue Pastourelle, off which (right), in the Rue de Beauce, Mlle de Scudéry (1607–1701) lived from 1670, and died.

To the left, at 70 Rue des Archives (the next main street), Lamennais (1782–1854), the subversive religious writer died. No. 78, to the right, was built by Bullet (c 1660), with a beautiful staircase by Le Muet, and was the residence of Marshal Tallard (1712). Further north at No. 90 are traces of the Hôpital des Enfants-Rouges, founded by François I and his sister Marguerite in 1534, so-called because the children wore a red uniform.

Just beyond is the Sq. du Temple (Pl. 9; 7), the centre of the densely populated **Quartier du Temple**, laid out in 1857 on the site of the late-12C stronghold of the Knights Templar. The headquarters of their order in Europe until 1313, it was then occupied by the Order of St. John.

The area owned by the Templars lay for the most part between this point and the Pl. de la République, to the north east (see latter part of Rte 22). Before the Revolution it was occupied by wealthy noble families, artisans who did not belong to the corporations and therefore were free from many restrictions, and debtors who were protected here from legal action.

The palace of the Grand Prior of the Knights of St. John was reputed for luxurious living but, with the Revolution, the Tour du Temple (1265) was transformed into a prison, and in August 1792 Louis XVI and the royal family were taken from the Tuileries and incarcerated here. On 21 January 1793, the king was driven from here to the guillotine; Marie Antoinette was transferred to the Conciergerie (cf.) on 2 August; and on 9 May 1794, Mme Elisabeth was carried off to execution. The Duc de Normandie ('Louis XVII'; born 1785 but never reigned) is believed to have died here on 9 June 1795. The sole survivor, Mme Royale (Marie Thérèse de France; 1778–1851), was released on 19 December of the same year. (Objects from the prison can be seen in the Musée Carnavalet, RR105–6.) Admiral Sir Sidney Smith, captured off La Havre, escaped from here in 1798 after two years' imprisonment. The tower was demolished by Napoleon I, and its last vestiges were razed under Napoleon III.

A short distance to the north (195 Rue du Temple) is **Ste.-Elisabeth**, founded in 1630 by Marie de Médicis. The façade is a copy of the original design of the façade Sta. Maria Novella in Florence. The main feature is the *boiseries* including, in the ambulatory, 16C carvings of scriptural scenes from the abbey of St.-Vaast at Arras.

The Rue Réaumur leads west from the Sq. du Temple, passing (left) the Rue Volta, in which No. 3, of c 1300, is possibly the oldest surviving house in Paris. The Rue Réaumur crosses the Rue de Turbigo to meet the Rue St.-Martin (the original Roman road to the north from Lutetia) between the former priory of St.-Martin-des-Champs (right) and (left) St.-Nicolas-des-Champs.

The **MUSEE NATIONAL DES TECHNIQUES**, or Conservatoire National des Arts et Métiers, with its entrance at 292 Rue St.-Martin (Pl. 9; 7), occupies the site of St.-Martin-des-Champs. The exterior of the church is best seen from the Rue Réaumur, to the south.

The priory, founded in 1060 by Henri I and presented to the Abbey of Cluny by Philippe I in 1079, stood outside the city walls until the early 14C. During the Revolution, it was taken over by the Société des Jeunes Français, an educational institution, and its dependencies were later used as a small-arms factory. In 1798 they were assigned to the Conservatoire des Arts et Métiers, which had been founded by a decree of the Convention in 1794, and here were assembled the collections of Vaucanson and other scientists. Its administrator was Joseph-Michel Montgolfier (1740–1810), who with his brother Jacques-Etienne (1745–99, a paper-manufacturer) were the inventors of the air-balloon (1783).

To the right of the entrance courtyard is the former *Refectory, a 13C masterpiece, built by Pierre de Montreuil (architect of the Ste.-Chapelle). This remarkable hall (42.80 by 11.70m), its vaulting supported by a central row of columns (recalling those of the Eglise des Jacobins at Toulouse), and with a reader's pulpit at the east end, now accommodates the library. The external side of the southern doorway is a good example of decorated Gothic, and the sole relic of the original cloisters. Further south is the restored 13C portal of the church (not entered from here; see below). The turret is a comparatively recent addition.

On the GROUND FLOOR are models of locomotives and rolling-stock; rooms on the left, and in the wing beyond, display an extensive collection of astronomical and surveying instruments; clocks (by Berthoud, Lepaute, Bréguet, Janvier and other famous 18C horologists); and a collection of elaborate automata, including Marie-Antoinette's 'Joueuse de Tympanon'.

On the FIRST FLOOR are rooms (left) displaying printing machinery; apparatus used by Daguerre, Niepce, Lumière and others, in the pioneering days of photography and cinematography; and historical equipment illustrating the development of recording, television, radio-astronomy, etc.

To the right on the first floor are rooms devoted to domestic lighting and heating; models of machines, including the 'Machine de Marly' (see end of Rte 35).

From the far end of this wing, steps descend to the former Abbey Church of **St.-Martin-des-Champs**, now sheltering a curious congregation of cars and planes. Although 'restored' in 1854–80, the fabric of the choir, with its apse chapels, is perhaps the earliest Gothic vault in Paris (1130–40), while the aisleless nave dates from the 13C.

Among the prototypes of the motor car are Cugnot's steam-carriage of 1770 and one by Serpollet (1888); petrol-driven vehicles include a Panhard (1896), Peugeots of 1893 and 1909, a Berliet phaeton (1898), a De Dion-Bouton (1899) and a Renault of 1900. Among the aeroplanes are those of Ader (1897), Esnault-Pelterie (1906), the plane in which Blériot made the first flight across the Channel (1909) and a Bréguet of 1911.

Most other sections of the museum, including that devoted to agriculture, are at present closed or are being reformed.

At the north-west corner of the building is the Fontaine du Vertbois (1712) which, with the adjoining tower, has been restored.

Adjacent is **St.-Nicolas-des-Champs**, with a square tower, built in 1420 but enlarged in 1541–87, when the choir was rebuilt and the outer nave aisles added. At the Revolution, it served as the 'Temple of Hymen'. The original west doors have survived, and the fine south portal (c 1576), after Philibert Delorme, also retains its contemporary doors.

There is good woodwork in the nave vestibule. Paintings include a Baptism of Christ by Gaudenzio Ferrari, and Madonna and Saints by Amico Aspertini (both c 1500). The ambulatory chapels have 17C wall-paintings; also (1st south chapel), Our Lady of Victories (c 1610–20) and (6th chapel) a 14C Italian altarpiece. The Apostles at the tomb of the Virgin, with the Assumption (on the 17C high-altar), is by Simon Vouet.

Guillaume Budé (or Budaeus; 1468–1540), Théophile de Viau (1590–1626), Gassendi (1592–1655), the astronomer, and Mlle de Scudéry (1607–1701) are buried here.

You return to the Rue du Temple by turning east along the Rue des Gravilliers (just south of St.-Nicolas-des-Champs). Balzac lived at 122 Rue du Temple in 1814–19; at 13 Rue Chapon (the first turning right, going south), with an interesting court, was the Paris residence of the archbishops of Reims. 115 Rue du Temple marks the probable site of a residence of Jean Bart (1650–1702), a privateer created Admiral of the Fleet by Louis XIV. Nos 101–103, the Hôtel de Montmorency, the residence of Fouquet in 1652, has its entrance at 5 Rue de Montmorency. No. 51 in this street, the Maison du Grand-Pignon, restored in 1900, was built in 1407 by Nicolas Flamel.

The Rue Michel-le-Comte, parallel to the south, retains a number of early 17C houses, including the Hôtel Le Tellier (No. 16), with a fine courtyard; No. 21, the home of the architect Edme Verniquet (1727–1804); and No. 28, the Hôtel d'Hallwyll, transformed by Ledoux in 1787, and the birthplace of Mme de Staël (1766–1817).

Nos 67–87, on the west side of the Rue du Temple, provide a charming ensemble of 17C houses, of which Nos 71, 73 and 75 form the Hôtel de St.-Aignan, built by Le Muet in 1640–50; the courtyards and gate are particularly elegant. No. 79, dating from c 1620, but altered after 1751, is the Hôtel de Montmor, also with a good gateway and an attractive pediment in the courtyard.

No. 62 was the site of a house in which Anne de Montmorency (1493–1567), Constable of France, died; No. 41, the Auberge de l'Aigle d'Or (17C), is the last remaining example in Paris of a coaching inn of the period. The square turret on No. 24 dates from 1610; and an inscription on No. 17 indicates the site of the house of Du Guesclin (1372–80).

You rejoin the Rue de Rivoli at the Hôtel de Ville (see Rte 19).

22 The Grands Boulevards: from La Madeleine to Pl. de la République La Madeleine; Opéra

METROS: Concorde, Madeleine, Opéra, Richelieu-Drouot, Rue Mont-martre, Bonne-Nouvelle, Strasbourg-St.-Denis, République.

The **Grands Boulevards**, a succession of wide thoroughfares extending in a curve from the Pl. de la Concorde to the Bastille, were laid out in 1670–85 on the site of the inner ramparts, demolished in previous decades. These had comprised the eastern part of the 'enceinte de Charles V', erected after 1370, and the new fortifications to the west built by Louis XIII in 1633–37.

Young visited them in 1787 after attending a theatre, and remarked: 'Coffee-houses ... music, noise and *filles* without end; everything but scavengers and lamps. The mud is a foot deep; and there are parts of the boulevards without a single light'. They have since changed in some respects.

Although the Western Boulevards are no longer the centre of fashion they once were, they are still busy shopping and commercial districts.

The **Rue Royale** forms a convenient approach to the Boulevards from the Pl. de la Concorde; see Rte 13. As far as the Rue St.-Honoré it is lined with uniform 18C houses, with shops below, including that of Lalique. René Lalique (1860–1945), also a goldsmith and jeweller, caused a sensation when he displayed his designs in glass at the International Exhibition of 1900. No. 3, Maxim's, was a haunt of 'high society' in the 1890s; the Café Weber, a literary rendezvous earlier this century, stood at No. 21. Mme de Staël lived briefly at No. 6 on her last visit to Paris (1816–17); No. 8 was the home of the architect Gabriel. No. 21 contains the Musée Bouilhet-Chris-tofle, devoted to the art of the silversmith (see also end of Rte 36).

The street is dominated by Ste.-Marie-Madeleine, or simply **La Madeleine** (Pl. 7; 6), built in the style of a Roman temple, and surrounded by a majestic Corinthian colonnade. It was being restored in 1991.

Two earlier churches had been demolished unfinished, in 1777 and 1789, before

Pierre-Alexandre Vignon (1763–1828) commenced work in 1806 on the orders of Napoléon, who, before he had thought of the Arc de Triomphe, intended it as a 'Temple of Glory' for the 'Grande Armée'. It was finished by Huvé in 1842. In the pediment is a relief of the Last Judgement (restored), by Lemaire; the bronze doors are adorned with bas-reliefs OF the Decalogue by Triqueti (1838). Some 300 insurgents were massacred here by M. Thiers's troops during the last days of the Commune.

The INTERIOR consists of a domed cella, meretriciously decorated and inadequately lit. In chapels on either side of the entrance are the Marriage of the Virgin, by Pradier, and the Baptism of Christ, by Rude; the affected group of the Ascension of the Magdalen, on the high-altar, is by Marochetti.

The statue of St. Luke at the back of the building was decapitated in May 1918 by a shell from 'Bertha', the German long-range gun.

On the eastern side of the Pl. de la Madeleine, is a small flower market. At No. 2 stood the Café Durand, which played a dominant role in the 1848 Revolution, and where Zola wrote 'J'Accuse', an open letter denouncing the army, and in defence of Dreyfus, published in 'L'Aurore', on 13 January 1898.

Stendhal lived at 14 (then No. 10) Rue Richepance, to the south east; and Pamela Fitzgerald, wife of Edward Fitzgerald (died 1798), the Irish patriot, died in the same street in 1831.

Marcel Proust spent much of his youth at 9 Blvd Malesherbes, leading north west from the Madeleine. Its southern is section dominated by St.-Augustin, an early example of the use of iron in church construction (1860–71), by Baltard, architect of the former Halles (cf.).

The Blvd de la Madeleine, the westernmost of the Grands Boulevards, leads north east. Marie Duplessis (1824–47), the prototype of 'La Dame aux Camélias', died at No. 15 (formerly 11). The Crédit Foncier occupies an 18C mansion in the neighbouring Rue des Capucines, leading south east towards the Pl. Vendôme (see Rte 17). The boulevard is continued by the Blvd des Capucines, crossing the Pl. de l'Opéra (see below). Offenbach (1819–80), who had lived in Paris since 1833, died at 8 Blvd des Capucines.

Off its north side the Rue Edouard-VII leads to a small Place containing an equestrian statue of Edward VII (by Landowski). As Prince of Wales and king he was a frequent visitor to Paris, and a promoter of the 'Entente Cordiale'.

At 14 Blvd des Capucines a tablet records the first exhibition of a cinema film (in the 'Salon Indien' of the Grand Café) given by the brothers Louis and Auguste Lumière (28 December 1895). The first demonstration of X-rays, a discovery of Dr Roentgen, took place in the same room a few days later. At No. 35, once the studio of Nadar (Félix Tournachon; 1820–1910), the portrait-photographer and aeronaut, paintings by Renoir, Manet, Pissarro and Monet were exhibited. Included in this exhibition of 1874 was Monet's 'Impression—Soleil levant' (in fact the port of Le Havre in mist), which gave the group its name. See Musée Marmottan.

The Pl. de l'Opéra (Pl. 7; 6), a busy focus of traffic, is dominated to the north by the opera-house, while to the north west is the Café de la Paix, once a fashionable meeting-place for visitors to Paris.

The grandiose *OPERA, an appropriate monument to the most extravagant and brilliant period of the Second Empire—as the Opéra de la Bastille is of M. Mitterrand's regime—was built in 1861–75 from the designs of Charles Garnier (1825–98), the successful entrant of 171 competitors.

Carpeaux's sculpture of The Dance from the Opéra

Although covering a huge area, it contains only 2158 seats, few in comparison with some other large theatres.

The first opera-house in Paris was established in 1669 by Perrin, Cambert and the Marquis de Sourdéac on the Left Bank, between the Rue de Seine and the Rue Mazarine. The first director was Lully (from 1674), under whom it acquired its secondary title of Académie Royale de Musique.

The façade, flanked by a flight of steps, is lavishly decorated with coloured marbles and sculpture. On either side of the arcade opening into the vestibule are allegorical groups, including (right) The Dance by Carpeaux (a copy of the original, which now graces the interior of the Musée d'Orsay). Above are medallions of composers; and bronze-gilt statues of other composers and librettists are seen between the monolithic columns of the loggia. Behind the low dome of the auditorium is a triangular pediment crowned by a statue of Apollo of the Golden Lyre.

The east pavilion in the Rue Halévy is the subscribers' entrance; to the west, in the Rue Auber, is the 'Pavillon d'Honneur', and the entrance to the museum and library. These contain a complete collection of the scores of all operas and ballets performed here since its foundation, and over 100,000 drawings of costumes, scenery and photographs of artistes, etc.

This latter entrance, originally known as the 'Pavillon de l'Empereur', was designed so that his coach could be driven up to the level of the dress circle—a precaution welcomed since Orsini's attempt on the life of Napoléon III on his way to the old Opera-house in 1858, and a device which won Garnier the competition, so it was rumoured: see Rue le Peletier, below.

The Hall d'Acceuil contains a shop selling objects on themes associated with the Ballets Russes, among others. The second vestibule contains the box-office, beyond which is the Grand Staircase, with its white marble steps 10m wide, and with a balustrade of onyx and rosso and verde antico. On the first floor, where the staircase divides, is the entrance to the stalls and the amphitheatre, flanked by caryatids, and on each floor are arcades of monolithic marble columns. The Avant-Foyer leads to the Grand Foyer; glass doors communicate with the Loggia overlooking the Pl. de l'Opéra, and by the middle door is a bust of Garnier by Carpeaux.

The auditorium, resplendent in red plush and gilt, and with five tiers of boxes, is—except during performances—not normally on view, but may seen during a guided tour. The dome, resting on eight pillars of scagliola, was redecorated in 1964, many would say inappropriately, by Chagall. The huge stage is 60m high, 52m wide and 37m deep, behind which is the Foyer de la Dance (the scene of many paintings of ballet dancers by Degas; see Musée d'Orsay), with a mirror measuring 7 by 10m. (There is at present much controversy as to whether ballet only, or both opera and ballet, will be performed here. The management of both opera-houses have been misguidedly combined.)

The Av. de l'Opéra leads south east to the Pl. André-Malraux (see Rte 17), and is crossed by the Rue Louis-le-Grand, in which (at No. 3) Mme de Montespan and the painter Hyacinthe Rigaud (1659–1743; who died at No. 1), had houses. Napoléon and Joséphine Beauharnais were married in 1796 at 3 Rue d'Antin (the next cross-street), which was then the Mairie of the 2nd arrondissement. The Fontaine Gaillon (1828), just to the east in the Rue St.-Augustin, is by Visconti and Jacquot.

Immediately behind the Opéra, facing the Pl. Diaghilev, are the department stores of Galeries Lafayette (1898) and, to the west, Du Printemps (1889; but remodelled after a fire in 1921, and since), with huge and remarkable central halls.

Just east of the former is the Rue de la Chaussée-d'Antin, leading north to La Trinité (see Rte 23). Rossini lived from 1857–68 at No. 2 in its southern section.

No. 5 (rebuilt) was the home of Baron Grimm, frequented by Mme d'Epinay, and which sheltered Mozart in 1778 after the death of his mother on 3 July of that year (see below): it was the residence of Chopin in 1833–36. At No. 7 stood the home of the Neckers, who entertained Gibbon here; in 1798 it was bought by Jules Récamier, the banker, whose wife presided over the most distinguished salon of the Directory here, frequented also by Lord and Lady Holland, and many other English *en passage*.

The Blvd des Italiens (the continuation north east of the Blvd des Capucines), whose many cafés have been largely replaced by cinemas and commercial buildings, derived its name from the Théâtre des Italiens (1783), where Donizetti's 'Don Pasquale' was first performed in 1843. Grétry lived at No. 7 from 1795 to 1813.

In 1784–85, Jefferson had lodgings in the Impasse Taitbout (now Rue du Helder), leading left. 5 Rue Taitbout, further east, was the home of Sir Richard Wallace, where Lord Hertford accumulated many of the works of art now in the Wallace Collection, London (see also p 228). Wagner lived at No. 25 in 1840–41.

At the corner of the next street, the Rue Laffitte (named after Jacques Laffitte, 1767–1844, the financier; see Maisons-Laffitte, Rte 35), stood the house of Mme Tallien (1773–1835), daughter of the Spanish financier Cabarrus, and wife of the revolutionary, and later Princesse de Chimay. Part of the building (No. 20) became the Café Hardy, rival of the Café Riche at No. 16 ('Il faut être bien riche pour diner chez Hardy, et bien hardi pour dîner chez Riche'). At the far end of the street you can see N.-D.-de-Lorette with Sacré-Cœur in the background (Rte 23 and 24 respectively). 17 Rue Laffitte was the residence of Queen Hortense of Holland, and Napoléon III was born here in 1808. From No. 27, then Laffitte's residence, was issued the manifesto of Thiers proposing the coronation of Louis-Philippe. At Nos 39 and 41 stood Ambroise Vollard's art gallery, where many paintings by Gauguin and Cézanne were first displayed. Vollard was also responsible for the first exhibitions in Paris of works by Picasso and Matisse (in 1901 and 1904 respectively).

It was in the parallel Rue Le Peletier (to the east) that the 'Carbonaro' Orsini flung a bomb at the carriage conveying Napoléon III to the opera in 1858, killing or injuring 156 people, but leaving the emperor unharmed. No. 3 was the Café du Divan, frequented by Balzac, Gautier, De Nerval and Baudelaire. On the site of No. 6 stood the Salle Le Peletier, an opera-house from 1821 until 1873, when it was burned out. It was here that the works of Meyerbeer, and Wagner's revised version of 'Tannhäuser' (1861; which was a flop), among many other operas, were first performed.

In the Rue de Marivaux (opposite) stands the **Salle Favart**, previously the Opéra-Comique, and now housing an experimental Opéra-Studio; it is also the venue of concerts.

The Opéra-Comique originated in a company which produced pieces during local fairs, and in 1715 purchased from the Opéra the right of playing vaudevilles interspersed with ariettas. Discord between the two theatres continued until in 1757 Charles Favart (1710–92) finally established the rights of the Opéra-Comique, which moved to this somewhat confined site in 1783, since rebuilt.

At the junction of the boulevard with that of the Blvd Montmartre and Blvd Haussmann (only extended to this point in 1927), the Rue Drouot leads north past (No. 6) the Mairie of the 9th arrondissement in a mansion of 1746–48, and No. 9 (left), the Hôtel des Ventes de Paris, or **Nouveau Drouot**, rebuilt in the 1980s, the main auction-rooms of Paris, where important sales are held from February to June. Since 1801 it has occupied the same place in Parisian life as Christie's or Sotheby's in London. Pissarro painted 13 views of the Blvd Montmartre from a window of the Grand Hôtel de Russie, which stood at 1 Rue Drouot.

To the south, Rue de Richelieu (where Thomas Paine wrote 'The Age of Reason' at No. 95 in 1793) leads to the Bibliothèque Nationale (see Rte 18).

The short Blvd Montmartre, in spite of its name, is some distance from Montmartre. At No. 10 (left) is the Musée Grévin, a waxwork collection equivalent to Mme Tussaud's in London. On the right is the Rue Vivienne, leading to the Bourse; the Passage des Panoramas (named after an entertainment displaying views of cities, introduced to Paris by the American Robert Fulton, who had also tested his first steamboat on the Seine in 1803). George Moore lived here as an art student. The Théâtre des Variétés was the scene of several of Offenbach's successes.

The Rue Montmartre, already so named in 1200, leads south east towards St.-Eustache (Rte 19). Emile Zola (1840–1902) was born at 10 Rue St.-Joseph, a short distance south; the family moved to Aix-en-Provence in 1842.

The Rue du Faubourg-Montmartre, heading north west towards the 'suburb' of Montmartre, recalls the time when the boulevard formed the city boundary. Lautréamont (1846–70) died at No. 7, where he had written 'Les Chants de Maldoror'. The Rue Geoffroy-Marie, a turning off to the right (commemorating a saddler and his wife who in 1260 presented to the Hôtel-Dieu a little farm which sold for over three million francs in 1840), leads through a mainly Jewish enclave and a centre of the diamond trade, towards the Rue Richer. Here at No. 32 is the cabaret known as the Folies-Bergère (originally the Café Sommier Elastique, founded in 1869 to produce vaudevilles). Manet's 'The Bar at the Folies-Bergère' was painted in 1881. Pissarro lived at 42 Rue des Petits-Ecuries, further east.

Continuing east along the Blvd Poissonnière (in which No. 27 was Chopin's first Paris home, in 1831–32), we pass (right) the Rue du Sentier, where, opposite the end of the Rue du Croissant, Mozart and his mother lodged in 1778. In the same year she was buried in the vanished Cimitière St.-Joseph nearby, also the original burial-place of Molière.

Necker lived in 1766–89 at the junction of the adjacent Rue de Mulhouse and the Rue de Cléry (in a house replaced by No. 29) and here Mme Necker (Suzanne Curchod; 1739–94) held her salon every Friday, frequented by Voltaire, Diderot, D'Alembert, Marmontel and Buffon, among others.

To the north, at 2 Rue du Conservatoire (beyond the Rue Rougemont), is the Conservatoire National d'Art Dramatique, a small theatre of 1802, reputed for its acoustics.

The boulevard is now crossed by the Rue Poissonnière (right) and its north extension, the Rue du Faubourg-Poissonnière, both named after the fishmongers who used to pass by on their way to the Halles. Corot (1796–1875) died at 56 Rue du Faubourg-Poissonière. Beyond this junction, the line of boulevards is continued by the Blvd de Bonne-Nouvelle, on the northern side of which is the façade (1887) of the Théâtre du Gymnase, where Rachel made her début in 1837.

To the south, steps lead up to N.-D. de Bonne-Nouvelle, rebuilt in 1824. André Chénier (1762–94) lived in 1793 at 97 Rue de Cléry, close by; the same street was Corneille's home in 1665–81.

The short Blvd St.-Denis (Pl. 9; 5) lies between the Porte St.-Denis and the Porte St.-Martin, beyond which the Blvd St.-Martin continues as far as the Pl. de la République. The **Porte St.-Denis**, a triumphal arch 23m high, designed by Blondel, was erected in 1672 to commemorate the victories of Louis XIV in Germany and Holland. The bas-reliefs were designed by Girardon and executed by the brothers Anguier. It faces the Rue St.-Denis, or 'Voie Royale', once the processional route of entry into Paris, and last so used on the occasion of Queen Victoria's visit in 1855.

On the far side of the Blvd de Sebastopol, which with its northern extension, the Blvd de Strasbourg, stretches from the Pl. du Châtelet to the Gare de l'Est, you pass the **Porte St.-Martin**, another triumphal arch in honour of Louis XIV, c 18m high, built in 1674 by Bullet, and decorated with bas-reliefs of contemporary campaigns, by Desjardins and Marsy (south side) and Le Hongre and the elder Legros (north).

At 6 Blvd St.-Denis stood the 'Cinéma St.-Denis', opened in 1896 by the brothers Lumière, which claims to be the first cinema.

The Rue St.-Martin (the original Roman road leading north from Lutetia) leads south to the Musée National des Techniques and St.-Nicolas-des-Champs (see Rte 21), off which the Rue N.-D. de Nazareth runs left. The façades of Nos 41–49 are of interest; Rudolf Diesel (1858–1913), inventor of the engine of that name, was born at No. 38.

You pass two famous theatres in the Blvd St.-Martin, just east of the arch, the Théâtre de la Renaissance, managed by Sarah Bernhardt in 1893–99, and the Théâtre de la Porte-St.-Martin, both rebuilt after being burnt down during the Commune.

The latter, in its original form a foundation of Marie-Antoinette (who had it built in 75 days in 1781 to house the opera), is remembered as being the theatre of Frédérick Lemaître (1800–76). Here Coquelin *aîné* (who created the name-part in Rostand's 'Cyrano de Bergerac') was seized by a fatal illness during a rehearsal of 'Chantecler' in 1909. Paul de Kock (1794–1871), the novelist, died at No. 8 in the boulevard.

The **Pl. de la République** (Pl. 9; 8), on the site of the Porte du Temple, and the junction of seven important thoroughfares, was laid out in 1856–65 by Haussmann for strategic reasons, but it has maintained a political role as the scene of radical demonstrations. The pedestal of the Monument de la République (1883; 25m high), has bronze bas-reliefs by Dalou.

At the corner of the Rue Léon-Jouhaux (previously Rue de la Douane) leading north east from the Place, was Daguerre's workshop in 1822–35. Gounod's 'Faust' was first performed in 1859 in the Théâtre Lyrique, one of many (including 'Des Funambules', 1816–62) which stood on a section of the Blvd du Temple demolished by Haussmann. It was known earlier in the 19C as the 'Boulevard du Crime', from the melodramas enacted here, as immortalised by Marcel Carné in the film 'Les Enfants du Paradis' (1945).

Beyond the Pl. de la République the boulevards are of slight interest, and change their character. The Blvd du Temple, with its continuations, leads south east to the Pl. de la Bastille (see Rte 21). Flaubert lived at No. 42 in this boulevard in 1856–69; and to the north is the site of the house from which Fieschi discharged his 'infernal machine' at Louis-Philippe in 1835, killing Marshal Mortier and several others, but not the king. To the west, at No. 5 in the parallel street named after him, Béranger died (1780–1857).

23 Gare de l'Est to Gare St.-Lazare (Faubourg St.-Martin and Faubourg St.-Denis)

METROS: République, Gare de l'Est, Gare du Nord, Poissonnière, N.-D.-de-Lorette, Trinité, St.-Lazare, St.-Augustin, Madeleine.

The Blvd de Magenta leads north west from the Pl. de la République to meet the outer boulevards beyond the Gare du Nord.

Just east of its intersection with the Blvd de Strasbourg is **St.-Laurent**, one of the oldest foundations in Paris. Gregory of Tours mentions that a church existed here near the Roman road as early as 583.

The present building, begun before 1429 but retaining an older north tower, was continued in the 16–17C, the nave having been vaulted and the choir remodelled in 1655–59, with a high-altar by Antoine le Pautre. The Lady Chapel dates from 1712. The 17C façade was demolished in 1862–65, when the Flamboyant west front was built and the spire erected. The roof has elegantly carved pendentives. Mme du Barry (Jeanne Bécu; 1746–93) was married here in 1764.

Just to the north, the courtyard of the **Gare de l'Est** (Pl. 9; 3) the future terminus of the projected TGV line to Strasbourg and Germany, to be completed by 1997, occupies the site of the medieval St. Lawrence fair.

To the west of the boulevard at this point stood the Prison de St.-Lazare (since 1935 partly demolished and rebuilt as a hospital), from 1632 the headquarters of the Lazarists or Priests of the Mission, founded in 1625 by Vincent de Paul (1576–1660). Among its temporary inmates were the poet André Chénier, and Hubert Robert.

The boulevard next crosses the Rue La Fayette before passing (right) the **Gare du Nord**, by Hittorff (1863), the terminus of the line from Calais, Boulogne, etc. (Pl. 9; 3), and also of a rapid shuttle service to the Charles de Gaulle airport. The station will also be the terminus of the TGV Transmanche (or Channel Tunnel line), and TGV to Brussels, Amsterdam and Cologne. The TGV Nord and the future RER EOLE line will be sited in the underground Gare du Nord-Est, being built between the two stations.

There is little of interest in the thickly populated cosmopolitan Quartier de la Chapelle to the north. Adjacent to an ugly modern basilica stands St.-Denis-de-la-Chapelle (13C, but much restored), where Joan of Arc received communion in November 1429 before besieging the walls of Paris.

Turning south west along the Rue la Fayette, you pass **St.-Vincent-de-Paul** (1824–44), by Lepère and Hittorf. With two square towers dominating a pedimented portico of 12 Ionic columns, it is approached by a monumental flight of steps.

At No. 58 Rue d'Hauteville, leading south, is the Hôtel de Bourrienne (1787), decorated in First Empire style by Napoléon's secretary. This street is crossed by the Rue de Paradis, where at No. 30 bis is the shop of the glass-maker Baccarat, replacing one existing since 1764, with a museum adjoining.

No. 9 Rue de Montholon (leading east from the Sq. de Montholon) was the residence of Liszt in 1831. Continuing west along the Rue la Fayette, you cross the Rue Cadet where, at No. 16, is the Musée du Grand Orient de France, with material relating to European Freemasonry. At this intersection, the Rue de Châteaudun leads west to pass **N.-D.-de-Lorette**, another drearily magnificent basilican church. It was built in 1823–36 by Hippolyte Lebas, and has a portico of four Corinthian columns.

Bizet (1838–75), born at 26 Rue de la Tour-d'Auvergne (leading off the Rue des Martyrs which ascends behind the church), was christened here. The Rue des Martyrs, the ancient approach to Montmartre, was already well known for its 'cabarets' in the 18C; Géricault (1791–1824) died at No. 49, later occupied by Béranger.

The Rue N.-D.-de-Lorette ascends north west from the church through a quarter whose name was synonymous with the *demi-mondaine* or *femmes entretenues* of the mid-19C who congregated here, and to whom newly-built dwellings in the neighbourhood were let off cheaply until the plaster dried! These 'Lorettes', a favourite subject of the caricaturist Gavarni (1801–66), are represented on his monument in the small Pl. St.-Georges, which the street crosses. Delacroix lived from 1844 to 1857 at No. 58 (then 54) in the Rue N.-D.-de-Lorette before moving to the Pl. de Furstemberg (cf.); Gauguin was born at No. 56 in 1848. Gavarni lived at 1 Rue Fontaine, its extension north, as did Degas between 1879 and 1886, at No. 19 bis.

27 Pl. St.-Georges is the Fondation Dosne-Thiers. The residence of President Thiers (1797–1877) from 1822 to 1871, burned down by the Communards and reconstructed at public expense, it now contains the Bibliothèque Thiers (80,000 vols on the history of France since the Revolution; and the Napoleonic collection of Frédéric Masson, of 30,000 vols; drawings by David; and a bust of Joséphine by Houdon, etc.). Contact the Librarian, Institut de France, 23 Quai de Conti, for permission to visit.

At No. 28, opposite, Thérèse Lachman, later Marquise de Païva, held her salons in 1851–66 (before moving to the Champs-Elysées), at which the brothers Goncourt, Gautier, Sainte-Beuve, Taine and Wagner were frequent visitors. The Symbolist poet Stéphane Mallarmé (1842–98) was born in the nearby Rue Laferrière (No. 12).

The Rue St.-Georges runs downhill, and crosses the Rue de Châteaudun. The Goncourt brothers lived at No. 43 from 1849 to 1868. Renoir had a studio at No. 35 and from 1897 at 64 Rue de la Rochefoucauld (see below). The composer Auber (1782–1871) lived for 30 years and died at No. 22; Henry Murger (1822–61), author of 'Scènes de la Vie de Bohème', was born the son of a concierge at No. 19.

In the Rue Taitbout (parallel to the west) lodged Rossini (at No. 28), when musical director of the Théâtre des Italiens (1824–25); and Mirabeau (1749–91) died at No. 42.

In 1842–47 Chopin and George Sand lived at Nos 5 and 9 respectively in the Sq. d'Orléans, off the east side of the northern end of this street. At 14 Rue de la Rochefoucauld, to the west at this level, is the **Musée Gustave Moreau** (admission 10.00–12.45, 14.00–17.15 except Tuesday), containing a collection of some 18,000 paintings and drawings left by Moreau (1826–98) to the State. Degas's Portrait of the artist, dated 1867, also hangs here.

To the west stands **La Trinité**, a conspicuously ugly church built in 1863–67 by Ballu in a hybrid style, with a tower 63m high. It was erected on the site of the disreputable Cabaret de la Grande Pinte, later Les Porcherons. It was here that Berlioz's funeral service took place (11 March 1869).

From a point north east of the church, the Rue Pigalle and Rue Blanche ascend north east and north towards Montmartre. Between the two, a short distance north, is Rue Chaptal. No. 16 is the so-called Musée de la Vie Romantique, with collections devoted to George Sand, Ernest Renan and his brother-in-law, Ary Scheffer. To the west of the church the Rue Clichy (in which Hugo lived at No. 21 in 1880) ascends north to the Pl. de Clichy. No. 16 is the Casino de Paris, a famous music-hall. To the south, the Rue de Mogador leads to the Opéra.

The Rue St.-Lazare leads west from the Sq. de la Trinité. Mme Vigée-le-Brun died at No. 29 in 1842. Just east of the **Gare St.-Lazare** (Pl. 7;4), the Rue d'Amsterdam leads north, in which lived Manet (at No. 77; in 1879–83) and Alexandre Dumas, *père* (No. 97; from 1854).

The station itself is a terminus of the western region of the SNCF. Its interior was the subject of paintings by Monet in 1877 (cf. Musée d'Orsay). The Hôtel Terminus was the home of Georges Feydeau, who, intending to stay a week while his family moved house, remained a decade (1909–19).

To the west of the station, the Rue de Rome leads north west (through the Pl. de l'Europe, painted by Caillebotte in 1877). No. 89 was the home of Mallarmé from 1885, and here his friends—among them George Moore— would congregate on Tuesday evenings. Jules Renard (1864–1910), author of 'Poil de Carotte', died at 44 Rue du Rocher, further west, where he had lived since 1888.

The Rue du Havre leads south from the Gare St.-Lazare, where No. 8, the Lycée Condorcet, founded in 1804, occupies the former buildings (with a Doric cloister court) of a Capuchin convent; on the site of its chapel (in the parallel street to the east) is St.-Louis d'Antin by Brongniart (1782). Proust, in 1882–87, was one of the school's many eminent pupils.

The street is continued south of the Blvd Haussmann by the Rue Tronchet (in which Chopin lived at No. 5 in 1839–42) to the Madeleine (see Rte 22).

The Blvd Haussmann, one of the main streets in the area, commemorates Eugène-Georges, Baron Haussmann (1809–91) who, as Préfet de la Seine, initiated extensive urban development in central Paris. Work began here in 1857 as part of a scheme to construct an unbroken thoroughfare from the Blvd Montmartre to the Arc de Triomphe, and was only completed in 1926. 'Nana', in Zola's novel, had an apartment in this boulevard.

A short distance to the west, on the south side of the Blvd Haussmann, is the Sq. Louis XVI (Pl. 7; 5), formerly the Cimetière de la Madeleine. Here lie the bodies of the victims of the panic of 1770 in the Pl. de la Concorde (see Rte 13), together with the Swiss guards massacred on 10 August 1792 and all those guillotined between 26 August 1792 and 24 March 1794 (among them Charlotte Corday and Philippe-Egalité). Near the south-west corner of the square stands the **Chapelle Expiatoire** (CNMH) erected in 1815–26 from the plans of Percier and Fontaine in the style of a classical funeral temenos. Built by order of Louis XVIII, it was dedicated to the memory of Louis XVI and Marie-Antoinette, whose remains, first interred in the graveyard on this site, were removed to St.-Denis in 1815; see Rte 36.

Inside are two marble groups: Louis XVI and his confessor Abbé Henry Essex Edgeworth (1745–1807) by Bosio (below which is inscribed the king's will, dated 25 December 1792) and Marie-Antoinette supported by Religion, by Cortot, the latter figure bearing the features of Mme Elisabeth. (Below is inscribed a letter said to have been written by the queen to her sister-in-law from the Conciergerie on 16 October 1793.) The bas-relief by Gérard above the doorway represents the removal of their remains.

24   Montmartre

Best approached from the METRO stations of Clichy, Lamarck-Caulain-court or Anvers.

The Pl. de Clichy (Pl. 7; 2) was the site of the 'Barrière de Clichy', which on 30 March 1814 was defended against the approaching Prussian troops by pupils from the Ecole Polytechnique and the Garde Nationale under Marshal Moncey. The action is commemorated by a bronze group by Doublemard (1869).

To the east lies the wide Blvd de Clichy, forming, with its continuation the Blvd de Rochechouart, the southern boundary of Montmartre proper. The Place and Blvd de Clichy were frequently painted by Renoir, Van Gogh (in 1887), Signac and many other artists working in the vicinity.

The first turning right off the Blvd de Clichy is the Rue de Douai: at No. 30, the home of Turgenev and Mme Pauline Viardot, Dickens met George Sand in 1856. Bonnard had a studio at 65 Rue de Douai in 1905. The street shortly crosses the Pl. Adolphe-Max (formerly Pl. Vintimille), in which Vuillard had a studio. Zola (1840–1902) died at 21 bis Rue de Bruxelles, crossing this square. Boudin lived at No. 11 in the Place, while Monet lived at 20 Rue Vintimille in 1879. Berlioz (1803–69) died at 4 Rue de Calais, leading south east; and Arnold Bennett lived in an apartment in this same building from late 1903 to late 1906, when writing 'The Old Wives' Tale' (1908).

The Blvds de Clichy and de Rochechouart are now the focus of the seedy night life of an increasingly sordid area, where colourful crowds congregate in the cafés and around the so-called 'cabarets artistiques' of the Pl. Pigalle and the Pl. Blanche, on the northern side of which stood the Moulin Rouge, founded by Joseph Oller, which was inaugurated on 1 May 1889. One of the star performers was Joseph Pujol, (1857–1945, 'Le Pétomane').

The Pl. Pigalle was the site of the 'Café de la Nouvelle Athènes', long an artistic rendezvous, notably of Manet and Degas. Puvis de Chavannes had a studio at No. 11 from 1852.

Over a century has passed since Montmartre was made more accessible by the construction of new streets ascending through the northern slums, and poor artists, migrating there because it was both picturesque and cheap, made it an artistic centre for about 30 years. Among those who vividly depicted this bohemian era was Toulouse-Lautrec (1864–1901), whose studio was at 5 Av. Frochot, near the Pl. Pigalle. No. 16 in the adjacent Rue Frochot was the home of Mme Sabatier (1822–89; 'La Présidente', the mistress of Richard Wallace after 1866), often the rendezvous of Alfred de Musset, Flaubert, Sainte-Beuve, Clésinger, Feydeau, Gautier and Baudelaire.

About 1881 the famous 'Le Chat Noir' (84 Blvd de Rochechouart; closed in 1897) was opened, advertising the attractions of the district and inviting a tide of pseudo-bohemians, tourists and less desirable hangers-on, before which the serious artists retired and have now all but vanished. There remain, however, a few old-fashioned streets and backwaters, made familiar in the paintings of Utrillo, among others, and an hour or two may be pleasantly spent wandering around the 'Butte' (see below), preferably during daylight.

Seurat (1859–91) had a studio at 128 bis Blvd de Clichy from 1886, and died at No. 39 Rue André-Antoine (leading north from the Pl. Pigalle). Signac's studio in 1886–88 was at No. 130 in the Boulevard, where Picasso lived in 1909. Degas died at No. 6 in 1917, where his protégée, Mary Cassatt, had painted.

The short Av. Rachel, the first turning on the left off the Blvd. de Clichy going east, leads to the main entrance of the **Cimetière de Montmartre**, on the western slope of the Butte (Pl. 7; 2), partly spanned by a viaduct.

Although less important than that of Père-Lachaise, it contains the graves of many famous 18–20C writers, including Gautier, De Vigny, the Goncourt brothers, Alexandre Dumas (*fils*), Stendhal, Heine, Murger, Zola, Feydeau, Maxime du Camp, Renan and Giraudoux; among composers, Berlioz, Delibes, Offenbach, Halévy, Adam and Ambroise Thomas; also Adolphe Sax; among artists, Fragonard, Greuze, Delaroche, Carle Vernet, Horace Vernet, Diaz de la Peña and Degas; the actors Frédéric Lemaître

Monument to Alexandre Dumas, fils, in the cemetery at Montmartre

and Louis Jouvet; the dancers Vestris, Taglioni and Nijinsky; Mme Récamier, Pauline Viardot and Marie Duplessis ('La Dame aux Camélias'); Waldeck Rousseau, Marshal Lannes (heart only), Hittorff, Fourier, Ampère, Dr Charcot and Miles Byrne, the United Irishman.

From the Pl. de Clichy, the Rue Caulaincourt is carried over the cemetery by a viaduct, which is the most convenient approach to Montmartre by car.

Toulous-Lautrec kept a studio for a decade prior to 1897 at No. 21 and Renoir at No. 73 c 1910, in the basement of which the Swiss artist Steinlen (1859–1923), who had lived in Paris since 1881, died. Continuing along the Blvd de Clichy, you pass (left) the once-famous Moulin Rouge (now a cinema; see above), facing the Pl. Blanche and turn left up the steep Rue Lepic. Vincent van Gogh and his brother, Théo, lived at No. 54 in 1886, towards the rebuilt Moulin de la Galette. The dancer 'La Goulue' began her career here, and it was painted by Renoir in 1876 and Bonnard in c 1905, among others. Turning east along the Rue Norvins, we shortly reach the central Pl. du Tertre (Pl. 8; 1–2), now much commercialised, and surrounded by cafés, etc.

To the east of the Pl. du Tertre stands **ST.-PIERRE-DE-MONTMARTRE**, the successor of an earlier church built to commemorate the martyrdom of St. Denis, a relic of a Benedictine nunnery founded in 1134 by Adélaïde de Savoie (died 1154). It was consecrated in the presence of her son Louis VII by Pope Eugenius III in 1147. In 1794 it served as the 'Temple of Reason'.

The façade dates from the time of Louis XIV. Inside, against the west wall, are two ancient columns with 7C capitals; two other capitals, one at the apse entrance and another in the north aisle, are of the same date. The nave has 15C vaulting; the aisle vaulting was added in a restoration of 1900–05. The apse has also been almost entirely rebuilt, but the choir retains perhaps the earliest example of an ogee arch in Paris (1147). The tomb of the foundress lies behind the altar.

In the adjacent Jardin du Calvaire are Stations of the Cross executed for Richelieu. Foundations of a Roman temple have been discovered to the north of the church, while in the derelict graveyard is the tomb of the navigator Bougainville (1729–1811); also buried here are the sculptor Pigalle (1714–85) and members of the Fitz-James family.

The Rue Azais, to the south, leads past a water-tower to the terrace below the Basilique du Sacré-Coeur, with extensive views south over the entire city with its changing skyline. Commanding Paris in this way, the history of the Butte Montmartre is one long series of sieges and battles.

The **Butte Montmartre** rises 130m above sea-level and 104m above the level of the Seine, and is traditionally the highest point in Paris; cf. Belleville. The name has been variously derived from Mons Mercurii, Mons Martis or Mons Martyrum; the two first presuppose the existence of a Roman temple on the hill; the last the probability that St. Denis and his companions, SS. Rusticus and Eleutherius, were beheaded at the foot of the hill, St. Denis afterwards walking to the site of the Basilica of St.-Denis (see Rte 36), 'with his head in his hands'. The Chapelle du Martyre (in the convent at 9 Rue Yvonne-le-Tac, just east of the Métro Abbesses) occupies the probable position of a chapel erected on the site of the martyrdom. It was in its crypt that Ignatius de Loyola and his six companions, including Francisco Xavier, taking the first Jesuit vows, founded the Society of Jesus (1534). The Butte was occupied by Henri of Navarre in 1589, and the final struggle between the French and the Allies took place here in 1814.

On 18 March 1871, at 6 Rue des Roses—then called des Rosiers—to the north east of the Butte, Generals Clément Thomas and Claude Martin Lecomte were captured and murdered by insurgents when attempting to seize cannon entrusted to the National Guards. Their deaths to a certain extent precipitated more drastic government action against the Communards.

In 1873 the National Assembly decreed the building of a basilica here as an expiatory offering after the Franco-Prussian War of 1870–71. The result, the **SACRE-COEUR**, only too visible from almost every part of Paris, is a conspicuous white stone edifice in a neo-Romanesque-Byzantine style derived from St.-Front at Périgueux.

Work began in 1876 from the plans of Abadie (who had restored St.-Front), and although used for services in 1891, it was not consecrated as a basilica until 1919. It is built of Château-Landon stone which whitens with age. The two statues at the front of the basilica depicting Joan of Arc and St. Louis are by Hippolyte Lefebvre.

100m long and 75m across the ambulatory, it is surmounted by a dome 83m high, and abutted by a square campanile in which hangs the Savoyarde, one of the world's heaviest bells: 19 tons.

Inside, this pilgrim church is extensively decorated with mosaics. That over the high altar, by Luc-Olivier Merson, shows Christ and the Sacred Heart worshipped by the Virgin, Joan of Arc and St. Michael, and is one of the largest in the world.

Both the crypt and the dome can be visited for a fee. From the dome there are views of the interior and from the external gallery of 80 columns (each with different capitals) extensive panoramas (50km) across Paris.

Flights of steps descend the steep slope of the Butte to the Sq. Willette (parallel to which a new funicular in projected). The Rue de Steinkerque continues downhill to Blvd de Rochechouart and the Pl. d'Anvers.

Not much remains of 'Old Montmartre', with its cottages and little gardens, although in the Rue des Saules, leading north from the Rue Norvins, you can see the last surviving vineyard of Paris. No. 4 in this street is 'Au Lapin Agile' (named after the rabbit of M. André Gill, who commissioned the sign), made famous by its artistic clientele. Harriet Smithson (Mme Berlioz; 1800–54, who had married the composer in 1833), Honegger (1892–1955) and Utrillo (1883–1956) are buried in the nearby Cimetière St.-Vincent.

At No. 42 Rue des Saules is the Musée d'Art Juif.

At No. 17 Rue St.-Vincent, to the right beyond the vineyard, steps climb to the Musée de Vieux-Montmartre (12 Rue Cortot), installed in a 17C house once belonging to Roze de Rosimond, a member of Molière's 'Illustre Théâtre'. It contains, apart from ephemera and material of very local interest, a small collection of Clignancourt (or Montmartre) porcelain, made in 1767–99 in a pottery at the junction of the Rues du Mont-Cenis and Marcadet. This house was occupied by Renoir in 1875, and later by Emile Bernard (who entertained Gauguin and Van Gogh here), Suzanne Valadon (in 1906–09), her son Maurice Utrillo, and Dufy, among others. Erik Satie lived at 6 Rue Cortot (parallel to the Rue St.-Vincent) in 1896–37. At the corner of the Rue St.-Vincent, at No. 24 Rue du Mont-Cenis (house rebuilt), Berlioz and Harriet Smithson lived in 1834–37.

Not far south of the Rue Norvins, the Pl. Emile-Goudeau was a favourite 'artistic' residence c 1910, where (at No. 13, the 'Bateau-Lavoir'; rebuilt since a fire in 1970) lived Modigliani, Van Dongen, Derain, Gris, Picasso, and Max Jacob, and where a banquet was given in honour of 'Douanier' Rousseau.

25 From Pl. de la Concorde to the Arc de Triomphe: Av. des Champs-Elysées; Petit Palais; Arc de Triomphe

METROS: Concorde, Champs-Elysées-Clemenceau, Franklin D. Roosevelt, George-V, Charles de Gaulle-Etoile.

To the west of the Pl. de la Concorde extend the Champs-Elysées, through which the wide Av. des Champs-Elysées gently ascends to the Arc de Triomphe. The lower-lying area, drained and planted in 1670 according to Le Nôtre's designs, was replanned in

1770 by the Marquis de Marigny (brother of Mme de Pompadour), who extended the avenue to the Pont de Neuilly in 1774. Cossacks encamped there in 1814, as did English troops in the following year. It was a fashionable promenade under the Second Empire, but time has treated it harshly, and although still crowded, few of its attractions are of an aesthetic nature, however imposing may be the vistas.

The **Champs-Elysées** consist of two parts; the first, forming a park, extends to the Rond-Point des Champs-Elysées; the increasingly commercialised avenue, flanked by the offices of airline companies, car showrooms, cinemas, banks and expensive cafés, continues north west towards the commanding bulk of the Arc de Triomphe, a striking silhouette against the setting sun.

Running parallel to the north side of the Champs-Elysées is the Av. Gabriel, with the American Embassy (1931–33) at the corner of the Rue Boissy-d'Anglas, built on the site of a mansion of 1769 belonging to Laurent Grimod de la Reynière, a noted gourmand, and later to his more famous son, Alexandre-Balthazar (1758–1838), author of the 'Almanach des Gourmands'. Further on (right) are the gardens of the British Embassy and then those of the Palais de l'Elysée; see Rte 26.

From the Pl. Clemenceau the Av. de Marigny leads north, passing (left) the Théâtre Marigny, and an open-air stamp market (Thursday and Sunday) to reach the walled gardens of the Palais de l'Elysée (see Rte 26) but pedestrians are forbidden to walk along the flanking *trottoir*.

To the south, the Av. Winston Churchill, with a fine view of Les Invalides (see Rte 11), leads between the Petit Palais (left) and Grand Palais, both built for the Exhibition of 1900, to the wide Pont Alexandre-III (1896–1900), a single steel arch 107.50m in length.

The **PETIT-PALAIS**, or Musée des Beaux-Arts de la Ville de Paris (Pl. 7; 7), with its domed entrance in the Av. Winston Churchill, is in itself a building of no great merit (by Girault), but it contains various ***Collections of paintings**, etc., donated to the city, which are often overlooked by the visitor. Unfortunately the quality of display leaves something to be desired.

The collections may be roughly divided into four sections. First the 19–early 20C **French** paintings, including representative canvases by *Vuillard* and *Bonnard*, and *Gustave Courbet's* portraits of M. Corbinaud, of his Father, of Pierre-Joseph Proudhon and his children, and Self-portrait with his dog. Among other important works are: *Fragonard*, Portrait of Lalande, the astronomer; *Cézanne*, Portrait of Ambroise Vollard, and wall-panels of the Seasons (signed 'Ingres' in derision); *Gauguin*, Old man with a stick; *Toulouse-Lautrec*, the Nice mail-coach, Portrait of André Rivoire; *Renoir*, Portrait of A. Vollard, Woman with a rose; *Mary Cassatt*, Head of a girl (pastel), Portraits of Lydia Cassatt and of 'M.D.'; Landscapes by *Sisley* and *Pissarro*; *Monet*, Sunset at Lavacourt; *Manet*, Portrait of M. Duret; *Marie Bashkirtseff*, Self-portrait; *Berthe Morisot*, A young girl, In the park; *Baudry*, Mme Singer; *Sargent*, Mme Allouard-Jouan; *Bonnat*, Mme Ehrler; and *Jongkind*, View of Notre-Dame from the Quai de la Tournelle.

Paintings of the **Dutch** school include: *Willem van de Velde*, Marine views; *Hobbema*, Mills, Forest scene; *van Goyen*, Landscapes; *Willem de Heusch*, Landscape; *Ter Borch*, The fiancée; Adriaen van Ostade, The gazette, Woman with a letter, The analyst; *Pot*, Portrait of a man; *Metsu*, The toilet, Woman playing the virginal; *Rembrandt*, Self-portrait in oriental costume; *Neefs*, Church interior; *Palamedes*, Palace interior, 'Réunion galante'; *Isaak van Ostade*, Farmyard; *Teniers the Younger*, Tavern scenes; *Jan Steen*, Idiot begging alms; *Willem Claesz. Heda*, Still life; *Wouwerman*,

Gypsies, The cavaliers' halt; *Jordaens,* Diana's repose; *Brakenburgh,* Tavern interior; *Adriaen van de Velde,* Landscape; *van der Meulen,* Cavalry combat; Both, Landscape; Berghem, The watering-place; Hackert and *Van de Velde,* Ash-trees; *Jouvet,* Portrait of Corneille.

The **Edward Tuck Collection:** Chinese porcelain of the K'ang-Hsi period (1662–1722; famille noire); Battersea enamels; Meissen figures; 18C Beauvais tapestries, *after Boucher* and *Huet; Greuze,* Portrait of Benjamin Franklin; terracotta bust of Franklin by *Houdon;* and a representative collection of Louis XV furniture.

The **Dutuit Collection:** among the paintings, *Cranach,* The burgomaster's daughter; *Brueghel* (de Velours), Wedding; and *Cima de Conegliano,* Madonna and Child. Also an impressive collection of Grolier bindings, among others; Gubbio and Urbino majolica; Limoges enamels; ivories; German and Burgundian wood carvings; Gallo-Roman bronzes; Egyptian statuettes; and an extensive collection of Greek ceramics, etc.

The **Grand Palais**, facing the Petit, with a classical façade, surmounted by a lofty portico, houses various exhibition-halls. Its western half contains a planetarium and the Palais de la Découverte, devoted to the popularisation of scientific knowledge (admission 10.00–20.00, except Tuesday).

Publications of the *Caisse Nationale des Monuments Historiques* are available from Porte F, facing the Cours-la-Reine; those of the *Inventaire général des Monuments et des Richesses artistiques de la France*, from Porte D.

Six avenues radiate from the Rond-Point des Champs-Elysées, with its six fountains. At 3 Av. Matignon, leading north east, the German poet and essayist Heinrich Heine (1799–1856) died; to the south west extends the wide Av. Montaigne.

On the right at the beginning of the built-up area of the Av. des Champs-Elysées are the offices of the newspaper *Le Figaro.* There is a project to repave the avenue and plant many more trees along either side.

Two streets beyond, at 107 Rue La Boétie, are showrooms of the **Institut Géographique Nationale**, where a large range of French maps may be bought. At the corner of the Rue de Berri, parallel to the west, a plaque marks the site of a mansion in which Thomas Jefferson lived in 1785–89 when American minister to France.

No. 25 in the Avenue, since 1904 the Travellers' Club, was built in 1855–66 by Pierre Maugin in an ostentatious Renaissance style for the Marquise de Païva. Here she continued to hold the artistic and political salon which advanced her career of adventuress and spy (cf. Pl. St.-Georges). Dickens lived at No. 49 in 1855–56. Byron stayed in the street named after him, north of and parallel to this section of the avenue.

At No. 127 (left) beyond the upper end of the Av. George-V, is the **Office de Tourisme de Paris**.

Twelve avenues radiate starwise from the Pl. Charles-de-Gaulle (formerly **Pl. de l'Etoile**, and still commonly known as such: Pl. 6; 5). The uniform façades facing it between each avenue were designed by Hittorff in 1854–57.

In the centre stands the grandiose ***ARC DE TRIOMPHE**, (CNMH) the largest triumphal arch in the world (almost 50m high, and 45m wide), recently restored.

Designed by Chalgrin, and begun in 1806, it was not completed until 1836. The main façades of the arch are adorned with colossal groups in high relief. Facing the Champs-Elysées are (right) the Departure of the Army in 1792 (otherwise known as

'La Marseillaise') by Rude and (left) the Triumph of Napoléon in 1810, by Cortot. Facing the Av. de la Grande-Armée are (right) the Resistance of the French in 1814, and (left) the Peace of 1815, both by Etex.

The four spandrels of the main archway contain figures of Fame by Pradier, and those of the smaller archways have sculptures by Vallois (south side) and Bra. Above the groups are panels in relief of incidents in the campaigns of 1792–1805. On the row of shields in the attic storey are inscribed the names of 172 (victorious) battles of the Republic and the Empire, including some claimed to be French victories, but in fact not so! Below the side arches are the names of some hundreds of generals who took part in these campaigns, those who fell in action being underlined. A discreet silence is maintained about the other hundreds of thousands of Frenchmen who fought for the Emperor, both in his victories and defeats, and who also died.

Beneath the arch is the Tomb of the Unknown Soldier, symbolic of the dead of both World Wars. Its flame has burnt constantly since 11 November 1923. At its foot is a bronze plaque representing the 'Shaef' shoulder-flash, and dated 25 August 1944, the day of the liberation of Paris from the German occupation. On the summit is a platform commanding panoramic views: admission 10.00–17.00 or 17.30 daily; fee.

Since 1840, when the route was followed by a cortège bearing Napoléon's body, watched, despite the intense cold, by 100,000 people, the Champs-Elysées has been used for state processions on a number of occasions, funereal, triumphal and in celebration of liberation.

Richard and Minna Wagner lived in the Rue Newton, a short distance to the south, in 1859–60.

To the west, the Av. de la Grande Armée leads gently downhill to Porte Maillot, with the towers of La Défense rising some distance beyond: see latter part of Rte 28. Maud Gonne (Mme Gonne MacBride), who founded the French society of Friends of Irish Freedom, lived in this Avenue in the 1890s.

26 From Rue du Faubourg-St.-Honoré to Parc Monceau
The British Embassy; Musée Jacquemart-André; Musée Nissim de Camondo; Musée Cernuschi

METROS: Concorde, Madeleine, St.-Philippe-du-Roule, Pl.-des-Ternes, Villiers, Monceau, Charles de Gaulle-Etoile.

The Rue du Faubourg-St.-Honoré is the north-west continuation of the Rue St.-Honoré. It extends from the Rue Royale (leading from the Pl. de la Concorde to the Pl. de la Madeleine, see Rte 22) to the Pl. des Ternes (north east of the Arc de Triomphe), following the course of the medieval road from Paris to the village of Roule.

It became fashionable at the end of Louis XIV's reign, and in the 18C its splendid mansions made it a rival to the Faubourg St.-Germain as an aristocratic quarter. Its pretensions are now largely sustained by a succession of luxurious and expensive boutiques, jewellers and fashion houses.

La Fayette (1757–1834) died at 8 Rue d'Anjou, leading north; Benjamin Constant (1767–1830) died at No. 29.

On the left in the Rue du Faubourg St.-Honoré is the exclusive Cercle Interallié (No. 33; of 1714), the Russian Embassy during the Second Empire; and adjacent (No. 35), the Hôtel de Charost, since 1825 the **British Embassy** (Pl. 7; 5), formerly at the Hôtel de Sagan (cf.) in the Faubourg St.-Germain, to which its earlier history refers.

The 4th Duc de Charost commissioned Antoine Mazin to build the mansion in 1722. In 1785 it was let to the Comte de la Marck, during whose tenancy much of its interior decoration was completed, and the 'jardin à l'anglaise' laid out. It was bought in 1803 by Pauline Bonaparte (later Princess Borghèse), much of whose furniture remains, and was sold by her to the Duke of Wellington in 1814 for £32,000, the figure including numerous clocks, chandeliers, candelabras and chimney-pieces, etc.

Sydney Smith preached an eloquent sermon in the dining-room (then serving as a chapel), and here Berlioz and Harriet Smithson were married (with Liszt as their best man) in 1833; and Thackeray to Isabella Shawe in 1836. Sir Edward Blount, attaché here in 1829, later promoted French railways, constructing lines from Paris to Rouen and from Amiens to Boulogne, in 1843 and 1845 respectively, thus making his contribution to the improvement in communications between the two countries. Bertram Russell was briefly attaché in 1894. Somerset Maugham (1874–1965), whose father was solicitor to the Embassy, was born at the residence, at No. 39 in the street. (A new law in 1870 proposed that anyone born on French soil was liable to conscription. His family lived at No. 25 Av. d'Antin, now Av. F.D. Roosevelt, until 1884.)

A few diplomatic representatives have distinguished themselves by throwing lavish parties, among them Duff Cooper (Ambassador just after the Second World War) and his wife, which some older men and women might prefer to forget, but protocol is perhaps now less lax; the scene more sober. Among ambassadors of consequence during the last 170 years were Granville, Cowley, Lyons, Lytton, Bertie, Derby, and Tyrrell.

In 1572, until shortly after the massacre of the Eve of St. Bartholomew, Sir Philip Sidney spent some months at a former embassy as guest of the Ambassador, Sir Francis Walsingham (who in 1583 was to be his father-in-law). John Dowland, the composer, attended the ambassador in 1580–84. In 1619–24 Lord Herbert of Cherbury (who had visited Paris in 1608, during the embassy of Sir George Carew) was Ambassador; his 'De Veritate' was published here in 1624. Thomas Carew, the poet, accompanied Herbert to Paris in 1619. The 2nd Earl of Stair, minister and later Ambassador here (1715–20), was responsible for the expulsion of James Edward, the 'Old Pretender' from Paris. In 1721–24 Sir Luke Schaub was Ambassador, and in 1730–40 James Waldegrave.

No. 41 is the Hôtel Pontalba, built by Visconti and restored by E. de Rothschild; No. 45 was the residence of Thiers at the end of his term as President, in 1873.

The **Palais de l'Elysée** (no admission), stands at the corner of the Av. de Marigny. This heavily guarded mansion was built by Molet as the Hôtel d'Evreux in 1718 but has been greatly altered and enlarged since.

It was occupied by Mme de Pompadour, Murat, Napoléon I (who signed his second abdication here in 1815), Wellington and Napoléon III, who lived here as Président from 1848 until he moved, as Emperor, to the Tuileries in 1852. It then reverted to its use as a residence for visiting heads of state (including Queen Victoria in 1855 and Elizabeth II in 1957). Since 1873 it has been the official residence of the President of the Republic. Here, in 1899, Felix Faure (President from 1895), died in the arms of Mme Steinheil.

To the right, the Rue des Saussaies (in which No. 11 was the Gestapo headquarters in Paris during 1940–44) leads to the Pl. des Saussaies where Francis Poulenc (1899–1963) was born at No. 2 and the Hôtel du Maréchal Suchet (No. 16 Rue de la Ville-l'Evêque), built by Boullée c 1750. Alexis de Tocqueville (1805–59), author of 'Democracy in America', was born at No. 12 in the same street.

Passing (right) the Ministère de l'Intérieur (Home Office), built in 1769—in which the poet Marquis de Saint-Lambert (1716–1803) died—flanking the Pl. Beauvau, continue along the Rue du Faubourg-St.-Honoré. Beyond the Av. Matignon is the Rue de Penthièvre (right), in which No. 26 may occupy the site of Benjamin Franklin's office. Meyerbeer (1791–1864) died in the Rue Jean-Mermoz, to the left.

Further on, to the right, stands **St.-Philippe-du-Roule**, built in 1769–84 by Chalgrin on the site of the parish church of Roule and later enlarged.

At 45 Rue La Boétie (to the right) is the Salle Gaveau, one of the more important concert-halls in Paris.

The Rue du Faubourg-St.-Honoré soon meets the wide Av. de Friedland, which leads west to the Arc de Triomphe (see Rte 25). Alfred de Vigny (1797–1863) died at 6 Rue d'Artois, parallel to and south of the Rue du Faubourg-St.-Honoré here.

At 208 Rue du Faubourg-St.-Honoré, beyond the Av. Friedland, are the buildings of the old Hôpital Beaujon (1784); opposite, at 11 Rue Berryer, is the former Hôtel Salomon de Rothschild, where Président Doumer was assassinated by a Russian emigré in 1932. At 12 Rue Balzac (then 22 Rue Fortuné, demolished), leading south west, is the site of the house where Honoré Balzac (1799–1850) died.

Just beyond the intersection with the Av. Hoche is the Salle Pleyel (1927), the largest concert-hall in Paris, radically revamped in 1981. Mme Arman de Caillavet held her salon, frequented by Anatole France, Maupassant and Proust, at 12 Av. Hoche.

In the Rue Daru, parallel to the north, is the neo-Byzantine Russian Orthodox church of St.-Alexandre-Nevsky (1859–61).

Gustave Flaubert (1821–80) lived from 1875 until his death at 240 Rue du Faubourg-St.-Honoré; from 1869 to 1875 he had lived at 4 Rue Murillo, just south of the Parc Monceau.

From behind St.-Philippe-du-Roule (see above) the Rue de Courcelles crosses the Blvd Haussmann. At 38 in the Rue de Courcelles (then 48) Dickens lodged in 1846; from 1901–05 Proust lived at No. 45, containing his cork-lined 'sound-proof' room, before moving to 102 Blvd Haussmann where he remained until 1919. Saint-Saëns lived at No. 83 bis. Henri Barbusse (1873–1935) died at No. 105.

The ***Musée Jacquemart-André** (Pl. 6; 4), at 158 Blvd Haussmann, contains collections of French art of the 18C (on the Ground Floor), and Renaissance and Italian art on the first floor. Although its contents are described, the museum is at present (1992) closed but should open in 1993.

The house was built c 1870 by Edouard André (died 1894), who in 1881 married the painter Nélie Jacquemart, who survived her husband until 1912, bequeathing their collection to the Institut de France.

From the entrance hall, turn left into **R2**, with four Gobelins tapestries and a Savonnerie carpet (1663), and displaying *Nattier*, Portrait of the Marquis d'Antin; *Prud'hon*, Cadet de Gassicourt; and busts of Caumartin by *Houdon*, the architect Gabriel by *Coysevox*, the artist Nicholas Vleugels by *Slodtz* and the Marquis de Marigny by *Lemoyne*. **R3**, with Beauvais tapestries of Russian games after *Le Prince*. **R4**. *Rubens*, Hercules strangling the lion and (from his studio) Portrait of a Flemish couple; *Van Dyck*, Count Henry of Peña; *Rembrandt*, Amalia von Solms, Pilgrims at Emmaus, Dr Arnold Tholinx; *Hals*, Portrait of a man; *Philippe de Champaigne*, Male portrait; *Ruysdael*, Landscape; Jan de Bray, Portrait; *School of Bruges*, Virgin and Child illuminating a book; and, in a case, the *Boucicaut Book of Hours, which belonged to Diane de Poitiers.

R5, *Canaletto*, St. Mark's Square and The Rialto, Venice; *Chardin*, Still life; and drawings by Lancret, Pater, Watteau and Boucher. **R6,** *Tocqué*, Male portrait; *Vigée-Lebrun*, Countess Skravonska; Greuze, Girl in confusion; *Perronneau*, Woman in a bonnet, Portrait of the artist Gillequin, and Chinard, A woman's head; in a case, book-bindings. Return to **R7**, with *Mantegna*, Madonna and Child between two saints, and Mocking of Christ; *Quintin Metsys*, Posthumous portrait of an old man; *Luini*, Virgin with SS. Margaret and Augustine; a bronze plaque of the Martyrdom of St. Sebastian, by *Donatello*; a horse in gilt bronze, *attrib. Leonardo da Vinci*; ivories; and an enamelled plaque by *Jean Pénicaud I*.

From the Winter Garden (**R8**) turn left into **R9**, dominated by Uccello, *St. George killing the dragon; *Di Conti*, Head of a man; *Pontormo*, An old woman; book-bindings. On the staircase, frescoes by *G.-B. Tiepolo*, including Henri III welcomed by Federigo Contarini to the Villa de Mira. **R10** is devoted to the arts of the Italian Renaissance. On its walls a number of 15C marble doorways have been re-erected, one with a sculpted frame attributed to Benedetto da Rovezzano. Among terracottas from the della Robbia workshops, a Madonna and Child by *Luca della Robbia*; the Legend of St. Emilian, a marble bas-relief in the form of a triptych (Venetian School); *Donatello*, two bronze winged torch-bearers, and bust of Lodovico Gonzaga, Marquis of Mantua; and *Ricciarelli*, posthumous Bust of Michelangelo (bronze).

R11, with Brussels tapestries, after *van Orley*; *Botticini*, The dead Christ with the Virgin, saints and others; Portrait of a young man (Venetian School); and marquetry choir-stalls, c 1505 (Northern Italian). **R12**, adjoining, retains 25 ceiling panels in grisaille attributed to *Girolamo Mocetto* (15C).

On the Ground Floor, **R13** contains a Bust of Richelieu by *Warin*, and a fine collection of Sèvres, Meissen, Vincennes and Vienna porcelain, and Chinese porcelain and stoneware.

The Rue de Téhéran, a few paces to the east, climbs north across the Av. de Messine to meet the Rue de Monceau, where at No. 8 Théodore Herzl, proselyte of Zionism, lived in 1891–95; No. 28 belonged to Prince Murat; and No. 32 was the birthplace of Oscar I of Sweden (1799–1859), son of Bernadotte and Désirée Clary.

The *MUSEE NISSIM DE CAMONDO**, 63 Rue de Monceau (Pl. 7; 3), an annexe to the Musée des Arts Décoratifs, is housed in a tastefully furnished mansion, containing a large number of Savonnerie and Aubusson carpets. It was bequeathed by Count Moise de Camondo (died 1935) as a memorial to his son Nissim, killed in 1917 (his daughter and grandchildren died at Auschwitz). A high proportion of the individual pieces of furniture are of outstanding quality. The museum has been restored recently, and the gardens, kitchens and orangerie will be shortly.

From the entrance hall, with a red marble fountain (1765) from the Château de St.-Prix, Montmorency, and a writing-desk by Riesener, stairs lead up past two lacquered Louis XV corner cupboards in the Chinese style, and a pair of Regency armchairs upholstered in Savonnerie tapestry.

FIRST FLOOR. Grand Bureau: white marble chimney-piece of c 1775, inlaid with bronze; a pair of low cabinets by *Leleu*; cylinder-top desk and secretaire by *Saunier*, the latter from the Château de Tanly; desk-armchair of 1778; a white marble-topped table by *Martin Carlin* from the Château de Bellevue; pair of low chairs by *Séné*; eight chairs by *Nicolas-Quinibert Foliot* covered in Aubusson tapestry (scenes from La Fontaine); Aubusson tapestries with six fables from La Fontaine *after Oudry*; a Beauvais screen with the fable of the Cock on the Dunghill; bronze bust of Mme Le Comte by *Guillaume Coustou*; *Vigée-Lebrun*, Bacchante.

Grand Salon: white and gold panelling of c 1775–80 from 11 Rue Royale; marquetry cabinet and tables by *Jean-Henri Riesener*; round table and *bureau de dame* (with Sèvres porcelain plaques) by *Carlin*; a pair of low tables by *Adam Weisweiler*; oval table by *David Roentgen* and one by *Lacroix* (Roger Vandercruse); suite of furniture (which belonged to Sir Richard Wallace), including two sofas and an armchair by *Georges Jacob*; four chairs by *Henri Jacob*; a six-leaved Savonnerie screen; 'L'Eté' (Hubert Robert's daughter), a marble bust by *Houdon*; *Vigée-Lebrun*, Mme Le Coulteux du Molay; 'La Pêcheuse', a Beauvais tapestry *after Boucher*; and among Savonnerie carpets, one ('L'Air') woven for the Grande Galerie of the Louvre (1678) and one made in 1660.

Salon Huet: seven panels and three *dessus de portes* of 'Scènes pastorales' painted by *Jean-Baptiste Huet*, dated 1776; cylinder-top desk by Oeben; pairs of small cabinets by *Garnier* and *Carlin*, the latter once belonging to Adm. de Penthièvre; sofa, two *bergères* and eight chairs by Séné; table with chased bronze given by Louis XVI to Vergennes; silver-gilt candlesticks by *François-Thomas Germain* (1762) embossed with the arms of Mme de Pompadour. Salle à Manger: console and a pair of ebony and chased bronze tables by *Weisweiler*; pair of small cabinets by *Leleu*; silver, including two tureens by *Auguste* and *Roettiers* (the latter's work was ordered by Catherine II of Russia for Orloff). Cabinet des Porcelaines (with a view of the Parc Monceau), with services of Sèvres, Chantilly and Meissen porcelain; silver-gilt service by *Dehanne* and *Cardeilhac*, etc. Galerie: sofa and chairs by *Pierre Gillier*; Aubusson tapestries *after Boucher* ('La Danse Chinoise', etc.).

Petit Bureau: furniture by *Topino*, *Riesener* and *Lacroix*, among others; snuffboxes, clocks, Chinese porcelain (Kien-Loung; 1736–95); terracotta medallions by *J.B. Nini*; marble bust of Mme le Comte by *Coustou*; four views of Venice by *Guardi*; portrait of Necker by *Duplessis*; *Oudry*, eight sketches for Gobelins tapestries of 'Les Chasses de Louis XV'; three paintings by *Hubert Robert*. On the stairs leading to the second floor, two Aubusson tapestries in the Chinese style, *after Boucher*.

SECOND FLOOR. Galerie: sofa and chairs by *Nogaret*; a series of engravings after *Chardin*; 18C Chinese porcelain. Turning right into the Salon Bleu: pair of tables attributed to Riesener; bookcase attributed to *Carlin*; red morocco casket embossed with the arms of Marie-Antoinette; views of Paris by *Bouhot* (1813), *Canella* (1830), *Demachy* (1774) and *Raguenet* (1754); a family portrait by *Gautier-Dagoty* (1740–86); watercolour of the Quai Malaquais by *Thomas Shotter Boys*; Chinese porcelain of the period 1662–1795.

Bibliothèque (oak-panelled): secretaire by *Leleu*; two bronze and Sèvres biscuit candelabras by *Blondeau* after Boucher; two paintings by *Hubert Robert*; Aubusson tapestry screen (1775). Chambre à Coucher: furniture by

Cramer, Topino and *Jacob Frères*; six-leaved screen by *Falconet* (1743). Among paintings: Danloux, Rosalie Duthé; *Lavreince*, The singing lesson; *Lancret*, Les Rémois; *Houdon*, Sabine Houdon (?), a plaster bust; *Drouais*, Alexandre de Beauharnais as a child; Savonnerie carpet (1760) for the chapel at Versailles. Deuxième Chambre: secretaire attributed to Riesener; screen by *Canabas*; 'Scènes de chasse' by *de Dreux, Shayer, Fontaine* and *Horace Vernet*.

At 7 Av. Vélasquez, a parallel street to the north, is the **MUSEE CER-NUSCHI**, bequeathed to the city in 1895 by the collector (of Maltese origin). In many ways it complements the more comprehensive collections of Oriental art in the Musée Guimet and Musée d'Ennery (see Rtes 27 and 28 respectively).

Of particular interest are the funerary figurines of the T'ang and Wei dynasties, neolithic terracottas, and bronze vases, etc., of the Chang dynasty (14–11C BC), while outstanding are the paintings on silk of horses and grooms of the T'ang period (8C). Note also the collections of clasps, mirrors, jade amulets, etc. On the FIRST FLOOR is an extensive collection of bronze objects from Louristan and Iran (8–7C BC), a bronze basin of 5–3C BC and porcelain of various periods.

The neighbouring *PARC MONCEAU* (Pl. 6; 4; 88 hectares) derives its name from a vanished village, and is a remnant of a private park laid out by Carmontel in 1778 for Philippe-Egalité d'Orléans, Duc de Chartres, and father of Louis-Philippe. Its gardener was Thomas Blaikie (1750–1838), a Scotsman. It was then known as the 'Folie de Chartres', and certain 'picturesque' details remain.

Near the north-east corner is the Naumachie, with a Corinthian colonnade which may have come from either the Château du Raincy or from the projected mausoleum at St.-Denis for Henri II and Catherine de Médicis. To the east of the lake is a Renaissance arcade from the old Hôtel de Ville; to the west is the Rotonde de Chartres, a toll-house (by Ledoux) of the 18C city wall erected by the Farmers-General. Used as a keeper's lodge, the building was disfigured in 1861 by fluting its columns and adding a dome.

There are a number of imposing mansions in the streets to the north, including those in the Rue de Prony, leading north west. Off this street the Rue Fortuny (where at No. 2 Edmond Rostand lived in 1891–97, and wrote 'Cyrano de Bergerac') turns north east to the re-named Pl. du Gén. Catroux (formerly Pl. Malesherbes but still métro Malesherbes). Slightly to the north is the Salle Cortot, a concert-hall (78 Rue Cardinet).

Further north east, in the **Batignolles**, some quaint areas still survive the pressures of modernisation, and deserve exploration. The Quartier gave its name to a school of Impressionist painters under the leadership of Manet (see the painting by Fantin-Latour in the Musée d'Orsay).

In the **Cimetière des Batignolles** (best approached by the Av. de Clichy, and some distance north west of the Cimetière de Montmartre) lie Verlaine, André Breton and Léon Bakst.

The Av. de Villiers leads north west from the Pl. du Gén. Catroux, in which No. 43 is the Musée Henner, devoted to the work of Jean-Jacques Henner (1829–1905). Some distance further west, near the Porte de Champerret, stands Ste.-Odile (1938–46), with a flattened dome and rocket-like tower. Nearby, at 41 Blvd Berthier, John Singer Sargent had his studio c 1883–86, which was taken over by Giovanni Boldini.

27 Chaillot, Passy and Auteuil
Musée d'Art Moderne; Musée Guimet; Palais de Chaillot; Musée de la Marine; Musée Marmottan

MÉTROS: Concorde, Alma-Marceau, Iéna, Trocadéro, Passy, Muette, Porte-d'Auteuil.

From the Pl. de la Concorde (see Rte 13), the Cours la Reine with its extension, the Cours Albert-1er (No. 40 has glass doors by Lalique, whose home it was), leads west to the Pl. de l'Alma. It was laid out in 1616, and followed the old road to the villages of Chaillot, St.-Cloud and Versailles, and the Roman canal which brought water from Chaillot.

The parallel Port de la Conférence, flanking the Seine, takes its name from the Porte de la Conférence (demolished in 1730), through which the Spanish ambassadors entered Paris in 1660 to discuss with Mazarin the projected marriage between Louis XIV and María Teresa.

The Pont des Invalides (west of the Pont Alexandre-III) dates from 1827–29, but was rebuilt in 1879–80 and enlarged in 1956. The Pont de l'Alma (1970) retains the figure of a zouave (a member of the French light infantry corps originally formed of Algerians) from its predecessor, which was long used as a gauge in estimating the height of the Seine in flood.

Immediately east of the south end of the Pont de l'Alma is the public entrance to the **Sewers** (*Egouts*) of Paris, a formidable system laid out by the engineer Eugène Belgrand (1810–78). Part of it may be visited between 11.00–17.00 except Thursday and Friday: closed when raining. The tour is not so hazardous as that experienced by Jean Valjean in 'Les Misérables'. The total combined length of the sewers of Paris which may be entered has been estimated at 2100km.

Several handsome streets radiate north from the Pl. de l'Alma (Pl. 11; 6), many of the mansions being the showrooms of *haut-couturiers*, who have replaced the once ubiquitous Parisian *midinette* in the folklore of fashion. At 13 Av. Montaigne, leading north east, is the Théâtre des Champs-Elysées, by A. and G. Perret (1911–13), with bas-reliefs by Bourdelle. On the west side of the Av. George-V, leading northwards, is the American church of the Holy Trinity (1885–88), built in a Gothic style by G.E. Street.

The Av. de New York, with its continuations, follows the north bank of the Seine for some distance before bearing west to the Porte de St.-Cloud. Parallel to the long narrow Allée des Cygnes ('Isle of Swans') lying mid-stream south of the Pont de Bir-Hakeim, is the cylindrical **Maison de la Radio** (or de l'ORTF), designed in 1960 by Henri Bernard, impressive in size even if its tower is out of proportion to the rest of the building, the only one of note in the area (Pl. 10; 8). A museum devoted to radio as a means of communication has been installed at 116 Av. du Président-Kennedy, 16e, but it may only be seen on a guided tour starting hourly from 10.30–16.30 (but not 12.30) on weekdays.

On the southern extremity of the Allée des Cygnes, crossed here by the Pont de Grenelle (rebuilt 1875), and facing downstream, is a reduced size bronze replica of Bartholdi's statue of Liberty, presented to France by the United States, where the original stands at the entrance to New York harbour.

The Av. du Président-Wilson leads west from the Pl. de l'Alma, from which the Av. Marceau immediately ascends right towards the Arc de Triomphe, passing (left) St.-Pierre-de-Chaillot (1937), built in a bogus Byzantine/Romanesque style by Emile Bois. It replaced the parish church of 1750, in which Proust's funeral service took place in November 1922.

To the right in the Av. du Président-Wilson, behind gardens, is the Hôtel Galliéra (1888), built to house the collections of the Duchesse de Galliéra (died 1889), who subsequently changed her mind and bequeathed the majority of them to the city of Genoa. At present it houses the **Musée de la Mode et du Costume** (of the Ville de Paris), with its entrance at 10 Av. Pierre-1er de Serbie. Parts of the extensive collections, enriched by numerous donations, are usually shown in rotation in a series of temporary exhibitions covering specific themes or periods.

Normally there is a display of dresses, designs, costume and fashion-plates, photographs and an astonishing variety of accessories: belts, buttons and ribbons; scarves, feathers and gloves; handbags and hats; fans and parasols; stays and stockings; and numerous other forms of clothing, from costume jewellery to shoes, as well as dolls, wigs, etc.

On the south side of the avenue stands the **Palais d'Art Moderne**, constructed for the Exhibition of 1937 (by Aubert, Dondel, Viard and Dastugue) on the site of a military bakery, itself replacing the old Savonnerie (cf. Gobelins). The wall of the terrace is decorated with bas-reliefs by Janniot; and here, with other statues by Bourdelle, is 'La France', in memory of French patriots who fell in the Second World War.

The building consists of two wings, that to the east housing the **Musée d'Art Moderne de la Ville de Paris**, often showing temporary exhibitions. The permanent collection is arranged on two floors but contains few canvases of great interest.

Near the entrance are two series of engravings: Picasso's Vollard Suite and Derain's suite 'Le Satyricon'. Notable is Modigliani, Woman with a fan; also on view are representative works by Jules Pascin, André Lhote, Chaim Soutine, Othon Friez, Marie Blanchard, Marcel Gromaire and Jean Lurçat. Among other works on the floor below are: Francis Gruber, Nude in a red waistcoat (sic); Buffet, three Nudes and Self-portrait; Foujita, The bistro; and Pierre Soulages, Composition.

The west wing, now styled the **Palais de Tokyo**, may house the **Centre National de la Photographie**. This will comprise a Cinemathèque, already functioning; a Bibliothèque and Médiathèque; the Mission Photographique du Patrimoine; the Service Photographique de la Délégation aux Arts Plastiques; and the Fondation Européenne des Métiers de l'Image et du Son (FEMIS).

To the west is the Pl. d'Iéna (Pl. 11; 5), from which seven streets diverge. 2 Av. d'Iéna is the residence of the US ambassador. To the north of the Place stands the Musée Guimet (see below).

At No. 24 Rue Boissière, to the north west, the poet Henri de Régnier (1864–1936) died; at 44 Rue Hamelin, leading north, Marcel Proust (1871–1922) died.

40 Rue Paul-Valéry (the continuation north west of the Rue Hamelin and formerly known as the Rue Villejuste), was the home of Paul Valéry (1871–1945) from 1902. From 1883 it had been the studio of his aunt by marriage, Berthe Morisot (died 1895), and a favourite literary and artistic rendezvous.

The *****MUSEE GUIMET**, at 6 Pl. d'Iéna, with its annex at 19 Av. d'Iéna, was founded at Lyon in 1879 by Emile Guimet (1836–1918), presented by him to the State, transferred to Paris and inaugurated in 1889. In 1945 it officially became the Département des Arts Asiatiques des Musées Nationaux,

Guimet's original collection having been considerably augmented, and now includes those of the Asiatic department of the Louvre, illustrating the arts of India and the Far East. The building also houses a library and photographic section.

GROUND FLOOR. From the vestibule you pass into **R'N'**, which together with **RR'L'**, **'O'**, and **'H'**, is devoted to Khmer sculpture from *Cambodia*, including a statue of Hari-Hara (pre-Angkorian style; late 6C), uniting in one person the two gods Siva and Vishnu; lintel of 7–12C; sculpture of 9–10C; Vishnu in the Kulen style; Brahma in the Koh Ker style; pediment from the temple of Banteai Srei (967); seated Buddha in the style of Angkor Wat (early 12C); carvings of a lion, an elephant and of the magic serpent, Naga (12C). Also sculptures in the Bayon style (12–13C); each meditative statue wears the enigmatic 'Angkorian smile'; portrait of King Jayavarman VII; frieze of dancing *apsaras*.

R'M': *Champa Art of Assam* (central Vietnam). Note the head of Buddha (9C) and a dancer with two young elephants (10C).

R'K' (left): *Java*: heads of Buddha (8–9C); lintel decorated in the Prambanan style (9C); bronzes (7–9C), and statuettes of Avalokitesvara and Kubera, gods of riches—note the seven treasure-pots at his feet; leather marionettes for a shadow-theatre; a painted fabric calendar from Bali.

(Centre): *Siam* (Thailand): stuccoes from P'ra Pathom (c 8C); Buddhas of the Schools of Sukhodava and U-Thong (14–15C); head of Buddha (16C); on the walls, painted and worked leather hangings. *Laos*: Buddha with a begging-bowl. *Burma*: lacquered wooden Buddha and illuminated MSS.

Tibetan Art (continued in **R'J'**): statue in gilded bronze of Dakini; and statuettes decorated with coloured stones; religious objects, jewellery, silverwork, etc. On the walls, paintings illustrating the life of Buddha, gods and saints. **R'I'**: *Nepal*: Buddhist paintings and statues of wood and gilded bronze.

FIRST FLOOR. **RR'K'** and **'J'**: *Indian Art*. Funerary furniture and stone sculpture from near Pondicherry; clay sarcophagus, pottery and jewellery. Mathurâ and Amarâvatî sculpture (2–4C); serpent-king (sandstone); marble bas-reliefs; Buddhas. Among objects of the 'classical' period (4–8C), a Buddha in the Gupta style; steles of Pâla Art (8–12C); South Indian stone sculpture; bronzes of Siva; *gouaches and watercolours of the Mogul, Rajput and Pahâri period (16–18C), including one of Louis XIV when young.

RR'M' and **'P'**: *Pakistan* and *Afghanistan*, including examples of Græco-Buddhist Gandara sculpture (1–5C); decorative bas-relief (schist); figurines from the Buddhist monastery of Hadda, including a Genie carrying a floral offering and a demon in a fur; fragments of frescoes from the monastery of Kakrak (c 5C); the Treasure of Begram (1–2C): Græco-Roman and Syrian objects, Indian ivories and Chinese lacquer-work discovered together by the French archaeological mission to Afghanistan in 1937 and 1939–40.

RR'N', **'F'**, **'G'** and **'H'**: the *Arts of China*. Carved bone objects of the Chang Dynasty (16–11C BC) and important collections of archaic bronze implements, ritual vases and arms, etc., from Ngan-Tang, capital city of the dynasty; ritual vase in the shape of an elephant; a 'p'an' bowl of the Chou Dynasty (11–5C BC); the Treasure of Li-Yu, a remarkable find from the 'Fighting Kingdoms' Dynasty (5–3C BC), notably a jade, turquoise and gold-ornamented sword. Jades: the earlier ones in the form of symbols (Pi, the sky; Tsong, the earth; Kwei, the mountain, etc.) and bronzes. Tombstone (Han Dynasty; 206 BC–AD 220); Buddha from Yun-Kang (5C); heads of Bodhisattva and Kasyapa, from Long-men (early 6C); Ananda and Kasyapa, disciples of Buddha (Suei Dynasty; 561–618), marble with traces of polychrome; Dvarapàla, guardian of the temple and funerary statuettes of the T'ang Dynasty (618–906); gilded bronzes of the Wei, Suei and T'ang dynasties (5–10C), including a small stele representing Sakyamuni and Pradhutaratna, dated 518; lacquer-work; polychrome bowls of the Han Dynasty and Sung Dynasty (960–1279); black lacquer cabinet decorated in gold (17C).

SECOND FLOOR. **R'K'**: the *Arts of Japan*. Jômon and Yayoi pottery (2000–1000 BC and 1C BC–3C AD respectively); figurines (Haniwa) of the era of the Great Tombs (5–6C); wooden Buddhas (8–9C); carved masks of the Nara Dynasty (8C); portraits of bonzes (14–15C); pottery for the Tea Ceremony ('Cha-no-yu'); Imari Kakiemon and Satsuma porcelain; sword-furniture (kozukas); screens, one illustrating the arrival of the Portuguese in Japan (16C). Also, from *Korea*: Gilded bronze crown and silverware from the kingdom of Silla (5–6C); and ceramics.

RR'D', 'L', 'P' and **'I'** contain an important collection of Chinese porcelain, formed principally from the Calmann Collection—'three colour' ware (T'ang Dynasty), celadon, black and white wares (Sung Dynasty)—and from the Grandidier Collection: Ming (1368–1643) and Ch'ing (1644–1912) dynasties.

R'M': *Central Asia*. Buddhist paintings from Touen-houang; votive banners, one representing Kasyapa in old age, dated 729.

Among recent acquisitions are the Torso of a finely sculpted sandstone Buddha (India; mid 5C), and of a Female divinity (Khmer sculpture, from Cambodia; early 9C).

Since April 1991, two floors in the former Hôtel Heidelbach, at 19 Av. d'Iéna, have displayed additional collections under the title **Galeries du Panthéon Bouddhique**, largely concentrating on sculptures related to the Buddhist cult in Japan (some 250 idols, etc.) and—to a lesser extent—in China. Its garden has been laid out in the Japanese style.

To the south west is the Palais du Conseil Economique et Social, by Auguste Perret (1937–38), originally designed for a Musée des Travaux Publics. The north wing was added in 1960–62 to house the Western European Union. 34 in the Av. du Président-Wilson was the home of Laure Haymann, the model for Proust's Odette de Crécy.

The Av. du Président-Wilson ends at the Pl. du Trocadéro (Pl. 10; 6), semi-circular in shape, from which six thoroughfares fan out. In the centre stands an equestrian statue of Maréchal Foch (1851–1929). It is flanked to the south east by the Palais de Chaillot (see below). The Place is situated on the 'Colline du Trocadéro' (named after a fort near Cádiz occupied by the French in 1823).

Catherine de Médicis built a country house on this hill; later embellished by Anne of Austria, it was sold to Maréchal de Bassompierre, and in 1651 Henrietta Maria bought it from his heirs and established the Convent of the Visitation here, frequented by Mary of Modena. This was destroyed during the Revolution, and Napoléon planned to use the site for a palace for his son which would be more magnificent than the Kremlin, but the disasters of 1812 intervened.

To the west, steps ascend to the small **Cimetière de Passy,** where Debussy, Gabriel Fauré, Manet, Berthe Morisot, Marie Bashkirtseff and Las Cases are buried.

The **PALAIS DE CHAILLOT**, on the south-east side of the Pl. du Trocadéro, was erected for the Paris Exhibition of 1937 and replaced the earlier Palais du Trocadéro, designed for the 1878 Exhibition. The building (by Carlu, Boileau and Azéma) encases in its two curved wings the two wings of the original structure. Between them is a square, its terrace affording a striking perspective towards the Eiffel Tower and across the Champ-de-Mars to the Ecole Militaire and the Unesco buildings beyond: see Rte 12.

Below the square, adorned with gilded bronze statues, is an aquarium and the Théâtre de Chaillot, seating over 2000, the home of the Théâtre National Populaire (decorated by Bonnard, Dufy and Vuillard, among others). The third General Assembly of the United Nations took place here in 1948.

To the right and left of the Colline du Trocadéro, gardens flank fountains which include a battery of 20 jets shooting almost horizontally towards the Seine, crossed here by the Pont d'Iéna (1806–13, since widened twice). The next bridge downstream is the Pont de Bir-Hakeim (formerly the Pont de Passy, 1903–06), a double bridge; the upper part being used by the métro. It is named after a French exploit in North Africa in 1942.

The Palais de Chaillot at present houses four museums: in the east wing, the Musée des Monuments Français and Musée du Cinéma; in the west wing, the Musée de la Marine and the Musée de l'Homme.

The **Musée des Monuments Français** was founded by Viollet-le-Duc in 1879 as the Musée de Sculpture Comparée, and although it only contains replicas of masterpieces of French sculpture, mural paintings and stained-glass, they are faithfully copied and are exhibited with ingenuity and taste.

It provides both an interesting introduction to the range of early French sculpture and architecture, displaying examples from all over France, and valuable reproductions of early wall-paintings, many of which have since deteriorated. The sculpture is arranged in a series of rooms to the left of the entrance. The wall-paintings occupy rooms to the right and on the three floors above, among which are:

FIRST FLOOR: mural and ceiling paintings from St.-Gilles (Montoire); Berzé-la-Ville (near Cluny); St.-Martin at Vicq (near Nohant); St. Michael from Le Puy cathedral; St.-Aignan-sur-Cher; St.-Chef (Isère); Rocamadour; and St.-Savin-sur-Gartemp.

SECOND FLOOR: Asnières-sur-Vè St.-Julien at Le Petit-Quevilly (near Rouen), St.-Jean at Vic-le-Comte (Puy-de-Dôme); dome of Cahors cathedral; Frétigny (Eure-et-Loire); Etigny (Yonne); La Clayette (Saône-et-Loire); Chapelle du Chalard, St.-Geniès (Dordogne); the Tour Ferrande, Pernes (Vaucluse); Chartreuse at Villeneuve-lès-Avignon; crypt of Auxerre cathedral; walls of the château of Ravel (Puy-de-Dôme); Les Brignes (Alpes-Maritime); and Transfiguration from Le Puy cathedral.

THIRD FLOOR: Kernascléden (Morbihan); Abondance (Haute-Savoie); La Chaise-Dieu; Château de Dissay (Vienne); Château du Pimpéan (near Angers); Ennezat (near Riom); Château de Rochechouart (Haute-Vienne); and Albi cathedral.

The devotee of the art of the film will find much of interest in the **Musée du Cinéma** located in the basement of this wing, established by Henri Langlois (1914–77). Over 3000 items are displayed in 60 sections, vividly presenting diverse aspects of the history of the film during its earlier decades.

On the GROUND FLOOR of the west wing of the Palais de Chaillot is the *MUSEE DE LA MARINE, with a remarkable collection of material illustrating French naval history, including an outstanding series of ship models and paintings of maritime subjects, among which are Vernet's Ports of France.

The main gallery, right of the entrance, is dominated by the richly carved poop of the 'Reale' (1690–1715), some of the sculpture of which is attributed to Puget. Note the paintings (Nos 61 and 62) of the Embarkation of Henry VIII for the Field of Cloth of Gold by Bouterwerke (a copy of the original by Vincent Volpi) and a View of Amsterdam by Bakhuysen (1664). Four anon. views of Malta (Nos 138–9) and two views of Port Mahon (Nos 147 and 416, the latter by Joseph Chiesa) are also of interest, and a number of marine paintings by Jean-François Hue (1751–1823).

In the centre of the gallery are displayed 13 (of the 15 completed of the original 24 commissioned) views of the *Ports of France painted between 1754–65 by Claude-Joseph Vernet (1714–89), depicting Dieppe, Antibes, tunny-fishing near Bandol, Rochefort, La Rochelle, Cette, two views of Toulon, two of Bordeaux, two of Bayonne, and Marseille.

You pass the Emperor's Barge (1811) before entering a section devoted to early steamships. **R15**, at the far end of the wing, contains recent models and paintings, and a section concentrating on the Fleet Air Arm, etc.

Along a parallel gallery are further sections displaying marine instruments, diving and underwater exploration equipment, a model of a nuclear submarine, models of the careening of a ship, and of the raising and transportation of the obelisk of Luxor (now embellishing the Pl. de la Concorde: see Rte 13), of ship construction, etc. Among individual items are a sectional view of the transatlantic liner 'Normandie' and Dr Bombard's raft.

The **Musée de l'Homme**, housed on the first and second floors of this wing, was formed by the amalgamation of the Galerie d'Anthropologie and the Musée d'Ethnographie du Trocadéro. A comprehensive library, photographic library, cinema and various technical services are also housed here.

In comparison with some more recently installed museums, its quality of display leaves something to be desired, but the items exhibited are more or less self-explanatory.The sections devoted to Anthropology, Paleoanthropology and Prehistory, Africa, the Near East and Europe are found on the FIRST FLOOR. On the SECOND are rooms displaying exhibits from the Arctic, Asia, Indonesia and Oceania, and America.

The Rue Franklin (No. 8 was Clemenceau's residence from 1883 to 1929) leads south west from the Pl. du Trocadéro, and is continued by the Rue Raynouard. From their junction, the Pl. de Costa Rica, the Rue de Passy, high street of the old village of **Passy**, runs west to the Jardin du Ranelagh (see below).

Steps descend to the left in the Rue Raynouard to the Sq. Charles Dickens, in which the vaulted medieval cellars of a 'Musée du Vin' may be visited.

No. 47 Rue Raynouard is the **Maison de Honoré de Balzac** (admission daily except Monday 10.00–17.40), the author's home in 1841–47, where he wrote 'La Cousine Bette' and 'La Cousin Pons' among other novels.

It is worthwhile entering the unexpected ivy-covered **Rue Berton**, behind the house, one of the more charming and once characteristic lanes remaining in Passy.

Earlier inhabitants of the Rue Raynouard include the architect Robert de Cotte, the Abbé Prévost and Benjamin Franklin (in 1777–85), who erected on his house (the Hôtel de Valentinois, which stood on the corner of the Rue Singer) the first lightning-conductor seen in France.

In the Rue d'Ankara, between Rue Berton and the Seine, No. 17, now the Turkish Embassy, was once the residence of the Princesse de Lamballe and later the private clinic of Dr Emile Blanche, where Maupassant died in 1893; Gérard de Nerval and Gounod had also sought treatment here.

Not far south west of Balzac's House (before reaching the Maison de l'ORTF), the Rue des Vignes leads north west, where at No. 32 Gabriel Fauré (1845–1924) died; James Joyce lived at No. 34 during the latter period of his stay in Paris.

Other distinguished residents of Passy include Frances ('Fanny') Burney (Mme d'Arblay; 1752–1840), in 1802–12; Béranger, in 1833–35; and Maeterlinck, in 1897–1910. Others were Rossini, from 1857–68; Gossec, from 1822–29; and Joseph Proudhon, from 1861–65, who all died here.

The Rue des Vignes also leads to the Chaussée de la Muette and the east end of the **Jardin du Ranelagh** (Pl. 10;7), part of the ancient royal park of La Muette. It was designed to emulate its fashionable namesake in London, and just before the Revolution was a favourite resort. The first balloon ascent in France was made nearby in 1783 by Pilâtre de Rozier and the Marquis d'Arlandes.

The royal Château de la Muette, originally a hunting-lodge, improved by the Regent Orléans and restored by Louis XV for Mme de Pompadour, has completely disappeared. It is also associated with Marie-Antoinette, who was welcomed here by Louis XVI on her arrival in Paris from Vienna in 1770. It also accommodated an establishment for spinning cotton under the direction of a manufacturer from Lancashire and under royal patronage. The château was later occupied by Philippe-Egalité, who stood on the terrace watching the mob bringing Louis XVI from Versailles to the Tuileries in 1789. From 1820 to 1920 it belonged to the Erard family, piano manufacturers.

The present mansion, just north of the Jardin du Ranelagh and east of the Porte de la Muette, was built by Baron Henri de Rothschild, and is now the property of the Organisation for Economic Cooperation and Development.

At 2 Rue Louis-Boilly, leading off the west side of the gardens, is the *MUSEE MARMOTTAN (Pl. 10; 5/7). It contains, apart from the Monet donation (see below), a number of interesting paintings, among which are works attributed to Van der Weyden and Schongauer. Some notable Empire furniture and bronzes are also to be seen. In October 1985 several paintings were stolen from the collection, including Berthe Morisot, Young girl at a ball; and Monet's Portrait of Renoir, of Poly, the fisherman from Belle Isle, and Impression—Soleil levant, which gave the name to the Impressionists. All these paintings were found in December 1990 in Corsica and are now rehung.

Also displayed are portraits of Talma by *Riesener* and of A young woman by *Lawrence*; of Désirée Clary by *Gérard*; and of the Duchesse de Feltre and her children by *François-Xavier Fabre*; also works by L. de France (1735–1805), Jean-Baptiste Mallet (1759–1835), Carmontel (1717–1806), A.-I. Melling (1763–1831), Louis Boilly (1761–1845) and Philibert-Louis Debucourt (1755–1832), together with drawings by *Fragonard* and *Hubert Robert*. There are also some pleasant views of Schönbrunn, etc. by Jean-Joseph-Xavier Bidault (1758–1846) and Carle Vernet, and of Rowing at Fontainebleau by Bidault and Boilly.

In a gallery to the left of the entrance are works by *Claude Monet* (1840–1926) and his friends, including Carolus Duran, Portrait of Monet; of Monet and his wife by *Renoir* and, by Monet himself, Argenteuil in the snow, Vertheuil in the mist, A train in the snow, and The beach at Trouville, together with sketches for his later canvases and several caricatures; also displayed are characteristic works by Caillebotte, Guillaumin, Jongkind,

Berthe Morisot, Au Bal (1875)

Berthe Morisot, Pissarro, Renoir and Sisley. The collection also contains drawings by Constantin Guys, Boudin and Signac, among others.

In November 1987 a new room was inaugurated to accommodate the Duhem Donation of some 60 oil-paintings, watercolours and drawings. Notable are *Gauguin*, Bowl of Tahitian flowers; *Corot*, The lake at Ville-d'Avray seen through trees; *Le Sidaner*, Daybreak at Quimperlé; *Monet*, Walking near Argenteuil; *Sisley*, The Canal du Loing in Spring; *Renoir*, Girl in a white hat (pastel); several works by Guillaumin and Lebourg and examples of paintings by Henri Duhem (1860–1941) himself.

The museum also houses the notable **Wildenstein Collection** of medieval illuminated miniatures, some 230 in all, assembled in one room as they were when in private hands. They deserve a better display and some examples are also in need of restoration. Among those of the Italian schools are several by *Lucchino Giovanni Belbello da Pavia* (fl. 1430–62); and among the French, some by Jean Colombe (fl. 1467–1529), Jean Perreal (1455–1530), Jean Bourdichon (c 1475–1521) and Jean Fouquet (c 1420–77/81), together with a depiction of a boar-hunt (late 15C); also some Flemish works of the period.

Stairs descend to an underground gallery built to house *Monet's* spectacular series of water-lilies, wisteria and other flower-pieces, largely painted at Giverny and the majority of them donated to the museum in 1971 by the artist's son Michel Monet; they form a complementary collection to those displayed in the Orangerie (see Rte 13).

In the residential district of **Auteuil**, to the south, Henri Bergson (1859–1941) lived and died at 47 Blvd de Beauséjour, skirting the Jardin du Ranelagh, and the Goncourt brothers (Edmond, 1822–96 and Jules, 1830–70) lived and died at 67 Blvd de Montmorency ('le Grenier', acquired by them in 1868), its continuation south, where they entertained Huysmans, Zola, Daudet and Maupassant among others. In parallel streets to the east of the latter lived Dr Emile Blanche and his son, the artist Jacques-Emile Blanche (19 Rue Docteur-Blanche). At 10 Sq. Dr-Blanche is the Le Corbusier Foundation, in a villa designed in 1923 by Le Corbusier (Charles-Edouard Jeanneret; 1887–1965) in 1923, which may be visited. André Gide lived in the nearby Av. des Sycomores. Paul Dukas (1865–1935) died at 82 Rue du Ranelagh, leading east from the Blvd de Beauséjour.

At the southern end of the Blvd de Montmorency is the Porte d'Auteuil, the south east entrance to the Bois de Boulogne (see Rte 28), and an approach to the A13 autoroute and Blvd Périphérique. From the Pl. de la Porte d'Auteuil the Blvd Exelmans swings south east to reach the Seine at the Pont du Garigliano. South west of the Porte d'Auteuil are the Municipal Nursery Gardens and the Roland-Garros tennis courts. South of the former is the restored Piscine Molitor from the Porte and several stadiums.

The Rue d'Auteuil leads east to N.-D. d'Auteuil, built in the Romanesque-Byzantine style (1877–88) on the site of the 12C parish church; in front is the tomb of the chancellor D'Aguesseau (died 1751) and his wife.

59 Rue d'Auteuil was the home of Maurice Quentin Delatour (1770–72), and then of Mme Helvétius until her death in 1800. Sir Benjamin Thompson, Count von Rumford (1753–1814), the scientist and administrator, lived here from 1808 until his death. Marcel Proust (1871–1922) was born at the home of his mother's uncle, which stood on the site of 96 Rue la Fontaine, a short distance to the north. François Mauriac lived at 38 Av. Théophile-Gautier for some 40 years until his death in 1970. Boileau and probably Molière (in 1667) were also residents of Auteuil.

In the small **Cimetière d'Auteuil**, in the Rue Claude-Lorrain (south of and parallel to the Blvd Exelmans), lie Rumford (see above; whose original tombstone was shattered by a shell from Mont Valérien in 1871), Hubert Robert, Mme Helvétius, Carpeaux, Gavarni and Gounod.

28 Bois de Boulogne, Neuilly and La Défense
Musée National des Arts et des Traditions Populaires; Bagatelle

METROS: Porte-d'Auteuil, Muette, Porte-Dauphine, Porte-Maillot, Les Sablons, Puteaux-Courbevoie, La Défense

NB. Visitors are strongly advised not to stray into the Bois at dusk or after dark.

The **Bois de Boulogne** (Pl. 10; 1–3), familiarly known as the 'Bois', lies immediately to the west of the 16th arrondissement of Paris (Chaillot, Passy and Auteuil: see Rte 27), and was originally bounded on the east by part of the peripheral fortifications of the city. Now the Blvd Périphérique tunnels below the east and south edges of the Bois, which is bounded on the north by Neuilly; the suburb of Boulogne-Billancourt to the south, and by the Seine to the west, on the far side of which rise the hills of Mont Valérien, St.-Cloud, Bellevue and Meudon.

Although the châteaux of La Muette, Madrid and Bagatelle, and the abbey of Longchamp were erected on its borders, the Bois was utterly neglected until the middle of the last century. Much timber was cut down for firewood during the Revolution, and a large part of the Allied army of occupation bivouacked here after Waterloo. It was the haunt of footpads and often the scene of suicides and duels.

In 1852 it was handed over by the State to the City, was transformed into an extensive park (863 hectares), and became a favourite promenade of the Parisians. The model was Hyde Park in London, which had so impressed Napoléon III. More trees were felled in 1870 to prevent them giving cover to the Prussians. The equestrian scenes which were such a favourite subject of Constantin Guys (1805–92) often had the Bois in the background. Carlyle condemned it as 'a dirty scrubby place', and in many respects it has little changed since.

There are four main entrances to the Bois from central Paris, namely the Porte Maillot (at its north-east corner); the Porte Dauphine (at the western end of the Av. Foch); the Porte de la Muette (at the south end of the Av. Victor-Hugo); and the Porte d'Auteuil (at its south-east corner). Between the last two is the subsidiary Porte de Passy.

The **'Bois'** is divided diagonally by the long Allée de Longchamp, leading south west from the Porte Maillot towards the Carrefour de Longchamp and a popular equestrian rendezvous. It is intersected by the Route de la Reine Marguerite (from the Carrefour de la Porte de Madrid to the Porte de Boulogne, on the south side of the Bois).

The usual approach to the Bois is by the imposingly wide, garden-flanked Av. Foch (opened in 1855 as the Av. de l'Impératrice), leading west from the Etoile to the Porte Dauphine. It was later known as the Av. du Bois de Boulogne, in which George Du Maurier (1834–96, author of 'Trilby'), who was born in Paris, attended a school in 1847–51. Note one of the original Art Nouveau entrances to the métro on the north side of the avenue here, designed by Hector Guimard.

Not far from the Etoile is a monument to Adolphe Alphand (1817–91), who laid out the Bois and many other parks in Paris in their present form.

At 59 Av. Foch, on the left, is the *Musée d'Ennery**, with an small important small collection of Oriental art formed by the dramatist Adolphe d'Ennery (Eugène Philippe; 1811–99); the building also houses a collection of Armenian art.

Anatole France (1844–1924) died at 5 Villa Said, leading north west off the avenue. 80 Av. Foch was the home of Claude Debussy (1862–1918), who died at 24 Square de l'Av. Foch (off the north-west end of the avenue). 82–6 Av. Foch were the German counter-espionage HQ in Paris during 1940–44.

South west of the park entrance is a huge building (1955–59) constructed for NATO but now housing university faculties. Paul Claudel (1868–1955) died at 11 Blvd Lannes, skirting the Bois to the south; Supervielle lived from 1918 to 1943 at No. 47.

To approach the Porte de la Muette directly from the Etoile, follow the Av. Victor-Hugo, in which Hugo (1802–85) died in a house on the site of No. 124. Lamartine (1790–1869) died near the square named after him off the southern section of this avenue (house demolished), beyond the Pl. Victor-Hugo. It was at the Porte de la Muette that Général Galliffet set up his HQ in 1871 and supervised the indiscriminate shooting of hundreds of Communards en route to Versailles.

Of particular interest in the northern section of the Bois is the *MUSEE NATIONAL DES ARTS ET DES TRADITIONS POPULAIRES (Pl. 10; 1), easily reached from either Porte Maillot or Porte Dauphine, or, more directly, from the métro: Les Sablons. The museum is housed in a not unattractive functional building by Jean Dubuisson, completed in 1966, standing just west of the Carrefour des Sablons.

Its contents are exceptionally well displayed on two floors. Several rooms are devoted to temporary exhibitions, but it is likely that these will take over entirely and there may not be any permanent display in future. However, the sections listed below will give some idea of the range of the collections.

The GROUND FLOOR contains the 'Galerie Culturelle', laid out in a series of convoluted sections covering aspects of rural life in the pre-industrial period, in which some 5000 objects are seen in context or 'ecological groups', among which are those concerned with sheep and shepherding; baking; the smithy; stone-splitting; forms of rural transport; wood-turning and furniture carving; viticulture; the fabrication of objects of horn and wood; the embellishment of metalwork; ceramic production; together with sections devoted to peasant costumes, coiffes, etc., with a charming painting of an Arlesienne (1858).

In the BASEMENT is the 'Galerie d'Etude', where similar objects are more systematically displayed in a series of nine parallel passages or 'rues'. By the entrance is a bell-forge.

Rue 1. Farming equipment: yokes, harnesses, traps, etc. 2. Harrows, hoes, rakes, flails, scythes, sickles and viticultural implements. 3. Cowbells, branding-irons, protective collars, crooks; bee-keeping equipment; sheepshearing and dairy implements. 4. Spinning, carding, rope-making and basket-weaving; brick and tile manufacture; surveying equipment and carpenters' tools. 5. Lamps and candlesticks; irons, jacks and bedwarmers; kitchen utensils—jars, waffle-irons, butter-moulds, etc.; furniture and lacework. 6. Ritual costumes; rural medicine; cradles and early toys; regional and traditional costumes: capes and sabots, etc. 7. Games and pastimes: archery, tennis, skittles and *boules*, marbles and croquet. Musical instruments: rattles, hurdy-gurdies, flutes and whistles; bagpipes, etc. 8. Fairs and circuses: puppets, marionettes and silhouettes. 9. Graphic arts: metal and wood blocks; engraving and lithographic equipment: stencils, etc.

There are audio-visual cabins adjacent. The library contains upward of 60,000 volumes and 2000 periodicals; the archives over 80,000 old post-cards, 40,000 designs, almost 200,000 photographs, among numerous other specialised collections of ethnographical studies, etc.; the record collection, some 50,000 recordings; an additional 70,000 objects may be seen on request, together with c 90,000 drawings, paintings, prints and other illustrative material. The building also contains an auditorium and labora-tories, the whole comprising an important centre for the study of French ethnography.

North west of the museum is the Jardin d'Acclimatation, with a small-scale zoo (its former inmates eaten in 1870) and children's playground. To the west, near the Porte de Madrid, stood the Château de Madrid, built in 1528 by François I (who is said to have named it in memory of his captivity in Spain, after the Battle of Pavia). It was gradually demolished between 1793 and 1847.

Further west, skirted by the Route de Sèvres à Neuilly, are the walls of the **Parc de Bagatelle** (24 hectares), famous for its rose-garden, at its best in mid-June. The attractive *Bagatelle Gardens are open to the public until dusk (fee); the restaurant is expensive. The elegant little **Château de Bagatelle**, replacing an earlier residence, was built for a wager within 64 days by Bélanger for the Comte d'Artois, later Charles X, in 1779. The dome was added in 1852. It was acquired by the Ville de Paris in 1904.

Henry Swinburne observed that during the Revolution it had been turned into a tavern. It was later the residence of Sir Richard Wallace (1818–90), supposed natural son of the Marchioness of Hertford. Wallace had a town house at 25 Rue Taitbout where he accumulated art treasures (now in the Wallace Collection, London) in addition to those he had inherited from his half-brother the eccentric Richard Seymour Conway, 4th Marquis of Hertford (1800–70), who had bought the mansion in 1835 and died here. Hertford's brother, Lord Henry Seymour (1805–59), was founder of the exclusive 'Jockey Club'. Wallace was also a great benefactor of Paris, which he provided with drinking fountains, and helped to equip ambulances during the 1870–71 war. He founded the Hertford British Hospital in Paris (opened 1879) and built the Anglican church of St. George (1887–88; Rue Auguste-Vacquerie, off the Av. d'Iéna).

To the west are various sports grounds (including polo and *tiercé*); to the south west is the Hippodrome de Longchamp, opened in 1857. Here on 29 June 1871 the French 'army', responsible for the massacre of thousands of Communards during previous weeks, was reviewed by MacMahon and Thiers. On the north side is a windmill (restored), almost the only relic of the Abbey of Longchamp, founded in 1256 by St. Isabel of France, sister of Louis IX.

From the Carrefour de Longchamp (just east of the windmill), a road leads due east past the Grande Cascade (an artificial waterfall) to skirt the enclosure of the Pré-Catelan (named after the troubadour Arnaud Catelan, murdered here c 1300), with a huge copper beech and a 'Jardin Shakespeare', said to contain specimens of all the plants and trees men-tioned in his plays.

Further east are buildings of the Racing Club de France, flanking the west bank of the Lac Inférieur, with two linked islands. Boats may be hired on the east bank. Further south is the Lac Supérieur, beyond the Carrefour des Cascades; in the south-east corner of the Bois, is the Hippodrome d'Auteuil (steeplechasing).

N.-D.-des-Menus, in the Av. J.-B. Clément, leading south west from the Porte de Boulogne, although frequently restored (by Viollet-le-Duc among others), retains its 14C nave. Beyond (right) are the Jardins Albert Kahn (including one laid out in the Japanese style), open daily April–November.

From the Arc de Triomphe (see Rte 25), the Av. de la Grande Armée descends north west to the **Porte Maillot** (Pl. 10; 2), the site of extensive blocks of buildings in recent years—and more are threatened—commanded on the north side by the Palais des Congrès (to receive a new façade) and one of the Aérogares (or air terminals) of Paris.

A short distance to the north west, near the Pl. du Gén. Koenig, or de la Porte des Ternes, stands N.-D. de la Compassion, a mausoleum in the Byzantine style (1843). It was moved here from its original neighbouring site, where stood an inn at which Ferdinand, Duc d'Orléans (1810–42), son of Louis-Philippe, died as the result of a carriage accident.

Beyond the Porte Maillot, the wide Av. Charles-de-Gaulle bisects **Neuilly-sur-Seine,** once the most fashionable suburb of Paris. It was partially laid out in what was formerly the park of Louis-Philippe's château (built in 1740 and burnt down in 1848), and later developed as a colony of elegant villas, but the construction of blocks of flats has overwhelmed the distinctive character of the neighbourhood.

Its southern half has the attraction of being adjacent to the Bois de Boulogne. At a house on the site of 33 Rue de Longchamp (leading south from near the bridge), Théophile Gautier died in 1872. Ossip Zadkine (1890–1967), the sculptor, also died at Neuilly. Further to the east, in the old cemetery, lie Anatole France and André Maurois.
   In the **Cimetière de Lavallois-Perret**, the suburb north of Neuilly, lie Louise Michel (1830–1905), the revolutionary, and Maurice Ravel (1875–1937).

The Av. Charles-de-Gaulle leads to Pont de Neuilly, a stone bridge by Perronet (1768–72, almost entirely rebuilt in 1935–39), which replaced an earlier bridge erected in 1606 after Henri IV and Marie de Médicis were almost drowned in the Seine here. The central section of the bridge stands on the northern extremity of the Ile de Puteaux; to the north is the Ile de la Grande Jatte, painted by Seurat in 1884.

LA DEFENSE, named after a monument commemorating the defence of Paris against the Prussians in 1871, designates an extensive area of 760 hectares which has been developed since 1958 by the Etablissement Public pour l'Aménagement de la région de la Défense, or EPAD. The first building of consequence was the triangular-shaped flat-domed exhibition hall, known as the CNIT Centre (1958), but with the construction of the RER line in 1970, bringing it within rapid reach of central Paris, tower blocks have proliferated, causing controversy in several quarters. One of the first, the Tour Roussel-Hoechst (then known as the Tour Nobel), of only 34 storeys, immediately south of the far end of the Pont de Neuilly, was built on the site of the house in which the composer Vincenzo Bellini (1801–35) died. His name in commemorated by the adjacent Terrace Bellini.
   It is already planned to demolish and rebuild the ESSO building, further west on the north side of the main axis of La Défense, and one of the earliest erected. It has been mooted that this was because it was not an aggressive enough example of the high-rise structures which have since mushroomed, housing a variety of national and international companies and corporations, and turning the area into a concrete jungle, in spite of the claims of

The view looking east from the Arche de la Défense

architects and town-planners. There are already some 30,000 residents and office space is available for at least 100,000.

At least rail and road traffic is sited underground, but the warren of passages leading from the car parks (with 26,000 spaces) and the RER station to the offices, commercial areas, banks, hotels, restaurants, fast-food establishments, residential blocks and schools is unalluring. The gardens and esplanades, embellished with a variety of sculptures, fountains and murals, provide some propitiatory but windswept space for the pedestrian.

The whole area has been divided into 11 sectors and it is preferable to know in advance the number of the sector you wish to visit. Emerging directly from the RER station or new extension of the métro (line 1), you will find yourself (in sector 4) on the Parvis close to *La Grande Arche, one of the more prestigious buildings.

The unusual design, by the Danish architect Johann Otto von Spreckelsen (1929–87), chosen by M. Mitterrand from 424 projects, was completed in mid 1989. Although referred to as an arch, it might be better described as a colossal hollow cube. It sits on 12 huge piles, sustaining a weight of 300,000 tonnes, is 110m square, and is open on two sides. It has the appearance from a distance of a marble 'picture frame'. It may be noticed that it is also pivoted slightly—over six degrees—from the main axis of La Défense. Below the arch (now housing several ministries and other offices), is suspended a cloud-like structure. A series of exterior elevators rise to the summit, which provides an awesome view over the surrounding chaos of buildings. Among these, several of which have façades of mirror-glass, the following stand out: to the south of the arch are the angular Pascal TowerS; to the east, the dark monolithic Fiat Tower (46 storeys), 235m high—so far the tallest—reflecting the prismatic ELF Tower adjacent. Further east rises the Descartes Tower; and beyond, the GAN Tower and triangular-shaped ASSUR Tower, and facing it, on the other side of the main axis, is the sharp-angled PFA Tower.

Among other projects are the Japan Tower and the innovative Tour Sans Fin, to the north of the CNIT building, designed by Jean Nouvel, which is expected to rise to a height of 400m, its base of black granite and summit of glass.

It is planned to exploit an extensive area further west, which will be flanked to the north by an extension of the main axis, and will incorporate the Parc André Malraux. This is part of an ambitious scheme to improve Nanterre, the préfecture of the département of Hauts-de-Seine, further north west, under which the new A14 motorway will tunnel to meet the A13.

29 From Pl. de la République to La Villette Hôpital St.-Louis; Cité des Sciences et de l'Industrie; Cité de la Musique; Buttes-Chaumont; Belleville

METROS: République, Colonel Fabien, Jaurès, Porte de la Villette, Porte de Pantin, Buttes-Chaumont, Jourdain, Télégraphe.

The Rue de Lancry, the first main turning right off the Blvd de Magenta (leading north from the Pl. de la République), shortly crosses the Canal St.-Martin, beyond which the Rue Bichat leads right to the entrance of the *Hôpital St.-Louis (Pl. 9; 6), founded by Henri IV and built by Claude Vellefaux in 1607–12. It is an excellent and now rare example of the Louis XIII style, and its courtyards and chapel may be visited on application at the porter's lodge; the chapel is normally open only on Sundays.

Follow the Rue de la Grange-aux-Belles (which skirts its north side), where to the north of the next crossroad stood a small Protestant cemetery, now built over. Paul Jones was buried there in 1792 (subsequently exhumed and now at Annapolis). Nearby stood the Gibet de Montfaucon, the 'Tyburn' of Paris, set up in the 13C and finally removed in 1790.

The gallows proved fatal to three Surintendants des Finances: Enguerrand de Marigny, who erected it; Jean de Montaigu, who repaired it; and Semblançay, who tried to avoid it. Olivier le Daim, confidential barber to Louis XI (1484; cf. 'Quentin Durward') was hanged here and, after the massacre of St. Bartholomew, Coligny's headless body was exposed, hanging by the feet. In 1608 it was visited by Thomas Coryate, who thought it 'the fayrest Gallows that ever I saw...which consisteth of fourteene fair pillars of free-stone'.

Further to the north is the Pl. du Colonel-Fabien, from which the Blvd de la Villette leads to the Pl. du Stalingrad. Here, in the shadow of the overhead métro line, on a small island site, stands the **Rotunde de la Villette**, built as a toll-house by Ledoux in 1789, and now a repository for archaeological finds in the Paris area.

At 44 Rue de Flandre, leading north east from the northern side of the Place, is a relic of the old Portuguese Jewish Cemetery, in use between 1780 and 1810.

The district of **LA VILLETTE** was known until the early 1970s for its cattle-market and abattoirs. Formerly an iron-foundry stood here, run by two English engineers, Davidson and Richardson, 'well-known for the beauty and precision of the machines which left their workshops'.

The ambitious project of converting the extensive site of some 55 hectares into a public park lying on both sides of the Canal de l'Ourcq, and the building of a science museum in its northern half, has now been largely realised.

The south entrance to the park and the buildings within it is best approached from the Métro: Porte de Pantin, while the Cité des Sciences (see below) is more conveniently reached from the métro: Porte de la Villette.

A complex of modernistic buildings known as the Cité de la Musique, designed by Christian de Portzamparc, has been laid out on either side of the south entrance to the park. On the west side, at 211 Av. Jean-Jaurès, stands the new **Conservatoire National Supérieur de Musique** (formerly—since 1911—in the Rue de Madrid, near the Gare St.-Lazare), containing practice studios and a small concert-hall. On the east side, with a student hostel, will be a large auditorium with a seating capacity of 2300, and a smaller rehearsal hall, etc. It is planned to house the formerly cramped Musée Instrumental in a Galerie des Instruments.

The Conservatoire was founded in 1765 as the Académie Royale de Chant, amalgamated with the Ecole de Déclamation Dramatique in 1786 and refounded by Bernard Sarrette in 1795. Among past directors have been Cherubini (1796–1842), Auber (1842–71), Ambroise Thomas (1871–96), the academic Théodore Dubois (1896–1905; during whose period the institution four times rejected Ravel's attempts to win the Prix de Rome), Gabriel Fauré (1905–20), Henri Rabaud (1920–40) and Marcel Dupré (1954–56). Among pupils were Berlioz (from 1826, taught by Lesueur and Reicha), Florent Schmitt, Charles Koechlin, Georges Enesco and Paul Dukas.

The ***MUSEE INSTRUMENTAL** originated in the Clapisson collection and now contains over 4000 instruments. Of particular importance and interest are the collections of medieval, Renaissance and 17C instruments, which have again come into their own. Among earlier items is a Bible-regal (16C German); a clavecin (Venice; 1543); a variety of lutes, viols, theorbos, basset-horns, spinets, harpsichords (outstanding amongst which is one of 1646 by Andreas II Ruckers), clavichords, virginals (including a fine example by Ruckers), square pianos, harps, finely decorated guitars, a curious one-stringed marine-trumpet and a unique octobasse (c 1850), constructed by J.-B. Vuillaume. Also shown are representative brass, woodwind and percussion instruments of all periods, and examples of the *vielle à roue* or hurdy-gurdy. The collections of stringed instruments (some owned by Lully, Kreutzer and Sarasate), include five violins by Antonio Stradivari and others by Amati and Guarneri. Among pianos are examples manufactured by Erard, Pleyel (including Chopin's and Bizet's) and Longman and Broderip. Other instruments of historic or artistic interest are Beethoven's clavichord (1786), Marie-Antoinette's harp and Adolphe Sax's saxophone.

Since 1967 a department for the restoration of old instruments has flourished, and constructional plans of early examples can be bought. The library contains an extensive collection of photographs of instruments, but the valuable series of scores, books on music and MSS (including Mozart's 'Don Giovanni') are now housed in the Bibliothèque Nationale.

Beyond an extensive paved forecourt three older buildings on the site have been retained, comprising two pavilions between which is the former Grande Halle aux Boeufs. Erected by Jules de Mérindol in 1867, it has been renovated and adapted by Bernard Reichen and Philippe Robert, and is now used for a variety of public performances and 'animations', exhibitions, trade fairs, etc. Its dimensions are 241m long, 86m wide and 19m high. The pavilion to the west now contains a small theatre for the production of contemporary plays.

An avenue of trees leads away from the east pavilion to the Zénith, a lightweight structure accommodating 6400, designed specifically for pop concerts and similar events.

A covered passageway parallel to the western side of the Grande Halle leads across the park and crosses the Canal de l'Ourcq (the south bank of which is skirted by another transverse passageway) to enter the northern sector. The **Park** itself, designed by Bernard Tschumi, containing a greenhouse and several other buildings, is studded by a variety of 'Follies', conspicuous structures of bright red enamelled metal, laid out on a grid pattern.

The northern half of the park is dominated by the spherical Géode (see below), beyond which is the huge rectangular building of the Cité des Sciences et de l'Industrie, entered more conveniently from the Porte de la Villette at 30 Av. Corentin-Cariou. Near this is a restored pavilion, formerly the rotunda of the Veterinary Surgeon, now housing a small museum devoted to the history of the abattoirs.

The impressive ***CITE DES SCIENCES ET DE L'INDUSTRIE** was inaugurated in March 1986. It measures 270m long, 110m wide and 47m high. It was built on the site of the auction-hall of the slaughter-house, but this structure was never completed. It consisted of 20 reinforced concrete piers supporting 16 lattice girders each 65m long, which formed the basis of the present building, radically adapted by Adrien Fainsilber, and employing several new technologies.

Among unusual innovative features are the three glazed sections of glass wall on its southern side, each 32m square, rising to the roof and in fact forming conservatories or hot-houses; the two rotatable roof cupolas, each

18m in diameter; and—within the conservatories—the transparent lifts or elevators ascending within a stainless steel framework. The whole structure is surrounded by a moat.

The Cité is normally entered from the north and most of the facilities and amenities, including a science bookshop, are grouped on the main entrance level. Opening times (including the Géode): Tues.–Sun. 10.00–18.00.

Details of the various sections of the Cité which may be visited are not given here, but a leaflet in English is available at information desks, specifying the whereabouts of the displays and exhibitions, both permanent and temporary.

The main hall is 100m long and 40m high, below which are two levels from which the Géode is reached (see below), accommodating a multimedia library, conference centre, etc. Escalators, with their mechanism visible, ascend to the upper three floors (on the second of which is the Planetarium) devoted to the permanent exhibitions, known as 'Explora', which occupy an area of 30,000m^2.

Although many visitors are of school age, this should not imply that the exhibits are designed largely for them; anyone interested in any aspect of modern science and technology will find more than enough displayed and explained here to satisfy their curiosity.

Among the several scale models which may be entered are the latest *Nautilus*, which can plunge to a depth of 6000m; a nose cone of the third stage of the *Ariane* satellite launcher; and a mock-up cockpit of an A320 airbus, which simulates take-off conditions, etc.

Another section displays three-dimensional models of the 2500 atomic nuclei currently known to exist, together with a 'particle accelerator', with a transparent skin, which may facilitate a better understanding of nuclear reactions. Several different types of robots are shown, and another section is devoted to computers and other radical changes in communications technology, but these are only a few of the sciences touched on.

Immediately to the south of the main building is the *Géode, a spherical dome of 36m diameter, its 630 tonne double shell composed of 6433 preformed triangular plates of polished stainless steel, with an inner framework of c 1600 triangles constructed with 2580 steel tubes linked by 835 assembly knots. The interior houses some 360 tiered seats facing a hemispheric cinema screen of 1000m^2 and 26m in diameter, on which a series of specially adapted films using the 'omnimax' technique are shown, projecting an image at an optical angle of 180°.

From the Pl. du Colonel-Fabien the Av. Mathurin-Moreau leads to the west entrance of the **Parc des Buttes Chaumont**, one of the more picturesque and least known of Parisian parks (23 hectares). It lies in the midst of the district of Belleville, which belies its name.

It was laid out under Haussmann's régime in 1866–67 by Alphand and Barillet on the bare hills ('*monts chauves*') which had long been used as a general rubbish-dump and slaughterhouse for horses, etc., its extensive gypsum ('plaster of Paris') quarries being ingeniously transformed into rock-scenery. These heights had been the scene of the 'Battle of Paris' in 1814, and in 1871 were held by the Communards until dislodged by bombardment from Montmartre, to the west.

From near the south-east end of the park, the Rue Fessart leads east, crossing the Rue de la Villette (where at No. 51 the artist Georges Rouault (1871–1958) was born) to Gothic-revival St. Jean-Baptiste (by Lassus,

1854–59). From the south side of the church, the Rue de Belleville continues east, passing a developing area to the north, to the Cimetière de Belleville, the second highest point in Paris (128m).

An inscription to the right of the entrance in the Rue du Télégraphe records that Claude Chappe experimented here with the aerial telegraph that was to announce the victories of the French Revolutionary Wars. Originally called 'Tachygraphe', it was set up in 1792 on this site and was the base of lines to Lille and Strasbourg.

At 79 Rue Haxo, parallel to the east, is the Chapelle des Otages, built in 1936–39 on the site of the Villa des Otages, behind which (at the end of the passage just north of the chapel) 52 hostages held by the Communards were shot on 26 May 1871.

You may return to the centre by the métro: Télégraphe, via République.

30 Père-Lachaise

METROS: Père-Lachaise, Alexandre-Dumas, Philippe-Auguste.

From the Pl. de la République, the Av. de la République leads east-south-east across the Blvd Richard-Lenoir, built over the Canal St.-Martin in 1860 by Haussmann, to the north-west corner of Père-Lachaise. The main entrance is in the Blvd de Ménilmontant.

The quarter of Ménilmontant, north of the cemetery, was the home of the philosophical fraternity of the Saint-Simoniens in the early 1830s.

The Cimetière de l'Est, better known as *PERE-LACHAISE, is the largest (47 hectares) and long the most 'fashionable' cemetery in Paris, and its tombs display the work of many 19C French sculptors, funerary and otherwise, several of which are of importance in themselves. Regrettably, a number of graves and statues have been vandalised or covered by graffiti.

Père François de La Chaise (1624–1709) was the confessor of Louis XIV, and lived in the Jesuit house rebuilt in 1682 on the site of a chapel. The property, situated on the side of a hill from which the king, during the Fronde, watched skirmishing between Condé and Turenne, was bought by the city in 1804 and laid out by Brongniart, and later extended.

The first interments were those of La Fontaine and Molière, whose remains were transferred here in 1804. The monument to Abélard and Héloïse, set up in 1779 at the abbey of the Paraclete (near Nogent-sur-Seine), was moved here in 1817, its canopy composed of fragments collected by Lenoir from the abbey of Nogent-sur-Seine.

In the eastern corner of the cemetery is the Mur des Fédérés, against which 147 Communards were shot in 1871 (28 May; see above also); and here also is a monument to the many thousand Frenchmen who died either in German concentration camps or during the Resistance of 1941–44. Thousands of Parisians still visit the cemetery on 1 and 2 November ('Jour de la Toussaint'—All Saints' Day—and 'Jour des Morts').

A guide-plan is available at a nominal sum from the keeper's lodge at the main entrance. The plan gives the position of a few of the tombs of the illustrious dead interred here, which indeed make an impressive list.

Among writers: Beaumarchais, Victor Hugo, Béranger, Proust, Balzac, Benjamin Constant, Mme de Genlis, Gérard de Nerval, Alfred de Musset, Daudet, Rémy de Gourmont, Anna de Noailles, Apollinaire, Henri de Régnier, Barbusse, Bernardin de Saint-Pierre, Villiers de l'Isle-Adam, Colette, Eluard and Sartre.

Among composers and musicians: Méhul, Gossec, Grétry, Boieldieu, Hérold, Pleyel, Lesueur, Rossini (later removed to Florence), Cherubini, Bellini (removed to Catania), Bizet, Reynaldo Hahn, Chausson, Kreutzer, Chopin, Lalo, Gustave Charpentier, Auber, Poulenc, Dukas and Georges Enesco; the librettist Scribe; Erard, the piano-maker, and the singer Adelina Patti.

Among artists and sculptors: David (? heart only), David d'Angers, Pradier, Pissarro, Corot, Doré, Ingres, Gros, Daumier, Daubigny, Clésinger, Guillaume Coustou, Alfred Steven, Barye, Prud'hon, Delacroix, Géricault, Seurat and Modigliani.

Among Napoléon's marshals: Davout, Kellermann, Lefèbvre, Masséna, Ney, Murat, Victor, Macdonald, Suchet, Gouvion-Saint-Cyr, Grouchy and Augereau; and generals Foy, Junot, Reille, Savary, Marbot and Baron Larrey.

Other famous names in their respective fields are: Mlle Mars, Rachel, Talma, Isadora Duncan, Sarah Bernhardt and Yvette Guilbert; Marie Walewska; Manuel Godoy; Mme de Genlis; De Sèze; Brillat-Savarin; Champollion; Parmentier; Blanqui; Baron Haussmann; Brongniart; Visconti; Percier; Fontaine; René Lalique; the philosophers Saint-Simon, 'Alain' and Comte; Lammennais; Michelet; Arago; Félix Pyat; Victor Noir (a journalist shot in cold blood by Pierre Bonaparte in 1870); Reclus; Cuvier; Monge; Branly; Barras; Sieyès, Chambacérès; and Thiers (see below).

Also interred here are Oscar Wilde (1856–1900, but not moved here until nine years after his death, with a monument by Epstein); Sir William Keppel (1702–54), second Earl of Albemarle; Gen. Lord John Murray (1711–87); Adm. Sir Sidney Smith (1764–1840); Gen. Sir Charles Doyle (1770–1842); and Sir Richard Hertford-Wallace (1818–90), the connoisseur and benefactor of Paris (see p 228) and Mary Clarke (Mme Mohl; 1793–1883).

North of the Rue de la Roquette, opposite the main entrance of the cemetery, stood the Prison de la Grande-Roquette, itself on the site of the convent of the Hospitalières de la Roquette, founded in 1639, replaced in 1899 by the Petite-Roquette (for women). From 1853 to 1899 condemned prisoners were held at La Roquette while awaiting execution. Here in 1871 some 50-odd Commune hostages were shot, although c 130 were also released. Thiers' victorious government forces 'of law and order' then proceeded to round up thousands of Communards—both repentant and unrepentant—and in two days shot out-of-hand 1900 of them in retaliation or 'in expiation'!

To the south east of the cemetery, approached by the Blvd de Charonne (forking off the Blvd de Ménilmontant) and Rue de Bagnolet, stands **St.-Germain-de Charonne**, a rustic church of the 13–14C, restored in the 19C, retaining its village cemetery (the only other in Paris being St.-Pierre-de-Montmartre). St.-Jean-Bosco (1937), of concrete and with a lofty tower, stands a short distance south east of the junction of the Blvd de Charonne and the Rue de Bagnolet.

31 Faubourg St.-Antoine

METROS: Bastille, Nation, Gare de Lyon, Bércy.

From Père-Lachaise (see above), the Blvd de Ménilmontant, with its continuation south, the Av. Philippe-Auguste, leads south east to the Pl. de la Nation, also approached direct from the Pl. de la Bastille by métro. The Rue du Faubourg-St.-Antoine leads east-south-east from the Pl. de la Bastille to the Pl. de la Nation, through an area memorable in the history of the Revolutions of 1789 and 1848. It was also the scene of skirmishing during the Fronde (1652), when Turenne defeated Condé.

Since the late 13C it has been a centre of cabinet-making, and many courtyards and passages still hide busy workshops behind 18C façades. The whole area is being spruced up and a number of antique shops and galleries now flourish here.

At No. 1 Rue du Faubourg-St.-Antoine, leading away from the Pl. de la Bastille (see Rte 21) and the new opera-house, Fieschi hatched the plot against Louis-Philippe (see Blvd du Temple). At No. 61 (left), at the corner of the Rue de Charonne, is the Fontaine Trogneux (1710). Further on (right) the Sq. Trousseau occupies the site of the Hospice des Enfants-Trouvés, in the graveyard of which the Princesse de Lamballe was buried after her corpse had been paraded through the streets (1792). In front of No. 151, Jean-Baptiste-Victor Baudin, representative of the people for the department of the Ain, was killed on a barricade while inciting the Parisians to protest against the coup d'état of Napoléon III (1851).

To the left, the Rue St.-Bernard leads to Ste.-Marguerite, built in 1634 but many times altered since. Behind the high altar is a Pietà by Girardon. It is believed that the 10-year-old Louis XVII, who in all probability died at the Temple (see p 193), was buried in the graveyard here in 1795, together with other victims of the Revolution.

South of the Rue du Faubourg-St.-Antoine at this point is the Hôpital St.-Antoine, rebuilt in 1905 but retaining part of Lenoir's 18C building for the former Abbaye de St.-Antoine-des-Champs.

Several thoroughfares converge on the spacious **Pl. de la Nation**, at the hub of which is a colossal bronze group representing the 'Triumph of the Republic', by Dalou (1899). It was known formerly as the Pl. du Trône (named after the throne erected for Louis XIV's triumphal entry in 1660 with Maria Thérèsa); in 1794 no fewer than 1306 victims of the Terror were guillotined here. Between 1793 and 1880 it was known as the Pl. du Trône-renversé.

To the east of the 'circus' are two pavilions, built as toll-houses by Ledoux in 1788, each surmounted by a Doric column 30.50m high; one with a statue of Philippe Auguste (by Dumont), the other, of Louis IX, by Etex.

The Cours de Vincennes (once the scene in Easter Week of the *Foire aux Pains d'épice*, a festival dating back to the 10C, when bread made with honey and aniseed was distributed by the monks of the Abbey of St.-Antoine) leads directly east from the Pl. de la Nation to the Porte de Vincennes, and beyond to the Château de Vincennes (see Rte 32), also reached direct by the métro.

The Rue Fabre-d'Eglantine leads south to the Rue de Picpus, where, at the end of the garden at No. 35, a convent of Augustinian nuns, is the little *Cimetière de Picpus (open 14.00–16.00 or 18.00, except Monday), a private burial ground for 'emigrés' and descendants of victims of the Revolution.

Among individuals interred here is La Fayette; among famous families, those of Chateaubriand, Crillon, Gontaut-Biron, Tascher de la Pagerie, Choiseul, La Rochefoucauld, Du Plessis, Montmorency, Talleyrand-Périgord, Rohan-Rochefort, Noailles, Quélen and Salignac-Fénelon, and sixteen Carmelites of Compiègne martyred in 1794. In a second section are buried members of the house of Salm-Kyrbourg and those guillotined in the Pl. du Trône-renversé, including André Chénier; see above.

A short distance south east of the Pl. de la Bastille, in the Rue de Charenton, is the rebuilt Hospice des Quinze-Vingts, founded as an asylum for 300 blind people by Louis IX in 1260. The previous building was later—until 1775—the Caserne des Mousquetaires-Noirs.
    Nos 40–60 in the street occupy the site of the Couvent des Filles-Anglaises de la Conception, which in 1634/5–55 accepted only daughters of English parents. It was suppressed in 1796 but later restored to its former owners. In 1817–20 George Sand was a boarder there.

The Rue de Lyon leads south from the Pl. de la Bastille to the modernised **Gare de Lyon** (Pl. 5; 6), terminus of lines to Dijon, Grenoble, Lyon, the south of France and Italy, including TGV. It preserves a fin-de-siècle buffet.

Opposite the station once stood the Mazas Prison, where 400 Communards were rounded up and massacred by Thiers' troops in 1871. Rimbaud had been briefly held there, in August 1870, for travelling from Charleville to Paris without a ticket.
    On its south side the station is now overlooked by tower blocks, including the Tour Gamma A, 195 Rue de Bercy, containing offices of the Observatoire économique de Paris (Institut National de la Statistique et des Etudes Economiques), a mine of such information.

Rue Van Gogh leads south east from the station to the projected Pont Charles-de-Gaulle, which will span the Seine to provide direct access to the Gare d'Austerlitz; see Rte 6.
    Not far south east of the station rises the new block of offices housing the Ministère de Finances, flanking the Blvd de Bercy, which leads to the widened Pont de Bercy (1864). On the far side of the boulevard stands the hexagonal **Palais Omnisports** (1984), a stunted pyramid topped by a tubular platform supported by four cylindrical towers. The structure accommodates 17,000 spectators.
    The area to the south east is to be laid out as the Parc de Bercy. Here stood the once extensive Entrepôt des Vins, with bonded warehouses and cellars. This spirituous district has suffered numerous calamities in the past, among them the floods of 1817, 1833, 1836 and 1850 and fires in 1820, 1823, 1853, 1859 and 1860.

On the far bank will rise the Bibliothèque de France (see Rte 10), with which it will be connected by a footbridge.
    Overlooking the north-east corner of the park will be the new American Center. At the far end of the park, between Pont de Tolbiac (1884) and Pont National (1852; enlarged 1942), among other developments, will be the establishment of a Maison International des Vins et Spiritueux, with a Musée des Vins et de la Gastronomie together with an Oenological centre, and departments of the Ministère de l'Agriculture.

Immediately beyond the Pont National is that carrying the Périphérique, and the Porte de Bercy, the beginning of the A4 motorway to the east.

The Blvd Diderot leads due west from the Gare de Lyon to the Quai de la Rapée, with the Institut Médico-Légal (no admission). This replaced the old Morgue, which formerly stood at the south end of the Ile de la Cité.

A few paces to the west is the Pont d'Austerlitz (also approached direct from Pl. de la Bastille by the Blvd de la Bastille). Dating from 1802–07, but rebuilt in stone in 1855 and widened in 1886, it spans the Seine to the Pl. Valhubert and Gare d'Austerlitz; see Rte 9.

32 Vincennes

Approximately 2km east of the Porte de Vincennes, and reached directly from the centre by the métro (Château de Vincennes), stands the impressive bulk of the historic *CHATEAU DE VINCENNES (CNMH), rectangular in plan, and flanked by nine square towers. All except the entrance tower, the finest and largest, which lost only its statues, were reduced to the level of the walls in the 19C. Michelet called it 'the Windsor of the Valois'.

The present castle, succeeding an earlier hunting-lodge fortified by Louis IX, was begun by Philippe VI in 1337. Its fortification was completed by his grandson Charles V (1364–73), who also commenced work on the Chapel, which was not finished until 1552. Some idea of how it once looked may be gained from the illustration of December in the 'Très Riches Heures du Duc de Berri', or Fouquet's panel of Etienne Chevalier. The foundations of the Pavillons du Roi and de la Reine (to the south) were laid in the 16C, but these buildings were not completed for nearly a century, when the château, then in Mazarin's possession, was altered and decorated by Le Vau.

With the completion of the palace at Versailles (c 1680), Vincennes was deserted by the court, and the château was occupied in turn by a porcelain factory (1745; transferred to Sèvres in 1756), a cadet school and, in 1757, a small-arms factory. Offered for sale in 1788, it found no purchaser, and in 1791 La Fayette rescued it from destruction by the Revolutionary mob. In 1808 Napoléon converted it into an arsenal, when the surviving 13C buildings were demolished. In 1840 it was made into a fortress and much of Le Vau's decoration was destroyed or masked by casemates.

During the Second World War, German occupying forces had a supply depot here, and the Pavillon de la Reine was partially destroyed by an explosion in 1944 during their evacuation of the building. Restoration continues to be undertaken sporadically, but much work is still to be done.

The historical associations of Vincennes are numerous. Here died Jeanne de Navarre in 1305, Louis X in 1316, Charles IV in 1328, Charles IX in 1574 and Mazarin in 1661; and Charles V was born here in 1337. In 1326 the 'Auld Alliance' or treaty between France and Scotland, was signed here. Henry V of England died here in 1422, seven weeks before the death of Charles VI, whom he was to succeed as king of France.

During the reign of Louis XIII, the keep was used as a state prison; and among its inmates were the Grand Condé, Card. de Retz, Fouquet, Diderot (visited there by Rousseau in 1749), and Mirabeau (who here wrote his 'Essai sur les lettres de cachet' in 1784). Among later prisoners were Jean Henry de Latude (1725–1805), who, for a fraudulent attempt to extract money from Mme de Pompadour, was incarcerated here (and elsewhere), untried, for 35 years.

In March 1804 the Duc d'Enghien (son of the Prince de Condé), arrested five days before on Napoléon's orders, was tried by court-martial and shot here the same night. Général Daumesnil was governor of the château from 1809 to 1814, during the Hundred Days, and from 1830 until his death in 1832. When summoned to surrender to the Allies in 1814, his answer was 'First give me back my leg' (which he had lost at Wagram). In 1830, when the mob broke into the building in search of some former ministers of Charles X, he dispersed them by threatening to blow up the powder-magazine. Mata Hari was shot here in 1917. In 1944, three days before evacuating it, the Germans shot some 30 hostages against the interior of the ramparts.

Crossing the moat, the fortress is entered beneath the imposing Tour du Village, 48m high, passing between a range of tawdry buildings in military occupation to reach the central courtyard. The *Keep, 50m in height, a square tower flanked with round turrets, is enclosed in a separate turreted enceinte, and is the finest of its type in France (since the Château de Coucy—north of Soissons—was blown up by the Germans in 1917), and as such deserves further restoration. The two doors on the ground floor facing the postern came from the prison of Louis XVI in the Temple. A wide spiral stair ascends to the first and second floors (third floor closed), supported by vaults springing from a central column; the corbels at each corner of the first floor room symbolise the Evangelists. Note the oak beams between the ribs.

The SECOND FLOOR, a favourite residence of Charles V, contains a fine chimney-piece, and an oratory in the north-west turret. Henry V (of England) and Charles IX died on this floor. 17C prisoners of state were lodged above. The roof commands a wide view of the area, with the main landmarks of central Paris easily discerned to the west. The kitchen, with its internal well, is shown on the ground floor.

The *Chapel opposite was founded by Charles V in 1379 and, retaining the Gothic style, was only completed in 1552. The Flamboyant façade has a magnificent rose-window surmounted by an ornamental gable filled with tracery. The bare interior contains graceful vaulting, and at the east end, seven stained-glass windows by Beaurain (16C), restored after an explosion in 1870. A monument to the Duc d'Enghien (see above; by Deseine, 1816) may be seen in the oratory.

To the south, approached through a portico, lies the immense Cour d'Honneur, and beyond, the monumental Tour du Bois. To the right stands the Pavillon du Roi (now containing military archives), and opposite, the Pavillon de la Reine, where Mazarin died in 1661. Both were completed by Le Vau in 1654–60.

Some 3.5km north east—as the crow flies—in the Parc de Montreau (to the east of Montreuil), at 31 Blvd Théophile Sueur, is the Musée de l'Histoire Vivante, largely devoted to the Socialist ethic and the history of the revolutions of 1830 and 1848, the Paris Commune and other proletarian movements.

For Champs, see Rte 41.

The **Bois de Vincennes**, first enclosed in the 12C, was replanted in 1731 by Louis XV and converted into a park for the citizens of Paris. It was further enlarged in 1860. To the south east of the château are floral gardens, and beyond are stadiums and sports grounds. Further east is the Lac des Minimes, a Jardin Tropical and an Indo-Chinese pagoda.

Towards the south-west end of the Bois, approached directly from the château by the Av. Daumesnil, is the Parc Zoölogique de Vincennes, the main zoo of Paris. Beyond it is the Lac Daumesnil, south of which is a Buddhist temple.

The Av. Daumesnil leaves the Bois at the Porte Dorée (or Porte Picpus), just north of which stands the *MUSEE NATIONAL DES ARTS AFRICAINS ET OCEANIENS, with an ornately sculpted façade. The building was erected in 1931 for a Colonial Exhibition. It also contains an aquarium.

As its name implies, it concentrates on the arts of the ci-devant French colonies rather than their ethnography, for which see Musée de l'Homme, Rte 27.

GROUND FLOOR: left, the Oceanian Collection: masks, wooden drums and statues from the New Hebrides: to the right, naïf bark paintings from Australia. FIRST FLOOR: left, arts of the West African coast, including gold figurines etc., from Akan; brass and gold powder figures from Ghana and the Ivory Coast; note also the carved wood woman and child from Kran (Liberia). To the right, work from the Niger and Congo basins, Yoruba (Nigeria) and the Cameroons; Benin bronzes; nail-studded magic statues from the Congo; Bembe figurines, masks, jewellery, and pottery.

SECOND FLOOR: left, Moroccan jewellery, including a fine necklace from Fez (16–17C); arms; and a section devoted to fabrics, brocades, embroidery, caftans, etc. To the right, the arts of Tunisia and Algeria, including bonnets, pendants, fibulas, etc.

The return to the centre may be made from the métro: Porte Dorée, adjacent.

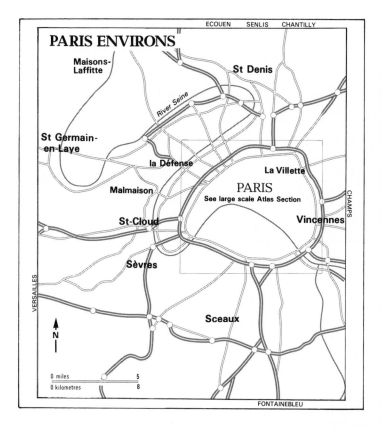

THE IMMEDIATE ENVIRONS OF PARIS

33 From Paris to Versailles

BY ROAD. Versailles is easily reached by taking the A13 motorway and turning left at the first exit after passing through the tunnel at St.-Cloud. A road leads south west towards the Château of Versailles (parking in the Pl. d'Armes).

An alternative is the N10, bearing south west from the Porte de St.-Cloud over the Pont de Sèvres, which our route follows.

BY RAIL. A convenient approach is the RER line running along the south bank of the Seine, where the train may be boarded at, for example, St.-Michel, Musée d'Orsay, Invalides, Champ-de-Mars or Javel. The terminus nearest the palace is **Versailles-Rive Gauche** There are also lines from the Gare St.-Lazare to Versailles-Rive Droit, and from the Gare Montparnasse to Versailles-Chantiers.

Alternatively, take the métro to the Pont de Sèvres, then bus 171.

Note that the **Château of Versailles** (see Rte 34) is **closed** on Mondays, although the gardens are open every day until dusk.

The N10, on leaving the Porte de St.-Cloud (south-east corner of the Bois de Boulogne, with fountains by Landowski), crosses the suburb of Boulogne-Billancourt before reaching the Pont de Sèvres (rebuilt 1963). **SEVRES** itself is famous for the porcelain factory founded in 1738; the *Musée National Céramique de Sévres** (4 Grande Rue) also displays ceramics and porcelain from other factories and countries. The museum is open 10.00–17.00, except Tues.

For guided tours of the adjacent workshops (no children under 16), telephone 45349905. The sale-room is open Mon. to Fri. 9.00–12.00; 13.30–18.00. Métro: Pont-de-Sèvres.

The factory was moved here from Vincennes in 1756 at the request of Mme de Pompadour, and since 1760 has been State-controlled. It was visited in 1776 by Thomas Bentley, Josiah Wedgwood's partner, who was impressed by its workshops, in which a dozen carvers or modellers and almost 100 painters were employed. Among designers of Sèvres porcelain were E.-M. Falconet (1716–91) and J.-B. Pigalle (1714–85).

On the FIRST FLOOR are Islamic ceramics (8–15C) and ceramics from Anatolia (16–18C); historical collections, mostly from France; Italian majolica; Hispano-Moresque ware, etc. from the Middle Ages to the 18C. SECOND FLOOR: North Gallery: Delft ware; faïence from Nevers; from Moustiers, Rouen, Strasbourg, Marseille and Sceaux; and copies of Oriental pieces manufactured at St.-Cloud, Mennecy, Meissen and Chantilly. South Gallery: porcelain from Vincennes and Sèvres, and Saxe (Meissen), etc.

Lully, the composer, once resided in a nearby pavilion, named after him.

Some distance to the west, in the suburb of Ville d'Avray, the 'Villa des Jardies' was the country retreat of Balzac in 1837–41. It was later the home of Léon Gambetta (1838–82), who died here. The 18C church contains frescoes by Corot, who often painted the lakes in the Bois de Fausses Reposes, further south west.

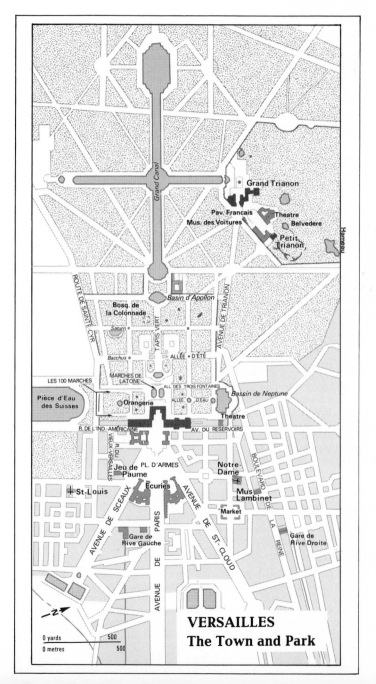

VERSAILLES
The Town and Park

0 yards   500
0 metres   500

Immediately south east of Sèvres is **Meudon** (Celtic *Mellodunum*), the benefice of which was enjoyed by Rabelais in 1551–52. Wagner composed 'The Flying Dutchman' here in 1841, at 27 Av. du Château; here too is the 'Villa des Brillants', the suburban home of Rodin from 1895 until his death in 1917, with a collection of his casts, and his grave. There is a museum of local history at 11 Rue des Pierres.

Further south is the Observatoire d'Astronomie Physique. The building, formerly the Château Neuf, was built for the Grand Dauphin ('Monseigneur', the son of Louis XIV), by Mansart, but a fire in 1870 reduced it to the single-storeyed building it is today. The terrace commands a wide view. The Forêt de Meudon extends to the south and west.

St.-Cloud, 2km north of Sèvres, was also the site of a porcelain factory from 1695 until 1773, when it was destroyed in a fire. The suburb was the birthplace of Hilaire Belloc (1870–1953). The royal castle was burned down during the German occupation in 1870 but its remains were not cleared away until 1891. It was here that Henri III was assassinated in 1589; Henrietta Anne (daughter of Charles I, and later Duchess of Orléans) died in 1670 (poisoned, according to Saint-Simon); and Philippe d'Orléans was born (1674); Napoléon's second marriage, to Marie-Louise, was celebrated in 1810; and Charles X signed his infamous 'Ordonnances' in 1830. The **Park** (392 hectares), with its cascades, fountains and views over Paris—which Queen Victoria thought splendid—is open to the public.

On a height some 3km north is seen the fort of Mont Valérien (1830), where Colonel Henry, implicated in the Dreyfus Affair, committed suicide in 1898; and where during the years 1941–44 some 4500 members of the Resistance, among others, were murdered. Off the Blvd Washington is an American Military Cemetery.

From Sèvres, the N10 continues south west (through the suburbs of Chaville and Viroflay) to (c 8km) Versailles.

VERSAILLES (95,000 inhab.), *préfecture* of the *département* of Yvelines, lies in a low sandy plain between two lines of wooded hills. With its regular streets and its imposing avenues converging on the palace, it seeks to retain its royal cachet, although the château, with which the history of the town is inextricably entwined, quite overshadows it in interest; see Rte 34. Nevertheless, the town does contain a certain number of buildings of importance, which are described below. See map on p 243.

Versailles was the birthplace of the Duc de Saint-Simon (1675–1755); Houdon (1741–1828) the sculptor; Marshal Berthier (1753–1815); Kreutzer (1766–1831), the violinist; Gén. Hoche (1768–97); and Ferdinand de Lesseps (1805–94; at 18 Rue des Réservoirs). The artist Georges Rouault (1871–1958) is buried in the St.-Louis cemetery. Sir Jonah Barrington (1760–1834), author of 'Personal Sketches'; and the art dealer Ambroise Vollard (1865–1939). Versailles was the 'Doncières' of Proust.

At 7 Rue des Réservoirs, north of the château, is the Hôtel des Réservoirs, built by Lassurance for Mme de Pompadour (but much altered), still bearing the marquise's arms. It now houses the local tourist office. Proust isolated himself here for almost five months in the latter half of 1906. The Théâtre Montansier (No. 13), founded by the actress Mlle Montansier, was built by Heurtier and Boulet in 1777, and since restored. La Bruyère (1645–96) lived and died at No. 22, the Hôtel du Prince de Condé.

A few minutes' walk to the north east is the Musée Lambinet, housed in a mid 18C mansion (at 54 Blvd de la Reine) and containing sculptures by Houdon. The collection of early prints and views of Versailles is of interest. Among paintings are Vigée-Lebrun, Portrait of Mme du Barry; and works by Corot, Le Sidaner and Bonington, among others.

At No. 1 Blvd de la Reine (further west) is the Trianon Palace, a hotel built by René Sergent, the architect of the Plaza Athénée in Paris, in 1910. For two years during the First World War it was a hospital for British troops. In April 1917 the Allied Military Committee installed its permanent War Council here and it was here that Clemenceau, Wilson, Lloyd George, Foch, Petain, Haig and Pershing held their meetings that preceded the signing of the Treaty of Versailles in the château. It was in a room, now the dining room, that Georges Clemenceau handed the conditions for peace to the German High Command on 7 May 1919. A plaque records the event. On 4 June 1920 the Trianon Treaty which decided the fate of Hungary was negotiated and signed at the Trianon Palace.

After the war the hotel once again became the haunt of the chic and the fashionable. Among its guests were the Duke and Duchess of Windsor, Colette and her cats, Marcel Proust, Sarah Bernhardt, François Coty and André Citroën.

The Trianon Palace was requisitioned by the Royal Air Force in 1939, by the Luftwaffe in 1940 and by the Americans in 1944 when it was again the meeting place for decisions that settled the peace.

Today the Trianon Palace has been restored. The hotel's original architectural splendours, the façades, the entrance hall, the gallery and the salons, have been elegantly refurbished.

A short distance south east stands Nôtre-Dame, by Jules Hardouin-Mansart (1684), with a pulpit of the period. To the south east are the restored market halls of Versailles

Hardouin-Mansart also designed the Grand-Commun, immediately south of the Château, built to accommodate court functionaries, which retains several fine bas-reliefs. It was converted into a small-arms factory at the Revolution, and later used as a military hospital. Adjacent is the former Hôtel de la Guerre (1759) and Hôtel de la Marine et des Affaires Etrangères (1761), now the municipal library, with Louis XV decoration. The Marquis de Louvois (1641–91) died at No. 6 in the street, once the Hôtel de la Surintendance.

From here the Rue du Vieux-Versailles (left) leads to the **Jeu de Paume**, the royal tennis-court (1686), but of little interest in itself (admission Wed. and Sat. 14.00–17.00; Sun. 10.00–12.00).

On 20 June 1789, the deputies of the Tiers-Etat, finding themselves locked out of the States-General, adjourned here, and with the astronomer Bailly as their president, swore not to separate until they had given France a proper constitution. It was later used as a studio by Gros and Horace Vernet.

To the south stands a rare but frigid example of a Louis XV church, **St.-Louis** (1742–54; by Jacques Mansart de Sagonne), designated a cathedral in 1802.

To the west is the former royal kitchen-garden, now a horticultural college (entrance 4 Rue du Potager). To the south east is the Pl. du Marché-St.-Louis, with 18C houses. Further on, at 4 Rue St.-Médéric, was the Parc-aux-Cerfs, purchased in 1755 by Louis XV for entertaining his mistresses. Its first occupant was Marie-Louise Murphy (1737–1814), born at Rouen and the daughter of an Irish shoemaker.

In the Av. de Paris, leading directly east from the château, No. 3 occupies the Hôtel de Mme du Barry (1751; admission on application), with contemporary *boiseries*. Comte Robert de Montesquiou (1855–1921), on whom Proust based his 'Baron Charlus' and Huysmans his 'Jean des Esseintes' in 'A Rebours', lived at No. 53, where he entertained many writers and dilettantes. Further on at Nos 57–61 are the Laiterie de Madame and Pavillon de Musique, built by Chalgrin in 1781 in emulation of the 'hameau' at the Petit Trianon, for Joséphine-Louise de Savoie, Comtesse de Provence, wife of the future Louis XVIII.

34 The Château and Gardens of Versailles: The Trianons

Visitors should be aware that it is almost impossible to see more than a small part of the Château, Park and Trianons in one day. The number of groups and coach-loads of people arriving at opening time means that the circuit of the State Apartments is virtually saturated throughout the morning. The individual visitor hoping to see anything at all is therefore advised to see the Grand Trianon first, later returning to the main building, by which time the crowds may have dispersed. See below about joining guided tours, the only way in which to see several of the less visited but equally interesting parts of the Château.

Study the following pages before deciding what to visit, as it may be necessary to request permission in advance to see certain sections which, unless there is sufficient demand, or if there are no guides available, may be closed.

Note that the room numbers in the description correspond with those printed in the Guide to Versialles and Trianon published by the Réunion des musées nationaux, which do not necessarily agree with those in some leaflets available.

The Château of Versailles. **Admission**. The **Château** is open every day **except** Monday. (Oct.–Apr. 09.00–17.30; May–Sept. 09.00–19.00.) Only the Galerie des Glaces and the Grands Appartements du Roi et de la Reine may be visited entirely without restriction. Regulations about visiting the Chapel and certain other galleries are liable to variation. Normally the Opéra, Appartements du Roi and those of de Mme de Maintenon and Mme du Barry, the Petits Appartements de la Reine and the Appartements du Dauphin et de la Dauphine, et des Mesdames may only be visited with a guided group (some with an English-speaking guide). Enquire in the main entrance hall, approached from the Cour de la Chapelle; see plan. Guided tours of the Appartements du Roi normally leave from adjacent to a passage (R39 on plan) every ten minutes or so between 09.00–15.30.

A bookshop will open adjacent to R40.

Enquire in advance to the *Bureau d'action culturelle* (Tel: (1) 30 84 74 00 and (1) 30 84 76 76) for details of rooms open to the public: certain sections may be closed for restoration. Others may only be visited on making a special request. See p 259 for the Gardens and Park (open year-round 07.00–dusk); and p 260 for the Trianons (closed Mon. Grand: Oct.–Apr. 09.45–12.30, 14.00–17.30; May–Sept. 11.00–16.30; Petit: Oct.–Apr. 14.00–17.30; May–Sept. 11.00–18.30).

Versailles emerged from obscurity in 1624, when Louis XIII built a hunting lodge here, which subsequently developed into a small château, with a garden laid out in 1639.

The royal estate originally covered an area of 6614 hectares, surrounded by a 43km-long wall and entered by 22 gates. The domain was reduced to 815 hectares after the Revolution. The real creator of Versailles was Louis XIV, who in 1661 conceived the idea of building a lasting monument to his reign—a trophy of self-glorification which was in the event to last until 1715. Louis le Vau was entrusted with the renovation and embellishment of the old building around the Cour de Marbre, while Le Nôtre laid out the park. After Le Vau's death in 1670 the work was continued by his pupil François d'Orbay, while the interior decoration was supervised by Charles le Brun. In 1682 Louis XIV transferred the court and seat of government here from St.-Germain. Jules Hardouin-Mansart, appointed chief architect in 1676, radically remodelled the main body of the château and built the two huge north and south wings, giving the immense façade (with its 375 windows) a total length of 580m, and began work on the chapel.

The workforce employed on the building and in laying out and draining the grounds was impressive. Dangeau noted in August 1684 that :'Each day there were 22,000 men and 6000 horses at work'. The cost, impoverishing France, amounted to over 60 million livres. In 1687 Mansart started work on the Grand Trianon. La Bruyère compared the Court itself to marble for, like the building, it was 'composed of men who are very hard but highly polished'. The life at Court, where its members would orbit, moth-like, around the imperious figure of the 'Roi soleil', obsessed with the concept of 'La Gloire', is inimitably described in the Duc de Saint-Simon's 'Memoires'. He was one of many not dazzled by the superficially scintillating scene, and his pages unremittingly reflect the monotonous routine, rigid protocol and ceremonious etiquette which, along with intriguing and hypocracy governed the drama played out on the stage of Versailles.

You may care to keep all this in mind and try to imagine the internal appearance of the main wings, which would have been compartmented into numerous diminutive suites to house—hutch-like—individual courtiers and their families; and perhaps even get wind of the malodorous state of that largely unwashed aristocratic society.

Under Louis XV a series of royal apartments, decorated in the current style, were incorporated; and one of the colonnaded pavilions in the entrance court, the interior of the opera-house and the Petit Trianon were built by Jacques-Ange Gabriel. Louis XVI redecorated a suite of apartments for Marie-Antoinette and built the 'rustic village' or Hameau.

Not all visitors from England were impressed by Versailles. The poet Thomas Gray, in 1739, wrote of it as 'a huge heap of littleness'; Dr Johnson, in 1775, was more interested by the menagerie than the palace; Smollett (1763), described it as a 'most fantastic composition of magnificence and littleness, taste and foppery'.

The independence of the United States was formally recognised by England, France and Spain in the Treaty of Versailles, signed in 1783. The meeting of the Assembly of the States-General was held in Versailles in 1789, where on 20 June the deputies of the Third Estate constituted themselves into the National Assembly. On 6 October a volatile mob, some 7000 strong, led by the women of Les Halles, marched to Versailles and forced the royal family to return with them to Paris, where they were confined to the Tuileries. The place was then pillaged.

In 1792, when Richard Twiss visited Versailles, he found it almost bare: glasses, tapestries and pictures removed. It had been uninhabited for over two years, and the Grand Canal—which Arthur Young in 1787 remarked 'was not in such good repair as a farmer's horsepond'—was quite dry. In 1814 the palace was occupied by Tsar Alexander I and Friedrich Wilhelm III of Prussia. Under the Restoration, the second colonnaded pavilion was completed by Dufour, but the building later deteriorated from neglect. Louis-Philippe did irreparable damage to the château in housing a pretentious museum here, containing few canvases of any importance and reflecting his prodigious lack of taste.

In the Franco-Prussian War Versailles became the HQ of the German armies operating against Paris, who had met near St.-Germain-en-Laye, when encircling the capital. The château was used as a hospital and Moltke occupied No. 38 Blvd de la Reine. On 18 January 1871, Wilhelm I of Prussia was crowned German Emperor in the Galerie des Glaces; on 26 January the peace preliminaries were signed at Bismarck's quarters at 20 Rue de Provence. In 1871–75 the National Assembly sat in the opera-house, and here the Third Republic was confirmed on 25 February 1875. The general restoration of the complex began after the appointment of Pierre de Nolhac as curator in 1887.

During the First World War Versailles was the seat of the Allied War Council, and the Peace Treaty with Germany was signed in the Galerie des Glaces on 28 June 1919. Further extensive restorations were made in 1928–32, thanks largely to the donations of the Rockefeller Foundation, and were continued after the Second World War under the curatorship of Gerald van der Kemp. During that war, the Allied GHQ was at Versailles from September 1944 until the following May, and many buildings were requisitioned by the military, which hardly improved them.

The château was the birthplace of Louis XV (1710–74), Louis XVI (1754–93), Louis XVIII (1755–1824) and Charles X (1757–1836).

The wide Avenues de St.-Cloud, de Paris and de Sceaux converge on the Pl. d'Armes, east of the château, bounded to the east by the **Grandes Ecuries** (south) and the **Petites Ecuries** (north), the royal stables, built by Mansart in 1679–85 to accommodate 200 carriages and 2400 horses. Communards were incarcerated here in 1871.

Their façades have been restored, and the Petites Ecuries converted into studios for the restoration of paintings in the national collections. They are also used for the storage of sculptures formerly in the gardens which have been replaced by casts. These will be displayed eventually in the projected museum (and carriage museum) to be installed here.

Flanking the gateway to the château, with Mansart's original grille, are groups of sculpture: (right) France victorious over the Empire by Marsy, and over Spain by Girardon; and left, Peace by Tuby and Abundance by Coysevox. The Avant-Cour or Cour des Ministres is flanked by detached wings once assigned to secretaries of state. Beyond the equestrian statue of Louis XIV (1837) is the Cour Royale, between two colonnaded pavilions dating from 1772 (right) and 1829.

In the time of Louis XIV, only those who possessed the honours of the Louvres—those called 'cousin' by the king, and who had the right to bring their coach or chair or liveried servants into the great Courtyard of the Louvre—could enter this court in a similar fashion.

The **˙˙CHATEAU DE VERSAILLES**. The visitors' entrance for individuals is in the Cour de la Chapelle, just north of the Pavillon Gabriel. Groups enter at the north side of the Cour Royale. Before entering, walk over to the Cour de Marbre, a deep, marble-paved recess at the end of the Cour Royale; this was the courtyard of Louis XIII's château and the nucleus of the whole, before being transformed by Le Vau and Mansart.

The information and ticket-offices, cloakroom (obligatory for umbrellas, parcels, etc.) and bookstalls are in the Vestibule Gabriel (**R23**).

Ground Floor. Adjacent to the Entrance Hall is the Vestibule de la Chapelle, with handsome carved and gilded doors and containing a marble relief by Nicolas and Guillaume Coustou of Louis XIV crossing the Rhine. From here you get a view of the **Chapel** (open only for occasional services; enquire at the information desk), with its colonnade of Corinthian columns, begun by Jules-Hardouin Mansart in 1699 and completed in 1710 by Robert de Cotte. The high altar is of marble and bronze with sculptures by Van Clève, above which is the organ. François Couperin was one of the great organists who played here. The central ceiling-painting is by Antoine Coypel, and above the royal pew is a Descent of the Holy Ghost by Jouvenet.

The 17C Gallery (Salles du Dixseptième Siècle)—at present not too well lit—consists of 21 rooms on two floors. It contains an impressive collection of portraits and historical scenes from the accession of the Bourbons to the throne of France to the death of Louis XIV.

R1. Anon., Henri IV in armour, and members of the royal family, including Rubens, Mary de Médicis. **R2**. Philippe de Champaigne, Card. Richelieu. **R3** is devoted to the Jansenists of Port-Royal, with Philippe de Champaigne, Angélique Arnauld and the architect Jacques Lemercier. **R4**. Anon. Card. Mazarin. **R5**. Portraits of the sculptors Jacques Sarrazin and Michel Angier, and the artists Jean Nocret and Samuel Bernard. **R7**. Portraits of Molière, Racine, La Fontaine, Le Brun, Le Nôtre, Louis le Vau, Couperin, Mme de Sévigné, Mme Dacier, and Jules Hardouin-Mansart by François de Troy. **R8**. Views of Versailles by Pierre-Denis Martin, and of this and other royal châteaux by Van der Meulen. **R9**. Carrousel at the Tuileries (6 June 1662) and Portraits of La Grande Mademoiselle, Henriette d'Angleterre and several court beauties painted by the Beaubrun brothers. **R10**. Portraits of members of the royal family, including Beaubrun, Marie-Thérèse; Nocret, Anne of Austria; and Le Brun, Turenne. **R11**. Claude Lefebvre, Colbert; Philippe Lallemand, Charles Perrault; and Gabriel de Rochechouart.

At the far end of this gallery is the Foyer de l'Opéra, retaining its 18C decoration by Pajou. Off the parallel Galerie de Pierre, to the right, displaying several good sculptures, are the Salles des Croisades, etc. (RR17–21), of very slight interest.

The **Opéra**, or Salle de Spectacles, although planned in the 1680s, was built for Louis XV by Gabriel in 1753–70. It was first used on the occasion of the marriage of the Dauphin (Louis XVI) and Marie-Antoinette, when Lully's 'Perseus' was performed.

It was later repainted in the poor taste of the period of Louis-Philippe, and in 1855 was the scene of a banquet given in honour of Queen Victoria.

Modelled on the King of Sardinia's theatre in Turin, it is a perfect example of Louis XV decoration, having been skilfully restored (1955–57) by Japy, even the upholstery being copied from the original specifications. Seating 700 spectators and with a stage second in size only to the Paris Opéra, it is now reserved for rare gala performances.

The mid 19C Questel Staircase ascends to the FIRST FLOOR and **RR12–13**, with battle-scenes by Van der Meulen and an Equestrian portrait of Louis XIV in 1672, by Houasse. **R14**. Views of royal châteaux: St.-Germain and Vincennes by J.-B. Martin, Marly and Trianon by P.-D. Martin, St.-Cloud by Allegrain; also a fine bust by Nicolas Coustou of Colbert. **R15**. Self-portraits by Antoine Coypel, Largillierre and Rigaud; Rigaud's portrait of the sculptor Martin Desjardins; Belle, François de Troy; Largillierre, Nicolas Coustou, among others. **R16**. Mignard, Mme de Maintenon, and the Marquis de Villacerf; Ferdinand Elle, Mme de Maintenon and her niece; and of Mignard by Rigaud. **R17**. Mignard, Family portrait of the Dauphin and Marie-Anne-Christine de Bavière and their sons (the Ducs de Bourgogne, d'Anjou and de Berry). **R18**. Rigaud, Marquis de Dangeau. **R19**. Princesses, among them the Duchesse de Bourgogne in a red dress, by Gobert. **R20**. Antoine Benoist, wax portrait of Louis XIV aged 68. **R21**. Rigaud, the Duchesse d'Orléans.

The Upper Vestibule **(R4)**, with figures of the Virtues by various sculptors, provides a striking view of the Chapel and Royal Gallery, the door of which has a chased lock by Desjardins.

Conveniently visited from the adjoining Salon d'Hercule (see below) is the Hall of the States General **(R2)**, near the head of the Grand Escalier, which formerly served as a foyer to the theatre.

The Salon d'Hercule **(R5)**, was fitted up by Louis XV in the Louis XIV

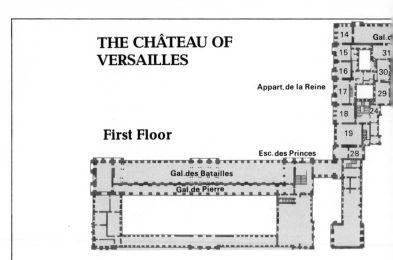

THE CHÂTEAU OF VERSAILLES

First Floor

Appart. de la Reine

Esc. des Princes

Gal. des Batailles

Gal. de Pierre

14
Gal. d
15
31
16
30
17
29
18
24
19
28

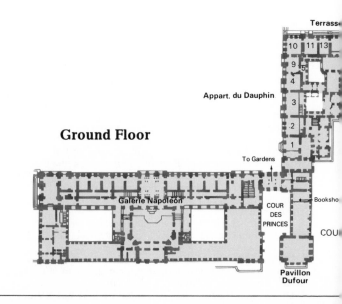

Ground Floor

Appart. du Dauphin

Galerie Napoléon

To Gardens

COUR DES PRINCES

Booksho

COU

Pavillon Dufour

Terrass

10 11 13
9 5
4
3
2
1

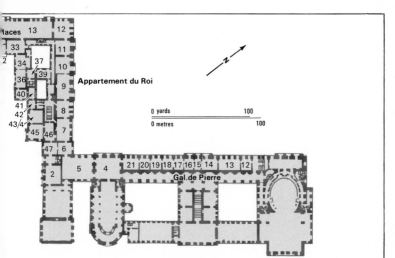

laces   13   12
33
2   34   37
39
36
40
41
42
43/4   45   46
47   6
2   5   4   21 20 19 18 17 16 15 14   13   12   Gal.de Pierre

Appartement du Roi

0 yards   100
0 metres   100

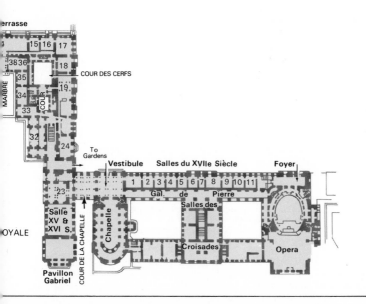

errasse
4   15 16   17
18   COUR DES CERFS
38 36
35
34   19
33   COUR
32
24

MARBRE

To
Gardens   **Vestibule**   **Salles du XVIIe Siècle**   **Foyer**

23   1   2   3   4   5   6   7   8   9 10 11
Gal.   de   Pierre
Salles des

**Salle
XV &
XVI S.**

OYALE

Chapelle

Croisades   **Opera**

COUR DE LA CHAPELLE

**Pavillon
Gabriel**

style. The elaborate decorations were sculpted by Antoine Vassé (1729–34). On the ceiling is the Apotheosis of Hercules by François Lemoyne; after three years' work (1733–36), he committed suicide on its completion. Swiss Guards used to be posted here to prevent the intrusion into the State Apartments of 'those freshly marked with smallpox, the shabbily dressed, petitioners, begging friars and dogs'.

The **Salon de l'Abondance** (**R6**)—used as a refreshment room at royal receptions—is the first of the **GRANDS APPARTEMENTS DU ROI** (King's State Apartments), which, although they have lost their original furniture, have kept their original decorations of marble inlay, sculptured and gilded bronzes, carved doors and painted ceilings, executed under the supervision of Charles le Brun. The ceiling-painting here is by Houasse (restored). The portraits are those of Louis XIV's eldest son, the Dauphin, and of his grandsons, the Duc de Bourgogne and Philip V of Spain, all by Rigaud; and those of Louis XV by J.-B. van Loo.

The **Salon de Vénus** (**R7**), named after its painted ceiling (also by Houasse), is noteworthy for its marble decorations in the early Louis XIV style. The carved doors are by Caffieri; above are bronze bas-reliefs. The mural decorations of this salon (and the succeeding one) are original. In the central alcove is a statue of Louis XIV in 'Roman' costume and wig, by Jean Warin; on either side of the room are trompe-l'oeil paintings by Jacques Rousseau.

The **Salon de Diane** (**R8**), the former billiard room, has a ceiling by Gabriel Blanchard and contains a bust of Louis XIV (then aged 27) by Bernini (1665).

The **Salon de Mars** (**R9**), once the Salle des Gardes, later a gaming-room and subsequently a ballroom and concert-room, has a ceiling by Audran, Jouvenet and Houasse. The *dessus de portes* are by Simon Vouet. The portraits of Louis XV and Marie Leczinska are by Carle van Loo.

The **Salon de Mercure** (**R10**), a card-room under Louis XIV and where after his death that monarch lay in state for eight days, has a ceiling by J.-B. Champaigne. The tapestry, by Le Brun, is one of the earliest woven at the Gobelins (1668–72); the clock, with automata, of 1706, is by Antoine Morand.

The **Salon d'Apollon** (**R11**), the former throne-room (in which the thone was silver), is the last of the King's State Apartments. In the centre of the ceiling, by Charles de la Fosse, is Louis XIV (the 'Roi Soleil') as Apollo in a chariot escorted by the Seasons. The portrait of the king in royal regalia is Rigaud's copy of that in the Louvre.

The three following rooms—the Galerie des Glaces, with its antechambers, the Salons de la Guerre and de la Paix—together form a grandiose decorative ensemble. The **Salon de la Guerre** (**R12**), completed in 1678, keeps its original decoration of coloured marble and bronze, and contains three of the six original busts of Roman emperors, bequeathed by Mazarin. Over the mantlepiece is a stucco relief of Louis XIV on horseback by Antoine Coysevox.

The ceiling-painting, the first of a series designed by Charles le Brun, represents France victorious, with a thunderbolt in one hand and a laurel-wreathed portrait of Louis XIV in the other; in the lunettes appear Bellona in anger, and figures of the defeated Empire, Holland and Spain.

The *****Galerie des Glaces**, or Grande Galerie (**R13**), 73m long, 10.5m wide and 12.3m high, is a masterpiece of the Louis XIV style. It was begun by Jules Hardouin-Mansart in 1678, and its decoration, from designs by Le Brun, was completed in 1686. Among the artists employed were Caffieri,

Coysevox, Le Comte and Tuby, for the sculptures; Cucci for the mirror frames; and Ladoireau for the trophies on the walls.

The gallery is lit by 17 windows looking on to the park, and facing these are as many bevelled mirrors of equal size. The red marble pilasters have bronze capitals decorated with cocks' heads, *fleurs-de-lys* and suns. The cornice of gilded stucco is adorned with crowns and the collars of the Orders of the Saint-Esprit and St. Michael. The marble statues of Venus, Paris, Mercury and Minerva in the niches are copies from the antique; some other statues are also copies of originals. Twenty silvered bronze and Bohemian glass chandeliers illuminate the gallery.

The central ceiling-painting represents Louis XIV omnipotent, while the numerous other paintings depict the subjection of Holland, the Empire and Spain, the Peace imposed by Louis on his enemies, his embassies abroad, the Protection of the Arts and of the People, and the great Foundations established during his reign.

You now enter the **Salon de la Paix (R14)**, the queen's card-room. The ceiling completes Le Brun's scheme, depicting France bringing the benefits of peace to Europe, etc. Over the chimneypiece (left unfinished by Le Brun) is a painting by Lemoyne (1729), showing Louis XV following his great-grandfather's example as the bringer of peace.

The **Chambre de la Reine (R15)**, the first of the **GRANDS APPARTEMENTS DE LA REINE** (Queen's State Apartments), has been restored to its appear-ance when Marie-Antoinette fled from it on the morning of 6 October 1789. The chimneypiece has been brought back from the Trianon; the silk hangings were copied at Lyon from pieces of the original material supplied by Lyon in 1787. The balustrade is a reconstruction. Both Marie-Thérèse and Marie Leczinska died in this room (1683 and 1768, respectively), and the confinements took place here of the queens of France. The jewel cabinet of Marie-Antoinette is by Schwerdfeger (1787); her bust was executed by Félix Lecomte. Above the doors are allegorical paintings of the children of Louis XV by Natoire and by De Troy; the grisaille panels of the ceiling are by Boucher.

R16, the **Salon des Nobles**, or **Salon de la Reine**, was the queen's presence-chamber. The ceiling is by Michel Corneille (died 1708); the tapestry portrait of Louis XIV is by Cozette (after L.-M. van Loo).

The **Antechamber (R17)**, where the king and queen dined in public, was formerly the Queen's Guardroom. The portrait of Marie-Antoinette in 1779 is by Mme Vigée-Lebrun, who also painted that of the queen with her children (1787). Three other portraits, by Adélaïde Labille-Guiard, depict the Duchess of Parma, and Mesdames Elizabeth, Adélaïde and Victoire (Louis XIV's aunts). It was in this room on 1 January 1764 that Mozart, not quite eight years old, was invited with his father to attend the Grand Couvert. Leopold Mozart records that 'Wolfgang stayed the whole time at the queen's table chattering almost continually, kissing her hands and eating from the dishes she offered him. The queen (Marie Leszinska) speaks German as well as we do and since the king does not understand a word, the queen translated everything Wolfgang said'.

The **Salle des Gardes de la Reine (R18)**, with marble decoration of the period of Louis XIV, retains its ceiling by Noël Coypel. It was here that the revolutionary mob, having ascended the adjacent staircase, burst in, and where three of the Swiss Guards died in the queen's defence.

The Chambre de la Reine leads to the ***Petits Appartements de la Reine** (guided tour), the small and cramped private suite of Marie-Antoinette, retaining its superb decoration, among them the Boudoir or Petite Mérid-ienne, with its gilded woodwork and mirror-frames, and the Library, with imitation bookshelves, which were designed by Richard Mique (c 1781). The Small Library was used by the ladies-in-waiting. In the Salon de la Reine, with elaborate decoration by the brothers Rousseau, she received her intimate friends, and her musicians, Gluck and Grétry, and sat to Mme Vigée-Lebrun for her portraits.

To the left of R18 is the landing of the Escalier de Marbre, or de la Reine, built by Le Vau and Mansart, with a perspective painting in the Italian style. Across the landing is a Loggia overlooking the Cour de Marbre, in which (right) a door admits to the Apartments of Mme de Maintenon (see below); to the left is the Salle des Gardes du Roi (see below).

R19, previously the Grande Salle des Gardes but now referred to as the **Salle du Sacre**, has been restored since its mutilation and decoration by Louis-Philippe. The ceiling-painting is by Callet and the *dessus de portes* by Gérard; on the walls are huge paintings depicting Napoléon presenting eagles in the Champ-de-Mars (1804), and his crowning of the Empress Josephine at Notre-Dame, both by David; and Murat at the battle of Aboukir (1799) by Gros.

R20 leads to the Salle de 1792 (**R21**), containing military portraits, and originally the 'Salle des Marchands', to which vendors of goods were admitted for the convenience of the inmates of the palace. The Escalier des Princes (**R22**), by Mansart, gave access to the south wing, once reserved for the princes of the blood.

Beyond this point extends the Galerie des Batailles, nearly 120m long, constructed under Louis-Philippe by combining most of the rooms on the first floor, displaying a sad selection of huge canvases representing French military achievements—perhaps the only one of note being The Battle of Taillebourg, by Delacroix. Thackeray considered them among 'the worst pictures that eye ever looked on'.

Adjoining the landing of the Escalier de la Reine is the Escalier de Stuc, which ascends to the SECOND FLOOR where, in the Attique de Chimay and Attique du Midi, are displayed an outstanding *Collection of Historical Paintings illustrating the early Napoleonic period. It may be necessary to make a special request, in advance, to visit these rooms.

Several rooms contain views of the many battles fought in the Revolutionary and Napoleonic campaigns, several of them by 'war artists' of the period, among them Louis-François Lejeune (1775–1848), Giuseppe-Pietro Bagetti (1746–1824), Nicolas-Antoine Taunay (1755–1830), Gén. Bacler d'Albe (1761–1824) and Carle Vernet (1758–1836), together with minor figures such as Hippolyte Lecomte, A.-A. Morel, R.-T. Berthon, F.-H. Mulard and Didier Boguet. Among the more remarkable are *Bacler d'Albe's* Arcole, and Lejeune's Battles of the Pyramids, Lodi and Marengo, and Napoléon visiting the bivouacs before Austerlitz; and *Adolph Roehn,* Napoléon at Wagram (a night scene). Also notable are *Gros,* Napoléon at Arcole; one of five copies made by *David* of his Napoléon crossing the Alps; *J.-F. Hue,* Napoléon visiting camp at Boulogne; *A.P. Mongin,* Passage of the army through the defile of Albaredo. Another section is devoted to the Peninsular campaigns, among them, *Lejeune's* Crossing the Somosierra, Assault on the monastery of Sta. Engracia, Zaragoza, and the battle of Chiclana (Barrosa) together with Taunay, Crossing the Guadarrama and F.-J. Heim, The defence of the castle of Burgos. Others depict the disastrous Russian campaign.

The war at sea is illustrated in *P.-J. Gilbert's* Combat between 'La

Canonniére' and 'The Tremendous' (1806) among other naval scenes, together with *George Healy's* copies of Hoppner's portraits of Lord Nelson and Lord St. Vincent, and of Lawrence's William Pitt, and *M.-I. van Bree*, Launching 'Le Friedland'.

Portraits of the imperial family are dominated by *Gérard's* Napoléon as Emperor of the French, also his 'Madame Mère'; *Robert Lefèvre*, Portrait Napoléon; *F.-A. Lethière*, Portrait of Josephine; *Vigée-Lebrun*, Portrait of Marie-Annunciade-Caroline Bonaparte; *Joseph Franque*, Marie-Louise and the King of Rome; apart from other members of the family.

Notable among other portraits of the period are an unfinished pastel of Marie-Antoinette by *Alexandre Kucharsky*; *François Kinson*, Bernadotte; *Charles Meynier*, Ney; *Levévre*, Augereau and Baron Denon; *J.-B.-F. Desoria*, Letourneur, member of the Directoire; *Girodet*, Chateaubriand and J.-B. Bellay, Deputy for St. Dominique; *David*, Pope Pius VII; *Gérard*, Comte Regnaud de St. Jean d'Angely and Murat. Also of interest are a series of miniatures by Louis Gauffier (1761–1801) and particularly the ***Collection of small portrait sketches** (or reduced versions of larger works) by Gérard.

The larger historical portraits and scenes are displayed on the GROUND FLOOR of the south wing, but although containing canvases by Gros, Horace Vernet and Carle Vernet, they impress more by their size than as great works of art.

Other rooms, devoted to the Restoration of the Bourbons, the July Monarchy, Second Empire and Third Republic are on the SECOND FLOOR of the north wing and include Horace Vernet's Louis-Philippe and his sons in front of the Château de Versailles; Lawrence, portrait of the Duchesse de Berry; Winterhalter, Louis-Philippe; Ingres, the Duc d'Orléans; and Flandrin, Napoléon III: but again, it is advisable to enquire in advance if these rooms may be visited.

The **Appartements du Roi** (guided tour) are approached by ascending the Escalier de la Reine to enter **R24**.

To the right is a suite of four rooms known as those of Mme de Maintenon (1635–1719), who married the poet Scarron in 1652, was widowed in 1660 and later became Louis XIV's confidante. As his morganatic wife, she occupied the suite from 1684 to 1715. Most of the business of state was transacted in her bedchamber, where every evening the king would work in her presence with one of his ministers before entering **R27**, where his family would gather. It was in the latter room also that he would enjoy listening to perfomances of music; and where Racine's 'Ester' was played before the king and in 1702 his 'Athalie' performed by the princes and princesses. No trace remains of the former decoration of Mme de Maintenon's apartments, which are now occasionally used for temporary exhibitions.

From the Salle du Gardes du Roi (R29) you enter **R30**, an antechamber in which Louis XIV supped in public at 10 o'clock, with his back to the fireplace. The second antechamber, adjacent (**R31**) is known as the Salon de l'Oeil-de-Boeuf because of its oval 'bull's-eye' window. It was in this room that the courtiers would wait for admission to the king's *lever*. Three doors open onto the Hall of Mirrors; and another on the left leads into the Queen's Apartments. Stairs behind a mirrored door descend to those of the Dauphin. The decorations are original, including the stucco frieze showing children's games on a gold background by Van Cleve, Hurtrelle and Flamen, among others. A curious picture by Nocret represents the royal family in mythological costume.

The lavishly restored **Chambre du Roi (R32)**, Louis XIV's bedchamber (in which he died on 1 September 1715), overlooks the Cour de Marbre. Here the ceremonious *lever* and *coucher* of the king, who used to lunch daily at a little table placed before the middle window, took place. It was from the balcony of this room that Marie-Antoinette and Louis XVI, at La Fayette's suggestion, showed themselves to the mob on 6 October 1789. The decorations of carved wood and the balustrade separating the (reconstructed) bed from the rest of the room have been regilded, but are in part original: most of the rich brocades and other fabrics are of recent manufacture, woven at Lyon, scrupulously copying the original materials. The sculpture of gilded stucco above is by Nicolas Coustou. The chimney-pieces date from 1761, with bronzes by Caffieri; the bust of Louis XIV is by Coysevox. Note the self-portrait by Van Dyck.

The adjacent **Cabinet du Conseil (R33)**, dates in its present form from 1755, with *boiseries* by Antoine Rousseau. Note the two Sèvres vases and the table on which the Treaty of Versailles was signed.

You now enter the **Cabinets du Roi** or **Petits Appartements du Roi**, a series of rooms constructed by Louis XV in 1735 to provide a retreat from the tedious etiquette of his court. **R34** was the Chambre de Louis XV, his bedroom, in which he died of smallpox on 10 May 1774; with *boiseries* by Jacques Verberckt and a bust of his mother, the Duchesse de Bourgogne, by Coysevox. **R36**, the Cabinet de la Pendule, derives its name from Passemant's clock, placed here in 1754, executed by Dauthiau, with chased designs by Caffieri, surmounted by a crystal globe marking the phases of the sun, moon and planets: note also the barometer by J.-B. Lemaire.

The Cabinet des Chiens (**R37**), with a frieze of hunting scenes and decorated with flower-paintings, was occupied by lackeys and the king's favourite hounds. On the staircase, Damiens attempted to assassinate Louis XV in 1757. Adjacent is a Salle à Manger (**R39**), overlooking the much-altered Cour des Cerfs.

Returning through **R36** (in which also note the meridian line marked on the floor) you enter **R40**, the Cabinet de Travail, with *boiseries* by Verberckt (1753) and a Savonnerie carpet; the ornate desk, the Bureau du Roi, ordered by the king in 1760 for this room, was designed by Oeben and Riesener (1769), with bronzes by Duplessis, Winant and Hervieux. **R41** was Louis XV's private study.

Adjoining is the **Cabinet de Mme Adélaïde (R42)**, also with *boiseries* by Verberckt, where, in December 1763, Mozart played the harpsichord before Mme Adélaïde (1732–1800, 4th daughter of Louis XV) and other members of the family. The Bibliothèque de Louis XVI (**R43**, with Louis-XV furniture) was decorated by Antoine Rousseau. The chimney-piece is by Boizot and Gouthière, and the candelabrum is attributed to Thomire.

The **Salon des Porcelaines (R45)**, with a desk by Leleu, was so called because of the annual sale of Sèvres ware arranged for the Court, which also occupied the two following rooms. These, the Salle de Billiard and Salon des Jeux (**RR46–47**), where Louis XIV's collections of paintings and gems were displayed, later became part of Mme Adélaïde's suite.

The adjoining staircase ascends to the **Apartments of Mme du Barry** (guided tour) on the second floor. (Mme du Barry (1743–93, lived here from 1769 to 1774 only.) The beautiful *boiseries* have been restored and repainted in their original colours. The attic floor contains the diminutive **Apartments of Mme de Pompadour**. Mme de Pompadour (1721–64) occupied the suite from 1745 to 1750 when, no longer the king's mistress but still his confidante, she moved to the ground floor.

A flight of stairs, built by Louise-Philippe, descends to the ground floor, from which a passage leads to the gardens: see below.

From the corresponding passage on the far side of the Cour Royale starts the guided tour of the **Appartements du Dauphin et de la Dauphine, et des Mesdames**, the restoration of which was completed in 1986. Looking out onto the gardens, they were occupied at various times by the Regent Orléans (1674–1723), who died here, and the sons and daughters of Louis XV. They have been repeatedly altered and much of the original decoration was spoiled—when not destroyed—by Louis-Philippe.

R1 contains Rigaud, Louis XV as a child; Santerre, The Regent Orléans; Largillierre, Louis-Urbain Le Pelletier; Pierre-Denis Martin (le Jeune), Departure of Louis XV from the Lit de Justice and The Consecration of Louis XV at Reims; and anon. Portraits of the Regent Orléans and of the Duc de Chartres. **R2**. Several portraits by Alexis Simon Belle, among them Marie-Anne-Victoire (Maria-Anna-Victoria; Infanta of Spain, betrothed to Louis XV when she was three, who in 1729 married the future José of Portugal); attributed to Pierre Gobert (after Nattier), Peter the Great of Russia (who visited Versailles in May 1717); François Stiemart, Marie Leczinska; J.-B. van Loo and Parrocel, Louis XV on horseback; J.-L. Lemoyne, Bust of Philippe, Duc d'Orléans. **R3**. Jean-Baptiste van Loo, Stanislas Leczinski and Catherine Opalinska, Queen of Poland; Belle, Marie Leczinska and the Dauphin; Rigaud, Samuel Bernard the banker; Stiemart (after Rigaud), Cardinal Fleury; School of Rigaud, Philibert Orry; Tocqué, Marquis de Matignon. **R4**. Bedroom of the Dauphine, with a *lit au polonaise* and containing a child's coach. Louis XVI, Louis XVIII and Charles X were born in this room, which was also the bedroom of Marie-Antoinette on her arrival in France from Vienna in May 1770. **R5** (green decoration), with Oudry, The Seasons, and Nattier, Marie-Josèphe de Saxe. **R9**, a small library, with Joseph Vernet, The times of day (seascape).

R10, at the corner of the building, has a splendid view of the gardens. Regilt, and with chairs by Georges Jacob, it contains portraits of the daughters of Louis XV by Nattier. **R11** (also with green decoration), the Regent's Study, where he died, and later the bedroom of the Dauphin Louis (1729–65), son of Louis XV, with Tocqué, Marie-Thérèse-Antoinette-Raphaelle d'Espagne; Louis-Michel van Loo, Felipe V of Spain and Elisabeth Farnese; Nattier, Louise-Elisabeth de France (Duchess of Parma). Note the *boiseries* by Verberckt and the marble chimney piece with figures by Caffieri, and attributed to Guillaume Coustou, Bust of Marie Leczinska. **R13**, retaining traces of Louis XIV decoration; Nattier, Marie Leczinska, and Mme Adélaïde.

R14, the Galerie Basse, below the Galerie des Glaces, has been completely altered since the reign of Louis XIV, when Molière gave several of his plays here, including the first performance of 'Tartuffe' (1664); it has recently been remodelled and contains several false arches.

R15 (once part of a suite of bathrooms) was later occupied by Mme de Montespan, Mme de Pompadour and, from 1769, by Mme Victoire (an accomplished musician to whom Mozart dedicated his first six harpsichord sonatas in 1784). It displays L.-M. van Loo, Duc de Choiseul (le Grand Choiseul), Self-portrait when painting that of his father Jean-Baptiste; and Tocque, Abel-France Poisson, Marquis de Marigny (Mme de Pompadour's brother); J.-B. Charpentier, The Cup of Chocolate; and Barthémy Ollivier,

The English tea-party with the Prince de Conti. **R16**, with *dessus des portes* by Oudry, and containing a commode by Riesener. **R17**, with a harpsichord by Blanchet. **R18**, with good *boiseries* and furniture, and Nattier, Mme Adélaïde. **R19**, with a commode by Foullet. **R21**, the first of Mme Adélaïde's apartments, with *dessus des portes* by J.-B. Restout of the The Seasons. **R22**, in which Mme de Pompadour died; the chairs are by Foliot; the bust of the Dauphin by Pajou. **R23** contains Nattier, Anne-Henriette, second daughter of Louis XV, playing a viola da gamba; a Gagliano violin belonging to Mme Adélaïde, and a small organ.

From **R24**, with restored 'perspective' decoration, you cross the foot of the Louis-Philippe staircase, which regrettably replaced the former Grand Escalier (a maquette of which is displayed), to enter an inner suite of rooms. One contains a painting of Marie-Antoinette, aged ten, dancing at Schönbrunn, and a remarkable suite of mahogany 'Etruscan' chairs by Georges Jacob, formerly at Rambouillet. **R32**. Roslin, Portraits of the Dauphin (son of Louis XV) in uniform; the Marquis de Marigny, and Joseph-Marie Terray; Mengs, a copy of his portrait of Carlos III of Spain. **R33**. Duplessis, a copy of his portrait of Louis XVI in 1776. **R34**. Batoni, The Bailli de Suffren. **R35**. Two Views of Versailles in 1775 by Hubert Robert; Gautier-Dagoty, Marie-Antoinette at Versailles. **R36**. Portraits by Vigée-Lebrun, including Marie-Antoinette holding a Rose (1784) and Labille-Guiard, Mme Elisabeth, the king's sister.

Passing through **R38**, formerly a bedroom, you enter the Marble Vestibule (**R37**), which had once served as a library, its 16 columns having been boxed in, off which is **R39**, a bathroom with aquatic decoration. From the vestibule you skirt the Galerie Basse and descend five steps to reach **R40**, the first antechamber of the Dauphin's apartment's (off which a spiral stair ascends to the Queen's private apartments), with a portrait of the Comte d'Angiviller by Duplessis. **R41**, a guardroom, contains Vigée-Lebrun, Marie-Antoinette seated (1788) and Labille-Guiard, the Prince de Bauffrémont. **R43–44** are being restored.

Château de Versailles

The *GARDENS OF VERSAILLES are conveniently approached by passages leading north and south of the Cour Royale.

André le Nôtre (1613–1708), the celebrated landscape-gardener (responsible for Greenwich Park, London and the Quirinal and Vatican Gardens, Rome), designed the gardens for Louis XIV. The fountains and hydraulic machinery were the work of Jules Hardouin-Mansart and the engineer François Francini, while the sculptural decoration was carried out under the supervision of Le Brun and Mignard.

The gardens were first laid out in 1661–68. The preliminary work of levelling and draining the site was prodigious, and thousands of trees were brought here from all parts. Inspired by Italian originals, interpreted with an amplitude and harmony hitherto unknown, Versailles is the masterpiece of French gardening. In their general lines and their 'classical' sculptural decoration, the gardens remain as they were planned, but it was not until the 18C that the planting of trees was developed to its present extent, so that what we now see are basically the gardens of Louis XV and Louis XVI.

They are essentially formal. Carefully planned vistas and straight tree-lined walks, their artificial lakes and ponds, arranged with geometrical precision, their groves and clumps of trees, lawns and terraces all interspersed with innumerable statues and vases of marble and bronze, and embellished with a variety of fountains. A number of the original statues, damaged by pollution or vandalised, have been placed in the Ecuries (stables) for safety, and replaced by casts.

The park and gardens were very seriously ravaged in the storm of February 1990, when some 1500 trees were blown down. The entire restoration has now been put in hand; but the replanting of trees (possibly as many as 20,000) will take several years.

Admission. The gardens and park are normally open from 07.00 until dusk to pedestrians (no picnics); cars are admitted to the park on payment, and to the Trianons (via the Blvd de la Reine, north of the Château).

The **Fountains** play on certain Sundays in May–October only. For further information contact the Tourist Office, 7 Rue des Réservoirs, just north of the Château.

The most direct pedestrian approach to the **Grand Trianon** is to follow the Allée d'Eau (see below), leading north from the terrace behind the central block of the palace to the Grille de Neptune, then turn left and veer slightly north west along the Av. de Trianon, approximately 20 minutes' brisk walk. By taking this route only, you see little of the main gardens. An alternative approach is to bear half left (north west) on reaching the Grand Canal (see below and on plan). This may be reserved for the return journey or vise versa.

The central axis of the main terrace commands splendid *views, and the terrace itself is adorned with bronze statues after the antique, cast by the Keller brothers, amongst them, Apollo, Bacchus and Silenus; also marble vases of War by Antoine Coysevox, and Peace by Tuby.

Beyond the Parterre d'Eau, two large ornamental pools decorated with bronzes (1690), are the **Marches de Latone**, monumental flights of steps, with an impressive view of the château and, in the opposite direction, a famous vista of the gardens. Flanking these steps are the Fontaines de Diane (right) and du Point-du-Jour (Dawn). By the former are statues of Air by Etienne le Hongre, and Diana the Huntress by Martin Desjardins.

On the right (north) of the terrace extend the Parterre du Nord, where the original design of Le Nôtre has been largely respected. Just beyond is the Fontaine de la Pyramide (in lead) by François Girardon, and among the sculptures in the cross-walk (left) is Winter, also by Girardon. The Allée d'Eau, designed by Perrault and Le Brun (1676–88), with its groups of children, leads directly to the **Bassin de Neptune** (1740), the largest fountain-basin in the gardens. The Bosquet des Trois Fontaines (parallel to the

Allée d'Eau), leads back to the main axis, passing (right) the Bains d'Apollon, within a grove laid out by Hubert Robert under Louis XVI, in a 'romantic' spirit very different from the formal symmetry of Le Nôtre.

The Marches de Latone (see above) descend to the oval **Bassin de Latone**. (Latona, or Leto, mother of Artemis and Apollo, insulted by Lycian peasants, had them turned into frogs by Zeus.)

Further west extends the so-called **Tapis Vert** (or Allée Royale), a lawn 330m long and 36m wide, lined with marble vases and statues, many of them copies from the antique. Note (on the left) Venus by Pierre le Gros and Achilles at Scyros by Vigier. Towards its far end (right) is the entrance to the Bosquet des Dômes, with several statues, including Acis and Galatea by Tuby.

Almost opposite, beyond the far side (south) of the Tapis Vert, in the Bosquet de la Colonnade, is a circle of marble arches by Mansart (1685–88), in the centre of which once stood the Rape of Proserpine by Girardon, now in reserve.

At the far end of the Tapis Vert is the **Bassin d'Apollon**, in the centre of which is the impressive group of Apollo's Chariot by Tuby. To the right is the Petite Venise, where Louis XIV's Venetian gondoliers were housed.

Beyond the Bassin d'Apollon, and separated from the gardens by railings, is the Petit Parc, divided by the **Grand Canal**, 1650m long and 62m wide, the scene of Louis XIV's boating parties. Almost at its central point it is crossed by a transverse arm (c 1070m), extending from the Grand Trianon, to the north, to the few remaining buildings of the former royal Menagerie.

To return to the château, cross the (so-called) 'Salle des Marronniers', a chestnut grove behind the Colonnade, to pass the Bassin de Saturne or de l'Hiver. South of this is the Bassin du Miroir, followed by the Bassin de Bacchus or de l'Automne, with sculptures by Girardon and Marsy. The walk now skirts (right) the **Bosquet de la Reine**, a glade notorious as the scene of the court scandal known as the 'Affair of the Necklace' (Affaire du collier; 1784–85), in which Cardinal de Rohan (seeking the favour of Marie-Antoinette by means of a costly gift) was duped by the Comtesse de la Motte.

The Parterre du Midi leads from here to the château. To the right (south) two flights of steps, known as the Cent Marches, descend alongside the **Orangerie** by Mansart, into which Communards were herded in 1871 prior to their imprisonment.

Further south, beyond the St.-Cyr road, is the Pièce d'Eau des Suisses (682m long by 134m wide), excavated in 1678–82 by the Swiss Guards, many of whom are said to have died of malaria during the operation.

The ***GRAND TRIANON**, a miniature palace designed by Jules Hardouin-Mansart and Robert de Cotte, was built for Louis XIV in 1687 as a retreat from the formality of court life, yet retaining sumptuous marble decorations comparable with those of Versailles itself. It replaced a flimsy summer-house for picnics, tiled inside with blue and white Delftware, and known as the 'Porcelain Trianon', erected on the site of the village of Trianon, which had been razed in 1663.

The buildings, sacked at the Revolution, were redecorated for Napoléon, who frequently stayed there with Marie-Louise, and the Empire furniture which he installed still remains. In 1818 the Duke of Wellington dined here with Louis XVIII. Louis-Philippe did his best to spoil the interior decoration in 1837. A restoration of both Trianons was carried out in 1925–27; the Grand Trianon (again) in 1963–66 and the Petit Trianon more recently.

The accurate work of reproduction of fabrics of the period, undertaken during the

1960s, is admirable, although the protective sheets of plastic detract from the splendid effect intended; however historically irreproachable the decoration may be, a little 'faded glory' would perhaps have been more becoming.

On the left of the courtyard, with the open colonnade or péristyle ahead, is the visitors' entrance. Off the entrance vestibules (**R1**), with views of Versailles and Chambord by Allegrain and Pierre-Denis Martin respectively, and a console table by Jacob-Desmalter. A corridor leads to a small Boudoir (**R2**), containing a gondola-shaped sofa, to the right of which is the splendidly mirrored Salon des Glaces (**R3**), furnished with a handsome set of white and gilt chairs covered with Beauvais tapestry. **R4**, the Salon des Colonnes, with Napoléon's bed (1809) from the Tuileries, later broadened and radically altered by Louis-Philippe. Beyond **R5** (formerly used as a chapel) and **R6**, we cross the open péristyle of Languedoc marble pillars to the RIGHT WING, first entering the circular Drawing-Room (**R8**), with paintings of American flowers and fruit by Desportes. **R11** (Salon de Musique): note the bronze table with Vosges granite top, two consoles by Jacob-Desmalter, and the Beauvais tapestry-covered set of chairs. You next visit the Grand Salon and Malachite Room (**RR12–13**), the latter with a malachite bowl given to Alexander I of Russia after the Treaty of Tilsit in 1807. From the adjoining Salon Frais **R14**, with paintings of Versailles by J.-B. Martin, you turn left into the Grande Galerie (**R16**), decorated by Mansart, with good views south over the terrace. It contains 24 allegorical views, almost all similarly framed, of the Gardens of Versailles and Trianon, 21 by Jean Cotelle (1645–1708), two by Allegrain and one by J.-B. Martin. The suite of rooms beyond, known as the Trianon-sous-Bois, in which Peter the Great lodged in May 1717, is not open to the public.

To the right of the Salon Frais is the Salon des Sources (**R15**), with Views of Versailles by P.-D. Martin (1663–1742) and Charles Chastelain (1672–1740).

The next five rooms (**R17–21**) are visited with a guide. They once formed the Apartments of Mme de Maintenon, and were later occupied by Stanislas Leczinski, former king of Poland (1741), Mme de Pompadour, and Napoléon and Marie-Louise. The remaining rooms (**RR9–10**) were installed on the site of a theatre which stood here until 1703, and from 1845 they formed an apartment for Louis-Philippe's daughter, Louise-Marie, and her husband, Leopold I of Belgium.

The gardens were laid out by Mansart and Le Nôtre. To the west is the Buffet (the main fountain), also designed by Mansart, with bas-reliefs and figures of Neptune and Amphitrite. A bridge leads from the Jardin du Roi, behind the palace, to the gardens of the Petit Trianon.

To the east is the ***PETIT TRIANON** (1751–68) on two floors and attic, unlike the Grand Trianon. It was built by Ange-Jacques Gabriel for Louis XV as a country retreat for himself and Mme de Pompadour, who did not survive its completion. Mme du Barry then occupied it. It was a favourite residence of Marie-Antoinette, and was subsequently occupied by Pauline Borghese, Napoléon's sister. To the left of the courtyard is a chapel.

Many of the rooms in the Petit Trianon retain their original decoration, including chimney-pieces by Guibert in the Dining Room and Grand Salon. In the dining room, traces of a trap-door, through which it was intended that tables would appear ready-laid, are still visible in the floor. The first floor (the Queen's Apartment) and the attic may be visited on a guided tour.

The **Gardens** of the Petit Trianon were originally a ménagerie and botanical garden laid out by Bernard de Jussieu for Louis XV, a keen botanist, but were altered for Marie-Antoinette in the English style (1774–86). Here, so Thicknesse was told, the king 'had a little garden...where he often picks his own salad, makes his own soup, and enjoys the conversation of a few select friends, without the plague, impertinence, and above all, the parade that generally attends royalty'.

The Temple d'Amour by Mique; 1778

To the west of the main building is the Pavillon Français, built in 1751 by Gabriel, with a good view of the façade of the palace. To the north is the Theatre (1780; by Richard Mique), where Marie-Antoinette made her début in court theatricals, beyond which is the octagonal Belvedere (also by Mique), with charming interior decoration by Le Riche, overlooking a small lake. The queen was resting in a grotto here when, on 5 October 1789, she was told the news that a revolting mob had broken into Versailles.

Some few minutes' walk to the north east, on the far side of a larger lake, are remains of the **Hameau**, a theatrical hamlet built in 1783 for Marie-Antoinette to indulge her taste for 'nature', as popularised by Rousseau, although, apart from churning butter, the queen left the work of the farm to real, not royal, peasants. It comprises a mill, the Maison de la Reine (with a dining-room, billiard-room, and card-room, with a kitchen or 'Réchauffoir' behind), and the 'Boudoir' on the right; a Colombier, with pigeon-cote and chicken-run; the Dairy; the 'Tour de Marlborough'; and farm-buildings.

You can return past the Temple d'Amour (1778; by Mique), with its Corinthian colonnade and Mouchy's copy (1780) of Bouchardon's statue of Cupid cutting his bow from the club of Hercules, to return to the courtyard of the Petit Trianon, and the exit.

35 From Paris to St.-Germain-en-Laye Malmaison; Bois-Préau; Musée des Antiquités Nationales; Musée du Prieuré; Maisons-Laffitte

Malmaison may be approached either by road (N13; 7.5km) from the Pont de Neuilly, or on the RER from Auber via Etoile to La Défense, there taking the 158A bus to within a few minutes' walk of the château. It is *not* advisable to take the RER to the Rueil-Malmaison stop, which is some distance from the château.

The *CHATEAU DE MALMAISON was built in 1622 on the site of a leper colony dependent on the Abbey of St.-Denis, which accounts for its name. From 1798 is was the home of Napoléon and Joséphine Beauharnais, remaining her main residence after their divorce. It now contains collections of considerable historic interest, concentrating on the earlier Napoleonic period, the Consulate and on Joséphine and her children. Its annexe (see below) is devoted to Napoléon in exile. The Empire period (1804–15) is covered by the Musée Napoléon I at Fontainebleau; see Rte 40.

The building was enlarged in 1800, and it was here that Joséphine held her literary and artistic salon when Bonaparte was at the height of his power, retiring here after their divorce in December 1809, and devoting herself to gardening. She died here only five years later of a chill caught while doing the honours of the grounds to the allied sovereigns.

Joséphine (Marie-Josèphe Rose) Tascher de la Pagerie (1763–1814), born in Martinique, had married Alexandre, Vicomte de Beauharnais, in December 1779; but in 1794 he was guillotined. She later became the mistress of Barras, among others, before captivating Bonaparte, who married her in 1796, and crowned her Empress in 1804.

Malmaison was later bought by María Cristina of Spain, and in 1861 was acquired by Napoléon III. Despoiled of most of its contents, it was sold in 1896 to the philanthropist Daniel Osiris (1828–1907), who refurnished it and presented the château to the State as a Napoleonic museum.

Malmaison contains superb collections of furniture and fittings, clocks, carpets, porcelain, silver and a variety of objets d'art of the early Napoleonic period: among the furniture are several pieces made specifically for the Consul and his wife by Jacob Frères and other *ébenistes*, and such personal pieces as Joséphine's bed (designed by Jacob-Desmalter), dressing-table, dressing case and embroidery frame, etc. Show-cases display a large number of smaller souvenirs.

The Entrance Vesitibule, in Antique style, contains marble busts of members of the Bonaparte family; a number of others are displayed throughout the building. Several rooms on the ground and first floors retain their original or restored decoration, notably the Salon Doré, with a chimney-piece given by Pope Pius VII (its embellishments torn off by the Prussians occupying the place in 1871), displaying Gérard's Ossian welcoming the dead to Valhalla, and Girodet's Apotheosis of the French who died in the Revolutionary Wars; the Music Room, containing instruments which may have belonged to the Empress; the Dining Room, with its frescoes of Pompeian dancers by Louis Lafitte; and the adjoining Library, with its decoration by Percier and Fontaine, and retaining a number of books from Napoléon's personal collection which, previously widely dispersed, have been purchased and reassembled on their original shelves.

Notable among the portraits in Malmaison are Gérard, Napoléon in grenadier uniform (1804/5), Joséphine seated, and Mme Mère; Isabey's drawing of Napoléon as First Consul at Malmaison; Bacler d'Albe, Gén. Bonaparte (1796/7); attrib. Girodet, Queen Hortense, and the First Consul wearing a black cravat; and another of the same subject by J.-M. Vien le jeune; David's replica of Bonaparte crossing the St.-Bernard Pass; Gros, the First Consul after Marengo; Pierre-Paul Prud'hon, the Empress Joséphine c 1809; and Constant (Napoléon's valet from 1800–14) probably by J.-H. Schmit.

The SECOND FLOOR is devoted in part to Joséphine's children by her first marriage: Eugène (1781–1824) and Hortense (1783–1837), who married Napoléon's brother Louis in 1802, becoming Queen of Holland in 1806 and mother of the future Napoléon III (1808–73) and his half-brother, the future Duc de Morny (1811–65). Other rooms contain mementoes of friends of Joséphine (including a bust of Charles James Fox by Ann Seymour Damer), or concern the history of Malmaison. Several watercolours of topographical interest by Auguste Garneray (1758–1824) may be on view.

The Gardens, of which only six hectares remain of 200, contain roses planted with those varieties grown by Joséphine herself, with the help, until 1805, of her English gardener, Mr Howatson. Her blooms were later drawn and coloured by Pierre-Joseph Redouté. The estate formerly contained a farm and dairy (with Swiss cows and dairymen), a range of greenhouses and a menagerie; black swans floated in the lake.

To the left of the entrance lodge, on your way out, is the **Coach House**, containing the 'Opale', the state carriage in which Joséphine drove to Malmaison after her divorce, a gala coach (of the time of Louis XIV) used by Napoléon; his '*dormeuse*' used at Waterloo and Blücher's *landau en berline*. Behind is the Pavillon Osiris, with collections of caricatures, medallions and snuffboxes propagating the Napoleonic legend, and a portrait of Tsar Alexander I by Gérard. Beyond the other side of the entrance drive is a summer-house used as a study by Napoléon when First Consul.

From opposite the entrance, a few minutes' walk through the park will take you to the ***Château de Bois-Préau**, dating from 1700, and acquired by

Joséphine in January 1810 as an annexe in which to accommodate her entourage and visitors, and to house part of her collections. It was later sold and in 1926 bequeathed to the State by its then American owner, Edward Tuck (see also Petit-Palais; Rte 25).

Rooms on the first floor are devoted exclusively to the period of Napoléon's years of exile. The deposed Emperor had spent only five days at Malmaison between his defeat at Waterloo and leaving France. On 17 October 1815 he disembarked from the 'Northumberland' and settled in his enforced residence at Longwood on the isolated south Atlantic island of St. Helena, where—under the eye of Sir Hudson Lowe, the governor—he was to remain until his death on 5 May 1821.

Here, in addition to the camp-bed in which he expired, are numerous souvenirs of his years of captivity, among them his *nécessaire* No. 3 (by Biennais), silver flasks and other plate, his grey coat and hat, boots and slippers, etc., apart from furniture; a book given to Napoléon by Lord Holland; Marchand's Sketch of the dead emperor; and his death-mask, moulded by Antommarchi, his Corsican doctor. His remains were brought back to France and placed in Les Invalides in December 1840; see Rte 11. A room contains souvenirs of Louis Marchand (1791–1876), his valet from 1814.

In the nearby church of **Rueil** (1584, with a west façade by Lemercier of 1635), is the tomb of the Empress Joséphine (1825); that of Hortense de Beauharnais (see above) in the chapel opposite, was erected in 1858 by her son, Napoléon III, who also donated the 15C Florentine organ-case by Baccio d'Agnolo.

The N13 skirts the south bank of the Seine, passing at **Bougival**, with a Romanesque church tower, the house where Bizet died (1875). Miss Elizabeth Harriet Howard (1823–65), mistress of the future Napoléon III, retired to La Celle-St.-Cloud, to the south, in 1853.

ST.-GERMAIN-EN-LAYE (40,800 inhab.), known as Montagne-Bon-Air during the Revolution, is easily reached from central Paris by the RER from Auber or Etoile (replacing the first railway constructed in France, in 1837).

By road, it may also be approached from the Pont de Neuilly by the N13 (taking in en route the Château of Malmaison, see above), or by the N190 branching right off the N13, which passes through the suburb of Le Vésinet.

Anthony Hamilton, the author of 'Mémoires du Comte de Grammont' (1703), who lived at St.-Germain in 1690–1720, was one of many Jacobites resident in the area during and after this period. Thicknesse rented a house here in 1766, and Henry Swinburne lived 5km north at Les Mesnils in 1786 and again in 1796. Claude Debussy (1862–1918) was born at 38 Rue au Pain, St.-Germain.

The Municipal Museum, from which 'The Juggler', by Bosch, was stolen in 1978, being reorganised. For the Musée du Prieuré, see below.

The strategically sited royal **Château**, dominating a bend of the Seine, was erected in the 12C by Louis VI and completely rebuilt (except for the keep) by François I in 1539–48. The infant Mary Stuart lived here from October 1548 until her marriage to François II in April 1558. In 1862 Eugène Millet restored the castle after it had been used to house a military prison for three decades, and it was adapted to house a Musée Gallo-Romain.

The so-called Château-Neuf, below the original castle, constructed for Henri II and Henri IV, was demolished in 1776, except for the Pavillon Henri IV and the Pavillon Sully, at the foot of the steep slope east of the town, in the suburb of Le Pecq.

It was in this 'new' castle that Louis XIV was born in 1638, five years before the death of his father in the same building; and the royal family escaped here in January 1649 during the Fronde. It remained one of the principal seats of the French Court until the completion of Versailles in 1682. Large sums were spent on its improvement during the years 1664–80. Meanwhile, the Château-Neuf afforded refuge to Henrietta Maria of England (1644–48). After 1688 what was then called the 'Vieux Château' was the residence—and Court—of James II (1633–1701) who died here, as did his wife, Mary of Modena (1658–1710). It is recorded that she gave as much as she could spare of the allowance she received from Louis XIV to the impoverished English who filled St.-Germain. John Caryll was secretary of state to the exiled dynasty. During this period it was a focus of Jacobite intrigue. St.-Germain has been the scene of several international treaties, the last being in 1919, the territorial clauses in which provided for the dismemberment of Austria-Hungary.

In 1962, a century after the setting-up of the earlier museum in the château, the *MUSEE DES ANTIQUITES NATIONALES** was installed here. It has more recently been tastefully reorganised to display its impressive collections in chronological order, which are well labelled and described.

On the GROUND FLOOR you can visit the Chapel (1230–38), just predating the Sainte-Chapelle in Paris, also by Pierre de Montreuil. François I and his first wife, Claude de France (1499–1524; daughter of Louis I), Louis XIV and his son, the Grand Dauphin, were baptised here. It has been sadly disfigured over the years and contains copies only of tombs from the Alyscamps at Arles.

Rooms on the MEZZANINE FLOOR are devoted to the Palaeolithic and Neolithic periods; the Bronze Age, with bracelets, torques and other gold objects; the Hallstatt period (1st Iron Age; 800–450) and the La Tène culture (450–52 BC), with a good collection of bronze vessels, jewellery, etc. Also a reconstituted chariot burial from La Gorge-Meillet and a maquette of the fortified site of Alèsia.

Stairs ascend to the FIRST FLOOR, concentrating on the Gallo-Roman period, with sections displaying Celtic divinities and those from the Graeco-Roman world, including notable figures of Venus and Mercury; ex-votos and their mould; an exemplary display of silver utensils, glassware, bronze lamps, scales, handles, keys, etc. and sigillate pottery. Other rooms contain small sculptured objects—birds, boars, horses and human figures: note the charming couple in bed, with a dog at their feet, from Bordeaux; a collection of jewellery, buckles, fibulae, games, etc. and a collection of arms. A large mosaic pavement of the 3C from St.-Romain-en-Gal (on the Rhône opposite Vienne) depicts a rustic calendar of the seasons. Adjacent are a variety of agricultural implements. Further collections of jewellery, plaques, glassware, and buckles from the Merovingian period are also to be seen, together with a section devoted to comparative archaeology.

To the north of the château is the Parterre, originally a park laid out by Le Nôtre, beyond which is a Jardin Anglais. At its south-east corner, at 21 Rue Thiers, is the Pavillon Henri-IV (see above), a hotel since 1836: Dumas wrote 'The Three Musketeers' and 'Monte Cristo' here; Thiers died here in 1877.

To the north east extends the Terrace of St.-Germain, which commands a splendid *view of Paris (and particularly of La Défense): Notre-Dame is approximately 21km to the east. James II once compared the view (unfavourably) to that from the Terrace at Richmond. At the far end is the Grille Royale, the entrance to the Forêt de St.-Germain, the former royal hunting preserve, once over 4000 hectares in extent, and still retaining a number of pleasant drives and walks (see IGN map 419).

St.-Louis (opposite the château), designed c 1765 by N.-M. Potain, but not completed until early 19C, contains the tomb of James II of England, erected at the request of George IV, and in which his partial remains were re-interred in 1824. From behind the church, the Rue au Pain leads south west. With its continuations, this approaches—after a few minutes' walk—the *Musée du Prieuré (2 Rue Maurice-Denis).

A former royal hospital founded by Mme de Montespan in 1678, it was the home of Maurice Denis (1870–1943) from 1914 until his death. The collection of his paintings bequeathed by his family, and those of the Symbolist School and the group of artists known as the Nabis ('Prophets' in Hebrew), was inaugurated in 1980. Denis had lived close by from 1893, and had rented one of its larger rooms as a studio in 1905.

Among the more important works are Maurice Denis, Self portrait (1921), with the Prieuré in the background; posthumous Portrait of Albert Besnard; Portrait of Paul Sérusier; The sewing lesson; Portrait of his mother; With Marthe, his first wife, in the garden at dusk; The ladder; Jacques Portelette aged four; Mme Ranson and her cat. Vuillard, Dr Viau, the dentist, The reservoir; Thérèse Debains (1907–74), Self-portrait; Paul Sérusier (1864–1927), Portrait of his wife, Breton girl; Félix Vallottan (1865–1900), Bookshelves; Georges Lacombe (1868–1916), carved wood Bust of Maurice Denis; Gauguin, The patron's daughter (in fact a boy; 1886); Louis Anquetin (1861–1932), Self-portrait, Woman in black; Odilon Redon (1840–1916), Portrait of Maurice Denis; and representative paintings by Charles Filiger (1863–1928).

Also displayed are several designs by Maurice Denis for wall-papers and stained glass. Several pieces of furniture and examples of the decorative arts of the period are also shown, including ceramics by the Daum brothers of Nancy, etc.

The Chapel was decorated entirely by Maurice Denis with blue frescoes, and Stations of the Cross, and he also designed the glass, with the exception of the round Visitation by Marcel Poncet.

The adjacent Studio was built by Auguste Perret in 1912 for Maurice Denis when he was working on the frieze for the Théâtre des Champs-Elysées. It now displays his sketches for the decoration of the apse of St.-Paul de Genève, and is the venue of temporary exhibitions.

At **Chambourcy**, 4km west of St.-Germain, famous for its cheese since the 17C, are the tombs of the Chevalier d'Orsay (1801–52) and Marguerite Power, Countess of Blessington (1789–1849), author of 'The Idler in Italy', etc.

Secluded in the Désert de Retz, c 2km south of Chambourcy, is a curious building in the form of a huge truncated Doric column, among other follies. Built in the 1770s by François de Monville, it has recently been restored.

Some 4km south of St.-Germain, to the west of the N386, stood the royal château of Marly (its name preserved in the town of **Marly-le-Roi**), built in 1679–86 by Jules Hardouin-Mansart for Louis XIV, and a favourite retreat from the formality of Versailles. Regular visits to Marly (and vice versa) were essential to allow the palaces to be cleaned and aired.

The château was destroyed at the Revolution, although vestiges remain of the park, where the famous hydraulic Machine de Marly stood. It was originally constructed in 1681 to raise water from the Seine to the Marly aqueduct, which in turn carried it to Versailles. New machinery had been installed in 1855–59, taking its water from an underground source, but the whole was dismantled in 1967.

The church of Marly-le-Roi was also built by Mansart (1689) and contains some works originally in Versailles.

For other sites west, south west and north west of St.-Germain, see Blue Guide France.

Some 4km north of St.-Germain-en-Laye is **Maisons-Laffitte** (23,900 inhab.), birthplace of Jean Cocteau (1889–1963). There are training-stables, a Musée du cheval de course and a racecourse.

The town, its station known as 'Maisons-Laffitte' as early as 1843 (after a nephew of the financier, himself a railway entrepeneur) was officially so-named in 1882.

Its celebrated *****Château de Maisons** (CNMH) was built for René de Longueil (1596–1677), first Marquis de Maisons, a Surintendant des Finances before Fouquet; the masterpiece of François Mansart (1642–51), it is also notable for its interior decoration.

The property was bought in 1777 by the Comte d'Artois and partly redecorated by Bellanger. It was deserted at the Revolution and its contents dispersed. In 1804 it was acquired by Marshal Lannes, Duc de Montebello, who died here in 1809 from wounds received at Essling. His widow sold it in 1818 to Jacques Laffitte (1767–1844), a banker and speculator who had profited out of the Napoleonic Wars. In 1833 he demolished the stables and sold off the estate. It later passed into the hands of Tilman Grommé, a Russian artist, who further fragmented the property, cutting it up into building plots. The shell of the château was saved from demolition in 1905, being acquired by the State, and the whole was restored.

From the present entrance, formerly a chapel, a series of rooms on the Ground Floor may be visited. These include the Salles des Graveurs, with a trompe l'oeil ceiling, and collections of prints and plans; and the Salon des Captifs, with a coffered ceiling, and a fireplace carved by Gilles Guérin. Passing through the Vestibule d'honneur, with reliefs by Jacques Sarrazin, you enter the south wing, redecorated by the Comte d'Artois (later Charles X). The main Staircase, embellished with putti executed by Philippe de Buyster, ascends to (left) the Salon d'Hercule, hung with early 18C Gobelins tapestries of the Hunts of Maximilian, among others, a musicians gallery and another fireplace by Guérin; the Chambre du Roi; the Salon à l'italienne, containing a portrait by Van Dyck of the Countess of Bedford; and the domed Cabinet aux miroirs, with a marquetry floor. In the south wing is the former Queen's suite, transformed by Lannes.

Voltaire wrote 'Marianne' when a guest here in 1723, and it is claimed that he was dosed with 200 pints of lemonade to avoid death by smallpox; he is also said to have set light to his bed. Later visitors were La Fayette and Benjamin Constant.

The N308 leads south east across a meander of the Seine towards La Défense (see latter part of Rte 28) and central Paris. The road passes, after crossing the Pont de Bezons (south of Colombes), the site of a château in which Henrietta Maria (1606–69) died. The widow of Charles I of England, she was buried at St.-Denis.

36   St.-Denis

St.-Denis (91,300 inhab.) is best approached by car by turning off the A1 autoroute about 3km north of the Porte de la Chapelle; or by taking the Métro, now extended to its terminus at **St.-Denis-Basilique**.

The Gothic **CATHEDRAL OF ST.-DENIS** (CNMH) stands in the centre of

St.-Denis (91,300 pop.), one of the more unattractive of the northern suburbs of Paris, spreading beyond the site of the celebrated 'Foire du Lendit', which was held here from Dagobert's time until 1552. It was founded on the probable site of *Catolacus*, where the missionary apostle of Lutetia was almost certainly buried.

The west front, although disfigured at the Revolution, retains one good 12C tower with a low modern steeple. The transeptal portals, each with a rose-window, are mid-13C work.

It is overshadowed in interest by the *tombs it contains. Admission 10.00–17.30, except Sunday during services.

The abbey of St.-Denis was founded c 475, perhaps at the instance of St. Geneviève, and rebuilt in 630–38 by Dagobert, who also founded a monastery for Benedictines. The first substantial church on the site was built by Abbot Fulrad in 750–75, and here in 754 Pope Stephen III consecrated Pepin le Bref and his wife and sons, thus establishing them securely on the throne. This church was itself replaced by another built by Abbot Suger, of which the narthex (west porch) and apse (c 1136–44) survive, ranking among the most important examples of the earliest Gothic architecture. Excavations in the crypt, also of this period and retaining the Romanesque arch, have brought to light Gallo-Roman Christian tombs and remains of the earlier churches. The rest of the building dates from 1231–81, following the designs of Pierre de Montreuil (died 1267), while the chapels on the north side of the nave were added c 1375.

Most of the effigies of earlier kings were made during the reign of Louis IX (St. Louis; died 1270), when St.-Denis became recognised as a royal mausoleum; others were brought here during the Revolution. With the exception of Philippe I, Louis XI, Louis-Philippe and Charles X, all the French kings since Hugues Capet are buried here. In 1422 the body of Henry V lay in state here on its way from Vincennes to Westminster, and seven years later Joan of Arc dedicated her armour here. In 1567 Condé's Huguenots captured the place, but he prevented them from despoiling the basilica: later in the year he was defeated in the plain to the south by Anne de Montmorency, who was himself mortally wounded. Henri IV abjured Protestantism here in 1593.

Henriette d'Angleterre, daughter of Charles I, was buried here in 1670, her funeral oration delivered by Bossuet. Her mother, Henrietta Maria, had been buried here the previous year.

It was visited in 1774 by Lady Mary Coke, who, on leaving, passed Louis XV's funeral cortège coming from Versailles: 'the Guards who follow'd the Coach gallop'd. The mob was very great & very indecent; so far from showing the least concern they hoop'd & hollow'd, as if they had been at a horse race instead of a funeral procession; never was a King less regretted'.

After injudicious alterations in the 18C, the abbey was suppressed at the Revolution and its roof stripped of lead. During the Terror, its tombs were rifled, their contents dispersed and the corpses of kings tosssed into a common pit and covered with quicklime. Only the remains of Turenne, also buried here, survived this macabre treatment.

The best of the monuments were saved from destruction by Alexandre Lenoir, who preserved them in his Musée des Petits-Augustins (Ecole des Beaux-Arts), from where they were later returned, and drastically restored. Restoration of the fabric of the basilica was taken in hand in 1813, but it was so incompetently carried out that the stability of the north tower was endangered, and in 1847 it had to be taken down. A subsequent 'restoration' by Viollet-le-Duc and Darcy went some way to repair the harm; but the explosion of a nearby bomb-dump in 1915 caused further damage.

INTERIOR. Only the more important tombs are listed. Smollett, who visited the abbey in October 1763, condemned the 'attitudes' of the sculptures as 'affected, unnatural, and desultory; and their draperies fantastic; or, as one of our English artists expressed himself, they are all of a flutter'.

The south aisle contains, among others, the tomb of Louis d'Orléans (died

1407), and Valentine de Milan (died 1408), a fine Italian work of 1502–15, commissioned by their grandson, Louis XII. Opposite, against the south-west pillar of the crossing, is the heart-tomb of François II (died 1560), by Germain Pilon and Ponce Jacquiau. Also in the south aisle, the urn (1549–55) by Bontemps, containing the heart of François I.

In the south transept: the *tomb of François I (died 1547) and Claude de France (died 1524), a masterpiece by Philibert Delorme, Pierre Bontemps, Primaticcio and others, begun in 1548. The royal pair appear both recumbent and (above) kneeling with their children: reliefs depict the king's military exploits. On the east side of this transept are the tombs of Charles V (died 1380) by André Beauneveu, and Charles VI (died 1422), with their queens; and of Bertrand du Guesclin (died 1380), one of the few commoners buried here (his heart is at Dinan; his entrails at Le Puy).

At the west end of the choir are the tombs of Philippe III, le Hardi (died 1285) by Pierre de Chelles and Jean d'Arras, remarkable as being one of the earliest known French portrait-statues. The effigy of his queen, Isabella of Aragón (died 1271), is particularly fine. Also Philippe IV, le Bel (died 1314). Following the ambulatory, you pass (to the left of the steps) the tomb of Dagobert (died 638), showing reliefs of the torment and redemption of the king's soul, and with a beautiful *statue (13C) of Queen Nanthilde: the figures of Dagobert and his son are 19C restorations. You next pass the tomb of Léon de Lusignan (died 1393).

Note the 12–13C glass in the Lady Chapel and adjacent chapels, including a Tree of Jesse. Turning west along the north side of the ambulatory, you pass (left) Blanche and Jean (both died 1243), children of Louis IX (from Royaumont), with fine enamelled plaques; Frédégonde (died 597), queen of Chilperic I, a remarkable slab in cloisonné mosaic (11C, from St.-Germain-des-Prés); and also from St.-Germain, Childebert I (died 558), a 12C statue. In the chapel at the top of the steps, draped statues of Henri II (died 1559) and Catherine de Médicis (died 1589) by Germain Pilon (1583). In the sanctuary is the Altar of the Relics (by Viollet-le-Duc), on which are placed the reliquaries, given by Louis XVIII, of St. Denis and his fellow-martyrs.

In the north transept is the splendid tomb of *Henri II and Catherine de Médicis, designed by Primaticcio in 1560–73, with recumbent and kneeling effigies of the king and queen, and supporters and reliefs by Germain Pilon and other contemporary sculptors. The king and queen were formerly kneeling at a bronze prie-dieu, which was melted down at the Revolution. Here also are the tombs of Philippe V (died 1322), Charles IV (died 1328), Philippe VI (died 1350) and Jean II (died 1364, prisoner at the Savoy, London), the last two by André Beauneveu. Opposite (left, in the choir) are tombs of Louis X (died 1316) and his son Jean I (died 1316).

In the north aisle is the *tomb of Louis XII (died 1515) and Anne de Bretagne (died 1514), made by Jean Juste (Giovanni di Giusto) in 1516–32. The royal pair are depicted naked and recumbent on the tombstone, and kneeling on the canopy above (the conventional design for Renaissance tombs); bas-reliefs illustrate episodes in the king's career.

Lastly, among other 13–14C tombs, that of Louis de France (died 1260), the eldest son of Louis IX, with Henry III of England as one of the bearers. Note, before entering the crypt, the High Stalls of the Ritual Choir (1501–07) from the chapel of the Château de Gaillon; the Low Stalls are 15C work from St.-Lucien, near Beauvais.

The Crypt, entered on either side of the choir, was constructed by Suger around the original Carolingian 'martyrium', the site of the grave of St. Denis and his companions, and retains some 12C capitals. Here also are the sarcophagi of Louis XVI, and Marie-Antoinette (see Chapelle Expiatore; Rte 23), and those of Louis XVIII among other 18–19C sovereigns.

The ossuary on the north side contains the bones that were thrown into a pit when many tombs were rifled in 1793, including those of Henrietta Maria and Maria of Modena, wives of Charles I and James II respectively. In a side chapel is a charming 12C Virgin, originally at the abbey of Longchamp.

To the south of the basilica are restored monastic dependencies. Rebuilt in the 18C by Robert de Cotte and Jacques Gabriel, they were occupied after 1809 as a Maison d'Education de la Légion d'Honneur.

Some five minutes' walk further south, at 22 bis Rue Gabriel Péri, the **Musée d'Art et d'Histoire** is installed in a Carmelite monastery founded in 1625. The compartmented cupola of its chapel (1784), by Mique, built while Louise de France was in residence (1770–87), is notable. It contains the reconstituted Pharmacy of the Hôtel-Dieu (demolished 1907), and the study of the poet Paul Eluard (Eugène Grindel; 1895–1952), born in St.-Denis; an archaeological section of interest; rooms devoted to the Commune de Paris (1870–71); some 4000 engravings and lithographs by Daumier; paintings and drawings by Albert André, Cézanne, Léger and Dufy, among others.

Also in St.-Denis, but best approached from the métro: Porte de Paris and following the Blvd Anatole France to the south west across the Canal St.-Denis, and there turning right, is the **Musée Bouilhet-Christofle** (open during working hours). Here are replicas of historical interest and original pieces of the art of the gold- and silversmith produced by the Société Christofle since its establishment.

37 Ecouen: Musée National de la Renaissance

Ecouen can be approached by public transport (métro to St.-Denis-Porte-de-Paris, and then the 268C bus, direction Ezanville.)

From the Porte de la Chapelle, take the N16 towards St.-Denis (see Rte 36), which may be by-passed. The road crosses a dreary dormitory area between (left) **Sarcelles**, with relics of a 12C church with a Gothic nave and Renaissance façade, and (right) **Villiers-le-Bel**, which belies its name, at 20km reaching (left) **Ecouen**. The town is of slight interest in itself, although the church of St.-Acceul retains some *stained-glass attributed to Jean Cousin in its choir (1544).

The town is dominated by the magnificent Renaissance *Château d'Ecouen**. It now houses the **MUSEE NATIONAL DE LA RENAIS-SANCE**, inaugurated in 1976, and displaying a number of outstanding objects from this epoch long stored at the Musée de Cluny.

Its construction began c 1535 for the Constable Anne de Montmorency, and among artists employed were Jean Goujon and Jean Bullant, to whom is ascribed the interior portico of the south wing (in the niches of which once stood Michelangelo's 'Chained Captives'). It was put to a variety of uses during the Revolutionary period, and in 1805 became a school for the daughters of members of the Légion d'Honneur, with Mme Campan as *directrice*. It later reverted to the Duc d'Aumale, who chose to remove a number of its embellishments to Chantilly, including an altar by Goujon from the chapel.

From the entrance turn left into the Chapel (**R1**), with painted ribbed vaulting and delicately carved stonework, before walking through a series of rooms on the ground floor ranged around the central courtyard. **R2**, with a painted mantelpiece (one of six depicting biblical themes) in the style of the School of Fontainebleau, contains arms and armour (including stirrups lost by François I at Pavia). The mantelpiece of **R3** backs onto that of the adjoining room, in which is a collection of Renaissance woodcarving; **R5** preserves a number of leather panels.

A series of smaller rooms is devoted to collections of carved wood plaques (**R6**), and larger panels (**R7**), including some remarkable examples in ebony. **R8**. Pear-wood and box-wood statuettes, mainly German or Flemish; coffers; a fine ivory flagon; bronze figurines, including fornicating fauns by Riccio. **R9** is devoted to metalwork, some damascened, cutlery and a collection of Renaissance door-furniture. **RR10–11** contain mathematical instruments and watches, and work in precious metals. **R12**, known as that of Catherine de Médicis, is crossed before reaching a room reserved for concerts and other functions, and another with collections of sculpture.

FIRST FLOOR. **R1**. Furniture, some ebony; and tapestries of the 'Labours of Hercules'. **R2**. Chairs and 'caquetoires'. **R3**, with notable carved doors. In **RR4–7** are hung a remarkable series of tapestries entitled 'The story of David and Bathsheba' (Brussels; 16C). Note also the finely carved stone fireplaces in **R5** from Châlons-sur-Marne (1562), with reliefs of Christ and the Samaritan, and Actaeon surprising Artemis/Diana in her bath. **R6** contains a collection of enamelled plaques by Pierre Courteys (Limoges; 1559) and tile-pictures. Beyond a carved wooden staircase, from the Chambre des Comptes of the Palais de la Cité is **R8**, with a made-up marble chimney-piece and a tiled pavement by Masséot Abaquesne (mid 16C). Beyond are rooms displaying glass panels of 1544–52, majolicas, including work by Luca della Robbia, furniture, embroideries, etc.

SECOND FLOOR. A remarkable collection of ceramics from Isnik (ancient Nicaea, in north-west Turkey), dating largely from 1555–1700; 16C French tile panels, and ceramics by Masséot Abaquesne and others; painted panels from Florentine marriage-chests (depicting the Trojan Horse and other Classical scenes); Limoges enamel plaques and portraits (by Léonard Limousin, Nardon Pénicaud, Pierre Reymond, Helie Poncet, Pierre Courtois and others); collections of majolica, glass and jewellery; silversmiths' work, notably a Daphne by Wenzel Jamnitzer, a goblet in the shape of a snail (Netherlands; c 1700) and several magnificent examples from Nuremberg and Augsburg; wax portraits, etc. Here also is a reconstruction of the Constable's Library.

For a detailed description of the area north of Ecouen, see Blue Guide France. For the excursion to Chantilly, see Rte 39.

38 Sceaux

The N20 leads south from the Porte d'Orléans to (10km) Sceaux, which is also be approached by the RER, stopping at Sceaux or Bourg-la-Reine.

You pass (left) 2km south of the Blvd Périphérique the double Aqueduct de Arceuil, crossing the valley of the Bièvre. The lower part was built in 1613–24 by Marie de Médicis to supply the Luxembourg fountains; it was preceded by a Roman aqueduct, built in the 4C to bring water to the Palais des Thermes (cf. Musée de Cluny). Both Erik Satie and Vasarley long resided in the suburb of Arceuil.

At 4.5km the broad Allée d'Honneur ascends west from the N20 to the entrance of the **Château de Sceaux**. A 19C building replaced the sumptuous 17C château built by Claude Perrault for Colbert, which, during the first half of the 18C, was the scene of the literary and artistic court of the ambitious Duchesse du Maine (1676–1753) as described by Mme de Launay, among others. Mme du Deffand was a frequent visitor, while Voltaire wrote 'Zadig' here; and works by Racine, Molière and Lully were performed in the adjacent Orangerie (left), constructed by Jules Hardouin-Mansart (1684; restored). To the right is the Pavillon de l'Aurore, also by Perrault.

Since 1937 the ***MUSEE DE L'ILE DE FRANCE** has been installed in the château. This illustrates the history and topography of the area now covered by the départements of Hauts-de-Seine, Seine-St.-Denis, Val-de-Marne, Essonne, Yvelines and Val-d'Oise. It is well worth visiting, not only for its site, but for the wealth of interesting material depicting the appearance of, and life in, the environs of the capital in past centuries. It also contains a reference library. Open Mon., Fri. 14.00–17.00; Wed., Thur., Sat., Sun. 10.00–12.00, 14.00–17.00; closed Tues.

The majority of the rooms are devoted to specific regions. **R2** contains a model of the château; **R3** portraits of Colbert attributed to Lefebvre, and of the Duchesse du Maine by De Troy. **R4** (providing a charming view): Sceaux ceramics (1754–95). **R5**. Sèvres and St.-Cloud ware. **R7**. Views of St.-Cloud by Dunouy, Fleury, and others. **R8** is devoted to Meudon. On the SECOND FLOOR, a series of rooms display views of the Machine de Marly; St.-Germain by James Basire (1730–1802); Mousseau by J.-M. Morel; drawings, watercolours and engravings by Dunoyer de Segonzac (1874–1946); two of Etry occupied by Cossacks in 1814 by J. Randon, and a number of views by Paul Huet (1803–69), among others of topographical value, including the Tower of Vincennes by Bonington.

The extensive ***park**, laid out by Le Nôtre, forms one of the more attractive open spaces near Paris and contains, south of the château, a series of cascades leading to the Octagon, to the west of which is the Grand Canal. From here you have a view of the Pavillon de Hanovre, moved here in 1832 from the Blvd des Capucines. It was built in 1760 with money extorted from the Hanoverians in the Seven Years War.

A short distance north west of the château, approached across the park, is the old churchyard of **Sceaux**, where the fabulist Florian (1755–94) is buried. The simple tombs of Pierre (1859–1906) and Marie Curie (née Sklodowska; 1867–1934), the discoverers of radium, may be found in the local cemetery. It was at the Lycée Lakanal at Sceaux that the writers Alain-Fournier and Jacques Rivière first met.

Some 2.5km west, in the Parc de la Vallé aux Loups, is the restored residence (in 1807–18) of Chateaubriand.

For the area south of Sceaux, see Blue Guide France.

EXCURSIONS FROM PARIS

The following routes describe three of the more important monuments and collections which may be conveniently visited in day trips from Paris. For more information on what may be seen *en route*, see Blue Guide France.

39 To Chantilly and Senlis

Distance from Paris 41km (25 miles) on the N16. Chantilly may also be approached by the N17 and D924A, a very slightly longer route; Senlis, 10km east of Chantilly, is also reached directly by the A1 motorway.

Two approaches to Chantilly are briefly described below.

The N16 skirts **Ecouen** (see Rte 37) and, 11km beyond, **Luzarches**, with a mid 16C church of interest, retaining part of its 12C predecessor.

A DETOUR may be made to **Royaumont**, 6.5km north west, with the considerable remains of a great Cistercian abbey, founded in 1228, in the dismantled church of which Louis IX was married in 1234; the beautiful *refectory, its vaulting sustained by five monolithic columns, contains the tomb by Coysevox of Henri of Lorraine (died 1666). Chantilly is 8.5km north east; or 9km directly north of Luzarches.

The N17 leaves Paris by the Porte de la Villette and at 16km passes (left) the former airport of Le Bourget, where the Musée de l'Air, with a collection of 140 aircraft, largely from 1919, but including earlier flying machines, has been installed. The first regular flights between Le Bourget and London (Croydon airport) started in 1919. A short distance beyond, the airport of Charles de Gaulle is passed to the right. At 18.5km the D924A forks left for (9.5km) Chantilly, first crossing part of the Fôret de Chantilly (2100 hectares in extent) before reaching the Château de Chantilly; the right fork leads 9.5km directly to Senlis; see below.

Chantilly (10,200 inhab.), the Newmarket of France, where race-meetings have been held since 1836, is principally famous for its château, housing the Musée Condé. It was formerly reputed for its silk lace, the manufacture of which was established in 1710; and for its porcelain, the potteries of which were opened by Christopher Potter (died 1817), an Englishman credited with introducing into France the art of painting on porcelain, and who settled in Paris in 1789.

The Rue du Connétable leads east past Notre-Dame (1692) to the vast *Grandes-Ecuries**, built for Louis IV, Duc de Bourbon (1692–1740) by Jean Aubert from 1719. They have been restored to house an equestrian museum; they once had stabling for 240 mounts. Passing through the Porte St.-Denis, just north of which is the Jeu de Paume of 1757, you approach the **Château de Chantilly**, comprising two conntected buildings standing on an island site in a carp-stocked lake. It houses the **MUSEE CONDE**, containing unique collections of French paintings and illuminations of the 15–16C, an important library and other works of art.

The domain came into the possession of the Montmorency family in 1484 and, after the execution of Henri II Montmorency (1595–32), it passed in 1643 to the Grand Condé (Louis II, Prince de Condé; 1621–86), whose mother was a Montmorency. The Petit

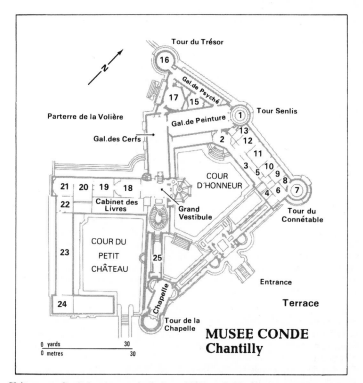

Tour du Trésor

16

Gal.de Psyché

17 15

Parterre de la Volière

Gal.de Peinture

1 Tour Senlis

Gal.des Cerfs

13

2 12

11

3 10

5 9 8

COUR
D'HONNEUR

4 6 7

21 20 19 18

Tour du
Connétable

22 Cabinet des
Livres

Grand
Vestibule

COUR DU

23 PETIT

CHÂTEAU

25

Entrance

24

Terrace

Chapelle

Tour de la
Chapelle

**MUSEE CONDE
Chantilly**

0 yards 30
0 metres 30

Château or Capitainerie was built in c 1560, probably by Jean Bullant, for the Constable Anne de Montmorency (1493–1567), whose adjacent mansion, the Grand Château, erected in 1528–32 by Pierre Chambiges, had been described by Lord Herbert of Cherbury as 'an incomparably fine residence, admired by the greatest princes in Europe'. Molière's 'Les Précieuse ridicules' was first performed here, in 1659; during the visit of Louis XIV in 1671, François Vatel, Condé's *maitre d'hôtel*, committed suicide because he thought the fish would be late for Friday repast (as described by Mme de Sévigne). In 1777 Philip Thicknesse saw the Prince de Condé at supper with some friends (eight people waited on by 25 servants) and complained that the music played during the meal 'was all wind instruments'. The Duc d'Enghien (1772–1804), shot at Vincennes on Napoléon's orders, was born here.

The Grand Château, rebuilt unimaginatively in 1686–91 by Hardouin-Mansart, was virtually razed at the Revolution, although the Petit Château survived. Some repairs were carried out after 1818 by the last of the Condés (who committed suicide in 1830), but it was left to his heir, the Duc d'Aumale (1822–97), fourth son of Louis-Philippe, to rebuild the Grand Château entirely, following the designs of Honoré Daumet. Unfortunately, Aumale also inherited his father's taste in many repects. After the confiscation of the property of the Orléans family in 1853, the château was acquired by the English banking firm of Coutts, but was returned to its rightful owner by a decree of the National Assembly in 1872. In spite of his banishment to Twickenham, the Duc d'Aumale bequeathed the whole domain, together with his art collections, to the Institut de France in 1886.

Chantilly marked the farthest advance in this direction of German troops in September 1914, but it remained undamaged, and soon after became the general HQ of the French high command, with Joffre and Nivelle, among others, in residence.

Passing the iron Grille d'Honneur, you leave on your right the Château d'Enghien (1770; by *Le Roy*), now the curator's residence. On the Terrasse du Connétable is a statue by *P. Dubois* of Anne de Montmorency. Passing between two bronze groups of hounds by *Cain*, you cross the moat and enter the Cour d'Honneur.

The Galerie des Cerfs displays the arms of successive owners of Chantilly, and is hung with 16C Gobelins tapestries of hunting scenes; above the chimneypiece is the Vision of St. Hubert.

Notable in the Galerie de Peinture are *Fromentin*, Hawking in Algeria; *Lancret*, 'Dejeuner au jambon'; *Philippe de Champaigne*, Mazarin, and Richelieu; *Lampi*, the Tsarina Féodorowna; *Nanteuil*, Colbert; and views of Chantilly by De Cort.

R1 on the plan is a rotunda formed by the Tour Senlis, with a mosaic pavement from Herculaneum, and containing *Jean Clouet*, Ode de Châtillon; *anon.*, Gabrielle d'Estrées in her bath; *Piero di Cosimo*, Simonetta Vespucci; and paintings by *Andrea del Sarto* and *Annibale Carracci*. In **RR3** and **5** are numerous portrait drawings, among them *Corneille de Lyon*, Anne, Duc de Joyeuse, Antoine de Bourbon, Duc de Nemours, Mary Tudor, Laure de Noves, Gabrielle d'Estrées, Marguerite-Charlotte de Montmorency; *Marc Duval*, Gaspard de Coligny; several others attributed to Le *Mannier* and *Quesnel,* are anonymous or after Clouet, Fouquet, Jean Perréal, Decourt, Dumoustier, etc.

R6, *Perrault's* copy of Horace Vernet's painting (at Versailles) of Louis-Philippe and his sons leaving Versailles; and *Bonnat*, Portrait of the Duc d'Aumale in 1890.

R7, another rotunda, formed by the Tour du Connétable, and **R8**, adjoining, display a Greek statuette of Minerva, the Portalés Amphora, bronze ewers from Herculaneum, Tanagra figures and other antiquities, including coins minted within ten years of the eruption of Vesuvius in AD 79, found at Pompeii; also a portrait of Franz I of Austria by *Lawrence*.

R9, *Enguerrand Quarton,* Virgin; *Iacopo del Sellaio*, Madonna; *School of Giotto*, Death of the Virgin; *Andrea del Sarto*, A Youth; *Ghirlandaio*, Portrait of Louis dela Trémoille. **R10**, landscape by *Théodore Rousseau* and seascapes by *W. van de Velde the Younger* and *J. van Ruisdael*. **R11**, *Bonnat*, The Duc d'Aumale in 1880; Jalabert, Queen Marie-Amélie in 1865; also portfolios of drawings by Primaticcio, the Clouets, Watteau and Cartmontel, among others, but not normally exhibited.

R12, Greuze, 'La Surprise', a study for the Village Marriage Contract (in the Louvre), and other works; *Watteau*, 'L'Amante inquiète' and 'La Sérenade'; among portraits, *Duplessis*, the Duchesse de Chartres watching her husband's departure for Ushant (1778); *Mignard*, the Comtesse de la Suze; Nattier, the Duchesse d'Orléans (as Hebe), and the Duchesse de Nantes, daughters of Mme de Montespan; *Carle Vernet*, the Duc d'Orléans and Duc de Chartres (1788); and *attrib. Rigaud*, the Princesse des Ursins.

More portraits are seen in **R13**, including *Marc Duval*, Jacques de Savoie; *Jean Decourt,* Henri III (?) and Albert de Gondi; *attrib. Corneille de Lyon* or his school, Gabrielle de Rochechouart (?), and the Dauphin François (son of François I); *attrib. Jean Clouet* or his school, Jeanne d'Albret, Charles IX, Elisabeth of Austria, Odet de Châtillon, Catherine de Médicis, Marguerite de Valois as a child, Henri II as a child; and *anon.*, François I, and his sister, Marguerite d'Angoulême, Henri d'Albret, Michel de l'Hôpital, Ferdinand of Austria, Claude de France (?), and Montaigne.

Returning through R5 (passing portraits by *Mierevelt* of Hugo Grotius and of Elisabeth of Bohemia) you cross the Galerie de Peinture to enter the

Galerie de Psyché, contining 42 of the original 46 stained-glass windows, representing the Loves of Cupid and Psyché, made c 1541 for the Montmorency château at Ecouen (cf.), and probably designed by *Michel Coxie*. At the end of the room is a bust by *Guillaume Dubois* of Henri IV (1610). Among more portrait drawings, many ascribed to the Clouets or Jean Perréal, are those of Diane de Poitiers, Marshal Strozzi, Hercule-François d'Alençon, Jeanne d'Albret (mother of Henri IV), Henri II, Henri, Duc de Guise, Jeanne of Navarre, François II, Marguerite de Valois (first wife of Henri IV), Charles IX as a child, Anne de Montmorency, Adm. Cologny, Henri II as a boy, and Marshal Brissac.

R15 contains some of the main treasures of the collection, including *Raphael*, Madonna of the House of Orléans, and the Three Graces or the Three Ages of Woman. The Esther and Ahasuerus, although catalogued as by *Filippino Lippi*, is probably by 'Amico di Sandro', a pupil of Botticelli. Reproductions only are on view of 40 of the original 47 miniatures ascribed to *Jean Fouquet* (1415–81), executed for the **Book of Hours of Etienne Chevalier**; that treasurer of France (1410–74) and his patron saint are depicted adoring the Virgin and Child.

R16, in the Tour du Trésor (view) displays an enamel of Apollo guiding the Chariot of the Sun, *attrib. to Cellini*, and the rose diamond known as the 'Grand Condé', a Cross from the treasury of Basel (15C); snuff boxes embellished with views of Chantilly by *Roussel* (1775); and collections of enamels, miniatures and fans, etc.

Passing a bas-relief of the Departure of Phaethon by *Jean Goujon*, you enter **R17**, an octagon containing a vase by Clodion; while on panels above the cornice are paintings of residences connected with the Duc d'Aumale: the Collège Henri-IV, Aumale, the Palais-Royal, Ecouen, Palermo, Guise, Villers-Cotterêts and Twickenham. On the walls, in unlikely juxtaposition, hang Reynolds, Countess Waldegrave and her daughter (1761); *Ary Scheffer*, Talleyrand; *Watteau*, 'Plaisir pastorale'; *Van Dyck*, Gaston, Duc d'Orléans; *Memling* (?), Diptych of the Virgin appearing to Jeanne de Bourbon (daughter of Charles VII), Christ on the Cross; *Perugino*, Madonna with SS Peter and Jerome; *Botticelli*, (?; once attrib. to Mantegna), Autumn; *François Clouet*, Card. Odet de Châtillon; Flemish School, Antoine, the 'Grand Bastard' of Burgundy (brother of Charles le Téméraire); *Sassetta*, Mystic Marriage of St. Francis; *Pesellino*, Madonna with SS Peter and Anthony; *Mignard*, Molière, and Mazarin; *Ingres*, Mme Devauçay (painted in Rome in 1807), and Self-portrait; *Philippe de Champaigne*, Angélique Arnaud; H.-G. Pot, Andres Hooftman; *after Rigaud*, the Abbé de Rancé; Rigaud, Louis XIV; three portraits by *Mme Vigée-Lebrun*; and *anon.* Marquise de Montespan, the Duc du Maine, Duc d'Anjou (later Philip V of Spain); also the Fall of Phaeton by *Goujon*, which complements that in the other vestibule.

Passing through the Galerie des Cerfs, you turn right to visit apartments in the **Petit Château** decorated by the Duc de Bourbon and furnished in the French Regency style with Beauvais tapestry, contemporary clocks, ornaments and *boiseries*. **R18** has *dessus de portes* by *Oudry* and *Desportes*; an enamel of Henri IV by *Claudius Popelin*; and Sèvres, Rouen and Chinese porcelain. **R19**, *Van Dyck*, Comte Henri de Bergues, and Princesse Marie de Brabançon; *Justus van Egmont*, the Grand Condé in 1658, and after Nanteuil, in 1662; four enamel portraits by Léonard Limousin; *anon.*, Abraham de Fabert, Maréchal de France; and François II de Montmorency, Duc de Luxembourg. The mosaic above the chimney-piece is from Herculaneum.

The richly decorated bedroom (**R20**), with panels by *J.-B. Huet*, contains a commode by Riesener, chairs by *J.-B. Sené* and a fine chandelier. **R21**, an equestrian statue of the Grand Condé be Frémiet. **R22**, the Salon des Singes, so-named from the chinoiserie panel-paintings by *Christophe Huet* of 'Singeries ou différentes actions de la vie humaine'. (The exquisite Petit Singerie, in a room below, may be viewed on making advance application.)

R23, the Galeries des Actions de M. le Prince, contains panels painted in 1686–96 by *Sauveur Lecomte* of scenes of battles fought by the Grand Condé (including Rocroi, Nördlingen and Lens), whose despatch-case lies on the bureau of the Duc de Choiseul. Over the fireplace is a trophy formed of his swords and pistols; above is his portrait, when only 26 years of age, at Rocroi (by *J. Stella*); below, a medallion by *Coysevox* of 1686, the year of the Prince's death. His bust in biscuit de Sèvres on the mantlepiece is by *Roland* (1785); those in marble of Turenne and of the Grand Condé are by *Derbais* (1695). **R24** contains Triophime Bigot, The Supper at Emmaus; a portrait of the Duc d'Enghien by *Vallain*; and a collection of miniatures.

Retracing your steps, you enter the Cabinet des Livres, containing some 12,500 volumes, many of great rarity or from an important provenance, and many are superbly bound. Perhaps the greatest treasure among some 1493 MSS is the '**Très Riches Heures du Duc de Berri**', with its brilliantly illuminated pages depicting the months, painted from nature and not treated conventionally as had been the practice previously. They were begun c 1415 by Pol de Limbourg and his brothers, and completed some 70 years later by Jean Colombe. Only reproductions of the delicate originals are now on view.

You return to the Grand Vestibule, on the right of which is the Grand Escalier, with its copper, brass and galvanised iron balustrade, designed by Daumet and executed by the brothers Moreau, with caryatids by Chapu, and Gobelins tapestries *after Boucher* and *De Troy*.

R25, leading to the chapel, displays drawings, among them *Dürer*, Annunciation (1526); *Domenichino*, Flight into Egypt; a head of Christ by *Sebastian del Piombo*; and a Madonna by Raphael.

The **chapel**, restored by Daumet in 1882, although founded in the early 14C, has been rebuilt several times, and was virtually destroyed during the Revolution. Behind the altar is the mausoleum of Henri II de Condé, with bronze sculptures by *Jacques Sarazin*. The altar itself (by Jean Bullant and Jean Goujon), the *boiseries* of 1548 and the stained glass (1544, with portraits of Anne de Montmorency's children), were all brought here from Ecouen (cf.). The flag was captured at Rocroi (1643).

The **park, with impressive parterres, was laid out for the most part by Le Nôtre for the Grand Condé, and is adorned with sculptures and ornamental ponds, etc. It was visited in November 1775 by Dr Johnson, who wrote, 'I walked till I was very weary, and next morning felt my feet battered, and with pains in my toes'. Among the buildings which may be seen are the Maison de Sylvie, to the south east behind the Château d'Enghien, to reach which you pass the Chapelle de St.-Sébastien (1552) and the Cabotière (early 17C). 'Sylvie' was the name given to Marie Félice Orsini, Duchesse de Montmorency, by Théophile de Viau, who when condemned to death in 1623 for his licentious verses, was hidden by her in this dwelling, later rebuilt by Condé. Here also, in 1724, the romantic affair of Mlle de Clermont (sister of the Duc de Bourbon) and Louis de Melun, killed in a 'hunting accident', took place.

To the north east stand a group of cottages, the Hameau (constructed by Le Roy in 1774 for the penultimate Condé) being the scene of many *fêtes champêtres* of the period.

Five and a half kilometres north east of Chantilly is the notable 12C church of *St.-Leu-d'Esserent, just north of which are priory cloisters. The local quarry supplied stone for the cathedrals of Chartres and Sens, and later the Château de Versailles. In 1944 they were used for the assembly of V1 and V2 rockets.

The D924 leads east from Chantilly via **Courteuil**, where Abbé Prévost (1697–1763), author of 'Manon Lescaut', died, to approach **SENLIS** (15,300 inhab.). The town retains several attractive old alleys within the Gallo-Roman ramparts of the Silvanectes, and has a cathedral of interest.

Probably built on the site of Ratomagnus, Senlis was a royal residence from the time of Clovis to Henri IV; Hugues Capet was elected 'Duc des Francs' here in 987; in 1358 it was the scene of a massacre of nobles by the Jacquerie. It was briefly in German hands in September 1914, when they set fire to some streets and plundered the town. It was also damaged in 1940.

A stretch of its medieval ramparts survives to the south east, while in the town centre is the Hôtel de Ville, rebuilt in 1495, from which the Rue du Châtel leads into the Gallo-Roman enceinte, of which 16 towers remain, although many are hidden by abutting houses. It approaches the Hôtel des Trois-Pots, first mentioned in 1292, but with a 16C façade, the entrance to the ruined castle, the Priory of St.-Maurice (14C), a hunting museum and the cathedral.

The *Cathedral was built in 1155–84 (almost coeval with St.-Denis and Notre-Dame), its south tower surmounted by a 13C spire. The central door of the west façade is embellished with statues and reliefs. The transepts were rebuilt in the mid 16C after a fire, and display Renaissance tendencies; the five east chapels and the side portals date from the same period.

The interior retains a beautiful triforium gallery, and a splendid 16C vault in the east chapel of the south transept. The late 14C chapter-house, with a remarkable central pillar, and the octagonal sacristy, a relic of the original church, are both notable.

To the east is the former Bishop's Palace, behind which is the former church of St.-Pierre (now a market). It has a Flamboyant façade of 1516, one tower with a dome of Renaissance date and the other partly Romanesque, with a spire of 1432.

To the west of the town are the relics of a Gallo-Roman amphitheatre. 2.5km south east are the picturesque ruins of the Abbaye de la Victoire, founded by Philippe Auguste to commemorate the Battle of Bouvines (1214), and rebuilt in the 15–16C.

For areas beyond Chantilly and Senlis, see Blue Guide France.

40 To Fontainebleau

Distance from Paris, 65km (40 miles). From the Gare de Lyon, you may take a train to Fontainebleu-Avon and then a bus to the château.

The A6 motorway provides a rapid route for the first 49km, then veer south east onto the N37. This skirts the western perimeter of Orly Airport, and bears south east past (left) Evry (29,600 inhab.) préfecture of the départe-ment of Essonne, and Corbeil-Essonnes (38,100 inhab.).

At 7km after leaving the motorway, a crossroad leads right 1km to the village of **Barbizon,** now the sophisticated resort of artists emulating the school of artists who made it their headquarters in the mid 19C, among them Millet, Théodore Rousseau, Corot, Diaz de la Peña and Daubigny. The first two were buried at Chailly-en-Bière, just north of the main road, where Bazille, Monet, Renoir, Sisley and Seurat also painted.

The N37 joins the 'N7 just beyond this crossroad, leading through part of the Fôret de Fontainebleau (see below) to approach (8km) the town of **Fontainebleau** (18,800 Bellifontains). It takes its name from *Fons Blandi* or *Fontaine de Bland,* and is one of the pleasantest resorts in the neighbourhood of Paris, even if Evelyn considered it 'encompassed with hideous rocks'; Arthur Young, who visited the place in September 1787, remarked that the landlord of the inn there 'thinks that royal palaces should not be seen for nothing; he made me pay 10 livres for a dinner which would have cost me not more than half the money at the Star and Garter at Richmond'.

Florent Dancourt (1661–1725), author of 'Chevalier à la mode', was born at Fontainebleau; Henry Swinburne spent the summer of 1797 here; Arnold Bennett lived here, when not in Paris, during the 1900s.

The Rue Royale and the Blvd Magenta (in which are several old mansions) converge on the Pl. du Gén. de Gaulle, in which the doorway of the Hôtel du Card. de Ferrara is the only authentic work of Serlio surviving.

Fontainebleau is mentioned as a royal hunting-seat in 1137, and it was later fortified. Thomas à Becket, then in exile, consecrated the chapel of St.-Saturnin in 1169; and in 1259 Louis IX founded a monastery of Trinitarians here. Philippe IV (1268–1314) was born and died here. James V of Scotland spent December 1536 at Fontainebleau, just before his marriage with Madeleine, daughter of François I.

The château owes its present form largely to François I, who had found the place almost derelict, Charles VII and his successors having deserted it for the Loire. After 1527 he assembled a group of Italian artists here to rebuild and decorate it, among them Serlio, G.B. Rosso, Francesco Primaticcio, Vignola and Nicolo dell'Abbate, with Gilles le Breton as architect. Work continued during the reign of Henri IV, who spent vast sums on the building. In 1601 his son Louis XIII was born here. (Both François II and Henri III had also been born here.)

At one time the poet Mellin de Saint-Gelais (1487–1558) was keeper of the library; and the humanist Pierre Duchâtel (1480–1552) was employed here. The manuscript of the cataloguer Ange Vergèce (died 1569) was imitated in type by his contemporary, Claude Garamond, and cut in 1541 for Robert Estienne's Greek classics.

In 1657 Christina of Sweden, who had abdicated in 1654, retired here briefly; among numerous distinguished visitors were James II, on several occasions between 1690–1700, during his exile, and in 1717 Peter the Great. Louis XIV signed the Revocation of the Edict of Nantes here in 1685.

Napoléon I spent 12 million francs on its restoration. He first received Pius VII here in 1804, who from June 1812 was to spend 19 months as his prisoner here, until he renounced temporal power. On 6 April 1814 Napoléon signed the act of abdication at Fontainebleau, before departing for Elba on the 20th, when he said farewell to his Old Guard—only to return on the 20th March 1815 via Grenoble to review his grenadiers and lead them to the Tuileries.

The château was again restored by Louis-Philippe, at enormous cost, but regrettably in his usual questionable taste. Nor was it improved by being occupied for six months in 1870–71 by the Prussians; while from 1941 it was the headquarters of General von Brauchitsch, until liberated by General Patton in August 1944. From 1949–66 it was the military HQ of the Allied powers in Europe.

The *****CHATEAU DE FONTAINEBLEAU** (closed Tuesdays) is composed of many distinct buildings erected over the years, for the most part of two storeys. As much of the stone is unsuitable for sculpture, its exterior is plain when compared to its richly decorated interior, which is described first.

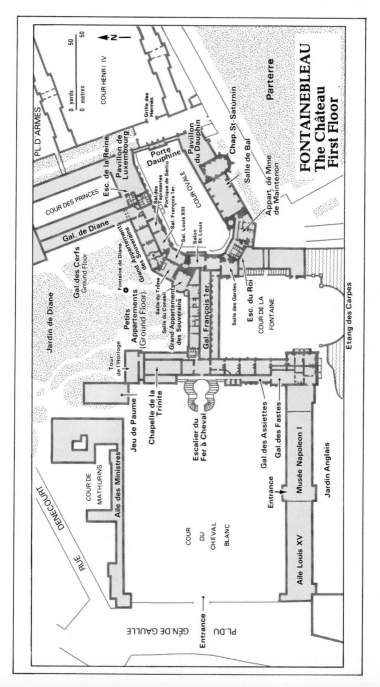

281

FONTAINEBLEAU
The Château
First Floor

N

0 yards 50
0 metres 50

COUR HENRI IV

PL.D'ARMES

Esc. de la Reine

Pavillon de Luxembourg

COUR DES PRINCES

Gal. de Diane

Porte Dauphine

Grille des Hermès

Pavillon du Dauphin

Chap. St-Saturnin

Salle de Bal

Parterre

Salle des Tapisseries

Portique de Serlio

Sal. François 1er.

Sal. Louis XIII

Salon St Louis

COUR OVALE

Appart. de Mme de Maintenon

Jardin de Diane

Gal. des Cerfs
Ground Floor

Fontaine de Diane

Grand Appartements des Souverains

Petits Appartements (Ground Floor)

Salle du Trône

Salle du Conseil

Grand Appartements des Souverains

Gal. François 1er.

Salle des Gardes

Esc. du Roi

COUR DE LA FONTAINE

Tour de l'Horloge

Jeu de Paume

Chapelle de la Trinité

Escalier du Fer à Cheval

Gal. des Assiettes

Gal. des Fastes

Entrance

Musée Napoleon I

Jardin Anglais

Aile Louis XV

COUR DU CHEVAL BLANC

Aile des Ministres

COUR DE MATHURINS

RUE

DENECOURT

PL.DU GÉN.DE GAULLE

Entrance

Etang des Carpes

The Pl. du Gén. de Gaulle provides a good view of the west front of the château; the massive grille marks the site of a former wing which closed the courtyard. This, the Cour du Cheval-Blanc (152m by 112m), is named after a vanished cast of the horse of an equestrian statue of Marcus Aurelius in Rome, which once stood by the horseshoe-shaped staircase of 1643 by Jean Androuet du Cerceau. It is also known as the Cour des Adieux, for it was here that Napoléon said farewell to his Guards.

The visitors' entrance is now in the Louis XV wing, to the right of the courtyard, which replaced the Galeries d'Ulysse, demolished in 1739.

For the Musée Napoléon I, see below.

Follow the corridor to the Escalier de Stuc and, on ascending to the FIRST FLOOR, turn right to enter **R48**, the Galerie des Fastes, built by Napoléon III on the site of a stair, and now displaying a collection of paintings, some by Oudry. You pass along the Galerie des Assiettes (**R49**), decorated with 128 Sèvres porcelain plates (1839–44) painted with views of Fontainebleau and other royal residences; the ceiling is decorated with frescoes by Ambroise Dubois (1543–1614).

(The Appartements des Reines Mères, of Pius VII, and those formerly of the 'grand maréchal' in this wing, are under restoration.)

R50 is the Vestibule du Fer à Cheval (alluding to the exterior entrance staircase), retaining three original massive oak doors of the Louis XIII period. Off this opens **R51**, the gallery or tribune of the Chapelle de la Trinité, built for Henri II by Philibert Delorme on the site of Louis IX's foundation. Martin Fréminet was largely responsible for its sumptuous decoration (1608–14), with its vault-paintings set in ornately moulded and heavily gilded stucco frames, while the elaborate altarpiece by Francesco Bordoni (1633) surrounds a painting of the Deposition by Jean Dubois, Ambroise Dubois' son. It was the scene of the marriage of Louis XV and Marie Leczinska in 1725; in 1810 of the baptism of the future Napoléon III; and in 1837 of the marriage of Ferdinand, Duc d'Orléans (1810–42; eldest son of Louis-Philippe) to Helen of Mecklenburg-Schwerin.

From the vestibule you enter the first of the Salles Renaissance, the 64m long **Galeries François I**, built in 1528–44, in which the initial and salamander device of the king are conspicuous. The paintings and stucco reliefs by Rosso were completed after his death by Primaticcio. The frescoes represent allegorical and mythological scenes, with reference to the life of François. Here the Italian influence in the decoration of the château is seen at its strongest.

Turning right at its far end, you pass through R63 (see below) into **R54**, a rotunda, and along the landing of the Escalier du Roi, built after a design by Gabriel in 1749. The upper part of the well was formerly the bedchamber of Anne de Pisseleu, Duchesse d'Etampes, long the mistress of François. The sculptures are ascribed to Primaticcio. The nude figures (some of the several 'Nymphs of Fontainebleau') are said to have been veiled at the request of Marie Leczinska. The frescoes, in which the king is depicted as Alexander the Great in eight episodes from the life of the Macedonian hero, were painted by Niccolo dell'Abbate from Primaticcio's designs. The stucco figures are of the period of Jean Goujon.

A passage ahead leads to **R56**, the splendid **Salle de Bal**, 30m long, the building of which was started by Gilles le Breton, but transformed by Delorme. Its windows command the best view of the Cour Ovale. The elaborate coffered ceiling is of walnut, the design of which is reproduced on the parquet floor, a conceit of Louise-Philippe. The interlaced monograms of Henri II and Diane de Poitiers and the emblems of Diana (bows and arrows and crescents) are ubiquitous. The mythological scenes, designed by Primaticcio and executed by Niccolo dell'Abbate in 1552, have been much restored. The satyrs flanking the fireplace are copies of the originals melted down at the Revolution.

(The adjacent Chapelle de St.-Saturnin (1541), replacing that consecrated by Becket, and the Pavillon du Dauphin are closed.)

Leaving the ballroom, you turn left to visit four rooms (**RR57–60**), originally the royal suite of François I, and converted by Louis XIV into the Appartements de Mme de Maintenon. The Boulle commode and clock by Lepaute in the bedroom are notable. It is said that Louis signed the Revocation of the Edict of Nantes, one of the more discreditable acts of his reign, in her Grand Salon (1685), in which the *boiseries* are in part of that date. **R62** is the antichamber of the former 'Salle de Spectacle' (closed). This wing had formerly contained the 'Belle Cheminée', dismantled in 1725 when the rooms were turned into a theatre, burnt out in 1856.

You now return to the **Salle des Gardes (R63)**. It was completed c 1570, but redecorated in 1836. This, the first of the 'Grands Appartements', retains its original frieze and ceiling (the design of which is reproduced on the marquetry floor), but the chimney-piece, with a bust of Henri IV attributed to Matthieu Jacquet, was made up from several pieces recovered from the 'Belle Cheminée' under the auspices of Louis-Philippe. Most of the furniture in this and the following suite of rooms dates from the first decades of the 19C, including a number of pieces by Alphonse Jacob-Desmalter (c 1840), placed as they were during the Second Empire.

Passing through **R64**, decorated with mythological scenes by Ambroise Dubois and others, you enter **R65**, in the original keep of the castle, which was the king's bedchamber until the 17C. It was transformed in 1757, redecorated in 1836 and embellished by paintings of the 1780s depicting episodes in the life of Henri IV. The fine marble bas-relief of Henri IV *à cheval* (1599; by Jacquet) comes from the above-mentioned 'Belle Cheminée'.

The Salon Louis III (**R66**), formerly the Cabinet du Roi or Chambre Ovale, retains some of its early 17C decoration, 'restored' in 1837, and most of its original paintings by Ambroise Dubois of The Loves of Theagenes and Chariclea, although three were removed in 1757 when the doors were widened to admit the voluminous dresses of the period. It was in this room that Marie de Médicis gave birth to Louis III in 1601.

R67, the Salon François I, retains its original chimney-piece, incorporating a medallion of Venus and Adonis by Primaticcio, while the walls are embellished by several Gobelins tapestries depicting hunting scenes (Chasse de Maximilien; after Van Orley). Those in the next room (**R68**) illustrate the Story of Psyche, while the adjoining antechamber contains three of The Seasons (Spring is missing).

Off this room is the Escalier de la Reine (**R83**) and **RR84–85**, known as the Appartements des Chasse, dating from 1601 but containing Second Empire furniture. These rooms were reserved for eminent guests until becoming those of the Prince Imperial (1856–79). Notable are the several large paintings by G.-B. Oudry of the Chasses de Louis XV in the forests of Compiègne and Fontainebleau.

R70, the Galerie de Diane, over 80m long, dates from 1600 and was originally part of the queen's apartments. It was decorated with paintings

illustrating the Myth of Diana and the Victories of Henri IV. Much dilapidated, it was tastelessly transformed during the Restoration and since 1858
has served as a library.

From its vestibule you turn right through **R71**, the first of the Appartements de la Reine, into **R72**, the Salon de Jeux, with its 'Pompeian'
decoration of 1786 by P.-L. Roland, and with Louis XVI and First Empire
furniture (among them, several pieces by Jacob Frères and Jacob-Desmalter). **R73**, the **Chambre de l'Impératrice**, with a notable ceiling and with its
walls covered by silk manufactured at Lyon, reproducing the original
designs. Marie-Antoinette's bed, by Sené and Laurent, made for this
position, has likewise been provided with replicas of the its former hangings. The room had been occupied successively by Marie de Médicis,
Marie-Thérèse, Marie Leczinska, Marie-Antoinette, Joséphine, Marie-
Louise, Marie-Amélie and the Empress Eugenie. **R74**, the Queen's Boudoir,
contains furniture by Riesener and Georges Jacob of 1786.

The sumptuously, but somewhat garishly, decorated Throne Room (**R75**),
first used as such by Napoléon in 1808, served previously as the Emperor's
bedchamber. Some of the decoration dates from the mid 17C, but most of
the *boiseries* were carved in the 1750s. The Savonnerie carpet, the lustre-
candelabra of rock crystal by Thomire, the standards flanking the throne
and surmounted by the initial N and an eagle, designed by Percier and
Fontaine for St.-Cloud and moved here in 1808, and the Napoleonic bees
on the baldaquin will be noted. The portrait of Louis XIII is after Philippe
de Champaigne. The adjacent cabinet served as the 'Brûle-tout', where
state papers were burned after council meetings.

R76, the richly decorated Salle de Conseil, contains paintings by Boucher,
Carle von Loo and J.-B. Pierre.

RR77–82, the Appartements de l'Empereur, are under restoration.

Stairs descend to the GROUND FLOOR and the Petits Appartements de
l'Empereur et de l'Impératrice (**R12–23**), most of them with their late 18C
decoration and Empire furniture. They were formerly occupied by the
members of the royal family; royal mistresses, among them Mme du Barry;
and later by distinguished visitors. Napoléon, his ushers and secretaries,
occupied **RR12–24**. His bedroom (**R18**) contains his richly canopied bed
(1804; by Jacob-Desmalter); **R22**, his main bureau (once the bathroom of
François I), is embellished by paintings of birds by Snyders and by Fyt; the
adjacent Antichambre du Col de Cygne (**R23**), a fountain by Roland and
Thomire; while **R24** was the map room (Cabinet topographique), displaying
furniture by Boulle, Jacob-Desmalter and attributed to Riesener.

The almost circular Study of the Empress (**R25**) has some *boiseries* of the
Louis XV period and more furniture by Jacob-Desmalter and Jacob-Frères,
ubiquitous throughout the suite, the most notable being in the Salon Jaune
(**R30**). (It was probably when attempting to enter Napoléon's apartments
from here, after having hurried from St.-Cloud to greet the Emperor on his
return from Wagram, that Joséphine found the door between their respective rooms walled up.)

Beyond **R33** you turn into the Galerie des Cerfs (74m long), so-called
because of the stags' heads which form part of its decoration. It has
undergone several alterations since 1600, notably in the 1860s, when
Napoléon III commissioned Alexandre Denuelle to decorate it. On the walls
are birds'-eye views of several châteaux and forests, while seven bronze
sculptures after antique originals are also displayed. It was in this gallery,
in November 1657, that Christine of Sweden had her favourite, the Marquis

de Monaldeschi, assassinated; his coat-of-mail did not offer sufficient protection to the fatal stab.

The ***Musée Napoléon I** is installed on two floors of the Louis XV wing (1738–74), on the south side of the Cour du Cheval Blanc. This is devoted to the period of the First Empire (1804–15): the collections at Malmaison and Bois-Préau concentrate on the Consulate and his years on St. Helena; see Rte 35.

Almost every room contains remarkable examples of the furniture of the period by the more eminent *ébenistes*.

It is better first to ascend the Escalier Central (**R45**) and then proceed along the corridor (**R35**), lined with busts and portraits of members of the Imperial family, to enter **R36**, displaying Napoléon I in his coronation robes, and Joséphine, seated, in her coronation robes, both by Gérard. Showcases display his ceremonial sword, surviving regalia, robes and decorations, etc. **R37** is devoted to items from the 'Grand Vermeil', the silver-gilt surtout of table decoration by Henry Auguste presented by the city of Paris, 19 of 72 Sèvres procelain plates, cutlery, etc. **R38** contains part of the surtout or epergne given by Carlos IV of Spain. **R39** displays the Emperor's personal belongings: his grey frock-coat; black beaver hat; campaign furniture; toilet equipment, including the Nécessaire No. 4, by Biennais, of 1809, and a smaller example, flasks, pistols, portfolio, etc. **R40** concentrates on his uniforms, arms, snuff-boxes, lorgnette and other items.

R41 is devoted to souvenirs of Marie-Louise (1791–1847), who Napoléon married in 1810 after his divorce from Joséphine, with a copy of Gérard's portrait. **RR42–44** concentrates on the Roi de Rome (1811–32; also known as the Prince de Parma, Duc de Reichstadt, L'Aiglon, etc.), born to Marie-Louise in the Tuileries and who died at Schönbrunn, Vienna. His cradle, by Thomire-Duterme, is one of several surviving pieces of furniture from his nursery and apartments shown here, together with his baby-clothes, toys and other souvenirs of his childhood.

Individual rooms on the GROUND FLOOR portray members of the extensive Bonaparte family to whom the Emperor was able to dispense largess in the way of kingdoms, etc. Conspicuous by his absence is Lucien (1775–1840), from whom he was estranged. **R3** is devoted to his mother, Mme Mère, née Maria Letizia Ramolino (1750–1836), widowed with eight children when aged 35. Her portrait is a copy of that by Gérard. **R4**, Joseph (1768–1844), whose portrait by Gérard depicts him when King of Spain, where many of his personal possessions were lost at the battle of Vitoria. **R5**, Louis (1778–1846), who married Hortense de Beauharnais and whose son became Napoléon III; his portrait as King of Holland was painted in 1809 by Charles Howard Hodges. **R6**, Jérôme (1784–1860), King of Westphalia, with a 'Romantic' portrait by F.-J. Kinson. **R7**, Elisa (1777–1820), Princesse de Lucques and later grand-duchess of Tuscany; her portrait attributed to Kinson. **R8**, Pauline (1780–1825), Princesse Borghèse. **R9**, Caroline (1782–1839), who married Joachim Murat (who became King of the Two Sicilies in 1808), is shown surrounded by her children in a painting by Gérard.

R2, at the west of this wing, is the Théâtre Napoléon III (1857; by Hector Lefuel) incorporated here after the former theatre burnt out.

At the east end of this wing is the restored Musée Chinois, containing a collection of Oriental art. The rooms of the Empress Eugénie have also been restored recently.

The exterior of the château may be seen by walking around from the north-east corner of the Cour de Cheval Blanc, first passing the Jeu de Paume (tennis court; right) to enter the Jardin de Diane, with a bronze fountain group of Diana (after an antique original) surmounting a plinth surrounded by dogs and stags' heads (by Pierre Biard; 1603). You bear round the wing of the Galerie de Diane and Galerie des Cerfs, following the line of the moat to reach the Porte Dauphine, by Primaticcio, an entrance to the Cour Ovale. Opposite is a gateway of 1640, decorated with heads of Hermes (Mercury) by Gilles Guérin, looking onto the Cour Henri-IV (1609), the main entrance to which is to the north, facing the Pl. d'Armes.

Continuing ahead, you reach the Parterre, a formal garden with ornamental ponds, laid out for Henri IV, and again, by Le Vau, for Louis XIV. To the right, beyond the poorly restored apse of the Chapelle St.-Saturnin, and the Porte d'Orée by Le Breton, a passage leads into the Cour de la Fontaine. To the south and south west extend the Etang des Carpes, with its island pavilion, and the Jardin Anglais, laid out for Napoléon. Thomas Coryate, when visiting Fontainebleau in May 1608, was amazed to see ostriches running wild in the gardens and apparently cormorants were kept here, with which to indulge in a form of aquatic falconry.

The park (84 hectares) extends to the east of the parterre. On the south side, beyond the canal dug by the order of Henri IV, are the buildings of the former School of Artillery.

Some distance to the east, beyond the walls, is the suburb of **Avon**, its 13–16C church containing the tombs of Monaldeschi (1657; Christina of Sweden's favourite, whose assassination she had ordered), the artist Ambroise Dubois (1543–1614) and the naturalist Daubentin (1706–99); while in the cemetery lies Katherine Mansfield (1888–1923) who died near here while under the malign influence of Gurdjieff. At **Valvins** (1.5km north east of the station), lived Mallarmé (1842–98) from 1884 until his death. He is buried in its cemetery.

The ***Forest of Fontainebleau**, surrounding the town, and approx. 17,000 hectares in extent, although crossed by a number of good roads, is best explored on foot. Its thick glades and picturesque wildernesses of rock interspersed by sandy clearings, make it a pleasant place for excursions. Two of the more attractive sites are the Gorges de Franchard and d'Apremont, some 4km west and north west respectively of the Carrefour de la Libération. See IGN Map 401.

For Melun (18km north), Vaux-le-Vicomte (6km north east of Melun) and areas beyond Fontainebleau, see Blue Guide France.

41 To Champs

The Château de Champs is not the easiest place to get to. By car, there are two alternatives: follow the N34 beyond Vincennes (see Rte 32) through Nogent-sur-Marne to Neuilly-sur-Marne, there turning onto the N370 for Champs-sur-Marne; or take the A4 motorway driving east from Porte de Bercy, turning off for Marne-la-Vallée and following signs for Champs.

The RER provides a fast service to Marne-la-Vallée; there change to a bus for Champs-Mairie; or by train from Gare de l'Est to Chelles, there also taking a bus to Champs-Mairie.

There is little of interest to see en route. The *Château de Beauté at **Nogent**, in which Charles V died in 1380, was demolished in 1622. Charles VII gave it to Agnés Sorel and it was later occupied by Diane de Poitiers. One of Baltard's market pavilions, which survived the demolition of Les Halles Centrales (see Rte 19), was re-erected here.

Watteau died at Nogent in 1721, while at Bry-sur-Marne, further east, was the birthplace of Louis Daguerre (1787–1851), who gave his name to the daguerreotype. Etienne de Silhouette (1709–67), controller-general of finances in 1759, is said to have decorated the walls of his château here with outline portraits. At Chelles stood a Merovingian palace in the 6C, where Chilperic I was murdered in 584 at the instigation of his wife Frédégone. Nothing remains of the abbey founded there in 660.

The *CHATEAU DE CHAMPS* was built in 1703–07 by J.-B. Bullet on the site of an earlier edifice. It was later the residence of the Princess de Conti (daughter of Louis XIV and Louise de la Vallière) and in 1757 of Mme de Pompadour. Pillaged during the Revolution, it was restored in the 1890s and since 1934 has been used occasionally by visiting heads of state. The gardens were laid out by Claude Despots, a nephew of Le Nôtre.

From the entrance vestibule you ascend to the FIRST FLOOR and turn into the Music Room, with a frieze of instruments, and *dessus de portes* by Monnoyer: those in the Guest Room are by Boucher; those in Mme de Pompadour's Bedroom (with its painted woodwork) by Carle van Loo. The next room contains Drouais' Portrait of Mme de Pompadour as 'La belle jardinière', and scenes of sheep and goats by Desportes.

The Grand Salon on the GROUND FLOOR contains furniture covered with Aubusson tapestry, and a Coromandel screen. The Dining-room, with *dessus de portes* by Desportes and Oudry, is embellished with pink marble fountains and serving tables, while a large canvas by J.-B. Martin (?) depicts a hunting scene at Champs. The Smoking-room, with good panelling, 18C Beauvais tapestries and a Boulle bookcase, displays Van Loo's Portrait of Louis XV given by the king to Mme de Pompadour. The Salon Chinois, decorated c 1740 by Christophe Huet, contains a fine chandelier, a Tabriz carpet, furniture covered with Beauvais tapestry depicting La Fontaine's fables and an onyx console table. In the adjoining room hangs Mignard's Portrait of Louis XIV in his minority. The Blue Room is also attractively decorated by Huet.

Some 7km further east is the Château de Guermantes (its name made familiar by Proust, but the building, with a wing added by Robert de Cotte, is in no way connected to the novel). Some 3.5km south of Guermantes stands the Château de Ferrières (rebuilt in the Renaissance style for the Rothschild family by Joseph Paxton in 1857); and 3.5km east of the last, that of Jossigny, of 1743, inexcusably dilapidated.

Twelve kilometres due east of Champs, and not far north east of Jossigny, is the frontier of the extensive site of **Euro Disneyland**, a commercial enterprise to be inaugurated in the spring of 1992 which, with all its sophisticated fantasy, should be seen to be believed. For further information, in English, telephone (1) 49 41 49 10.

Seven kilometres south east of Jossigny lies **Villeneuve-le-Comte**, a planned village of 1230, with a good church, standing on the edge of the Forêt de Crécy (not to be confused with that near Abbeville where the battle of 1346 took place). Here in September 1914 the British army rested after its retreat from Mons, before advancing on the Marne.

For areas further east, see Blue Guide France.

INDEX

Topographical names in Paris are in Roman type; those outside Paris are in **bold**. Subject entries are in CAPITALS. Note that streets, etc. named after people are known by and indexed under the full name: i.e. Rue Antoine-Bourdelle, not Rue Bourdelle. The names of Ministères are subject to change. These, together with Avenues, Bibliothèques, Boulevards, Cafés, Canals, Carrefours, Chapelles, Cimetières, Collèges, Ecoles, Fontaines, Forêts, Gares, Hôpitals, Hôtels (mansions), Instituts, Jardins, Musées, Palais, Parcs, Places, Ponts, Portes, Prisons, Quais, Rues, Squares, Théâtres and Tours in Paris, are index alphabetically in sub-groups under these headings, as are departments of the Musée du Louvre, etc.

ATLAS CONTENTS

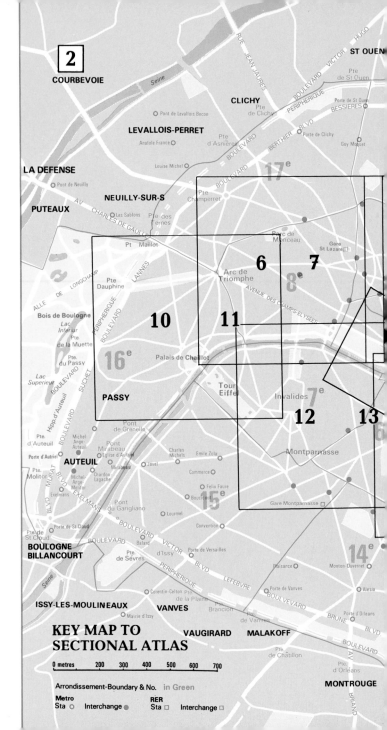

KEY MAP TO SECTIONAL ATLAS

| 0 metres | 200 | 300 | 400 | 500 | 600 | 700 |

Arrondissement-Boundary & No. in Green

Metro
Sta ○   Interchange ●

RER
Sta □   Interchange ▨

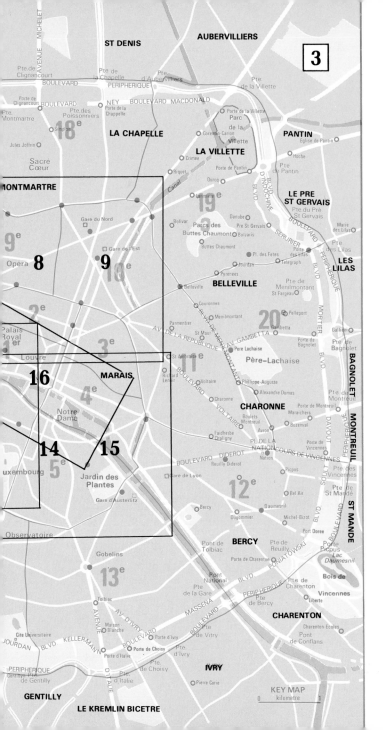

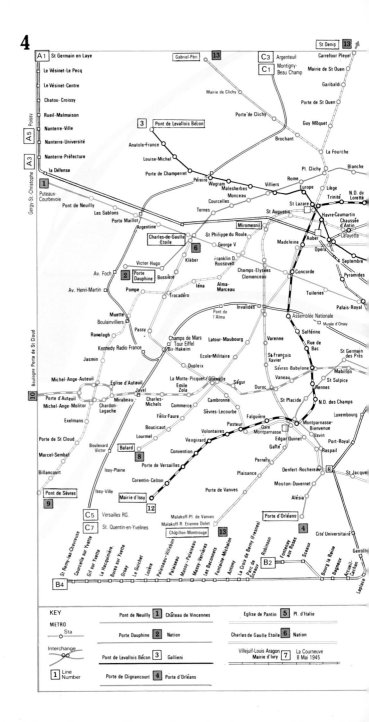

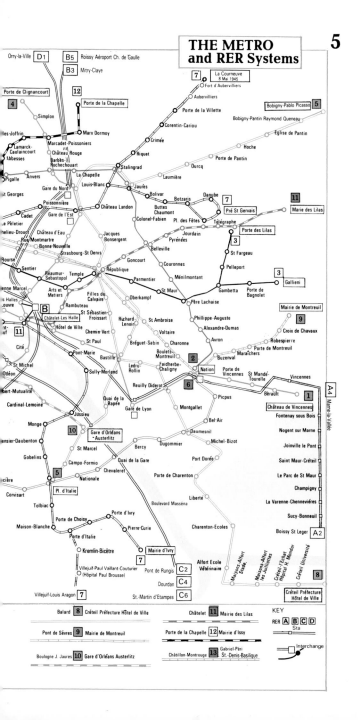

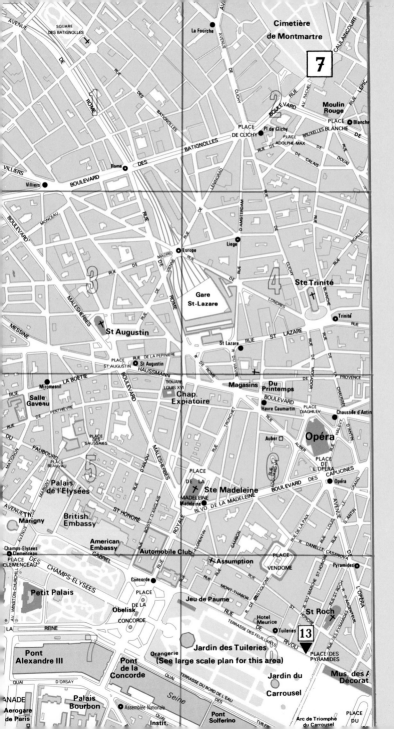

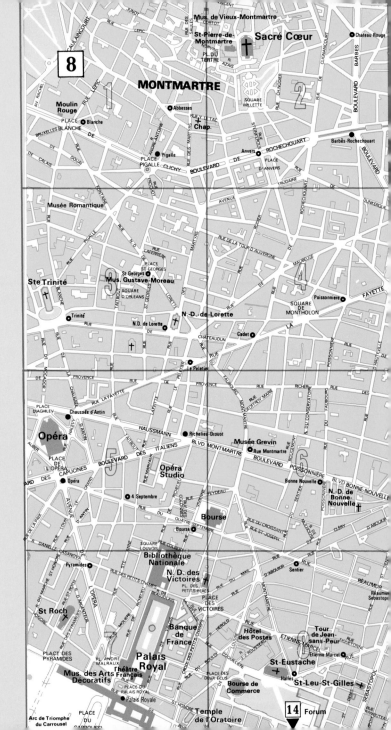

St Bernard

La Villette

9

RUE MARX DORMOY

RUE D'AUBERVILLIERS

RUE DE FLANDRE

BOULEVARD DE LA CHAPELLE
La Chapelle
BOULEVARD DE
Stalingrad

PLACE DE
STALINGRAD
Rotonde de la Villette

Jaurès

RUE ST MARTIN
DE FAYETTE
Louis Blanc

RUE DU FAUBOURG

RUE DE LA VILLETTE

BOULEVARD DE MALHEBERGE

RUE DE MAUBEUGE

RUE DE DUNKERQUE

RUE DE MAGENTA

RUE DE ST DENIS

Gare du Nord
Gare du Nord

St Vincent de Paul

3

Chateau Landon

Gare de l'Est
Gare de l'Est

RUE ST MARTIN

Canal St Martin

PLACE DU COLONEL
FABIEN
Colonel Fabien

4

PARADIS

St Laurent

RUE DE STRASBOURG

BOULEVARD DE MAGENTA

RUE DE L'AQUEDUC

RUE DE LANCRY

RUE GRANGE AUX BELLES

AVENUE RICHERAND

Hôp. St-Louis

PETITES ECURES

Chateau d'Eau

5

RUE DE ROUGEMONT

RUE DE LENCRY

Jacques Bonsergent

RUE LEON JOUHAUX

6

Goncourt

RUE PARMENTIER

Porte St-Denis

Porte St-Martin

BLVD ST DENIS
Strasbourg-St Denis

BOULEVARD ST MARTIN

RUE DU FAUBOURG DU TEMPLE

AVENUE DE LA REPUBLIQUE

BOULEVARD DE LA VILLETTE

PLACE DE LA REPUBLIQUE
République

RUE DE NAZARETH

RUE VOLTA

Mus. Nat. des Techniques

St-Martin-des-Champs

RUE TURBIGO

Temple

RUE DU TEMPLE

Ste-Elisabeth

BOULEVARD DU TEMPLE

St-Nicolas des-Champs

Arts et Metiers

RUE DE BEAUMUR

RUE DE GRAVILLIERS

SQUARE DU TEMPLE

7

8
VOLTAIRE
Oberkampf

CHAPON

RUE DE MONTMORENCY

RUE PASTOURELLE

RUE DE BRETAGNE

RUE SAINTONGE

Fils du Calvaire

MICHEL LE COMTE

BLVD DES FILLES

MARAIS
(See large scale plan for this area)

15

Musée de

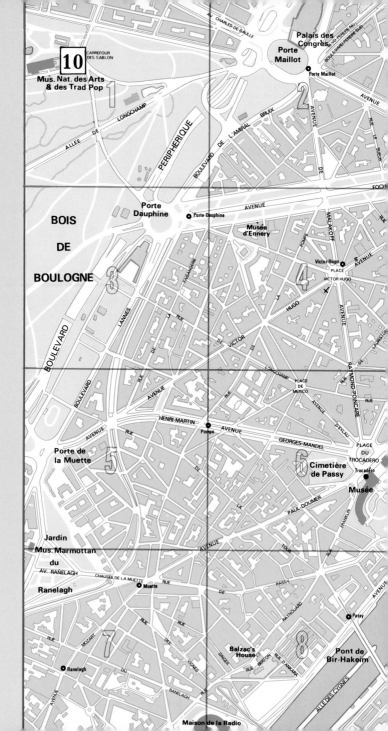

10

CARREFOUR
DES SABLONS

Mus. Nat. des Arts
& des Trad Pop

Palais des
Congrès

Porte
Maillot

Porte Maillot

AV. CHARLES-DE-GAULLE

ALLEE DE LONGCHAMP

PERIPHERIQUE

BOULEVARD DE L'AMIRAL BRUIX

AVENUE

BOULEVARD VICTOR HUGO PERE SUD

AVENUE

RUE LE SUEUR

FOCH

Porte
Dauphine

Porte-Dauphine

AVENUE

Musée
d'Ennery

MALAKOFF

POMPE

Victor Hugo

PLACE
VICTOR HUGO

S AVENUE

RUE

BOIS

DE

BOULOGNE

LANNES

DE LA RUE

RUE

DE VICTOR HUGO

DE

RAYMOND-POINCARÉ

RUE LAURISTON

BOULEVARD

RUE

AVENUE

LONGCHAMP

PLACE
DE
MEXICO

RUE

AVENUE D'EYLAU

RUE

HENRI-MARTIN

Pompe

AVENUE

GEORGES-MANDEL

PLACE
DU
TROCADERO

Porte de
la Muette

AVENUE

RUE

DE

Cimetière
de Passy

Trocadéro

Musée

PAUL-DOUMER

FRANKLIN

Jardin

Mus. Marmottan
du

AV. RANELAGH

Ranelagh

CHAUSSÉE DE LA MUETTE

Muette

RUE

AVENUE

DE

TOUR

PASSY

RAYNOUARD

AVENUE

Passy

RUE

RUE

MOZART

RUE

DES

VIGNES

SINGER

Balzac's
House

RUE BERTON

RUE D'ANKARA

Pont de
Bir-Hakeim

Ranelagh

DU

RANELAGH

RUE

AVENUE

ALLÉE DES CYGNES

Maison de la Radio

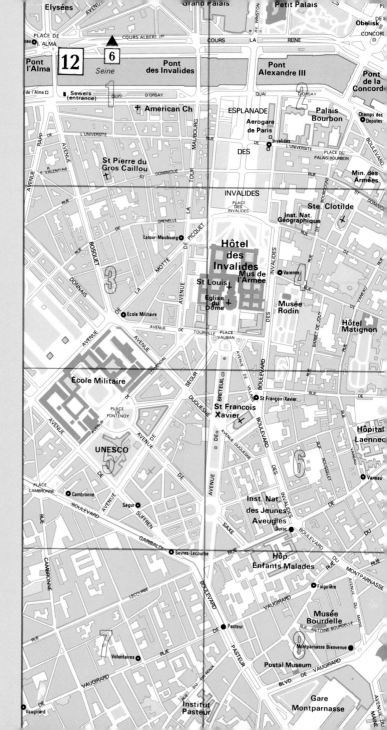

Elysées

Grand Palais Petit Palais

PLACE DE
l'ALMA

Obelisk

DE

CONCORD

Pont
l'Alma

12

6
Seine

Pont
des Invalides

COURS ALBERT 1er

COURS   LA   REINE

Pont
Alexandre III

Pont
de la
Concord

Sewers
(entrance)

de l'Alma

QUAI   D'ORSAY

QUAI   D'ORSAY

+ American Ch

ESPLANADE

RUE

Aerogare
de Paris

Palais
Bourbon

Champs des
Deputes

DE   L'UNIVERSITE

RAPP

AVENUE

DE

DES

PLACE DU
PALAIS BOURBON

BOULEVARD

R. E. VALENTINE

MAUBOURG

Invalides

L'UNIVERSITE

St Pierre du
Gros Caillou

DOMINIQUE

LA

TOUR

RUE

Min. des
Armées

St.

DOMINIQUE

INVALIDES

PLACE
DES
INVALIDES

Ste. Clotilde

BOURDONNE

GRENELLE

Inst. Nat.
Géographique

DE

BOSQUET

Latour-Maubourg

DE   PICQUET

DE

RUE

Hôtel
des
Invalides

INVALIDES

Varenne

RUE

YANKEL

DONNAIS

LA

MOTTE

St Louis +
Mus de
l'Armée

DES

RUE

Musée
Rodin

Ecole Militaire

Eglise
du
Dôme +

BARBET-DE-JOUY

Hôtel
Matignon

AVENUE

AVENUE

DE

TOURVILLE

PLACE
VAUBAN

AVENUE   DE   VILLARS

AVENUE

DE

TOURNON

SEGUR

BRETEUIL

St François-Xavier

École Militaire

DUQUESNE

St François
Xavier +

BOULEVARD

Hôpital
Laennec

PLACE
DE
FONTENOY

DE

AVENUE   DUQUESNE

DES

ROUSSELET

AVENUE

DE

SAXE

INVALIDES

Vaneau

UNESCO

DE

SUFFREN

Inst. Nat.
des Jeunes
Aveugles

PLACE
CAMBRONNE

Cambronne

AVENUE

Segur

GARIBALDI

Duroc

BOULEVARD

DU

RUE

BOULEVARD

Sèvres-Lecourbe

RUE

Hôp.
Enfants Malades

DU

MONTPARNASSE

CAMBRONNE

LECOURBE

Falguière

AVENUE   DU   MAINE

RUE

DE

Pasteur

VAUGIRARD

Musée
Bourdelle

RUE   ANTOINE   BOURDELLE

Volontaires

RUE

Montparnasse Bienvenue

Postal Museum

DE

VAUGIRARD

PASTEUR

BLVD.   DE   VAUGIRARD

Vaugirard

Institut
Pasteur

Gare
Montparnasse

AVENUE DU
MAINE

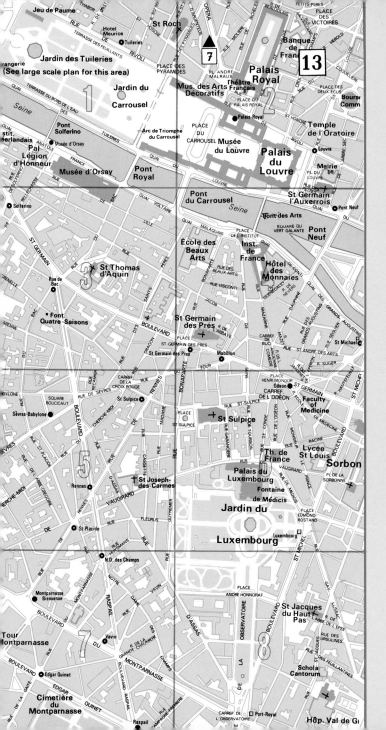

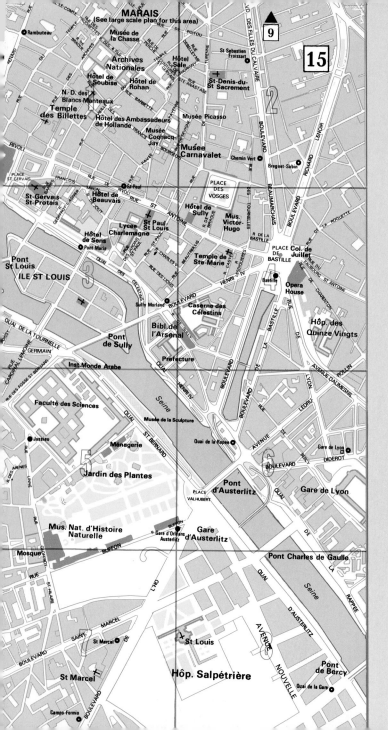